Masao Abe
A Zen Life of Dialogue

For Masao Abe
on the occasion of his eightieth birthday

First published in 1998 by Tuttle Publishing, an imprint of Periplus Editions (HK) Ltd., with editorial offices at 153 Milk Street, Boston, Massachusetts 02109.

Cataloging-in-Publication-Data

Masao Abe : a Zen life of dialogue / edited by Donald W. Mitchell.
-- 1st ed.
      p. cm.
    Includes bibliographical references and index.
    ISBN 0-8048-3123-8 (pbk.)
     1. Abe, Masao, 1915– . 2. Zen Buddhism--Relations.
    3. Philosophy, Comparative. I. Mitchell, Donald W. (Donald
William), 1943– .
    BQ940.B3M36 1998
    294.3'927'092--dc21   98-6073
    [B]   CIP

Distributed by

USA
Charles E. Tuttle Co., Inc.
RR 1 Box 231-5
North Clarendon, VT 05759
Tel: (802) 773-8930
Fax: (802) 773-6993

Japan
Tuttle Shokai Ltd.
1-21-13, Seki
Tama-ku, Kawasaki-shi
Kanagawa-ken 214, Japan
Tel: (044) 833-0225
Fax: (044) 822-0413

Southeast Asia
Berkeley Books Pte. Ltd.
5 Little Road #08-01
Singapore 536983
Tel: (65) 280-3320
Fax: (65) 280-6290

First edition
07 06 05 04 03 02 01 00 99 98   10 9 8 7 6 5 4 3 2 1

Cover design by Kathryn Sky-Peck
Text design by Deborah Hodgdon

Printed in the United States of America

CONTENTS

PART IV. THE BUDDHIST-CHRISTIAN DIALOGUE

PART V. COMPARATIVE PHILOSOPHY

FOREWORD

Huston Smith

WHEN IN 1974 the man who was arguably the best soccer player ever, Pelé, announced his intention to retire, his fellow Brazilians took him to court to contest his right to do so. Brazilians take soccer seriously. The supreme court ruled that Pelé was not legally bound to defend his nation's honor. Now there is reason to connect that incident with this present volume because those of us who take dialogue seriously want Masao Abe to understand that it is to honor his eightieth birthday only; it is not an invitation for him to retire. We continue to expect much from his pen and serve notice that—"Brazilians" that we are in our regard for his work—we, too, may resort to the law if that proves necessary to keep him writing. Having made that point, I turn from the present to the past.

I cannot recall when I first met Masao Abe, but I do recall the incident that brought him permanently to my attention. The year was 1977, and Kendra and I were staying in Kyoto in an apartment in Chōtokuin that Mrs. Ogata reserved for foreign visitors. Mrs. Ogata was the widow of Sōhaku Ogata, priest of Chōtokuin in the Shōkoku-ji Temple complex that abuts Dōshisha University. Had he lived out his normal lifespan, he would have shared, with Abe, D. T. Suzuki's mantle as Zen's ambassador to the West. But cancer claimed him prematurely. Ogata's first—and as fate decreed, his only—project in that capacity was to translate into English a large section of Tao-yuan Shih's *Ching-te Chuan Teng Lu,* which he originally titled *The Transmission of the Lamp* and which carries the title *Records of the Transmission of the Lamp* in its posthumously revised edition. Ogata died before he had put the finishing touches on his translation; and in the moment I am recalling, Masao Abe was standing before Mrs. Ogata's door, her husband's carefully cloth-wrapped typescript in his hands, to promise her that he would see her husband's project to term.

That scene remains permanently framed in my memory, for it gathers into a single visual image the traits that all of us who know Masao Abe have come to recognize as the signatures of his distinguished career: sincerity, generosity, diligence, and single-minded dedication to the task of moving Zen Buddhism into the mainstream of humanity's efforts to plumb the human spirit and give it larger play in human history. While a foreword is not the place to rehearse what Masao Abe has already accomplished in his distinguished career (collectively the contributors to this book do that well), it will be enough if I set the tone for what follows by adding a second recollection. This one is of Abe's mentor, D. T. Suzuki, whose pioneering work Abe memorialized in *A Zen Life: D. T. Suzuki Remembered.*

I had the honor of hosting D. T. Suzuki in his appearance on NBC's 1958 *Wisdom* series, and as we neared the wrap-up I asked him, point-blank and by way of summary, "What is Zen?" He answered in words I have not forgotten: "Psychologically, to become conscious of the unconscious; ethically, to be detached while attached; and metaphysically, to see the infinite in the finite." This formula is not Masao Abe's, but it rings true to things I have come to know in and through him. So with palms together, I join my colleagues in deep *gassho*. We hope that these essays on his life and work will bring him the satisfaction he so richly deserves.

PREFACE

MANY OF THE ESSAYS in this volume, dedicated to Masao Abe's life of dialogue in the West, contain stories, vignettes that give the reader a glimpse into the personality of one of the truly great Zen Buddhist figures of the twentieth century. So it seems appropriate for me to begin this preface with such a story. During the fall of 1992, I was driving Masao and Ikuko Abe to Chicago for a weekend. On the way, Masao Abe began talking about the twelve or so years during which he had been living here in the United States. Some weeks before this trip to Chicago, he had finally reached the decision to retire after completing his visiting professorship at Purdue in the spring of 1993. I might add that this was not an easy decision for him to make. And as we drove to Chicago, he began to reflect on what his years of dialogue in the West had meant and what he would do during his retirement back in Japan. In regard to the latter, it was clear that he was not going to retire from the historic dialogue between Buddhism and the West. Rather, he was contemplating what new directions his life of dialogue would take.

When Abe had finished speaking, I said that it seemed to me that his life of dialogue could be divided into three periods. The first period began in Japan with his early practice of Pure Land Buddhism as well as the ensuing spiritual struggle and academic preparation at Kyoto University. Then there was his spiritual conversion to Zen Buddhism, under the guidance of Shin'ichi Hisamatsu, and his involvement in the F.A.S. Society. Finally there was his life as a professor of philosophy at Nara University, during which time he became involved in the Buddhist-Christian dialogue. His study of Western philosophy and religion during this first period led him to visit the United States as a student and then as a visiting professor and lecturer on Buddhism and its dialogue with Christianity.

The second period of his life of dialogue began after his retirement from Nara University in 1980. It was then that he came to the United

States on a more permanent basis. In the West it seemed that his dialogical work progressed on a number of fronts. His academic work in the Buddhist-Christian dialogue became more focused and productive, and even expanded to include Judaism. His comparative philosophical scholarship developed as he introduced Kitarō Nishida's philosophy, the Kyoto School, and Dōgen scholarship to a Western audience. Finally he was more intensely involved in the effort to foster world peace through interfaith dialogue. I also mentioned that because of this life of dialogue, some people were referring to him as the heir to D. T. Suzuki, who was one of Abe's early teachers.

I concluded by suggesting that perhaps the third period of Abe's life of dialogue would be carried out in Japan, where he could complete the enormous task of publishing the many and important philosophical and comparative works he has written over the years. He could also spend more time being a mentor to the many younger scholars who will carry on the kind of dialogue to which Abe's life has been so devoted. And finally, since he is still probing the deepest subjects of religious experience and life, I would hope that new vistas would appear on the horizon.

On the way back home from Chicago, I told Abe about an idea I had from the previous day's conversation. I suggested that while his life of dialogue in the West was still fresh in the minds of the many persons he has influenced during his stay in the United States, perhaps a collection of essays on his dialogue in the West could be published. This collection would document both the intellectual content of Abe's encounter with the West as well as the dialogical process and interpersonal dynamics of that encounter. It seemed that the occasion of Abe's retirement back to Japan was the proper time for such a volume. Abe was excited about this idea and asked if I would be willing to edit the proposed collection of essays. I said that it would be an honor to do so.

LET ME TURN NOW TO A BRIEF REVIEW of Masao Abe's fascinating life of dialogue that we are celebrating in this volume. Masao Abe began his academic career after completing the graduate course (in the old Japanese system) in Buddhism and comparative religion at Kyoto University in 1949. After teaching a short time at Otani University, he

accepted an assistant professorship in the Department of Philosophy at
Nara University of Education in 1952. As time passed, Abe became more
and more engaged in researching comparative East-West philosophy and
religion. Therefore, he sought an opportunity to study Western philosophy and theology in the United States in order to strengthen his knowledge of the Western tradition. This opportunity came in 1955 when he
was awarded a Rockefeller Foundation Research Fellowship. He used the
fellowship to study Western philosophy at Columbia University, and systematic theology and Christian ethics at Union Theological Seminary
from 1955 to 1957.

Upon his return to Japan, Abe continued his academic work at Nara
University and also lectured on philosophy of religion at Kyoto University and Hanazono University. He began more actively to publish his ideas
concerning the relation between Zen Buddhist thought on the one hand
and Western philosophy and Christian theology on the other. The focus
of this work was to introduce the philosophy of the Kyoto School, especially Kitarō Nishida's philosophy, to the West. At the request of William
Theodore de Bary of Columbia University, in 1958 Abe, along with
Richard DeMartino, translated an excerpt of Nishida's *Problem of Japanese Culture* to contribute to de Bary's *Sources of the Japanese Traditions*.
This was the first English translation of Nishida's writings.

In the 1960s Abe's comparative work led to numerous invitations
to be a visiting professor in American universities. In 1965 he served as a
visiting professor of Buddhism and Japanese philosophy at Claremont
Graduate School. He returned to Columbia as a visiting professor in 1966
and was the Charles Gooding Lecturer in 1969 at the Divinity School of
the University of Chicago. While at Columbia, Abe conducted a seminar
on Nishida's seminal work, *A Study of the Good*. This was the first seminar on Nishida's philosophy at the university level outside of Japan. During these years, Abe offered lectures and seminars on the philosophy of
the Kyoto School and stimulated the intellectual encounter of East and
West. The growing American interest in Nishida's philosophy and the
Kyoto School in the 1970s and 1980s was due to a large extent to Abe's
groundbreaking work in the 1960s.

In the 1970s Abe continued to travel to the United States as a visiting professor. In 1974 he taught at Carleton College and in 1976 was again
at the Claremont Graduate School. Then from 1977 to 1979, he was a

visiting professor at Princeton University. Also from 1975 to 1979, Abe served as vice president on the executive board of the International Association for the History of Religions.

During these three decades of comparative work and interfaith dialogue both in Japan and in the United States, Abe was active as a scholar at Nara University and also played a spiritual leadership role in the F.A.S. Society in Kyoto. This society was founded at Kyoto University during World War II by Shin'ichi Hisamatsu and a number of university students, including Masao Abe. It provided a spiritual standpoint for Abe's comparative dialogue because the society was devoted to personal achievement of Awakening, on the basis of which its members could work to create a more united humankind through, among other things, interreligious dialogue and cooperation.

This spiritual and intellectual goal, defined by the F.A.S. Society, along with his personal commitment to Hisamatsu, led Abe to move from Japan to the United States on a more permanent basis in the spring of 1980, following his retirement from Nara University. It was Abe's intent to devote all his time and energy to the development of the religio-philosophical encounter between East and West that he had been nurturing for thirty years. He especially wanted to focus on the emerging Buddhist-Christian dialogue that was beginning to play such a central role in East-West interfaith relations. Each summer he and his wife would return to Japan to maintain contact with the intellectual world in Kyoto as well as the spiritual activities of the F.A.S. Society. Between 1980 and 1993, when he again retired from academic life and returned to Japan, Abe resided in the United States at the Claremont Graduate School (1980–83), the School of Theology at Claremont (1984), the University of Hawai'i (1984–85), Haverford College (1985–87), The Divinity School of the University of Chicago (1987), the Pacific School of Religion (1988–91), the California Institute of Integral Studies (1990–91), and Purdue University (1991–93). At these institutions, Abe taught courses on Zen Buddhism, the philosophy of the Kyoto School (especially Nishida's philosophy), the comparative study of philosophy and theology, and the Buddhist-Christian dialogue. In regard to the Buddhist-Christian dialogue, it is noteworthy that Abe broadened this encounter to include Judaism. His essay "A Buddhist View of the Holocaust" created a vigorous discussion of post-Auschwitz theology between Abe and Jewish theologians.

Also during the 1980s Masao Abe and John B. Cobb, Jr., collaborated to form a group of Christian theologians and Buddhist scholars that would meet each year for five years beginning in 1984. This group, informally called the "Abe-Cobb group," was intended to help the American seminary communities to broaden their theological horizons to include a dialogical dimension. The group included some of the best known Christian theologians in the West: John B. Cobb, John Hick, Gordon Kaufman, Langdon Gilkey, Schubert Ogden, Rosemary Ruether, David Tracy, and Hans Küng. Because of the success of this initial, historic project, the group has grown and continues to meet. It is now known as the International Buddhist-Christian Theological Encounter Group.

It was also during this time that Abe was actively involved in the International Buddhist-Christian Conferences. The first two were held in 1980 and 1984 in Hawaii. At the third conference in Berkeley in 1987, a committee was formed to establish a new Society for Buddhist-Christian Studies. This society came into being the following year, with Masao Abe as one of its founding members. During that same year (1988), Abe traveled to Europe to give a series of lectures on the Buddhist-Christian dialogue. He lectured at the Universities of Oslo, Bonn, Tübingen, Heidelberg, and Munich. Finally, through a major grant from the Lilly Endowment, Inc., Abe participated in the four Purdue Buddhist-Christian-Jewish dialogues. These four public conversations, held on different university campuses, were between Masao Abe and Marjorie Suchocki, Wolfhart Pannenberg, Richard L. Rubenstein, and Keith J. Egan. They brought the Buddhist-Christian encounter to a broader audience in a way that demonstrated the challenge and promise of interfaith dialogue in a pluralistic society.

Masao Abe is a prolific writer. Besides numerous publications in Japanese, he has published in English, as of this writing, more than sixty academic articles, thirty book chapters, and six books. His 1985 book, *Zen and Western Thought* (University of Hawai'i Press), was selected by the American Academy of Religion to receive its Award for Excellence in 1987. In 1986 he edited *A Zen Life: D. T. Suzuki Remembered* (Weatherhill) in memory of the twentieth anniversary of Suzuki's death. Then in 1990 Abe and Christopher Ives published a new translation of Kitarō Nishida's *Inquiry into the Good* (Yale University Press). This edition has become the standard translation of this important comparative philosophical text. Perhaps the most significant of Abe's publications for the Buddhist-Christian dialogue has been his long essay "Kenotic God and Dynamic Sunyata," which appeared in the 1990 book *The Emptying God: A Buddhist-Jewish-Christian Conversation* (Orbis Books). This book includes responses to Abe's essay by noted Christian and Jewish theologians as well as Abe's rejoinders. A second volume of theological responses to Abe's essay appeared in 1995 under the title of *Divine Emptiness and Historical Fullness: A Buddhist-Jewish-Christian Conversation with Masao Abe* (Trinity Press). In 1992 Abe published *A Study of Dōgen: His Philosophy and Religion* (State University of New York Press). And most recently he published *Buddhism and Interfaith Dialogue* (University of Hawai'i Press) in 1995 and *Zen and Comparative Thought* (University of Hawai'i Press) in 1996. As of this writing, Abe is working on publishing even more books on Zen Buddhism, Dōgen, Buddhism, comparative studies/interfaith dialogue, and the philosophy of the Kyoto School.

BEFORE PREVIEWING THE ESSAYS about Abe's work and life of dialogue that we have collected here, it may be helpful to take a look at the origin and nature of his philosophical and religious standpoint for interfaith dialogue. Influences on the philosophical side of Abe's work include such Western philosophers as Plato, Aristotle, Saint Augustine, Kant, Hegel, Nietzsche, Kierkegaard, Heidegger, and Whitehead. His religious thought is strongly influenced by Paul Tillich and Reinhold Niebuhr, with whom he studied at Union Theological Seminary, as well as the many other Christian theologians with whom he has been in dialogue over the years. Abe has participated in the activities of the Tillich Society; and Niebuhr's Christian realism stimulated Abe's interest in social thought. In terms of Buddhist influences, Dōgen, Shinran, Kitarō Nishida, Keiji Nishitani, Shin'ichi Hisamatsu, and D. T. Suzuki played central roles in the formation of his thought in the context of the Kyoto School.

Abe's own comparative philosophy of religion, as I would attempt to characterize it, is developed at the meeting point of two crossing lines of intellectual encounter today. On the one hand, there is the interreligious encounter of East and West. On the other hand, there is the modern encounter of religion and atheism, and the resulting rejection of the value of religion by such social forces as secularization and scientism. At the juncture of these two lines of encounter, religions East and West are meeting one another in the climate of an unbelieving world, that is, in a world where their religions are playing less and less of a formative role in society.

So, it seems to me that for Abe the historical importance of inter-faith encounter is that it offers the dialoguing religions the opportunity to be transformed by one another in a manner that can make each of them more able to face the challenges of antireligion in the modern world. And this mutual transformation can better enable each religion to play a more formative role in the building of a new postmodern world. Indeed, Abe's efforts in his intellectual work are inspired by his vision of this emergence of a more peaceful, harmonious global community of peoples of different cultures and religions. Abe feels that such a new world must have a spiritual foundation. Therefore, all religions must discover a depth of spiritual life that can contribute to such a world transformation. And this depth, he feels, can be discovered through the profoundly self-transformative means of interfaith dialogue.

As a student, Abe himself struggled with modern religious skepticism—especially Nietzsche's nihilism. Through Zen, under the guidance of his teacher Shin'ichi Hisamatsu, he was able to go beyond this existential anguish by awakening to the True Self. Abe saw this spiritual Awakening, and its intellectual expression in the Kyoto School's philosophy of Emptiness, as the contribution that Zen can make to the interfaith project of overcoming modern antireligious ideologies in a manner that can also provide a spiritual standpoint for the creation of a more united and peaceful postmodern world. I must add that I do not think that Abe wanted just to add this Zen contribution to the other religions he encountered. Rather, he was hopeful, according to my interpretation, that the nondualistic depth dimension of Emptiness beyond dualistic and theistic distinctions could be found in the deepest experience of other traditions. What he could do in interfaith dialogue was to provide a Zen mirror, as it were, by which other faiths could come to deeper spiritual self-discovery. This depth awakening to Emptiness would then prompt the other religions to give Awakening and its understanding of Emptiness a more central place than it presently has in their traditions. In so doing, these religions would find, as Abe did in his own life, that this depth dimension of spiritual life would enable them to counter the antireligious ideologies of today and would empower them to contribute to a more united and peaceful world community.

Following in the footsteps of D. T. Suzuki, but with much greater philosophical and theological preparation, Abe entered into dialogue first with Christianity and then with Judaism. In line with the Kyoto School's use of Western philosophy to present the Zen understanding of life, especially Emptiness as ultimate reality, Abe engaged Western philosophers and theologians in comparative conversations in which he always put before them the notion of Buddhist Emptiness. Using their own philosophical and theological concepts to do so, Abe, like a Zen master, always pushed the conversation to its deepest level in order to help his dialogue partners face as clearly as they could the Zen notion of Emptiness. I believe that Abe hoped that by so doing, his dialogue partners would then be better able to find this deeper spiritual dimension in their own traditions. In most of his dialogues, this presentation of Emptiness was made in explicit comparison to the Western notions of God. I believe that the culmination of this dialogical task was reached by Abe in his comparison of Buddhist Emptiness to the Christian notion of kenosis, or self-emptying. His seminal essay "Kenotic God and Dynamic Sunyata" is the high point of Abe's comparative work in this regard. As we have seen, it has elicited numerous responses from the most respected Christian and Jewish theologians from around the world.

WITH THESE COMMENTS on Abe's dialogical project as background, we can now turn to a preview of the essays we have collected on his extraordinary life of dialogue in the West, which this book seeks to document and celebrate. In Abe's work, one finds a dialogue of East and West that has taken their cultures, philosophies, and religions an enormous step forward in their historical encounter. To commemorate Abe's retirement from the West and return to Japan, we have asked a broad range of scholars to contribute essays on Abe's life of dialogue in the West so that we can record the full scope of one of the truly significant philosophical and religious encounters of East and West in the twentieth century. However, this is not just a collection of essays that praise Abe, but a collection that puts his ideas under critical scrutiny in a manner that challenges Abe's work as well as celebrates it. This is what Abe wants. His dialogical method always welcomes criticism in order to push the comparative inquiry to a deeper level of encounter so as to uncover a deeper level of truth. In order to pursue this goal, Abe has agreed to write a response to the papers collected here. Therefore, this book is not just a retrospective but is itself an important contribution to furthering East-West dialogue.

We have divided this text into six parts. Part I is a section devoted to essays on Abe's foundational work in Japan in the fields of comparative philosophy and religion as well as to the intellectual/spiritual journey that led him to dialogue with the West. The first essay is by Jeff M. Shore, who has been involved with Abe in the F.A.S. Society. With Abe's collaboration, Shore presents the fascinating story of Abe's spiritual quest for Awakening, a story that throws light on why Abe takes the religious stance he does in his later scholarly work. Shore's essay is followed by Steven Antinoff's striking portrait of Abe as a Zen disciple of Shin'ichi Hisamatsu as well as a Zen teacher of Antinoff himself. Antinoff's essay gives the reader a deeper glimpse into Abe's Zen experience and personality that he brings to interfaith dialogue in the West. Valdo H. Viglielmo's essay also describes encounters with Abe as a Zen teacher but adds a picture of Abe as a Japanese scholar in the Kyoto School. Felix E. Prieto relates Abe's life and scholarship to the philosophy and goals of the F.A.S. Society. Prieto shows how the F.A.S. ideals motivate Abe's concern for the future of humankind, which is such a driving force behind his work in interfaith dialogue. Richard DeMartino's essay traces the origins of Abe's thought as a Zen Buddhist philosopher in the Kyoto School back through the works of Shaku Sōen, D. T. Suzuki, Kitarō Nishida, and Keiji Nishitani. Finally, Hans Waldenfels traces Abe's dialogical work from its beginnings in Japan to its development in the West, and also presents a critical analysis of Abe's comparative method.

Part II of the book is devoted to essays that present a picture of Abe's activities at different periods of time during his stay in the West. John B. Cobb, Jr., discusses his own encounter with Abe at the School of Theology at Claremont and their discussions concerning process theology. Cobb also tells the story of the founding and development of the International Buddhist-Christian Theological Encounter Group, also known as the Abe-Cobb group. William R. LaFleur describes Abe's classroom use of a Zenlike dialogical or interrogative textual hermeneutic at the University of Chicago and Princeton University. Abe's method of teaching a text seeks to establish an interactive relationship between the reader and the text itself in a way that confronts the reader with existential life-and-death questions. David W. Chappell, from the University of Hawai'i, where Abe resided for two years, not only presents the positions Abe took there on different comparative issues but also questions him about these positions: especially his logic, his claims concerning the ultimacy and centrality of Emptiness in Buddhism, and his approach to ethical issues. Ashok Gangadean places the many activities Abe undertook at Haverford College in a larger historical perspective. He also explicates Nishida's logic of place as he understands it from Abe's lectures at Haverford. In so doing, he demonstrates Abe's contribution to the emergence of intercultural philosophy. Durwood Foster presents Abe as a Zen teacher at the Pacific School of Religion and describes the difficulties one faces in keeping the presence of a Buddhist scholar of Abe's stature in what Walter Kaufman has called "modernity's worst intellectual ghetto"—the Christian seminary. My own essay traces my personal relationship with Abe and his influence on my work leading to his coming to Purdue University. I also describe his activities at Purdue and his four Purdue dialogues. I explain how our dialogue moved to a deeper level through his encounter with the Focolare movement, which in turn led to his visit to the Vatican. In terms of the latter, I recount his fascinating and historical meetings with theologians in the Congregation for the Doctrine of the Faith, with Cardinal Joseph Ratzinger, and with Pope John Paul II.

Part III of the book presents essays by six prominent Christian and Jewish theologians who discuss their engagement with Abe in interreligious dialogue. John Hick advances his own dialogue with Abe by questioning the latter about his way of understanding *Śūnyatā* as ultimate reality. Abe, it seems, often speaks of *Śūnyatā* in a manner that rejects the notions of ultimacy found in other religions. Thomas J. J. Altizer discusses Abe's comparison of the Buddhist notion of *Śūnyatā* with his interpretation of a kenotic God as a possible Christian notion of the ultimate. In doing so, Altizer tries to show the relevance of this comparison by referring to the ideas of Heidegger, Hegel, Kierkegaard, and especially Nietzsche. Heinrich Ott has offered us a very suggestive essay based on

Heidegger's notion of "neighborhood." Speaking from his own experience, Ott reflects on what happened to his own theological reflection when Masao Abe entered his "neighborhood." He goes on to suggest that this notion of neighborhood can serve as a paradigm for the theology of religions. In the final Christian essay, Langdon Gilkey tells how an early personal encounter with Abe helped him understand the spiritual foundation from which Abe would later engage in dialogue with Christianity. Gilkey shows that sometimes profound theological insight comes not from words but from the dialogue of spiritual life. Eugene B. Borowitz places his own Buddhist-Jewish encounter with Abe in the context of the intellectual development of modern Jewish theology in a way that shows some significant differences between his own thinking about God and Abe's views. In the final essay of this section, Richard L. Rubenstein challenges Borowitz's position concerning Abe's notion of ultimate reality. Rubenstein affirms the similarities between his notion of Holy Nothingness and Abe's notion of Dynamic *Śūnyatā* while also criticizing Abe's Buddhist tendency to diminish the sociohistorical dimension of human existence.

Part IV of the book presents essays on Abe's involvement in the Buddhist-Christian dialogue. Each essay explores Abe's dialogue with a particular Christian theologian. Joseph A. Bracken, S.J., presents Abe's dialogues with Wolfhart Pannenberg on the topics of the self and ultimate reality. Pannenberg adds an epilogue concerning his disagreement with Abe concerning the latter's notion of a kenotic God. Ruben L. F. Habito examines Abe's dialogue with Hans Küng. Habito raises serious questions about whether Abe's notion of *Śūnyatā* can be an adequate ontological ground for the kind of global ethic proposed by Küng. Harold H. Oliver discusses Fritz Buri's thought-provoking assessments of Abe's legacy in the areas of comparative philosophy and interfaith dialogue. Leslie D. Alldritt explores the thesis that Abe has found in the theology of Paul Tillich an analysis of the human condition and human potential that parallels his own Buddhist thought. Alldritt suggests that Tillich had a strong influence on the way Abe presents his own views to a Western, Christian audience. Finally, James L. Fredericks relates a story about Abe's criticism that Karl Rahner's view of "mystery" suffers from "traces of dualism." Fredericks admits that Christianity has to resist the tendency toward dualism, but he also charges that Buddhism, especially Zen, must resist a tendency to decay into monism. He suggests that while Abe is aware of this fact, he would do well to take more seriously the Pure Land notion of otherness in order to challenge Buddhism in as radical a manner as he has challenged Christianity.

Part V of the book is a collection of essays by persons working in the field of comparative philosophy. Each essay critically examines an aspect of Abe's contribution to this field. In the first essay, Thomas Kasulis positions Abe's philosophical work in the historical context of comparative philosophy. He shows how Abe corrected a misunderstanding about Zen and philosophy that was fostered in the West by D. T. Suzuki. Kasulis also explains how Abe brought to the West's encounter with Zen a new and distinctively philosophical element by introducing the West to the comparative ideas of the Kyoto School and Dōgen studies. He also demonstrates how Abe has become a unique and significant comparative philosopher in his own right. John E. Smith then outlines Kitarō Nishida's comparative philosophical project, one that Abe himself follows, that seeks to build a new "world philosophy" drawing from both Eastern and Western traditions. Smith shows how, for Nishida, this project is informed by William James's attempt to move beyond Hegel. Smith critiques Nishida's and Abe's understanding of James's notion of "pure experience" but seems to support Nishida's overall comparative project and applauds Abe's attempt to present it to the Western philosophical community. On the other hand, Thomas Dean challenges this kind of comparative project. Dean questions Abe's dialogical approach that seems to judge Christianity from a Zen standpoint, demanding fundamental changes in Christian ontology but not in Zen. He also questions Abe's view that the ontology of Emptiness is a "positionless position" that lets every other position stand as it is. Dean questions Abe's use of Western concepts and the Western notion of philosophy in his comparative work, as well as Abe's tendency to place categories from one tradition into the other. Joel R. Smith argues in his essay that while Abe criticizes the West for its ontological bias in favor of being, Abe himself has a bias toward non-being that in itself does not resolve the antinomy between being and non-being—which is one of Abe's philosophical projects. Joan Stambaugh responds to Abe's criticisms of the philosophy of Martin Heidegger on the issues of "thinking," the ontological difference, and the priority of time over being. Finally, Robert E. Carter has written a fascinating and poetic essay on Abe's influence on Carter's own philosophical attempts to understand the meaning of Emptiness as ultimate reality.

The sixth and final part of the book gathers together a selection of essays on Abe's ideas in the field of interfaith relations. William Theodore de Bary asks the provocative question: Can Buddhism provide what is necessary to achieve what Abe sees as the goal of interfaith dialogue, namely, a united and peaceful world community? De Bary raises serious reservations in this regard based on Buddhism's history in East Asia; but then goes on to make an important suggestion that would affect Buddhism's relation to Western religions. Arvind Sharma has written an intriguing essay about his encounters with Abe and how they led him to reflect on the relation of Buddhism to Hinduism. Steven Heine explores the dialogical methodology by which Abe tries to move beyond the traditional divisions between Zen and Shin Buddhism, and between Sōtō and Rinzai Buddhism, by promoting an "intrafaith" dialogue between them in the larger context of his interfaith dialogue with the West. Christopher Ives tells how Abe's personality furthers his dialogical mission in interfaith relations. He also raises the question as to how much of Abe's "Buddhism" is actually created through that dialogical mission. Stephen C. Rowe shows how Abe's presence in the West has been itself a dialogical praxis, a practice that has greatly affected interfaith relations in the West. Finally, Steven Morris's essay examines Abe's existential Zen stance in the absolute present from which he encounters other religions. Abe's dialogical focus from this stance is ultimately reaching for a level of spirituality that produces human transformation and freedom.

ONE FINAL EDITORIAL NOTE: Following the custom Masao Abe has adopted, we will capitalize *Śūnyatā* and its English translations as Emptiness, Absolute Nothingness, etc. We do this to indicate that *Śūnyatā* is absolute Non-being rather than relative non-being. To maintain consistency and to avoid confusion, we will do this in all the essays in this volume.

Let me conclude by thanking a number of people for their important assistance in producing this book. First and foremost, I want to thank

Masao Abe for his central role in this project. He provided me with many crucial bits of information about his life and work in the West, as well as with a list of potential contributors to this volume. I would also like to thank Ikuko Abe for her support of both Masao Abe's and my own work on this project. I want to express my appreciation to all the persons who contributed to this volume: the quality of their essays has made this book the definitive work on Masao Abe's life. Thanks also to Sharon Yamamoto for her many helpful suggestions and support, and to Manfred Kuehn who translated Heinrich Ott's essay. And finally, I want to thank the persons who helped me with the many technical details of editing this work: Jered Moses, Steven Cordiviola, and especially Pamela Connelly.

Donald W. Mitchell
Purdue University

Part One

FROM JAPAN TO THE WEST

chapter One

THE TRUE BUDDHA IS FORMLESS: MASAO ABE'S RELIGIOUS QUEST

Jeff M. Shore

HUMAN BEINGS SHOULD HAVE COMPASSION for all living things—not only animals but plants, all things. And yet one must eat to survive. If one is to truly live out this compassion, however, one should not eat a thing. But then one would be taking one's own life. In short, one must either take life to survive or give up one's own so as not to take the life of another. This moral contradiction was the first real philosophical problem for young Masao Abe. The sensitive and intelligent young man had heard one of his teachers at school speak of the importance of compassion for all living things. He was about fifteen at the time, and as he mulled the contradiction over, it caused him considerable distress. He continued to struggle with the issue as he grew, and the problem deepened.

Born in 1915 in Osaka, Masao Abe was the third of six children. His father was a doctor. His mother was the only one in the family devoted to religion—the Pure Land Buddhism of Shinran (1173–1262). Young Abe went on to what is now Osaka Municipal University to study economics and law. There, a friend urged him to read *The Tannishō*, a collection of talks by Shinran. Doing so, he was shocked to see how it served as a kind of searchlight into his own soul, revealing for the first time the deep sinfulness within him.

He then realized the utter futility of "self power" for salvation and accepted the "other power" faith in the grace of Amida Buddha that is taught in Shin Buddhism. This decision was the first step on his religious path. Yet truly to be embraced by Amida Buddha's grace, one must relinquish all self-centered calculation and discrimination. However, that was the one thing that Masao Abe just could not do. He *understood* only too well the necessity of relinquishing all self power; it was another thing altogether to *realize* it in himself.

After graduation, he wanted to go on to Kyoto University and pursue his study of Buddhism but was unable to because of family matters. Instead, he had to find employment. He entered a trading company in Kobe and worked in an office for four years. Even though he tried his best to live the life of a businessman, typing up invoices and answering the phone, his inner turmoil would not abate. Looking around at his fellow workers as they spoke with clients and went about their business, he was so plagued with a sense of utter futility and meaninglessness that he felt as if he were in a land of the living dead. Desperate to find some way out of this spiritual wasteland, he decided to study Western philosophy rather than Buddhism. He hoped to resolve his religious impasse by taking the reasoning mind, of which he had been unable to divest himself, to its very limits and thus break through to a pure faith. This decision was the second major step in his religious quest.

But when he quit his job and entered Kyoto University, it was April of 1942, four months after the Japanese attack on Pearl Harbor. Thus, Abe had to endure the criticism and rebuke of family and friends for being a traitor and a coward during his nation's hour of need. Still, he pursued his study of Western philosophy under the renowned Hajime Tanabe (1885–1962). Tanabe was strongly influenced by Shin Buddhism. But it was Abe's meetings with Shin'ichi Hisamatsu (1889–1980) that served as the decisive religious inspiration—and challenge—in his life. Abe had never even heard of Hisamatsu, but since Hisamatsu was then associate professor of Buddhism at Kyoto University, Abe naturally attended his lectures. Hisamatsu was a Zen layman, yet he had attained a profound religious Awakening, or *satori*. Watching Hisamatsu standing at the lectern, Abe immediately sensed that here was a man living truth with complete sincerity.

When Hisamatsu opened his mouth, however, Abe was shocked to hear him using the same basic Buddhist terminology that Abe was used to, but with what seemed to be the completely opposite interpretation! Hisamatsu clearly stated that the Pure Land teaching of Shinran, which speaks of Amida Buddha as an object of devotion, was a "lower form" of Buddhism and that true Buddhism was the standpoint of the "formless" Buddha. Furthermore, he said that this formless Buddha was not something in which one had faith. Rather, genuine Buddhism is Awakening to this formless Buddha as one's own True Self.

Once Abe asked Hisamatsu, "I'm nothing more than a lump of selfish passions. And yet isn't the standpoint of Mahāyāna Buddhism that one can be saved just as one is, selfish passions and all?" Hisamatsu immediately and decisively replied, "The very thought that there are selfish passions is a selfish passion. Originally there is no such thing." Abe could not accept this viewpoint and persistently, obstinately argued with Hisamatsu. For if what Hisamatsu said were really true, Abe's decision to leave his job and study philosophy was pointless. As Abe and other students at Kyoto University wrestled with these kinds of problems in the shadow of World War II, it became clear that a religious practice was necessary to supplement their academic studies. Thus, under the guiding inspiration of Hisamatsu, the Buddhist Youth Organization at Kyoto University was transformed gradually into the F.A.S. Society.

Eventually Abe was able to confirm his Pure Land faith through an experience of Amida Buddha's infinite grace. Until then Abe had been unwittingly running away from Amida even as he thought he was running toward him. Finally he realized that Amida had been waiting there all the time; then Amida's boundless compassion enveloped him. At that moment, Abe threw himself on the tatami floor and wept. When he told Hisamatsu of his experience, Hisamatsu was delighted and never again criticized Abe's standpoint. And Abe no longer felt the need to challenge his teacher's standpoint. This experience was the third decisive step on Abe's religious path.

Abe now felt he could embrace any and all with his newfound faith. But gradually he came to realize that there was still one person he just could not embrace—Shin'ichi Hisamatsu. Hisamatsu's presence, his living truth and inviolable dignity, presented Abe with mute testimony of an essential disparity with his own faith. Thus, he was forced to inquire into which standpoint was really true: Hisamatsu's or his own.

It was at this time, during the December 1951 intensive retreat held at the Reiun-in Temple on the grounds of the Rinzai Zen monastery complex of Myōshin-ji in western Kyoto, that Abe leaped up from his sitting cushions and raced toward Hisamatsu as if to attack him. Others were so frightened at his intensity that they jumped up to protect their teacher. The traditional silence and decorum of the retreat was violently disrupted. As Abe struggled to get through to him, Hisamatsu neither moved nor said a word. Finally Abe was able to get free and grabbed Hisamatsu. Hisamatsu freed one of his hands and placed it against Abe's forehead, eyeing him all the while. Then Abe screamed, "Is that the True Self?!" Hisamatsu solemnly replied, "That's the True Self." "Thank you." Abe bowed and left the room.

That evening during the tea break, Abe returned, approached Hisamatsu, and started tapping him on the head. Someone sitting next to Hisamatsu said, "Is that all you can do?" Hisamatsu responded, "Do it more!" Abe slapped him with all his might, but Hisamatsu just laughed calmly. Here we can discern Abe struggling heart and soul to test and discover Hisamatsu's inviolable standpoint—and to make it his own. This event was another milestone in Abe's spiritual journey.

At another of the winter retreats at Reiun-in, it gradually became clear to Abe that an element of ego-self still remained in his faith. To try to get rid of it, Abe suddenly broke out of line during the walking meditation and ran to the temple's well a few yards away. He filled the bucket with ice-cold water and was about to throw it out in a desperate attempt to throw out everything within himself. Yet even then he was conscious of the eyes of others upon him. Unable to contain himself, he just burst forth, "It's all a lie!" and doused himself with the water. Readers may be familiar with Abe's penetrating critique of Nietzsche and his interpretation of "God is a sacred lie" (heilige Lüge). This incident indicates the point in Abe's spiritual struggle when he realized the falseness of *everything*. Even the Pure Land faith he had been living in up until then collapsed. He now entered a phase of sheer nihilism.

Out of this nihilistic standpoint, the final form of Abe's religious problem naturally came to the fore: the problem of the devil. In freeing oneself from the duality of good and evil, one gains a kind of enlightenment. Such freedom may indicate divine salvation, but it can also turn into the working of the devil. Saint Augustine says that while we are touching God, we are touching the devil. Behind the mask of the so-called Buddha, behind the very face of God, the devil's eyes are flashing. It was this duplicity *within himself* that was the core of Abe's problem. His early inability to attain singleness of faith in Amida, his later sense of lack even after he had attained faith, and the agonizing nihilism and self-consciousness following the collapse of his faith—all were rooted in this devilish ego charading as Buddha. This is what Abe calls "*the self-realization of the devil*—a realization that I was doing the work of the devil in the name of faith."

Realizing the self-deception he was embroiled in, he knew he had to get free even of Nietzsche's nihilism and find a truly positive standpoint, yet he did not know how. He had sat in concentrated *zazen* through many, many F.A.S. Society retreats and had even done some formal *kōan* training with Zen masters Rekidō Ōtsu and Sōnin Kajitani, both of the Shōkoku-ji Monastery in Kyoto. But it was during a "mutual inquiry" encounter with Hisamatsu that Abe was finally able to find complete release. Abe said, "I have tried all kinds of ways, but to be frank, none have been true. I just cannot find any place where I can stand." "*Stand right at that place where there is nowhere to stand,*" Hisamatsu replied without missing a beat. At that instant, the final vestige of ego-self dropped away, and Masao Abe realized the boundless expanse of his own formless True Self. Now there is no longer any devil, nor is there any trace of Buddha.

It is important to see this Awakening, and the enormous struggle that preceded it, as the existential basis for all Abe's later thought and activity. Abe speaks, for example, of *complete reversibility* between God and humanity. This *reversible autonomy* stands as the basis of a "religion of Awakening" even as it serves as a fundamental challenge to all "religions of faith":

> *For the true encounter between Zen and Christianity, I believe we*
> *must deal with this self-realization of the devil. In failing to do so,*
> *the encounter of Zen and Christianity will end in "talks" in the*

dimension of thought or concepts, and no path will be found by which both Zen and Christianity can break through the existing framework and creatively and developmentally give life to the self. In other words, Christians must somehow become aware of the unobjectifiable devil lurking behind the indispensable divine normativeness and accompanying irreversibility in their theistic faith. Only when through this self-realization theistic normativeness and irreversibility are transcended, one comes into contact with the Zen insight of "Wherever you are, total Reality reveals itself" for the first time.[1]

Abe then goes on to reveal a blind spot in Zen:

On the other hand, Zen Buddhists must realize that their reversible autonomy is never a mere point of destination; it is nothing other than the point of departure. If this is taken merely as a destination, reversible autonomy will immediately fall into anarchic self-indulgence, and, moreover, one will become a devil assuming the title of "absolute being" for himself. Reversible autonomy must be grasped as the point of departure for establishing all ethics, culture, and history. To this end, Zen Buddhists must realize that reversible autonomy continuously includes the possibility of becoming the devil. For establishing the world and history from the Zen point of view, they must transcend the possibility of becoming the devil included in Zen autonomy. At that point, they first comprehend the meaning of the divine normativeness in Christian theistic faith. Herein, the irreversibility between God and man is also first embraced by reversible autonomy.[2]

These passages clearly reveal the inseparability of Abe's *religious struggle* and the *religious philosophy* that developed from it. I beg the reader to keep in mind this inseparability, and that the latter gains true meaning and life only through the former.

In the spring 1981 issue of *The Eastern Buddhist*, Abe included the following reflections on the "philosophy of Awakening" of his teacher, who passed away in 1980:

*Hisamatsu's philosophy, then, however important it may be, was
but one of many self-expressions of his Awakening, all stemming
from the same source. The philosophy of Awakening differs in no
way from a flower arranged by Hisamatsu for the tea ceremony. In
that one flower his philosophy is fully manifested. Those who cannot see the philosophy of Awakening in that flower will fail to see
it in his philosophical works as well. The same can be said of an
ordinary word of greeting spoken by Hisamatsu. Containing the
philosophy of Awakening, his greeting of "How are you?" inquires
directly into the foundation of the other's existence, and turns him
towards the Awakening of himself. Only someone able to respond
to the question contained in such a greeting can comprehend
Hisamatsu's philosophy of Awakening.[3]*

This last statement applies to Masao Abe and his philosophy as well.
Whether speaking slowly in his careful English, laughing, knitting his
brow, asking an unanswerable question—and then waiting, waiting for
that unquestionable answer—or simply chatting with students, Abe is
patiently and calmly doing his religious philosophy. We are forever in
his debt.

chapter Two

THE FIRE IN THE LOTUS

Steven Antinoff

WALKING THROUGH THE GROUNDS of the Shōkoku-ji, the monastic compound where I lived in a three-mat room five minutes from his home, Masao Abe let out one of the occasional pieces of autobiography he would divulge when he thought it might help me advance. "In my late thirties and early forties, I was pressed to the wall. It was a situation of near collapse, and it impelled me during the *sesshin*[1] to resume *zazen* practice immediately after the midday meal and to sit without respite, forgoing supper, until the meditations concluded at nine. Later I had some problems with my knees." With this last sentence we both laughed, but there was an infinity of difference in our laughter: his nonchalant in its relaxed recollection of a hardship borne and long since cast off, mine nervous, apprehensive at the abysmal difficulty before me.

This was one of those fascinating glimpses of the Abe of a previous incarnation, when age had not yet blended with compassion to give him the tinge of the grandfatherly. It was rather the Abe of the tales of his friend (and my teacher) Richard DeMartino, who told the story of an American who appeared in the circle surrounding Suzuki in the 1950s and who, "thinking he had something," challenged Abe as he stood opposite him outside the Lion's Den at Columbia University only to have the pipe ripped from his mouth and thrown back in his face.

It is said that the lotus born in water can be destroyed by fire, but the lotus bloomed in fire cannot be burned. Abe told how during a talk on the Pure Land the words "Amida Buddha is not far from here" pressed him to the ground and had him clawing at the tatami in anguished recognition that it was he who would not permit Amida to enter. He recalled how in the after years of a conversion that he felt had empowered him to embrace the whole world, the nihilism that at the depths of his religious experience had been dissolved through Amida's grace had broke forth anew in a second, now God-resistant strain; how, in the midst of a last-ditch effort during a winter *sesshin* to achieve the "no-mind" through which he sought to undercut the force of this disclosure, he had run from the meditation hall and, tearing the kimono from his shoulders, doused himself repeatedly with the freezing water of the temple well, only to hear the words "Everything is a lie! Everything is a lie!" pour unexpectedly from his mouth and draw even the *nembutsu* into their nihilating caress. Above all, there was Hisamatsu, the great lay Zen master and his teacher, the one being in the world who had remained, of course without intent, elusive to Abe's all-encompassing faith and who in existence as well as in word had rejected Abe's realization as not thoroughgoing, reprimanding simply, "No noise in the *zendo*," when Abe, though formally in the *zazen* posture, was so absorbed in the *nembutsu* that he unwittingly blurted, "*Namu Amida Butsu*."

Hisamatsu himself had been reared in a Pure Land milieu, only to see his faith give way to the demands of a human reason that at length likewise proved powerless against the crisis of being human. The resulting double impotency, of human existence and of God, stood at the root of his insistence on a "religious atheism," religious in that it broke through the "I," atheistic in that this breakthrough was obtained in the absence of any divine agency. Short of this radical position, nothing could be of any avail. "Whether walking, standing, sitting, or lying, whatever you do will not do. Then, what do you do? Absolute negation; death. But this at the same time is absolute affirmation." This, a few seconds of talk once thrust before a student, is the core of Hisamatsu's existence as well as his religious teaching; and a chronicle exists, in the writings of fellow disciple Ryutarō Kitahara, of an episode in Abe's attempt during the postwar years to contend with both:

> *Following Hisamatsu's lecture [during a* sesshin *at Reiun-in Temple in 1951], when the chanting of the* sutras *had also been*

completed and the group in its entirety was sitting together, Abe-san, seated in one of the spots on the row to the left of the front gate and diagonally opposite Hisamatsu, suddenly shouted, "Sensei! If sitting will not do, what do you do?" I was astounded. This was the very koan I had been struggling with day and night for the past seven days, in fact, for the last three years. Hisamatsu engaged him in an aggressive exchange:

"That's your problem."

"I am asking you."

"You're the one with the problem."

"Deceiver! I am asking you. If sitting will not do, what do you do?"

"In your doing it, I do it."

Without warning Abe burst from his seat onto the area of wooden floor in the center of the room, and was about to pounce on Hisamatsu. I was sitting next to Sensei, and caught up in the bystander's curiosity as to how the situation would unfold, was a second slow in reacting. But when I realized what was happening I grabbed Abe from behind, pinning his arms, like the man who seized hold of Asano Takumi no kami as he slashed Kira Kozuke no suke.[2] The oldest among us, Tokuho Nishitani, sitting in the furthest corner, dashed towards Hisamatsu as soon as he saw him in danger, trampling the fallen Abe just like the statue of Vaisuravana stomping out evil spirits in the Sangatsu Hall of the Todaiji temple. Reiun-in was now unexpectedly transformed to a scene of sheer chaos.

Abe, trying to writhe free, at the same time maintained his grip on Hisamatsu and could not be made to relinquish his hold. Finally Hisamatsu shook an arm free, and pressing his hand against Abe's forehead, watched him intently. "Is this the True Self?" Abe shouted at him. "This is the True Self," Hisamatsu replied solemnly. Abe bowed and said, "Thank you very much," then darted off somewhere.

That evening, as we were drinking tea in the shoin, Abe reappeared, staring fixedly at Hisamatsu—who had his back to the tokonoma—with a strange look. Suddenly with his open palm he slapped Hisamatsu's balding skull. Sekuin Koretsune, sitting next

to Hisamatsu, said, "Is that all?" Hisamatsu replied, "More, more."
Abe then struck him with all his power, but Sensei was just smil-
ing calmly.

Later, when I came across the Zen phrase: "An angry fist
cannot strike a smiling face," I thought, "So that's it!" and remem-
bered that scene, strange even for this world.[3]

Close to three decades later, in the same room, this same Koretsune, now
over seventy, criticized Abe, as we drank tea during a *sesshin* break, for the
inappropriateness of his action. Abe simply laughed. "You don't understand. I had no choice. I was completely cornered."

THE MASAO ABE I FIRST MET IN 1972 seemed *kalpas* removed from
these struggles. Two monks brought me to his home the day of my entry
into Shōkoku-ji. He explained the monastery routine to me in English.
There was about him an intimation of ripened virtue, very much the man
who when asked how he was doing would respond, as he appeared at the
gate in his kimono, "Always very busy; always very free." One remark from
that first occasion especially intrigued me—that enlightenment was also
the goal of the Shōkoku-ji *rōshi's* life. This was a man, I thought, who
would not yield even to a Zen master, an impression subsequently
strengthened when Abe confirmed an account I'd heard from DeMartino: He'd been barred from the monastery where he trained for accusing
the *rōshi* in a *sanzen* interview of acting.

My own first tenure at the monastery turned out to be a failed one.
Within three months I was down to 107 pounds. Life hitherto had been
too devoid of suffering, of persistence, to be readied for the physical and
psychic shock that was abruptly to ensue. Abe visited frequently to bail
me out. I could not bow properly or even dress myself. I could not fold a
kimono were it to cost the world. Abe noted simply, "The forms are dead.
Only you can give them life."

Later I learned that for Abe this "life" was engendered not by mastery but by compassion. "It is the law of the Buddha," he said, "not to
destroy life. If so, one cannot eat. The notion that it is justifiable to kill
plants but not animals is an illusion of anthropocentrism. But if we do

not eat, we destroy ourselves, still violating the Buddhist law. This is the significance of the *gassho*, the pressing together of the palms, before partaking of a meal. One destroys life so as not to destroy life, but one does so only at the ultimate heartfelt limit."

What beauty of man, what ferocity of inner struggle was requisite to create such simple beauty of phrase! And thus the *gassho*, formed by my hands before each sitting, each bow, each meal and after, *dead*, illimitably far from an ultimate heartfelt limit I had not the humanity to achieve, became, as with every other form of this universe, a wall. One that, it soon became clear, would have to be scaled from an encampment somewhat distanced from those of the monastery. Still, as I regrouped in America, something of Abe seemed to abide. He had instilled my failure with dignity, always referring to me in the presence of others as his friend, even as I succumbed to my downward spiral. He had been able, at a time when the pain of *zazen* thwarted me in my most critical aspiration, to convey to me its beauty, as if to know it in its depths turned the breath to champagne. He had been uncompromising in his insistence that I must be able to persist in *zazen* alone. And he set before me a cliff that at once gave partial illumination to the austerity of his own undertaking with a spare piece of advice: "You must kill yourself at every instant."

Three years later, a few days after my return, I met him in his study. He seemed to be testing my resolve. I had arranged a new strategy, sitting the nightly hours with the monks and moving into the monastery only for the week-long *sesshins* several times per year. The *rōshi* had already acceded to this arrangement. Abe, too, seemed satisfied. He described me with the phrase *kendo jurai o kisuru*—to emerge from a setback with redoubled effort.

But the Zen path has its own inevitable logic, "inevitable" in Abe's sense of the word meaning an existential necessity that one might not come to, yet must come to if one is to prevail. "What will you do at the edge of life and death?" he demanded, patrol stick poised over his shoulder amid what Hisamatsu called "the murderous tension of the meditation hall" at a *sesshin* of the F.A.S. Society, in which I, too, had become a participant. But how does one achieve the edge of life and death, without which an answer to the challenge is impossible? DeMartino, in an exposition of the "right aspiration" of Gautama's Eightfold Path, had said, "It's not enough to want Enlightenment. You've got to need it." The disparity between the two tore at my heart and legs with dramatic force, and the thought of dying without Awakening generated an anguish matched only by the bewilderment that the force of this anguish could not be converted into anything more than a hopscotch between sporadic effort and evasion. One may volunteer for the Zen quest, but one is conscripted into the Zen wars.

I was, then, as I suppose must always be the case, pulled into the vacuum in spite of myself. The abandonment of the half for the full lotus became for me the personal symbol in the struggle against the impulse to shrink back from the edge, resulting in an unintended asceticism that bared me to the grid of my ambivalence. As I sat tears fell onto my clasped hands, the realization that the last thing I wanted in this world was to maintain my posture even one more period clawing against the thought that the last thing I *could* do was to waver. Abe observed only that the struggle with pain and the doubting of its validity was a problem that every serious practitioner of Zen must confront. He assured me that the question would remain in my mind as long as I had the luxury to raise it.

He would say, "Ordinary education is to add on. Zen education is to take away." And he knew well the paradox that an ever increasing honing of the power of the will could bear fruit only when this power expended itself to exhaustion. At my explanation in the back of a trolley that intensified effort had merely brought greater awareness of my powerlessness, he was almost incredulous: "You still think *you* have power! Self-negation is the only ultimate power."

Presenting me with an English translation of the *Record of Rinzai*, he inscribed in Chinese characters the phrase "Seeking Buddha and seeking Dharma is only making hell karma." He remarked that at the point of his life when he came upon this sentence, it had brought him to the verge of collapse. Intrigued, I asked what had transpired in the wake of that encounter. But letting me know once and for all that curiosity is barren where it really counts, he responded coolly, "Find out for yourself."

DURING MY INITIAL STINT IN KYOTO, when I would not persevere at the monastery, Abe met my dejection and, more important, my fear, which was far less transient, with a *juzu*, or Buddhist "rosary," made from dried fruit of the Bodhi tree in Bodh Gayā, where Gautama, unable to marshal a further step, was brought to the final impasse. It was a precious gift, a symbol of his faith in my capacity to carry my quest to its consummation in the absence of any warranting sign, too large for my wrist and so worn around my bicep. Eventually it was to slip unnoticed from my arm, to my great regret. But the Bodhi tree is without form and does not slip off so easily. It is planted where a person is planted, the contradiction around which human existence is coiled and from which it recoils.

I now see that all of Abe's offerings were the fruit of this tree, beads on a *juzu* that with each addition shrank the circumference of its circle, choking off the possibility of escape. Inexhaustible in his unwillingness to renounce discussion until I was satisfied how next to proceed, that he held finally that one was to be deprived of every way of proceeding is not to be doubted. This, regarding what might be called "method" in Zen, was the jewel of his inheritance from Hisamatsu. "When cornered, there is a change; where there is a change, there is a passing through"—words I would later encounter with frequency in Hisamatsu's writings—I first heard from Abe. And though of course it was not his style to press me with this method, he knew that I and anyone else who sought to win out in the battle for Awakening would have to come that way, just as Hisamatsu knew Abe would have to. It was only in response to my overt indication that I might no longer have the option *not* to bear up to its mandate that he held out "You must try to corner yourself as much as possible." When I showed that I could not, there was not the slightest trace of disappointment or disapproval. To my confession that my whole life had been reduced to the duality of confronting the Zen quest and evading it, he merely remarked, "You need not try to find some third position. You need only to get to the bottom of that opposition."

I understood him to mean that the attempt to achieve a "pure effort" that would eliminate the impulse to evade was vain, that what was essential by contrast was to be deadlocked in the depths of the inescapable oscillation between the two poles. This deadlock, the final cornering, was the "great-doubt-mass" in Hisamatsu's meaning of the term, which he describes in the autobiographical account of the situation immediately prior to his own Awakening as "black, and with no means of escape left open in the entirety of his existence, not even one the size of a hole in a needle . . . as though one were to climb to the tip of a pole 300 feet tall, and then find oneself unable to advance, to descend again, or to maintain one's position." I still own the napkin on which Abe scrawled the diagram wherein he argued that *zazen* alone, while approaching it, could never achieve the crown of that pole, that sitting, too, would have to be under-cut if "doubt," in Hisamatsu's sense of absolute contradiction, absolute agony, and absolute dilemma, is to be achieved. Hisamatsu had driven home this point most emphatically. "I was at an extremity," Abe recount-ed to me in his study. "I said to Hisamatsu, 'For many years I have strug-gled for a place to stand but have not been able to find one.' His reply, as usual, was without hesitation: 'You must stand where there is no place to stand.'"

This was in thorough consonance with Hisamatsu's strong advoca-cy of a cherished phrase from *The Gateless Barrier*: "In order to attain the wondrous Awakening, it is necessary for all routes of mind [and body] to be brought to the extremity and extinguished." I, who could find no way to bring my paths to an end, ran forward but could not get free of the starting blocks, ran away but could not get free of the need to run forward. Abe made a gift of a calligraphy he had in his turn been given by Hisamatsu, "Extinguish-in-sitting the dusty world," and a year later a copy of the painting, attributed to Sesshu, of Hui-k'o presenting to Bod-hidharma his severed arm. But these affirmations of my exertions were invariably countered by the insistence that they be brought to a standstill at the cusp of maximum effort and the impossibility of advance. "Gauta-ma deadlocked at the Bodhi tree is the negation of Buddhist practice," he said, adding, before I could respond, "Gautama at the Bodhi tree is the fulfillment of Buddhist practice."

I found myself increasingly pulled apart: a tautening of contradicto-ry forces thrusting the mouth open and the eyes dangerously shut as I bicycled from English lessons to the interview with the *rōshi*; an inex-orably expanded balloon whose air is anguish in *zazen*; neck lashing back-ward in hundreds of paroxysms during a three-month season of *sesshin*. Still, I remained what characterizes, contrary to *Exodus*, man and *not* God, a tangle of branches that burns and burns but cannot burn out. Lay-ing this "intensity" before Abe mid-*sesshin* outside the gate of the Reiun-in, he dismissed it with singular indifference: "Psychological, not ontological." This was disturbing, not because he was rejecting any attempt on my part to exhibit a resolution—I had none. Rather, after so much heartache on what I took to be the Zen path, I had been confiscated in my attempt to express even the problem at the first move. Feeling I had no recourse, I challenged his characterization. To this he pressed me gently, just firmly enough between the shoulder and heart for me to fall backward, and said, as he turned to other business, "What are you going to do with that?"

THUS DOES ONE TOUCH render impossible an entire world, though one touch is sure to redeem it. And when I ask myself why I was worth his bother on so many occasions over so many years, I know it is because he honors a man in what he calls his "burning problem." My inability to as yet face up to the final implications of that burning seemed never to be a concern. He responded to whatever was brought before him. And yet I believe he knew I was thoroughly aware of the nature of those implications: a kind of reverse Indian rope trick whose moment of final descent is the *mondo*: "What is Zen?" "Boiling oil over a blazing fire."

The first time Abe visited me in the monastery he had said that *zazen* must be without either bodily or mental tension, though a "spiritual" tension was imperative. But these are not so readily separated. I remember that once when the bell marking the transition from the seated to the walking form of meditation rang, the release from the full lotus set me into uncontrollable laughter as we circled and recircled the veranda. The next afternoon as we were both rinsing our hands, Abe was ebullient. "Last night I heard you laughing during the walking. That's the tension. . . . Oh, very good sign!" Later, inquiring if when the physical torment made concentration on the *kōan* difficult it was better to abandon the *kōan* and try until the period's end to become one with the pain, he advised against it: "You may not be able to achieve this oneness before the bell rings, but if you throw yourself into the *kōan*, it is sure to be intense."

Yet it was without words that Abe gave portent of what intensity would have to come to mean. The initial block of the evening sitting periods had terminated, and the bell rang for the walking meditation. Abe fronted the queue, and I, on the cushions next to him, was second in line. As we stepped barefoot along the inner side of the veranda, I noticed a thick line of icy slush along its outer edge parallel to the garden, remnants from a recent snow. It was directly in our course as we turned into the third leg of the circle, but Abe could have easily avoided it by establishing the path a foot to the inside. Since I was highly susceptible to the cold, my mind urged him on to the dry wood. Instead, he accelerated, trampling right into the slush, and there was no choice but to follow. Coming back from the bathroom, I prepared to resume my place in line. Palms pressed in the *gassho*, I watched him steadily as he stormed round the veranda, for as soon as he was past, I was obliged to bow quickly and step in behind him. Two seconds from me I caught the full force of his visage. I knew then he had not simply stomped into that snow; he had blowtorched it.

As an episode it is inconsequential, but it gave me a glimpse of some decisions Abe had obviously made a long time ago. Such things cannot be settled by another. Nonetheless, in response to a letter I had written him at Princeton, he made it quite clear that in the end there is no retreat. It reads, in part, as follows:

> *It is true that Gautama rejected asceticism. But asceticism means undergoing pain for its own sake, or enduring the pain as if that itself were the means of attaining Awakening. This is simply a form of morbidity. The unintended pain which may accompany hard zazen practice in the quest for the True Self, on the other hand, was never rejected by Gautama.*

Enclosed with the letter was a photocopy, one passage, a reference to Ta-hui, marked in red. When I read it, I knew that I was boxed in, just as I was locked out.

The postmark dates from more than a decade ago. Though other discussions ensued, mostly toward the preparation of Abe's work in English, I consider it our last critical exchange. Perhaps there will be from me a response, but none could be made now that I would accept. For as the letter makes clear, to be valid my rejoinder will have to be spawned, as in the verse of Tung-shan, from where "one returns home and sits among the ashes."

I PREFER NOT TO REPEAT what I have elsewhere written about the day Abe took me to meet Hisamatsu, who, having slain self and universe in what Zen calls the Great Death, stood where there is no place to stand. I believe I learned that afternoon what Rilke must have meant when he wrote that beauty deigns to destroy us; for though not his design, the encounter with Hisamatsu tore me to shreds, reducing me to a spasmodic wailing of unprecedented intensity and duration. At the time, I saw the meaning of my reaction in the cross formed through the intersection of coming face to face with Hisamatsu's Great Peace and the terrifying dread of the path that loomed before me if that peace were in fact to be attained. But subsequently I came to know that those tears possess an additional meaning. They brought me to the certitude of what Abe had always maintained—"Compassion is the supreme inner reality." That it was not as its embodiment but as its negation that I found this certainty does not diminish it. Those tears remain the rare "ocular proof" that when Jesus says to lose yourself is to find yourself, when Socrates replies to his accusers that if he is put to death, "you will hurt yourselves more than you hurt me," they spoke truth.

It interests me that Abe's direct comment on those tears was silence. Neither at Hisamatsu's house nor in the taxi back to Gifu station, where my sobbing perdured unabated, nor at any point on the return train to Kyoto did he offer a word. Only in response to a question as we rode the bus toward the neighborhood where we both resided did he finally talk, as if unwilling to intrude on what had transpired for me alone. Then he said only that I had experienced a "great encounter," and in reply to my confessed fright of being plunged into the abyss, "Today you met a man who leapt into that abyss. Look at the result!"

But though he made no mention of them, I am convinced that he knew those tears even before I had wept them. Abe once told the *sūtra* parable of doves ardently in love with a forest that they discover desperately ablaze. Their sole remedy, soaking their wings in the water of a nearby lake, is hopeless, the water evaporating in the air en route. The doves repeat the process—again without effect—and repeat it again. A rare droplet douses a flame, no more. But love is its own destiny, and the doves are impelled to the perpetual recapitulation of virtually doomed passion. This, without its sentiment, is the vow of the bodhisattva.

Sixteen years have evaporated since Abe voiced those words to the members of the lay group (of the retired, absent Hisamatsu) circled on the tatami of the Reiun-in Temple on a lovely evening infused with the stillness of *zazen*. I am now of the mind that the lake consists of the bod-hisattva's tears, hidden in the flames, hidden even from the bodhisattva himself. This, in Hisamatsu's explication of Zen art, is "austere sublimity" or "lofty dryness," and it explains to me the meaning of tears met with silence. It is this that I first beheld in the passage "As we go to part, a tall bamboo stands by the gate; its leaves stir the clear breeze for you in farewell" and sensed the pierced heart of the master, his task completed, who would never see again his greatest disciple; this that I was honored to witness in the unshaven countenance of DeMartino the afternoon he made his farewell *mondo* to his departed friend Bernard Phillips, comrade in the pioneering American quest for Zen, as he sat cross-legged in a small room of students common to them both; this that I have loved so well, though from an infinite distance, in Wu-tsu Fa-yen's sole response to his long-struggling disciple Fu-kuo at the moment of his Enlightenment, and in which can be traced the imprint of Abe's utter-most aspiration: "The great affair of life that has caused the Buddhas and patriarchs to appear among us is not meant for small characters and inferior vessels. I am glad to have been a help to your delight."

Chapter Three

MY ENCOUNTERS
WITH MASAO ABE
IN JAPAN AND
THE WEST

Valdo H. Viglielmo

I AM BOTH HONORED AND DELIGHTED to have been asked to commemorate Masao Abe's achievements in his life of dialogue in the West. But at the outset I should state that my essay will, I am fairly certain, differ considerably from the others in that, unlike most of the other contributors, I am not a specialist in the area of comparative religion, comparative East-West philosophy, or the philosophy of religion. Rather, my field of specialization is Japanese literature, especially that of the modern (post-1868) period, and my involvement in the study of modern Japanese philosophy, particularly that of the Kyoto School, has been peripheral to that specialization. Nevertheless, such involvement has been a source of tremendous personal satisfaction to me, a satisfaction deriving in no small measure from my encounter with many of the prominent figures of the Kyoto School, among whom Masao Abe must surely be counted. Indeed, although my teaching and research continue to be focused primarily upon modern Japanese literature, my interest in modern Japanese philosophy has in no way waned over the past thirty-five years, and I am profoundly grateful for my association with those figures of the Kyoto School and for the influence of their writings on me.

To trace the stages of my encounter with Masao Abe, I think it appropriate to give a brief account of my encounter with the aforementioned Kyoto School prior to actually meeting him. For one year beginning in the summer of 1954, as a Harvard graduate student studying Japanese literature at Tokyo University and the Gakushuin University under a Ford Fellowship, I was boarding at the home of a woman whose son-in-law happened to be a professor of philosophy and younger member of the Kyoto School, Yasumasa Ōshima. We struck up a friendship, and it was through him that I later became acquainted with the major surviving figures of the Kyoto School, especially his own revered *sensei*, Hajime Tanabe. Tanabe had succeeded to the mantle of Kitarō Nishida, by consensus of both Japanese and Western authorities the acknowledged founder and principal exponent of the Kyoto School. I did not then intend to work in the area of modern Japanese philosophy, because I had not yet obtained my Ph.D. from Harvard in Japanese literature, but my curiosity was piqued and I was gradually persuaded by Ōshima of the intrinsic significance of the philosophy produced by the members of that school. It was during my next visit to Japan, in the summer of 1957 after a two-year absence, that I bought the complete works of Nishida and actually began to explore his philosophy, which at the time I found extremely difficult. And during that summer as well as during my subsequent trip to Japan, in the late summer and fall of 1958, I resumed my friendship with Ōshima, discussing with him various aspects of modern Japanese philosophy. Thus it was that Ōshima, as a member of the Japan UNESCO Commission, became instrumental in my being nominated to translate Nishida's *Zen no kenkyū*, the second major work in a series of Japanese philosophical works to be translated into English. I accepted the task with considerable trepidation since I did not feel truly competent, given the fact that my own formal academic background in philosophy was virtually nil. Nevertheless, I persevered and in the process developed a deep admiration for Nishida's philosophy as well as a determination to introduce it, through translation, to the Western world, although I still continued to specialize in Japanese literature. I recognized only too keenly my own inadequacies, but I vowed to continue my work because almost no other Western scholar in Japanese studies appeared interested in studying the philosophy of the Kyoto School at that time. (Robert Schinzinger, a German scholar and philosopher teaching in Japan, with whom I also developed a friendship, was a notable exception. He had already published a German translation of several of Nishida's essays and later published an English translation of those same essays.)

This discussion may appear to digress from my encounter with Abe, but it is actually quite relevant in that it was my translation of Nishida's maiden work, under the title *A Study of Good*, that was largely responsible for my first meeting with Abe. My translation was published in 1960 and was already being used in a seminar conducted at Columbia University during the 1961–62 academic year by another philosopher of the Kyoto School, the renowned Yoshinori Takeuchi. I learned of this fact, and since I was teaching Japanese language and literature at Princeton University at the time, it was a simple matter to go to Columbia and meet Takeuchi. Thus began a close relationship extending down to the present day. We later embarked on an ambitious project of helping each other in our respective tasks of translating Tanabe's immensely difficult major postwar work *Philosophy as Metanoetics* (Takeuchi had been asked to undertake it by the same Japan UNESCO Commission) and Nishida's equally difficult second major work, *Intuition and Reflection in Self-Consciousness*, which I had somewhat foolhardily decided to translate on my own. Takeuchi and I worked together on these translations intermittently over many years, and it was during one of my trips to Japan, in the summer of 1966, to work with him on them at his Kyoto home (he was then still teaching philosophy of religion at Kyoto University, continuing in the direct tradition of Nishida and Tanabe) that he informed me that a Kyoto School colleague, Masao Abe, had just returned from teaching at Columbia University, where he, too, had used *A Study of Good* in a seminar. As I recall, Takeuchi kindly arranged my first meeting with Abe at the latter's home.

I vividly recall that first meeting because of the exhilaration I felt in becoming acquainted with yet another scholar of the Kyoto School, one who, like Takeuchi, sought to introduce American students—and the American academic world in general—to Nishida's philosophy and who had used my translation in doing so. The time passed extremely rapidly as I asked him many questions about his particular philosophical interests while he in turn inquired about my own academic work and how I had come to translate *A Study of Good*. Already at that first meeting, I learned of Abe's deep involvement in—indeed, commitment to—Zen Buddhism, in the line of D. T. Suzuki and Shin'ichi Hisamatsu, both of whom he considered to be *his* teachers. I was happy to be able to discuss Zen Buddhism (in which I, too, had developed a strong interest) with a specialist and practitioner because Takeuchi, as a priest of the Shin sect, was naturally somewhat less knowledgeable about Zen, despite his vast erudition. Moreover, I had been fortunate to meet both Suzuki and Hisamatsu at Harvard when the two had delivered lectures there, so I was happy to share those experiences with Abe.

If my memory does not fail me, at that first meeting I gave Abe a copy of my lengthy biographical article "Nishida Kitarō: The Early Years," which I had presented at a symposium in Puerto Rico that January. He very kindly agreed to read it and at a subsequent meeting that summer went over it carefully with me, making several valuable suggestions. In the process I was impressed with his meticulousness and with his concern that Nishida's life and work be presented to the Western world as accurately and fairly as possible. (Such concern was undoubtedly responsible for his later retranslation, with Christopher Ives, of *Zen no kenkyū* under the title *An Inquiry into the Good*.) In this way began our association or, more aptly, dialogue, focusing primarily on Nishida's philosophy and Zen Buddhism but extending to a broad range of topics in philosophy, religion, and comparative East-West culture. And in addition to finding Abe an extraordinarily stimulating person intellectually, I sensed in him great personal warmth and understanding—so much so that I felt I could share with him many of my personal and family concerns in a way that I have done with very few of my academic associates, even fellow Americans.

Yet another important aspect of my first meeting with Abe that warm summer day (only those who have experienced Kyoto summers can know how hot and humid they can be!) was his mentioning to me the work of one of his American graduate students who had participated in his Nishida seminar, David Dilworth. He lent me a copy of one of Dilworth's papers in the seminar, a study of the religious thought of Nishida as expressed in *A Study of Good*. Little did I realize at the time that I was then being introduced to the American scholar of the Kyoto School with whom I would also have a long and fruitful association. However, it was only in January 1968, during yet another visit to Kyoto (this time during the bitter cold of a Kyoto winter!), that I actually met him. Abe accompanied me to Dilworth's temporary home where he was living while writing his Ph.D. dissertation on Nishida's philosophy. (I cannot but reflect on the strange chain of "coincidences" mediated by the philosophy of the Kyoto School—Ōshima to Takeuchi to Abe to Dilworth—which began in 1954 by my happening to board at the home of the mother-in-law of Ō shima. Is it frivolous of me to say that I seem to have discerned a karmic link in all of this?)

My friendship with Abe deepened during the next six years through correspondence and in several meetings with him in both Japan and the United States. The spring and early summer of 1972, however, clearly represent the period of my closest association with him, for he became at that time not only my *sensei* in the area of Nishida studies but actually my *rōshi* during intense sessions of *zazen*. But here, too, I think I should provide some background as to why I came to participate in such *zazen* practice. I had arrived in Japan with my family (my wife, Frances; son, Marc; and daughter, Emily) in the late summer of 1971 to do research in both Japanese literature and philosophy during my sabbatical year. (I was then teaching at the University of Hawai'i.) But our living arrangements in Tokyo were so unsatisfactory that finally my wife and I agreed that it would be best that she and the children return to Honolulu and that I continue on alone in Japan to pursue my research. After they left in early February 1972, I made another decision: to move to Kyoto to continue my translation work with Takeuchi even though I had not really completed my literature project in Tokyo. The major reason for this change of plans was that I was able to make the excellent arrangement of boarding at the home of Presbyterian missionary friends, very near Kyoto University. I was happy to be able to continue working with Takeuchi in pleasant surroundings and also to enjoy the more relaxed atmosphere of Kyoto, with its many Buddhist temples and gardens, for an extended period. Nevertheless, I missed my wife and children, and my health was not good since I had not fully recovered from a major operation the previous year. Such was my mental and physical state when I learned, again through Takeuchi, that Abe was then conducting *zazen* sessions at the Myōshin-ji, a famous Buddhist temple in western Kyoto, the very place where Nishida had himself done *zazen* precisely three-quarters of a century earlier, during the summer of 1897.

I rather quickly made the important decision to ask Abe's permission to participate in those sessions at Myōshin-ji because I felt that it was a splendid opportunity for me, unencumbered for the moment by family responsibilities, actually to *practice* Zen rather than merely to *study* it. I also was in the frame of mind that in the broader sense I wished to deepen my religious experience after so many years of considering both Christianity and Buddhism primarily from an intellectual standpoint. I was then an active member of the well-known Church of the Crossroads in Honolulu, a church of the mainstream Protestant denomination the United Church of Christ. Of course, Abe kindly acceded to my request, and I began to go once a week to the sessions he conducted. I discovered that I was not the only Westerner in the group, which consisted of about a dozen people, mostly men but women also.

I shall not burden the reader with a detailed account of those sessions; there are many excellent accounts of the practice of Zen meditation. (Philip Kapleau's *The Three Pillars of Zen* comes to mind as a particularly vivid and moving account of a Westerner's experience in Zen Buddhism.) I wish merely to emphasize how extraordinarily important those weekly sessions were to me and how appreciative I was for Abe's conducting them and for allowing me to participate. I found them to be a spiritual oasis at a time when I was questioning many of the assumptions on which I had built my life. This in no way means that I considered *zazen* to be easy. On the contrary, I found even the half-lotus sitting posture extremely painful and could not begin to achieve the full-lotus position. Also, because of my poor health the damp cold in the early months was especially hard to bear. Moreover, as Kapleau and others have described, a thousand extraneous thoughts obtrude as one tries to concentrate on counting breaths; often I felt myself to be a total failure. But while I was under Abe's expert guidance, something significant was clearly happening to me, and I never considered canceling a single session. (The only major interruption in my attendance came when I had to go to the city of Kamakura in the Tokyo area to attend the funeral of Yasunari Kawabata, Japan's first recipient, in 1968, of the Nobel Prize for literature, who committed suicide in mid-April. His death saddened me greatly because I had come to know him very well during his lengthy stay in Honolulu in the spring of 1969. But his self-inflicted death also made me more determined than ever to continue with the *zazen* sessions and grapple, as best I could, with the deepest problems of human existence.) I also found the discussion period after the long meditation sessions to be fruitful, although, of course, intellectual discussion *about* Zen had not been lacking in my life.

Although nothing truly startling or dramatic (or at least observable as such by others) happened to me during those sessions, I did have one experience toward the end of my stay in Kyoto that gave me a brief glimpse of the Zen goal—or perhaps simply "state" is more appropriate—of *satori*. I did not mention it to Abe at the time, nor have I mentioned it to him since, because somehow I felt hesitant to do so, but I should like to describe it now, as I reflect on my almost three decades of association with him. As he reads this essay, I think he may find this episode to be of interest and may even wish to comment on it.

I was sitting in the prescribed half-lotus position (as I have indicated, I could not possibly manage the *full* lotus) and looking out through half-closed eyes at the beautiful Myōshin-ji garden. As I recall, Abe, as *rōshi*, was sitting facing me—and the rest of us—diagonally to my right. But as I was concentrating on counting my breaths, I gradually lost consciousness of being there in Kyoto and instead felt that I was back in my Honolulu home, looking out at the green lawn of my backyard through the closed glass lanai doors. And then, utterly without my willing it—or at least my *conscious* mind's willing it—I was aware that an unseen hand was removing a faint smudge that prevented the glass from being invisible. But as soon as that one smudge was removed, another yet fainter smudge appeared somewhere else on the glass doors and was similarly removed. This process continued without interruption, as if some power within me were absolutely intent on removing every single smudge, however faint, so that the glass in the doors would be *perfectly* invisible and I could see the lawn without the slightest impediment. I do not know how long this trancelike state continued—probably not more than three or four minutes—but it was extraordinarily vivid and gave me a feeling of heightened awareness, and intense joy, the memory of which has remained with me. And, of course, although this experience *could* have happened to me anywhere at any time, it *actually* happened to me in Kyoto in 1972 under the direct guidance of Abe.

One might very well think that with such an experience, however brief, behind me, I would have been impelled to pursue my *zazen* with even greater fervor and that my association with Abe thereafter, even though we might be separated geographically, would have deepened precisely in this area of "discipleship" to him as a Zen master. That it did not do so is no reflection whatsoever upon his skill or wisdom as a Zen teacher but almost wholly because of the particular course my life took after my return to Honolulu in August 1972. For my interest in Zen and the interior religious life in the spring and early summer of that year occurred within the broader context of my consciousness as a U.S. citizen and as a thinking, feeling member of the late-twentieth-century world community. By this I mean, quite specifically, that even as I was going to the weekly sessions at the Myōshin-ji, I was keenly aware of the fact that a United States–initiated war was raging in Vietnam, causing immense suffering there as well as intense social turmoil in the United States itself.

Thus, after my return to the United States, and increasingly throughout the 1970s, I found myself caught up in political developments. I had been opposed to the Vietnam War from its inception, but I had not taken an active role in the many antiwar demonstrations and rallies of the late 1960s and early 1970s. My opposition was largely limited to writing in the "Letters to the Editor" section of the two Honolulu daily newspapers. But ironically, with Watergate, Ford's pardon of Nixon, and the events leading up to the final debacle in Vietnam in the spring of 1975—in fact, just as the broad antiwar movement was subsiding—I became much more active in expressing myself against the actions of the U.S. government and in opposing imperialism throughout the world. (It was as if I wanted to compensate for not having been active enough at the height of the Vietnam War.) This more active political stance inevitably came to affect my academic life as well, which included my continuing involvement in the study and translation of the works of the Kyoto School. (In 1973 David Dilworth and I published a joint English translation of an important work of Nishida's middle years, *Art and Morality*.) My heightened political consciousness made me look at modern Japanese history in a different light, and I gradually became more critical of the political activity and philosophical writings of the members of the Kyoto School—even of Nishida—in the Japan of the 1930s and early 1940s.

This important change in my thinking had manifested itself already in my relationship with Abe during several conversations I had with him in the mid- and late 1970s, both in Japan and the United States, as we engaged in free-ranging discussion on the various topics I have mentioned. One meeting with him that is especially vivid took place at Princeton University in November 1978, while I was on the East Coast doing research at Columbia University during my second sabbatical from the University of Hawai'i. William LaFleur, who was teaching at Princeton at the time, was with us during the early part of the meeting. But it was when Abe and I were alone together that I felt I could share with him some of my political concerns, especially my opposition to imperialism in all its forms, as well as my conviction that religion, if genuine, should involve itself with important political problems. He listened most sympathetically, as I recall, even commenting on his own interest in left-wing thought as a young man in the 1930s. He, too, felt that religion should address pressing contemporary political issues, and I think it was at that time (but it may have been later, when he was teaching at the University of Hawai'i) that he told me, with a touch of justifiable pride, that his Zen study group (which was the same group that had met at the Myōshin-ji six years earlier) had sent a telegram to the French government protesting nuclear testing in Tahiti. Nevertheless, I still sensed that a large gap existed between his emphasis on the more formal aspects of religion and my own pressing need to participate actively in the peace movement (during that summer I had gone to Hiroshima and Nagasaki with the Gensuikin, the Japanese antinuclear group loosely affiliated with the then-Socialist Party, to observe the thirty-third anniversary of the atomic bombing of both cities) and to work in solidarity with the liberation struggles of the Third World. In sum, my own life trajectory had moved me to a point where, while I was still greatly appreciative of his life and work—especially of his pioneering in the area of the Buddhist-Christian dialogue and, of course, of his personal guidance in Zen—I felt that I had to express my religious convictions primarily by working for peace and social justice.

With our differing emphasis on the role of politics in the religious life, it is perhaps not surprising that our relationship in subsequent years, down to the time of this writing (September 1993), should have become primarily one of friendship and mutual respect on a horizontal basis, although still retaining many aspects of the uniquely Japanese *sensei-deshi* (teacher-disciple) relationship. For example, in the spring of 1983 I was utterly delighted to learn that he was coming to teach at the University of Hawai'i and was happy to try to be of assistance to him in getting settled and in finding a place for him and Mrs. Abe to stay in Honolulu, a city in which housing is notoriously difficult to obtain.

One episode that took place shortly after their arrival in Honolulu, in June 1983, stands out in my mind as epitomizing everything I have admired in Abe, for it showed me how thoroughly his personal religious life and his life in the workaday world merged. I am certain that when he reads this he will be surprised that I should bother to comment on it, because for him his behavior at that time must seem the most natural thing in the world. And that is precisely the point I am trying to make. On a particularly muggy day (Honolulu, unlike Kyoto, has few of them, thanks to the tradewinds) I offered to drive Abe and his wife to the warehouse in the airport district where their many boxes of personal effects had arrived and required their inspection and clearance. Because of major construction in the area I had great difficulty in finding the correct warehouse, and there were further complications in finding someone to let us enter the warehouse and to supervise the clearance process. It was a most trying time, and Mrs. Abe was justifiably distressed at the confusion in the numbering of the boxes and at the fact that the entire process had to be conducted in what was for her a foreign language, English. I, too, was feeling the heat and undoubtedly showed that I hoped everything would end soon (which it gave no indication whatsoever of doing). But Abe, about a dozen years older than I and surely still tired from the exertion of the trip to Hawaii, as was Mrs. Abe, showed not the slightest sign of impatience or irritation at the situation. In fact, he behaved with perfect equanimity and composure until everything was completed satisfactorily.

The above episode may seem to be (and actually is, on the face of it) an extremely minor and mundane one, but for me it was more instructive of the spirit of Zen—and indeed of all genuine religion—than all the erudite lectures and treatises on the subject. Thus, even though Abe and I have come to differ in the area of politics and even though I have undoubtedly strayed from the role of his faithful *deshi* in the religious realm, I must acknowledge how deeply I admire those personal qualities he manifested so elegantly and so eloquently that muggy June day ten years ago.

During his two-year stay at the University of Hawai'i, I naturally had many more occasions to meet him, but because of the factors I have already mentioned and also because departmental lines are ridiculously sharp here (I teach in the Department of East Asian Languages and Literatures, *not* in either Religion or Philosophy), I regret to say that we did not have as close an association as we had in Kyoto more than a decade earlier. But I do remember that he showed me great sympathy at a time, in the course of those two years, when my wife and I were experiencing great distress at the severe personal difficulties both our son and daughter were undergoing. Indeed, there clearly has been a strong bond between us that far transcends our common academic concerns in the area of modern Japanese philosophy or even that of the Buddhist-Christian dialogue, a topic of the greatest interest to me over many years.

But I must touch upon another topic, which it would be so much easier for me to avoid. In fact, upon being asked to contribute to this volume, I pondered precisely the question, Should I mention what for me has become a burning issue, especially in the past five years, knowing how sensitive a topic it is and how easily it can arouse controversy? Yet I feel I cannot avoid it, because it is so germane to my entire almost-four-decade-long involvement in the study of the writings of the Kyoto School, and thereby germane to "My Encounters with Masao Abe" as well. I refer to the vexed question of the stance of the Kyoto School members toward the Japanese imperial institution, more commonly referred to in English as "the emperor system." For many scholars in the field, even other contributors to this book, this topic may seem an unimportant one, especially now in the postwar period after Emperor Hirohito's (since his death referred to as the Shōwa Emperor) renunciation of his "divinity" on January 1, 1946. But, of course, Hirohito's renunciation in no way cancels out the views of the members of the Kyoto School toward the imperial institution before the end of the Pacific War, particularly during the fourteen-year period beginning with the Japanese invasion of Manchuria in 1931. Moreover, this topic is not unimportant even now, in the 1990s, for a glance at the daily newspaper shows that the imperial institution is thriving in its new postwar, "symbolic" guise. Indeed, as I write, the present emperor and empress are in Italy, performing various "symbolic" duties, including having an audience with Pope John Paul II. (One might even say that the present emperor is no longer merely a symbol but rather has become "divine" by cohabiting with the spirit of the Sun Goddess, Amaterasu, during the Daijōsai ceremony of November 1990.)

During the first approximately twenty years of my study of the Kyoto School, I too thought the imperial institution was of minimal importance to an understanding of the writings of the school's members. But since the late 1970s, and increasingly throughout the 1980s, I became convinced that it was not only important but *critically* important to an understanding of the writings of its most prominent member, Nishida, during the last fifteen years of his life (1930–45). As I worked on his biography, I perceived that what at the turn of the century was a relatively benign interpretation of the role of the imperial institution became by the 1930s total acceptance of its divine role. Even more to the point, Nishida articulated in sophisticated philosophical terms a justification for the unique mission of the imperial institution in world history. Although much of Nishida's philosophical legacy remains untouched by this particular interpretation of modern history, and by his obvious espousal of nationalism through such absolutizing of the imperial institution in his later years, it would be wrong not to address it and to attempt to understand it. That is what I alluded to, in a very cursory way, toward the end of a review article on David Dilworth's translation of Nishida's last major philosophical work, "Nishida's Final Statement" (*Monumenta Nipponica*, Autumn 1988). Although my statements prompted a vigorous rebuttal from Michiko Yusa—herself a distinguished scholar of Nishida's philosophy—in a later issue, I continue to believe that the question of Nishida's nationalism and exaltation of the imperial institution requires much, much more study and cannot be dismissed so easily.

How this problem relates to Abe is, of course, a matter of how *he* assesses Nishida's writings on the imperial institution and other aspects of the "national polity" (*kokutai*, in Japanese) and how he himself views the Japanese imperial institution, both in the prewar period and in the present. As I continue my dialogue with him through this essay, I must ask him these questions. I especially hope he will respond to them because I find his statement in the introduction to his and Christopher Ives's translation of Nishida's first work, *An Inquiry into the Good*, to be quite enigmatic: "Nishida was, however, neither anti-nationalistic nor nationalistic" (xxv). I am perplexed also that he does not mention Nishida's views on the imperial institution at all, despite extensive references to it by Nishida in his later writings. Thus, I cannot but think that the topic is somehow taboo; and in keeping with everything I have learned from Abe himself, both from his writings and in person, I think it is proper finally to break all taboos. For surely, if religion has any function at all, it is to seek the truth and overcome all obstacles on the road to it.

I realize, in conclusion, that this essay is a most curious mélange of personal anecdotes, impressionistic descriptions, and polemical statements. But somehow I am confident that Abe will read it in the spirit in which it was written, as both a tribute to him and as an extension of what I can truly affirm to be one of the most fruitful encounters of my life.

Chapter Four

THE F.A.S. ACRONYM IN MASAO ABE'S LIFE TRAJECTORY

Felix E. Prieto

THIS ESSAY, OFFERED TO MASAO ABE as an appreciation of his work in American universities, is structured according to the three stages in which his teacher Shin'ichi Hisamatsu (1889–1980) encapsulated his basic understanding of human existence in his use of the acronym F.A.S. I shall try to show how Abe's life trajectory represents an outstanding embodiment of the development of the selfless Self, which lies at the foundation of Hisamatsu's philosophy of Awakening, of which Abe is the most brilliant example in the academic arena.

Let me begin with a brief description of what F.A.S. means. *F* stands for an Awakening to the Formless Self, which refers to the dimension of *depth* in human existence, i.e., the True Self as the fundamental ground of human existence. *A* stands for this Formless Self as the standpoint of *a*ll-humankind and refers to the *width* of human existence, which also includes all beings in their entirety. The dimension of the *S* stands for the activity of creating history supra-historically and refers to the chronological *length* of human existence as awakened human history.

Masao Abe's main academic efforts were first directed at a provisional synthesis of Christianity as a religion of faith or grace and Buddhism as a religion of self-awakening or self-realization. Both religious trends coexist in Japanese Buddhism as well, where they find expression in Pure Land Buddhism and Zen Buddhism. As a devoted follower of Pure Land Buddhism in his younger days, Abe was directly confronted with the tension represented by the two contrasting ways of self-realization: the one based on the other power (*tariki*), in which one's efforts at human emancipation prove totally ineffective without the helping grace of Amida, and the other based on self power (*jiriki*), in which the seeker relies exclusively on his or her own efforts to obtain freedom from the human condition. This dialectical tension took for Abe at that time the shape of an existential impasse leading to a genuine philosophical *aporia* that his remarkable dialectical power was not able to overcome. In a conversation with John Cobb, Abe refers to this transition as a very painful one, which he was able to solve only under the guidance of his teacher Hisamatsu.

Upon the resolution of the contradictory tension inherent in the *tariki-jiriki* existential conflict, Abe undertook to apply consistently an analogous methodology regarding the Buddhist-Christian contrast:

> *Through that experience I was, in a sense, forced to compare Pure Land Buddhism and Zen—not intellectually, but existentially. This problem overlaps comparative studies of Buddhism and Christianity. Thus my personal interest is not merely to compare these two religions, Buddhism and Christianity, but rather to find the deeper root for the two types of religion they embody. To realize such a deeper truth is a very urgent task for us today. This is the main motif of my interest in the Buddhist-Christian dialogue.*[1]

The failure of reason to solve the vital problems created by the intellect points to the reason's inherent weakness to solve any truly fundamental contradiction in human existence. Hisamatsu distinguishes between a relative antinomy in the process of rational activity and an ultimate or absolute one that points to a fatal limitation in the structure of reason in which there appears the extremity of reason itself. This absolute antinomy characterizes the unavoidable limitations of the person as a rational being. Humans are not aware of this fact themselves and continue to rely on this antinomic standpoint. But without the realization and solution of this problem, one cannot help falling into anxiety and desperation.

When the fundamental antinomy has become one with the person who wrestles with it, there appears the great-doubt-mass (*dai-gi-dan*), an ultimate negation of the thinking itself. However, a great-doubt-mass that remains a *particular* doubt mass can yield only a *particular* form of *satori*, one that still has *form*, and as such cannot really be called Great Awakening. The great-doubt-mass stands in proportion to its effects. The greater and more thoroughgoing the doubt, the more exhaustive and shattering its results.

It is worth emphasizing, however, that a theoretical description of the process does not at all provide the real problematic to start the quest of self-discovery. It is not that in doubting myself I am truly doubting, but only when I have become a total doubt myself. The overcoming of the great-doubt-mass cannot be undertaken only by reading a literary description of it, unless one has previously become the very doubt mass itself.

This existential problem, as Abe says, overlaps the comparative study of Buddhism and Christianity. Upon resolving the initial antinomy eventually transformed into the great-doubt-mass, Abe would not start digging up relics and bones of the Buddhist tradition as a heritage for the future. On the basis of his awakening to the Formless Self, and working in the present historical situation, he would now undertake the task of finding and working out the deeper roots of the two types of religious realization embodied in his initial problematic. A religious experience should, in his view, be grasped in terms of reflective thought. Philosophy and religion ought to build a strict and inseparable unity, inasmuch as a religion without philosophy is blind to its own articulation, and philosophy without religion is an abstract endeavor with no transforming power. In the West both are strictly separated departments, which explains why at present there are so many religious movements based on simply emotional reasons, blind to any philosophical articulation, and philosophies that are powerless because they are limited to a positivistic approach. Abe's thinking is not only concerned with establishing the necessary demarcations between philosophy and religion either in the East or the West. If the cultural and religious meeting of both hemispheres is now taking place and creatively developing their religious and philosophical standpoints, it is because of people of Abe's stature. And those of us who by one way or another have come within his personal world as friends or devoted readers are greatly indebted to him. The meeting of East and West, as an overcoming of the historical preconceptions between the Buddhist and Christian antagonism hitherto firmly entrenched, is one of a processual character meant to be accomplished in time, as mutual love and understanding develop. It is in this sense that Abe's dialogue has been a model for the coming generation.

Throughout his teaching career, through his remarkable books and articles confronting Buddhist thought with the West's most outstanding thinkers, and through his interpretative book on Japan's foremost religious philosopher-priest, Dōgen, Abe has offered us a truly penetrating view of the so-called Kyoto School of philosophy, of which he has been its living representative in the West. The nature of this essay does not call for a critical evaluation of Masao Abe's output. Others who are more qualified can do that. Nor is here the place to assess how far his possible development of the Kyoto School's conception of Nothingness has succeeded to advance its articulation after Kitarō Nishida's initial formulation. In the case of Masao Abe, we are offered an interpretation of Buddhist thought that in my view had already attained its full development in the foregoing generation. Abe's task has been the formulation in straightforward language of a process of Buddhist speculation far from easy to assimilate and follow. Criticism has been voiced of his use of Western terminology when submitting Western thinkers to a *pāramitā* dialectic, especially regarding the process thinking of Whitehead or the onto-theology of Heidegger. But since this criticism is only external, it in no way invalidates or calls for a radical revision of Abe's position inasmuch as his initial aim is to establish a way of thinking that is truly universal and common to East and West. To note the separations and differences is but a way to a better understanding of their common and fundamental agreements for a world philosophy.

But this philosophical task is not Abe's *ultimate* concern. More important to him is the discovery of our common humanity. Given our focus on F.A.S., this is the aspect of Abe's thought that needs to be stressed here. Humankind is today a scattering of individuals, an aggregate or conglomeration of single entities, windowless monads wandering aimlessly in a world without meaning. This means that "all humankind as a whole" does not exist at all. The world today should aim to abolish the nation-states with which people identify themselves. Abe is pressing upon us the urgency of investigating the religious reasons to take as our destiny the state of being persons belonging to a single and united world. It is because there is no true humankind that there is at present no true world history. When the individual transcends the ego-centered structure of the nation-states and thereby creates the universal sovereignty of humankind, true history may begin in a postmodern world. In Abe's estimate, what we need most at present is not a new humanism but a new cosmology. Human existence is now in great need of clarifying authentic religiosity with the aim of overcoming the antireligious ideologies now threatening the world in a blind alley of nihility, and in need of establishing a self-awakened cosmos based on the realization of Emptiness, the Formless Self.

Now Masao Abe returns to Japan and concludes his teaching career in the Western academic world, thus entering into the *length* dimension of his trajectory, the dimension of the extension of life in which the awakened individual embarks on the creation of history supra-historically (S). For the creation of true history, a third dimension of human existence is called for, because true history cannot be created by any means immanent in conventional history. History is something that should always be created anew rather than being the record of what has already been created. When fettered by our own creation, history becomes mere scholarship. Living without continuously creating the future belongs already to the past and, as such, is historically worthless. Therefore, after awakening to the Formless Self (F) and having helped to form the world on the standpoint of All-Humankind (A), Abe's concluding stage of supra-historically creating history at all times (S) is now opening up. After the brilliant actualization of its previous stages, without being fettered by the already created history, the last stage for the completion of the F.A.S. acronym now looms large in Abe's trajectory as the actualization of the ultimate postmodern Mahāyāna career.

I have ventured, perhaps somewhat arbitrarily, to establish in a cursory way Abe's trajectory with the scheme of spiritual development traced by Hisamatsu's notion of F.A.S. If Abe's work is read under this light, we can find implicit an evaluation, both in terms of its potential development as well as in terms of what has already been achieved. With some qualifications, the F.A.S. acronym thus exemplified also throws a personal challenge to every one of us to be worthy of the Dharma rain so generously poured with wisdom and compassion upon our parched hemisphere.

chapter Five

THE
ZEN ROOTS OF
MASAO ABE'S
THOUGHT

Richard J. DeMartino

IN HIS FOREWORD to Masao Abe's award-winning book, *Zen and Western Thought*,[1] John Hick, with much justification, described Abe (who "belongs to the vigorous Kyoto School and is a successor of its greater figures, Nishida, Hisamatsu, and Nishitani")[2] as "the leading philosophical exponent of Zen to the West since the death of D. T. Suzuki."[3] Indeed, since 1958,[4] Abe's many years of translating, lecturing, and publishing in English concerning Zen carry on a long-standing interaction of Zen with Western thought and Western expression that goes back in fact through Suzuki to Suzuki's teacher Shaku Sōen (1859–1919). For the first serious, probing engagement between Zen and Western thought began, from the side of Zen, possibly as early as 1885. It was then that Shaku Sōen, recently having received his final Zen approval from his Zen teacher, Imagita Kōsen (1816–92), decided—in a startling departure for a Zen monk of his time (and over the objections of his teacher)[5]—to enter Keiō-Gijuku (later Keiō University) in Tokyo. This was an upper-level school formally established about two decades earlier by Yukichi Fukuzawa (1835–1901) under patently discernible influences of Western thought. Sōen entered expressly "in order to study Western science."[6]

Perhaps as an offshoot of his experience at that school, this same Shaku Sōen in 1893 became the first Zen master to visit the United States. Having in 1892 succeeded Imagita Kōsen as head of the Engaku-ji monastery compound (in Kita-Kamakura, south of Tokyo), Sōen in August of 1893 went to America as a delegate to the World Parliament of Religions, held the following month in Chicago. At that conference his paper was read in an English translation prepared back in Japan initially by D. T. Suzuki.[7] As a result of friendships stemming directly or indirectly from that conference, Sōen was once again in the United States during 1905–06. An assemblage of some of the verbal presentations he made in America, translated into English and edited by Suzuki (who, through Sōen's contacts, had been in America since 1897), was published in 1906.[8]

The topics dealt with in this collection were wide-ranging. Of special interest for what shall be a major focus here (since it came to be one of Abe's primary concerns) is that in explaining the central or pivotal Buddhist notion of *Śūnyatā*, or "Emptiness," great care was taken to prevent a dualistic or exclusively one-sided negative or nihilistic misunderstanding. That is, not only was *Śūnyatā* presented and discussed along with the companion Buddhist notion of *tathatā*, and *bhūtatathatā*, or "suchness," as equivalent "philosophical terms for Dharmakaya"[9] or the "totality of existence,"[10] but further spelled out were the implications of this for the Zen Awakened Self (or "Mind"): that "it is perfectly empty when it is filled to the brim,"[11] and, because of this, that "it has no abode whatever where it finds itself located"[12]—i.e., that it occupies what could be called a "place-of-no-place."[13]

This same theme of the non-nihilistic, nondualistic nature of Emptiness (particularly in its relation to suchness) was taken up and treated by Suzuki in his own way in some of his early works in English, *Açvaghosha's Discourse on the Awakening of Faith in the Mahayana* (1900)[14] and *Outlines of Mahayana Buddhism* (1907).[15] Although the emphasis in the Açvaghosha treatise, supposedly one of the earliest Mahāyāna Buddhist texts, was not on Emptiness, but on suchness, Suzuki, in the introduction to his translation of this work, commented: "Whatever the origin of the idea of suchness might have been, its 'absolute aspect' evidently foreshadows the *Çūnyatā* philosophy of the Mādhyamika school."[16] In the glossary he supplied at the end of his translation, Suzuki explicitly spoke of "emptiness [or] *çūnyatā* [as] an aspect of suchness."[17]

This position was disclosed more fully in Suzuki's footnote to a portion of *Açvaghosha's Discourse* (on which the position was apparently based), which stated that

> there is a twofold aspect in suchness. . . . The first is trueness
> as . . . (çūnyatā) in the sense that it is completely set apart from
> the attributes of all things unreal, that it is the real reality. The
> second is trueness as . . . (açūnyatā) in the sense that . . . it is
> self-existent.[18]

The footnote Suzuki gave to this was "Açvaghosha here states that bhūtatathatā is at once çūnyā and açūnyā. It is çūnyā because it transcends all forms of separation and individuation (i.e., it is nonparticular); it is açūnyā because all possible things in the world emanate from it (i.e., it is the font or source of all particulars)."[19]

Thus, for Suzuki, "philosophically speaking, Suchness or Bhūtatathatā is an ontological term. . . ."[20] Yet in one of his last published books, Suzuki announced: "Ontologically, Emptiness is Being *per se*."[21] His rationale for this was, as he wrote elsewhere, "Emptiness is not a negative idea, nor does it mean mere privation."[22] "Emptiness is not sheer nothingness."[23] "Emptiness which is conceptually liable to be mistaken for sheer nothingness is in fact the reservoir (*ālaya*) of infinite possibilities."[24] Hence, for Suzuki, "Śūnyatā, properly speaking, has no negative connotation. It is another name for Tathatā, that is, emptiness is suchness and suchness is emptiness."[25] Inasmuch as "Emptiness . . . is synonymous with suchness (*tathatā*),"[26] because "in reality Śūnyatā is Tathatā, and Tathatā Śūnyatā,"[27] Suzuki maintained, "Buddhist philosophy, therefore, is the philosophy of Suchness, or philosophy of Emptiness."[28]

With Suzuki, then, besides its being spoken of as an aspect of suchness, Śūnyatā is also used interchangeably—or even equated—with suchness. This, too, had a basis in *Açvaghosha's Discourse*, which reports: "It is said in the *Sūtras* that all things in the world without exception are perfect emptiness (*atyantaçūnyatā*), that even Nirvana or suchness is also perfect emptiness."[29] Actually, the text goes beyond this, holding that not alone is *tathatā* or suchness empty, but "the truth is that . . . (çūnyatā) is also void (çūnyā) in its nature."[30] A similar pronouncement is found in the *Prajñāpāramitā* tomes. Rendered by Suzuki, "'Emptiness itself is empty' (*sūnyatāsūnyatā*)."[31] It likewise appears in the Mādhyamika literature. As quoted by Abe, "'Emptiness too is empty' . . . sunyata-sunyata.'"[32] And, as further amplified by Abe, "In other words, true emptiness is *pure activity of emptying* which empties everything including itself."[33]

Since it is avowed that suchness is empty, that Emptiness itself is empty, and that suchness and Emptiness are synonymous, the key in all this, clearly, is precisely "sunyata-sunyata." For the contended relation between suchness and Emptiness can prevail solely if suchness is a self-emptying suchness, and Emptiness a self-emptying Emptiness—which means solely if each bespeaks equally a self-emptying emptying, or a self-emptying-self-emptying: "sunyata-sunyata."[34] This would account for Suzuki's assertion that "Buddhism [would say,] 'This universe is . . . emptiness itself (*çūnyatā*)'";[35] that "Emptiness is in truth no less than the concreteness of reality itself";[36] that "it is only possible in Emptiness to see 'something and nothing alike.' 'Something' here is Buddhist *asti*, and 'nothing' *nāsti*, and true *Prajñā* obtains only when the dualism of being and non-being is transcended."[37] In addition, it would serve to explain his including a reference to Hinduism in another of the footnotes to his translation of *Açvaghosha's Discourse*: "Cf. the *Bhagavadgītā*, Chapter IX, p. 84: 'I am immortality and also death; and I, O Arjuna! am that which is and that which is not.'"[38] In what might be considered a Buddhist parallel, it may be noted that in his characterizing a bodhisattva of "the eighth stage" (or what could be called the Self-awakened-Self-actualization of this "ontology" of the self-emptying-self-emptying or nondualistic-duality of suchness and Emptiness), Suzuki exclaimed, "He is nature herself,"[39] or, as he was later to put it, "The Buddha is Nature personified."[40]

This is the reason Suzuki started to emphasize, as early as he did, that "bhūtatathatā (suchness) . . . does not fall under the category of [dualistic] being and non-being. . . . Says Nāgārjuna in his Çāstra (Chapter XV):

To think 'it is,' is eternalism,
To think 'it is not,' is nihilism:
Being and non-being,
The wise cling not to either.

Again,

> *The dualism of 'to be' and 'not to be,'*
> *The dualism of pure and not-pure:*
> *Such dualism having abandoned,*
> *The wise stand not even in the middle."*[41]

"So the Mahāyānists generally designate absolute Suchness as Çūnyatā or void."[42] Hence, "absolute Suchness [also designated as Çūnyatā] is empty and not empty, çūnyā and açūnyā, being and non-being, sat and asat."[43] Expressed otherwise: "When considered absolutely [they] can neither be empty nor not-empty, neither *çūnyā* nor *açūnyā*, neither *asti* nor *nāsti*."[44] This prompted Suzuki to query, "Could a doctrine be called nihilistic when it defines the absolute as neither void (*çūnyā*) nor not-void (*açūnyā*)?"[45] Thus did Suzuki, as far back as the first decade of this century, elucidate "the nature of Suchness [and Emptiness] or the 'Dharma of Non-duality,' as it is termed in the [Vimalakīrti] Sūtra."[46]

Shortly thereafter (in 1911), there was published in Japan, in Japanese, the first really sustained religio-philosophical treatment of Zen thought under the perceptible influence of Western thought. This was the intellectually groundbreaking *Inquiry into the Good*, by Kitarō Nishida, Suzuki's lifelong intimate friend. In the view of Masao Abe, as set forth in his introduction to his joint translation of this work: "*An Inquiry into the Good* stands upon [the] mutual transformation of Zen and philosophy. As both a philosopher and a Zen Buddhist, Nishida transformed Zen into philosophy for the first time in the history of this religious tradition and, also for the first time, transformed Western philosophy into a Zen-oriented philosophy."[47] As Abe went on to explain, "At this time, Nishida clearly [took what he] regarded [to be Zen's] *pure experience* as the sole reality and wanted to develop his philosophy on this basis."[48]

At the outset, then, Nishida's own distinctive use of "pure experience" was the vehicle through which he sought to explicate what the *Vimalakīrti Sūtra* epitomized as the "Dharma of Non-duality." Nishida spoke of "the state of pure experience in which there is no separation of subject and object and no distinction between the self and other things."[49] In Abe's explanation, "Pure experience is realized prior to the distinction between subject and object. . . . In Nishida's understanding of pure experience . . . the knower and the known are not two."[50] Though Nishida's explication developed and changed somewhat over the years, Abe, after examining the complete corpus of Nishida's writings, concluded, "Given Nishida's philosophical work after *An Inquiry into the Good*, we can argue that his entire philosophy is a development and deepening of his initial notion of pure experience. *An Inquiry into the Good* provided not only the point of departure but also the foundation of his philosophy."[51]

Unquestionably, there can be found in Nishida's overall maiden effort such rudimentary statements that were germinal for his future philosophy as, "When we assert that 'there are no things'—from the perspective of intuition that transcends the distinction between subject and object—a consciousness of nothingness lies behind our assertion. Nothingness is not merely a word: its concrete meaning indicates the lack of certain qualities and also the possession of certain positive qualities."[52] This means "absolute nothingness . . . is not . . . mere nothingness."[53] So, "Non-being separate from being is not true non-being."[54]

Concerning Nishida's ensuing developed thought, Abe has observed, "Realizing the uniqueness of the Eastern way of thinking, Nishida [eventually] took absolute nothingness as ultimate reality and tried to give it a logical foundation through his confrontation with Western philosophy."[55] As Nishida himself professed, "At the basis of Asian culture . . . lies something that can be called seeing the form of the formless and hearing the sound of the soundless. Our minds are compelled to seek for this. I would like to give a philosophical foundation to this demand."[56] "[In this undertaking,] through the mediation of Greek philosophy I developed . . . the idea of 'place.' In this way I began to lay a logical base for my ideas."[57] Working out this "logical base" in terms of "the idea of place," Nishida evolved what he came to call "the logic of place," which, as Abe saw it, was linked to Śūnyatā. "[Nishida's] logical foundation for ultimate reality [was] formulated in terms of the logic of place or the logic of absolute nothingness. . . . It is a logic of Oriental *nothingness* (*śūnyatā*) and is essentially different from Western logic."[58]

While Nishida evidently did not make too much use of the specific term Śūnyatā—or, for that matter, of the term *suchness*—Abe is not alone in associating Nishida's use of *nothingness* with *Emptiness* or Śūnyatā. For this coupling of Nishida's Eastern—or absolute—nothingness with *Śūn-yatā* or Emptiness can be discerned as well in the writings of Keiji Nishitani, one of the more well known of Nishida's direct disciples. "The Eastern spirit is . . . intuitive as well as active. This is the standpoint of nothingness or emptiness. Nishida's philosophy was also based on the standpoint of an absolute nothingness, but here nothingness and emptiness do not mean that there is nothing. On the contrary, nothingness is the 'actual form of all dharmas.'"[59] Similarly, Suzuki once stated: "Sunyata. . . . is a 'nothing' which is absolute 'nothingness.'"[60]

This commingling the notions of a non-nihilistic Emptiness and nothingness apparently goes back, in the Zen tradition, at least to the Fifth Chinese Zen Patriarch, Hung-jēn. As Abe has brought to light in another connection, "With Hung-jēn, Dōgen emphasizes: 'Since the Buddha-nature is empty it is called *mu* (no-thing).'"[61] Actually, Abe sees the relation between these two notions going back much further. For him, already "in the doctrine of dependent co-origination expounded by the Buddha, the notion of absolute Nothingness was implicit. It was Nāgārjuna who explicitly enunciated this absolute Nothingness in terms of *Śūnyatā*."[62] That is, "It is Nāgārjuna who established the idea of *Śūnyatā* or Emptiness by clearly realizing the implication of the basic ideas transmitted by the earlier Buddhist tradition."[63] Again, Abe presses the crucial point:

> *It must be emphasized that Nāgārjuna's idea of Emptiness is not nihilistic. . . . In fact, Nāgārjuna . . . denounced the so-called "nihilistic" view, which insisted that true reality is empty and non-existent. . . . Therefore, his idea of Emptiness is not a mere emptiness as opposed to fullness. . . . Thus, in* Śūnyatā, *Emptiness as it is is Fullness and Fullness as it is is Emptiness.*[64]

Suzuki has been equally emphatic: "Absolute fullness is the same as absolute emptiness."[65]

Although Nishida did allude to "the *śūnyatā* logic of the *Prajñā-pāramitā Sūtra* tradition,"[66] instead of *Śūnyatā* or Emptiness, he rather accentuated, besides "absolute nothingness," the notion of "absolute self-negation," which he alternately formulated as an absolute "self-contradiction." Thus, for example, in his last complete essay, he argued, "Since there can be nothing at all that objectively opposes the absolute, the absolute must relate to itself as a form of self-contradiction. It must express itself by negating itself."[67] "The absolute must . . . possess absolute self-negation within itself. In this respect the absolute must be absolutely nothing."[68] "A true absolute must possess itself through self-negation."[69] "The true absolute must be an identity of absolute contradiction in this sense."[70] Furthermore,

> Because . . . the absolute stands to itself in the form of a contradictory identity—namely as its own absolute self-negation, or as possessing self-negation within itself—it exists and expresses itself through itself. Because it is absolute nothingness, it is absolute being. It is because of this coincidence of absolute nothingness and absolute being that we can speak of . . . divine omniscience and omnipotence.[71]

So it is that "the true absolute possesses absolute negation within itself. It is by negating its own nothingness that it is infinitely self-affirming."[72] For Nishida, then, it is consistently a matter of "the Absolute's own self-affirmation through self-negation,"[73] "the absolute's affirmation through its own negation."[74] Given this sort of delineation, "nothingness separated from being is not true nothingness."[75]

With respect to Nishida's "logic of place," in the *Diamond Sūtra*, there is a celebrated injunction that is quoted often in Zen: "Give rise to the Mind [or Self] that has no abiding place!" I believe it may be said that Nishida sought in effect to give a logical formulation—or a logical grounding—to what could be called this self-negating or self-emptying place-less-place, or place of no-abode. He did so in what he denominated variously "the logic of place," the "logic of contradictory identity,"[76] the "logic of nothingness,"[77] "the logic of absolute nothingness," "the place of absolute nothingness,"[78] "the logic of the place of nothingness,"[79] or, simply "the place of nothingness."[80] Regardless of how it is designated, such a place may be said to be at once no-place and yet every-place—nowhere and yet everywhere, in an "absolutely contradictory self-identity." Hence, Nishida, in his usage of the term *God*, could make reference to what he characterized as "the old phrase that God is 'nowhere and yet everywhere in this world.'"[81] That is, "because God is no-thing, there is no place where God is not."[82]

Addressing his understanding explicitly to Christianity and its notion of kenosis (self-emptying), Nishida held that "God must always, in Saint Paul's words, empty himself. . . . If it is said that God creates the world out of love, then God's absolute love must be essential to the creative act as God's own absolute self-negation."[83] For "a God who does not empty himself, a God who does not express himself through his own self-negation, is not the true absolute."[84] To Nishida, this constituted "the paradox of God, of God's own self-affirmation through self-negation."[85] On the other hand, this paradox, for Nishida, was not limited, restricted, or exclusive. Anything that "stands in relation to itself must negate itself. But by negating itself it is paradoxically one with itself."[86] This is what Nishida meant by—and gave voice to as—an "absolutely contradictory self-identity."

As Nishida learned from Suzuki that "Buddhism expresses this paradox through the dialectic of 'is' and 'is not' (*soku hi*). I am indebted to Daisetsu Suzuki for showing me the following passage in the *Diamond Sūtra*:

> *Because all dharmas are not all dharmas,*
> *Therefore they are called all dharmas.*
> *Because there is no Buddha, there is Buddha:*
> *Because there are no sentient beings, there are sentient beings."*[87]

In fact, when Suzuki first heard from Nishida of the latter's now famous phrase "*zettai-mujun-teki-jiko-dōitsu*" (herein translated as "absolutely contradictory self-identity"),[88] Suzuki informed Nishida that this was akin to what Suzuki, under the influence of the aforementioned *Diamond Sūtra*, was calling "*soku-hi-no-ronri*"[89] ("the logic of soku-hi," which could, accordingly, be translated as "the logic of even-as-it-is-it-is-not"). In Suzuki's own English articulations: "A is A because it is not A";[90] or, "A is not-A, therefore it is A."[91] In his employment of the term *God*, this meant, "To be God is not to be God";[92] that "God is God when God is not God";[93] just as "Being is Being because Being is Not-Being."[94] In brief, for Suzuki, "To be itself is not to be itself—this is the logic of Zen."[95]

In this understanding then, these contradictory dualities are neither simply contradictory nor simply dualities. As each component of the duality is a component of a self-emptying or self-negating duality—or perhaps better, a self-emptying-self-emptying or a self-negating-self-negating—it is at once itself and not-itself, and so at once itself and the other in a non-dualistic and therefore noncontradictory-contradictory-duality. It is exactly this "logic of Zen," logic of *soku-hi*, or what may comparably be deemed logic of the nondualistic paradox that undergirds Suzuki's seemingly quizzical statements: "Emptiness is not sheer emptiness. . . . It is and at the same time it is not."[96] "Zen emptiness is . . . the emptiness of fullness."[97] "Perfect poverty is recovered only when perfect emptiness is perfect fullness."[98] "Tathatā is Śūnyatā, and Śūnyatā is Tathatā."[99] Hence, "To be absolutely nothing is to be everything."[100] In sum, "Emptiness is Suchness and Suchness is Emptiness. A world of *rupa* is no other than sunyata, and sunyata is no other than this *rupaloka*, which is a Buddhist term for Nature."[101]

Consequently, with Suzuki, a truly thorough self-emptying, kenosis, self-negation, "dying," or "being killed" is not, in Christian terms, a matter of the Son emptying himself of his divinity and taking on the form of a human servant. On the contrary, it would rather be a matter of the total spiritual coincident death-rebirth of the human person Jesus. "[In Zen] there is no half-killing. The killing is to be so complete that there will be a rebirth. The half-dead can never be resuscitated."[102] "We must negate ourselves to affirm ourselves."[103]

This call for what in Zen is known as the Great Death was equally prominent in Nishida:

> The method through which we can know the true self . . . is our
> self-attainment of the power of the union of subject and object. To
> acquire this power is to kill our false self [or "ego completely"] and,
> after dying once [and for all] to gain new life [by being "born
> again"].[104]

This makes intelligible Nishida's exclamation: "Those without a self—those who have extinguished the self—are the greatest."[105]

Tendering his own comprehension of this self-emptying, kenosis, or "making oneself empty," Nishitani has proposed that

> [*as for*] *"making oneself empty," [in] the case of Christ, it meant
> taking the form of man and becoming a servant, in accordance
> with the will of God, who is the origin of the* ekkenōsis *or
> "making himself empty" of Christ. . . . Accordingly, the meaning
> of self-emptying may be said to be contained within God
> himself. . . . What is* ekkenōsis *for the Son is* kenōsis *for
> the Father.*[106]

For Nishitani as well then, there "must be a point within God where God
is not God."[107]

In Nishitani's more strictly Buddhist (or Zen) perspective,

> *When the standpoint of emptiness is radicalized—and the
> corresponding orientation is one in which emptiness itself is also
> emptied—this . . . point at which emptiness is emptied to become
> true emptiness is the very point at which each and every thing
> becomes manifest in possession of its own suchness.*[108]

Coming about through an emptying of the very Emptiness (or, in
other words, through a self-emptying of the self-emptying), this being "in
possession of its own suchness" has been further elaborated by Nishitani
in terms of "being so of itself," or of being "what it is of its own accord"—
both of which are revealed to be characteristics of "nature."

> *In [Japanese], the meaning of the word "nature"* (jinen, shizen)
> *is said to be* onozukara shikari—*being so of itself. Nature* (jinen),
> *being so of itself, being what it is of itself—[means that the being
> of] something . . . is of-itself . . . that no power from outside forced
> it to be what it is. Or we can say that it is what it is of its own
> accord. This "of its own accord"* (hitorideni) *corresponds to the
> meaning of the Chinese character* ji *of* jiko *("self"), or the* shi *of*
> shizen *[or* ji *of* jinen*] ("nature"). This character [*ji*] has both the
> meaning of "of itself"* (onozukara) *and "for itself"* (mizukara).[109]

Moreover, "this latter [being "of itself" and "for itself"] is the great standpoint of the true self, the standpoint of no-ego, of the Life of the universe."[110] That is,

> the standpoint of no-ego is one that smashes that pattern we
> call [ego] to become one with the Life of the universe, of nature.
> When one stands there, all things, just as they are, become the
> actual form and actual reality that they are—the truth of their
> "suchness."[111]

Turning attention to these same interrelated themes, Abe declared:

> As long as the human self tries to grasp itself through [its
> ordinary] self-consciousness . . . the human ego-self falls into
> an ever-deepening dilemma. . . . It is essential that one face this
> dilemma and break through it, in order to realize Emptiness or
> suchness. This realization of Emptiness is the liberation from that
> dilemma which is existentially rooted in human consciousness.
> Awakening to Emptiness, which is disclosed through the death of
> the ego, you realize your "suchness." This is because the realization
> of suchness is the positive aspect of the realization of Emptiness.[112]

This viewpoint is the basis of Abe's claim that "'Emptiness' and 'suchness' are simply different verbal expressions of one and the same Reality."[113] Alternately conveyed, "'Emptiness' is also called as-it-is-ness or suchness. Emptiness is not a mere emptiness, but rather fullness."[114] In another statement, "Buddhism advocates Sunyata (Emptiness), which is not a nihilistic emptiness but rather a fullness of particular things and individual persons functioning in their full capacity and without mutual impediment."[115]

So, for Abe, "the ultimate in Zen (and in Buddhism) is . . . 'absolute Nothingness' or 'Emptiness,' which is dynamically identical with 'wondrous Being' or 'Fullness.'"[116] Always to be remembered is that "the real Nothingness is not the nothingness as distinguished from somethingness."[117] Quite the reverse, "in true Emptiness the . . . 'emptying' is also 'emptied,'"[118] and "precisely because it is Emptiness which 'empties' even Emptiness, true Emptiness (Absolute Nothingness) is absolute Reality."[119] This, for him, is "the dynamism of 'Emptiness' which is simultaneously Fullness."[120] Reformulating this self-emptying-Emptiness—or what is, in effect, also a self-emptying-fullness, or a self-full-filling-Emptiness—in yet other terms, Abe has ventured, "Thus we may say that absolute negation is absolute affirmation and absolute affirmation is absolute negation. This paradoxical statement well expresses the dialectical and dynamic structure of *Śūnyatā* in which Emptiness is Fullness and Fullness is Emptiness."[121]

What is especially notable in Abe's explication is his interpretive application of this view of Emptiness to the Christian notion of kenosis. In his provocative and challenging essay "Kenotic God and Dynamic Sunyata," which became the centerpiece of two volumes of responses by Western religious thinkers,[122] Abe proposed that

> *we should understand the doctrine of Christ's kenosis to mean*
> *that Christ as the Son of God is* essentially *and* fundamentally
> *self-emptying or self-negating—because of this fundamental*
> *nature, the Son of God is Christ—that is, the Messiah. It is not*
> *that the Son of God became a person through the process of his*
> *self-emptying but that fundamentally he is true person and true*
> *God at one and the same time in his dynamic work and activity*
> *of self-emptying.*[123]

From this, in Abe's view, it follows that

> *the problem of the kenosis of Christ inevitably leads us to face the*
> *problem of the kenosis of God. In other words, if Christ the Son of*
> *God empties himself, should we not consider the self-emptying of*
> *God—that is, the kenosis of the very God?*[124]

> *Is it not that the kenosis of Christ—that is, the self-emptying of*
> *the Son of God—has its origin in God "the Father"—that is, the*
> *kenosis of God? Without the self-emptying of God "the Father,"*
> *the self-emptying of the Son of God is inconceivable.*[125]

Abe therefore insists, "This kenotic God is the ground of the kenotic Christ. The God who does not cease to be God even in the self-emptying of the Son of God, that is, the kenosis of Christ, is not the true God."[126]

By this Abe is "contending that through the kenosis of God, 'God is truly God.'"[127]

Relating his interpretation to Buddhism—or to Zen—Abe has argued:

Only when the ego-self negates itself completely does it come to understand who the kenotic God is and what God's total self-emptying means to the self. Accordingly, the . . . statement, "God is not God, and precisely because God is not a self-affirmative God, God is truly God," can be properly grasped [only] by the parallel existential realization that "self is not self, and precisely because it is not, self is truly self."[128]

Or, once more:

God is not God; precisely because of this, God is truly God. And, as . . . emphasized before, this statement of God cannot be properly understood without our own parallel existential realization that "Self is not self, and precisely because it is not, Self is truly Self."[129]

However, recapitulating in even more traditional Buddhist terminology, Abe is careful to note that

the ultimate reality for Buddhism is neither Being nor God, but Sunyata. Sunyata literally means "emptiness" or "voidness" and can imply "absolute nothingness." This is because . . . true Sunyata is not even that which is represented and conceived as "Sunyata." . . . Instead, Mahayana Buddhism emphasizes that "Sunyata is non-Sunyata (aśūnyatā): therefore it is ultimate Sunyata (atyanta-Śūnyatā)." Sunyata not only is not Being or God, but [is] also not emptiness as distinguished from somethingness or fullness. . . . In other words, emptiness not only empties everything else but also empties itself.[130]

Thus, while *Śūnyatā* is formless[131]—that is, "'Emptiness' is also termed 'formlessness' because it completely overcomes 'form,'"[132] nevertheless, as highlighted in the Prajñāpāramitā-Hridaya-Sūtra, formless and form, nothingness and somethingness, Emptiness and fullness go together non-dualisticly. As presented to Abe, "In the realization of true Sunyata, form is ceaselessly emptied, turning into formless emptiness, and formless emptiness is ceaselessly emptied and forever freely taking form."[133] So it is that "true emptiness is the ever self-emptying activity which is incessantly turning into being."[134]

Inasmuch as what is involved is an emptying-forming that is always a self-emptying-self-forming, it is not surprising that Abe should touch upon the relation of *Śūnyatā* to *jinen*. "Sunyata [is] translated by *jinen* in Japanese, or *svayambhū* in Sanskrit, which means 'self-so,' 'so of itself.' . . . It also means 'natural-ness.' . . . It is the most basic original 'nature' of things."[135] Furthermore, as Abe in his own way understands and has intimated, when speaking of Nature, or *jinen*, and of what may be termed its self-emptying-self-full-filling-self-activity, it is possible to speak of an unawakened *jinen*, or Nature, as distinguished from a Self-awakened *jinen*, or Nature. For "in the. . . . Self-awakening of each one of us, not only is mankind awakened to its own true nature but indeed the myriad phenomena of the universe are awakened to their true nature."[136] That is, "At the same time that the Self-awakening wherein each of us awakens to his or her original Self is the true . . . Self-awakening of each of us, it is the Self-awakening of the world itself."[137] Again, "This immediate self-realization of Self-Mind by Self-Mind itself is nothing other than the realization of 'Emptiness.' When Self-Mind immediately awakens to Self-Mind itself, the world is simultaneously awakened to as the world itself."[138] In short, "in this Awakening . . . 'being so of itself' (*jinen*) . . . presents itself."[139]

As Suzuki has phrased it, "[this Self-awakening or] Satori is seeing into one's own nature; and this 'nature' is not an entity belonging to oneself as distinguished from others; . . . 'Nature' is the seer as well as the object seen."[140] In the words of the Sixth Chinese Zen Patriarch, Hui-neng, translated by Suzuki, "Nature reflects itself in itself, which is self-illumination."[141] This understanding of *satori* explains why, for Suzuki, "to understand truthfully, *yathābhūtam*, what Emptiness is, the awakening (*sambodhi*) is indispensable."[142] "All that is needed is the experience of nothingness, which is suchness."[143] This means "it is for us to bring into full consciousness . . . Nature."[144] Or in Abe's phraseology, "Sunyata is the very ground of the self and thereby the ground of everything to which we are related. The realization of Sunyata-as-such is nothing but the Self-Awakening of Dharma . . . our Self-Awakening of Dharma."[145] "It is precisely within this 'expanse of Self-awakening' that all things exist in the true sense."[146]

Along with Suzuki, Nishida, Nishitani, and especially Hisamatsu,[147] Abe, too, has proclaimed that in order to come to this Self-awakening, there is the necessity "for man . . . to 'die' in the death of his own ego. For only through the death of his own ego is the cosmological dimension, the dimension of *jinen*, opened up to him. And only in that moment does he awaken to his true self."[148] Since this breakup-break-through, or "death," of what may be said to be the ego's dualistic structure-and-functioning is specified in Zen as the Great Death, Abe has underscored that,

> *The realization of the Great Death is the crucial point for the*
> *seemingly paradoxical Mahayana doctrines. This is simply another*
> *expression for the . . . statement that the realization of absolute*
> *Nothingness is indispensable for attaining the Mahayana notion*
> *of Emptiness which is no other than Fullness.*[149]

The end result for Abe is that "in the true breaking through of the ego-self, the true Self emerges within an unending 'expanse' of Self-Awakening [wherein] there is a realization of the true suchness of the world and the Self."[150]

This being the case, with this Self-awakening there is overcome "not only the duality of life and death but also the wider dualities, i.e., the dualities of generation-extinction and appearance-disappearance . . . i.e., the duality of being-nonbeing."[151] For this reason, as Abe sees it, "Buddhism . . . transcends [the duality of] man and nature in the direction of [a nondualistic] 'naturalness' or *jinen*, which is identical with Buddha-nature or suchness,"[152] which, in turn for him, as already indicated, is identical with Śūnyatā, or Emptiness.[153]

This then, briefly sketched, is the position that Abe has worked out and elucidated most extensively in comparison with—and in contrast to—Western religious and philosophical thought. In so doing, he has not simply carried on but has also carried forward the work of his predecessors. Not that this work has ended. Far from it. Abe is today as prolific and as provocative as ever, continually stimulating—and evoking comments and responses from—numerous Western thinkers.

In the spirit of this continuing dialogue, and in the interest of engaging avowedly secular as well as religious thinkers, I wonder how Abe would react to the following question-proposal that would adopt as its central or pivotal focus precisely *jinen*, or Nature. That is, may it not also be said that initially there is primordial Nature-in-itself functioning unreflectively and so in an unawakened, unbroken absence of duality in what could be called the ongoing simultaneity of its self-creation, self-destruction, and self-re-creation? (In Buddhist terminology, this probably would be primeval, unreflective *pratītya-samutpāda*, that is, Nature's unreflective or unawakened interdependent co-origination-co-cessation.)[154] Then, with the emergence of the ordinary human person, "I," or ego with its dualistically reflective consciousness-and-being, Nature comes to its first awakening to itself, but in—or as—a broken contradictory duality of Nature and not-Nature, in which the ordinary, regressively dualistic person or ego stands at the same time within, as a part of, and outside or even against Nature.

With the actualization of what Zen takes to be the ultimate limit-barrier or great doubt mass, this ego-engendered contradiction or broken reflective duality of Nature and not-Nature, self and not-self, being and not-being, subject and object, ego and other, is actualized-in-itself nonregressively.[155] When this affected and so immobilized contradictory dualistic structure breaks up nondualistically in what Zen terms the Great-Death-Great-Re-Birth or Great-Awakening, Nature comes to a nondualistically reflective and so nonfragmented and noncontradictory—or consummate—Awakening to, or of, Itself. For with this nondualistic, noncontradictory Self-less-Self-Awakening to—or of—Itself, Nature becomes awakened to the paradoxical not-two-ness-of-the-two or nondualistic-duality of Its sundry self-emptying-self-forming formless-forms. As a Self-Awakened nonparticular-particular[156] formless-form, Nature thereby is a nondualistic egoless-ego, Self-less-Person, or Self-less-Self.

Tied together in summary fashion, may it not also be said that the Great Awakening (or Great Death-Great-Re-Birth) is the (Nonpersonal-Personal) Self-less-Self-Awakening of Nature's ongoing simultaneous self-generation, self-extinction, and self-regeneration—in other words, of

Its self-emptying (of Its) self-emptying and, therefore, of Its self-full-filling-self-emptying?

> *Self-emptying-Self-emptying*
> *Self-Awakened Nature*
> *Awakened by, to, and as*
> *Its Self-less-Self*
> jinen
> tathatā
> śūnyatā
> *fullness*
> *emptiness*
> *Self-filling*
> *Self-emptying-filling*
> *Self-filling-emptying*
> *Self-affirming negation*
> *Self-negating affirmation*
> *the True Person of No-self*
> *of No-title*
> *of No-place*
> *of*
> *Every-place*

chapter six

MASAO ABE'S INTELLECTUAL JOURNEY TO THE WEST: A PERSONAL REFLECTION

Hans Waldenfels

MY FIRST ENCOUNTER WITH MASAO ABE occurred in Kyoto sometime in 1965 when I joined the study group gathering around Keiji Nishitani. Abe belonged to the scholars and disciples who continued to see Nishitani, after his retirement from Kyoto University, every fortnight to discuss modern philosophy, medieval mysticism, Zen Buddhism, and the like in a seminarlike meeting. When I joined the group, they were reading texts written by Tauler in medieval German. It was a wonderful experience, all the more so since at the time I happened to be the only foreigner in the group.

I do not remember any significant contribution made by Abe at that time. I recall only that he spoke rather hesitantly and slowly. It was another fact that impressed me more at the time. Nishitani had published his famous *Shūkyō towa nanika?* (Religion—what is that?) in 1962. The only important review I had come across was written by Abe and published in

Tetsugaku Kenkyū in 1962. Most probably it was the first text of Abe's that I ever read. At first, he heartily admitted that he learned very much from Nishitani's book; consequently, he showed his admiration. However, little by little he manifested the doubts and problems that surely enough grew in the process of his own thought. It revealed the Masao Abe as I should come to know him better in the years to come.

A discussion he launched in *Japanese Religions* in 1963 revolving around an article titled "Buddhism and Christianity as a Problem of Today" was supposed to be published as a book in the United States. Unfortunately, it has never come out. Abe very clearly stated that Buddhism and Christianity are challenged by the developments in modern life. The thesis behind Abe's observation, however, called for a threefold clarification: (1) What kind of Buddhism is at stake? (2) What kind of Christianity is presupposed? (3) What is the understanding of "modern life?" Considering that Abe is a pioneer of intercultural discourse, he cannot be blamed when his understanding of the various factors involved appear somewhat simplified and slanted.

Quite a few people were invited to comment on Abe's point of view and his proposals. Most of them were Westerners, scholars, Christians of various denominations—but there were also those searching for a way of life beyond Christianity. Reviewing the series of respondents, I still feel that the Japanese as well as the larger Asian side was rather missing, or at least not very well represented. Somehow Abe was facing the Western world by himself. Accordingly, the question of hermeneutics was more or less left aside. The approach to Christian doctrine and Buddhist self-understanding appeared somehow deficient, subjective, anyway incomplete. As a Roman Catholic, I realized certain shortcomings from my perspective; I am sure that a Protestant reader, too, could not have the impression of being fully understood. Even Buddhists could call for more detailed explications from their respective points of view. And yet the series of statements, responses, and rejoinders was one of the most exciting attempts to start a dialogue about the needs of our times and the possible contributions to their solutions from the two world religions. And, after all, it was Masao Abe who started and kept it going with great patience.

In the meantime, I returned to Europe and Abe moved to the United States. We stayed in contact, exchanged letters, and met again in

Japan, the United States, and the Netherlands. I consider the collection of Abe's essays in *Zen and Western Thought* (1985) his most inspiring publication so far. Different from D. T. Suzuki, with whom he is compared as one of the champions of interreligious dialogue (at least in North America), he did not engage so much in the transfer and translation of original Buddhist texts and writings. His main concern was with ideas, Eastern and Western. He knew about the importance and danger of Western technology and science. He was aware of the divorce between godless Western science and theistic Christian thought, but also about the apparent closeness of science and Eastern thought. And yet he felt challenged by the anthropocentric scientific attitudes of the West and drew from the non-self attitudes in Buddhist schools, especially Zen Buddhism. His interest concentrated on the search for bridges and companionship on the way to discover convictions and behavior suitable to modern life.

In this connection Abe stressed Emptiness and nature in their East Asian understanding. He understood the argument that because of Buddhism's lack of concern about the concrete features of history, victories and defeats, its ethical questions and sense of social responsibility must appear underdeveloped—all the more so considering that Buddhist thought aims at overcoming all kinds of dichotomies and dualisms. However, how can a nondualism beyond good and evil strengthen human responsibility? Abe knew well enough that the enlightened one is not allowed to withdraw from the everyday business of helping others find the way to true salvation. Wisdom and compassion are twins in his view. And yet to my mind, the question is still very much on the table.

On his way to the West, Abe discovered many arguments and tried them out. Understandably he found them mostly in the U.S. scene. Whitehead's process philosophy and its influence upon Christian theology piqued his interest. Go-betweens like John B. Cobb, Jr., and others became his interlocutors. He looked out for prominent theologians and philosophers, though I got the impression that he did not care much for the original Christian understanding, preferring conceptions that seemed adaptable to his own standpoint and confirmed it. For although nondualism should imply an extreme richness of flexibilities, Abe's own standpoint appears nevertheless rather firm and inflexible. As the enlightened one lives and survives on the field of nothingness and Emptiness, and thus nothingness itself is surrounded by sparkling light, Abe's thought seems to be unmovable and unmoved even amid the most challenging questions.

To my mind, the last step in Abe's intellectual journey to the West was reached when he gradually became aware of the closeness between Christ's kenotic attitude and the central Buddhist notion of *Śūnyatā*. This time Abe succeeded in starting a broad discussion that includes American and European theologians and thinkers. However, I still regret that Abe did not succeed in inviting Asian thinkers to the roundtable talk. This omission weakens Abe's own position again, as I pointed out before. Undoubtedly Abe's dealing with the question of Buddhist *Śūnyatā* and Christian kenosis will remain an important contribution not only to the Buddhist-Christian dialogue but to Christian theology itself. As *Śūnyatā* is traced to its roots in Nāgārjuna's life and thought, it will prove to be a complex field of logic, metaphysics, ethics, and religious spirituality. So, too, Christian kenosis is to be seen as a challenge to reflective thought as well as to lived existence.

When I met Masao Abe the last time in the Netherlands, he gave me a surprise. For at the international conference in which he was the main speaker, he did not present himself in the gray suit of a Japanese intellectual and scholar but in the dress of a Zen master. Of course, it was well known that he practiced Zen in Buddhist temples. I had seen him at various occasions relaxing in his Japanese home gown. What surprised me, however, was that Abe evidently appealed to the hidden Western religious sense that is about to lose its grounding in Christian traditions. To me, the question is not whether Abe himself received the qualification of an authority as a Zen master. What struck me was the sight of a person who—beyond all discursive thought—is grounded in non-thought and non-mind. As such, I can greet him only with a big silent smile.

Part Two

PERIODS OF DIALOGUE IN THE WEST

chapter Seven

MASAO ABE, PROCESS THEOLOGY, AND THE BUDDHIST-CHRISTIAN-JEWISH DIALOGUE

John B. Cobb, Jr.

MASAO ABE HAS UNDERSTOOD HIMSELF, at least in part, to carry on the work of D. T. Suzuki. Since Suzuki lived in Claremont for some time, it was natural that Abe knew of Claremont and was interested in it. This interest was reciprocated and led to Abe's appointment as visiting professor in the Claremont Graduate School in the fall of 1965. I was on sabbatical in Germany at that time but heard about Abe's impact on Claremont upon my return. I became acquainted with him in the years that followed. When the establishment of the Center for Process Studies in 1973 made it possible for us to take the initiative in developing relations, Masao Abe was one of the first whom we cultivated.

The first step was a conference we held at the University of Hawai'i on Buddhism and process thought in the fall of 1974. Abe was one of the key spokespersons for the Buddhist perspective. I remember stopping him after some of the sessions to press him for clarification of what he had said and vividly recall how from time to time his explanations, often through illustrations, gave me insight into the real significance of what he was saying. For example, he would talk about the difference between the perspectives of the swimmer in the stream and of the observer on the bank. He argued that Buddhist thought was that of the swimmer, whereas Western thought was from the perspective of the observer. He acknowledged that process thought said many things about the swimmer similar to what the swimmer experienced, but he insisted that the fundamental objectifying was not overcome. This issue has been important to me ever since. I thought then and still think now that he exaggerated the difference. But as I expound process thought myself and listen to others do so, I listen for the perspective. Indeed, often it is an objectifying one, trying to describe something that is other than the momentary experience itself. But at its best, it is—and calls for—reflection on what is going on in the swimming itself.

Abe, of course, never denied that there is a place for the discourse of the observer on the shore. But for him, it was a different level of discourse playing a different role in society. It does not lead toward Enlightenment. As a Westerner, I have wondered whether this is not too sharp a separation. I learn about myself profoundly from what others observe in me as well as from attention to the immediacy of what is happening. Can these viewpoints not interact fruitfully? That would seem more appropriate for a process perspective. And I have learned since that it is not alien to all forms of Buddhism, either.

I have offered these reflections to illustrate the impact that Abe has had on me at least since 1974. As through him I came to understand something of Buddhism, or at least of his version of Zen, I was grasped by its wisdom and truth. It became important to me to appropriate that wisdom and truth. It never seemed to me to be the whole of wisdom and truth; so I was not tempted to convert. But it has seemed to me important to adjust the way I as a Western Christian thought, so as to incorporate such insights as I grasped.

Abe would agree, I think, that coming to Buddhism from a process perspective made it possible to understand much of what Buddhists say with relative ease. The Buddhist polemic against substance thinking was more intense and powerful than that of process thought, but process thought posed no resistance. For me, it came as a surprise that what I thought of as intellectually helpful ideas were so closely bound up with soteriology. Process theology was deepened for me and took on new dimensions of meaning.

The existence of the Center for Process Studies also enabled us to invite Abe to spend another semester in Claremont, this time in the fall of 1976. We were thus able to continue our discussion, one in which I was the learner. By then, I think, Abe was troubled that I thought I was grasping so much of what he was saying without surrendering my framework of Western process thought. It became increasingly important to him to contrast Buddhism with that framework.

In part, this may have been a Zen master's way of shocking his student and blocking his reliance on conceptual thinking. However, it was also in part a philosophical difference that could be and was discussed in objectifying terms. There have been two main sources of contention between us.

First, as I tried to understand codependent origination in terms of Whitehead's concrescence of the many into one, my understanding of Whitehead deepened. But I continued to see the many as the past forming the present, and the one as the new emergent in the present. This relation of the present to the past, both in Whitehead's account and in my experience, differs from the relation to the future. Hence, reflection on the immediacy of the moment does not do away with temporality. And more important, reflection *in* the immediacy of the moment does not, either.

Abe more and more emphatically disagreed. In the Buddhist view, based on full immersion in the moment, there is no difference between past and future. That distinction belongs to the observer's perspective, or the horizontal, historical line. In the vertical, or depth, dimension, he insisted, time is overcome. And the more I tried to accommodate to the sense in which—indeed, in the momentary concrescence—there is no time, the more Abe insisted that I had not understood, that my perspective in terms of Western process philosophy blocked me.

This interchange both frustrated and stimulated me. It was frustrating because, having found so much wisdom in Buddhism, and knowing that I had not experienced *satori*, I was not able to dismiss Abe's idea. But it remained unintelligible to me. It was stimulating because it suggested to me that here I might find the deepest roots of the difference between Western and Christian experience on the one side and Eastern and Buddhist experience on the other. In process thought, the element of novelty in each concrescence was thematized. In Buddhist thought, it was not. With emergent novelty, the relation to the future cannot be the same as that to the past. Without it, it can.

The second topic was closely related. For Whitehead, the entry of novelty into concrescence is the presence of God in that concrescence. For Buddhist thought, especially Abe's Zen, there is no God. I argued that the Buddhist polemic against God was usually against a substantial God and against divine power acting on events from without. Process thought also opposed those notions and appreciated the Buddhist polemic. It spoke of God as another instance of codependent origination, and Buddhism, I insisted, should have no principled objection to there being a variety of types of such instances.

Abe was adamant in rejecting this idea of God, but he recognized that the standard Buddhist arguments were not relevant. If, as Whitehead said, God is not an exception to metaphysical principles but rather another instance of creativity, then Buddhists might be skeptical that this instance occurs, but they would have no reason to deny that it might. However, Abe rightly pointed out that God plays functions in relation to other entities that they do not play in respect to God or to one another. This he regarded as unacceptable. Even if God is not metaphysically different, God is certainly cosmologically different, and Abe regarded any such assertion as unacceptable to the Buddhist.

We have continued this argument. I have pointed out that in Pure Land Buddhism, Amida plays a unique role, analogous in many ways to the one played by God in process theology. This analogy suggests to me that it is not necessarily Buddhism in general but Abe's Zen in particular that cannot tolerate any divine reality of this sort. The truth is that Abe shares a widespread Zen view of Pure Land as a halfway house to authentic Buddhism. He was himself converted to Zen from Pure Land, and this conversion involved his giving up faith in Amida. He might allow process theology to be something of a halfway house for Christians on the way to Buddhism, although I never heard him make such a concession.

Meanwhile, Abe's teaching had a profound impact. His extended study of Christianity enabled him to explain the relation of Christianity and Buddhism to his students in ways that were convincing. The implication of Buddhist superiority was clear. For some seminary students, this caused a crisis of faith. For others, it initiated ongoing critical reflection of a sort that is rarely begun by the study of Christian theology alone.

Abe's longest stay in Claremont was from 1980 to 1984. He came to the United States after retiring from Nara University, hoping to establish an institute for scholarly Buddhist studies that would deepen and extend Buddhist scholarship here. He discussed this possibility with several institutions. As long as the funding came from Japan, more than one university was ready to welcome it. The Claremont Graduate School agreed to help try to raise money. Abe arranged a Japan Foundation grant that funded him at Claremont for three years. A special arrangement was made to continue his stay with one additional year at the School of Theology. But the funds were not raised, and the hopes for an institute faded.

During that time we began discussing the possibility of an international Buddhist-Christian dialogue. Of course, there were dialogues already taking place. In 1980 David Chappell had organized a successful meeting in Honolulu that brought together persons interested in Buddhist-Christian studies from Japan and the United States. But there were few Christian theologians there. The assumption of most theologians who knew about the meeting, rightly or wrongly, was that it was for those in North America who were already involved in teaching or studying Buddhism.

My interest was in bringing leading Christian theologians together with leading Buddhist thinkers so that the Christian theologians would experience firsthand the wisdom of Buddhist teachers, learn from it, and rethink their Christian theology accordingly. Of course, any advance knowledge of Buddhism would be helpful, but a theologian was welcome to begin the conversation with minimal previous study. The ideas of Buddhism that are most important for Christians to understand can be learned in dialogue even without prior study. But the dialogue must be extended. I wanted participants to commit themselves to take part in annual meetings for five years. I was confident that necessary study would take place between sessions.

We were quite successful in getting commitments from the persons we invited to join the group. Expecting our resources to be limited, we restricted ourselves to ten or eleven on each side. Of the eight U.S. theologians I invited, only Rosemary Ruether declined; in fact, she later changed her mind and became an important member of the group. James Cone, on the other hand, who accepted, was never able to come. The excellent response made it clear that the time was ripe, theologically speaking, for this kind of encounter.

Our efforts to raise money, on the other hand, were not successful. Hence, we were delighted when David Chappell agreed to include our group in the second meeting of his larger organization in 1984. At that time, John Berthrong, then working for the United Church of Canada, agreed to assume responsibility for funding subsequent meetings.

The original group was international chiefly in the sense of bringing Americans and Japanese together. Hans Küng was our only European connection. Similarly, the forms of Christianity and Buddhism involved were limited. There were Roman Catholics and Protestants on the Christian side, and Zen and Pure Land scholars on the Buddhist, with David Kalupahana our token representative of Theravada. Worse still, the group that gathered in Hawaii was initially all male!

It was this last limitation that precipitated immediate action. The Christians added a Canadian woman. The Buddhists added an American woman who is a Tibetan Buddhist. This addition proved the most important development because several other Tibetan Buddhists then joined and thereby changed the character of the conversations.

During successive meetings it became clear that Japanese and Tibetan Buddhists are not well acquainted with each other. In some respects their interaction was most painful for the Japanese and especially for the Zen Buddhists. Their efforts to speak for Buddhism were disrupted by the effective presence of a quite different voice. Nevertheless, Abe retained his poise and his leadership. I have frequently commented that in Buddhist-Christian dialogue the Christians change but the Buddhists remain where they are. This may be viewed as favoring either group. From my point of view, as one who sees truth and wisdom as always in the future, the willingness and ability of Christians to change is usually healthy—although it sometimes may reflect simply giving up and caving in. From the point of view of a Buddhist who believes that Enlightenment is a sometimes realized possibility at all times and places, there is no need to change. One can encourage Christians as they shed those teachings that block the way to that Enlightenment, but that engagement need involve no movement on the Buddhist side.

On the other hand, Abe—although he may subscribe ultimately to the view that the Buddhists are already there and do not need to change—also believes that at other levels they have something to learn from Christians. On one occasion he used his role as leader of the Buddhist group to chastise them for failing to learn and change in their interaction with Christians. Actually, in my observation, this was in any case less true for the American Tibetan Buddhists.

Back in Claremont, the Center for Process Studies continued to sponsor occasional seminars dealing with Buddhism. Ryusei Takeda was in Claremont for part of this time. He is professor at one of the Pure Land Buddhist universities in Kyoto. He had studied in Claremont earlier; he and I had collaborated on an article. Just as it was through Abe that I gained my understanding and admiration for Zen, so it was through Takeda that I gained my understanding and admiration for Pure Land.

Takeda's presence introduced welcome complexities into my ongoing arguments with Abe. We enjoyed three-cornered debates. On some issues, such as those related to grace and faith and even deity, Takeda and I would tend to agree against Abe. Of course, on others, Takeda and Abe were allied in their Buddhism.

During Abe's four-year stay in Claremont, he attracted some fine students. One in particular was Christopher Ives. Ives had worked with Abe in Japan and came to Claremont to complete a doctorate under his guidance. When Abe left to go to the philosophy department at the University of Hawai'i, Ives wanted to follow him. But it turned out that doing so would have involved a shift from a department of religion to a department of philosophy, which would require extending his program for a couple of years. Ives stayed in Claremont to finish his degree, with the understanding that Abe would help supervise his dissertation from afar.

This was a happy circumstance for me. Abe has long confessed that Buddhism is weak in its social ethics and has something to learn here from Christians. He had himself worked with Paul Tillich and Reinhold Niebuhr at Union Theological Seminary. Ives wanted to write on Zen social ethics. This idea interested me greatly, and I agreed to work with Ives on the understanding that his dissertation would be accepted only with Abe's approval.

This introduced me to a different relation to Buddhist thought. Working with Ives on the development of Zen social ethics encouraged me to play a role with Buddhist thought similar to that often played by Abe with Christians. Abe proposes Christian theological solutions to Christian problems. I tried to help Ives make authentically Zen moves that would ground social ethics. My role in the dissertation was very small, but I am proud of the results anyway. Abe was pleased with them, too.

Abe's presence encouraged a Pure Land Buddhist student, John Ishihara, who had earlier studied with Takeda in Japan, to undertake a somewhat analogous dissertation on a Pure Land social ethic. Again, I had the opportunity to advise with the assurance of Abe's ultimate guidance. It was striking how different were the moves he made from Pure Land teaching to social ethics in comparison with Ives's moves from Zen. But he, too, I believe, was successful.

Working with these gifted young Buddhists convinced me of the accuracy of the Christian critique of Mahāyāna Buddhism for being undeveloped in its understanding of social ethics. It also convinced me that the stimulus of Christianity can lead Buddhists to find resources within their own traditions for developing social ethics that may be able to avoid some of the pitfalls into which Christian involvement with society has fallen. Finally it became clear that this is not a simple matter, with one grounds for social ethics common to all Buddhist schools. Each school of Buddhism will have to work out its own grounds for involvement in society and its own principles for action there.

Abe has pushed the Buddhist-Christian dialogue in other ways as well. Of these, publishing is an important one. He has written not only on Buddhism but also on the contributions Buddhism can make to Christianity. His penetrating studies of classical Christian themes have opened Christian eyes to unexpected possibilities for Christian theology.

He has been particularly fascinated by the New Testament idea of kenosis. This concept has obvious connections with the Buddhist idea of Emptiness, but the way it has been employed in Christianity generally moves in quite different directions. Abe has written an extended essay interpreting kenosis in a Buddhist way. He has tried out this essay in lectures and in different forms of publication. He continues to be eager to get responses from leading Christian theologians.

I agreed to work with him on this project with the understanding that I would share the labor with Chris Ives, now teaching at the University of Puget Sound. Once again, the willingness to respond by those invited was impressive, reflecting both a high level of Christian interest in Buddhism in general and the universal respect for Abe personally. Unfortunately, not all who promised to write did so promptly, but eventually all the responses were received.

Abe, in his turn, responded with his usual care to each response.

The interaction is frank and real. Criticisms are honest in both directions, although there is no lack of mutual respect and appreciation. The days when dialogue was characterized by superficial courtesy are happily over, and *The Emptying God: A Buddhist-Jewish-Christian Conversation* is now in print.

The insatiable Abe has wanted to keep this dialogue going. Hence, he had me gather responses to his responses. Not all the earlier respondents wished to continue in this way, but several have appeared in *Buddhist-Christian Studies* along with Abe's further reply.

To me, the most interesting development in this dialogue has been its extending beyond Buddhists and Christians. Abe reached out to Jewish thinkers by including a Buddhist discussion of the Holocaust in his essay. This encouraged Eugene Borowitz to respond, and his participation in turn justified including "Jewish" in the subtitle of the book. There has been to date very little Buddhist-Jewish dialogue, although a considerable number of individual Jews have turned enthusiastically to Buddhist disciplines for spiritual nurture. Borowitz has made an important contribution to changing this situation, and he has continued his dialogue with Abe.

Meanwhile, Abe has continued to seek new respondents. I declined to be actively involved in this new venture. It was time that fresh perspectives come to play. But I am particularly pleased that in this new volume (*Divine Emptiness and Historical Fullness: A Buddhist-Christian-Jewish Conversation with Masao Abe*), there are also Jewish voices. This extension of the conversation is indeed welcome and represents an important added achievement for Abe.

Thanks to the leadership of John Berthrong, the Buddhist-Christian Theological Encounter Group proceeded through the five sessions to which the original participants committed themselves. During that period I refrained from committing myself to any other ongoing group. But as the fifth, and I thought final, meeting approached, I agreed to join another (annual) international dialogue group, this one of Jews, Christians, and Muslims. As it turned out, the other participants in the Buddhist-Christian Theological Encounter Group wanted to continue. Indeed, to my great embarrassment, I was the only one who dropped out! I am afraid that Abe was quite offended.

Plans for a sixth meeting in Taiwan did not work out, and the group held its sixth meeting in connection with the Fourth International Buddhist-Christian Conference (1992) in Boston, where I was in attendance. As a result, I was able to take part in this session as well. I missed the seventh meeting, which was held in Japan in 1994. Then in 1997, Donald Mitchell at Purdue University received a major grant from the Lilly Endowment, Inc. that will fund the group to meet annually five more times beginning in 1998. The group will add new members from North America, Europe, and Asia, and will turn its attention from purely theological to social issues. It is now assured that the dialogue will continue its historic conversations into the new millennium.

Abe and I take great satisfaction in what has occurred in this dialogue group. Leading Protestant and Catholic theologians have interacted with Zen, Pure Land, and Tibetan Buddhists at a level of openness and honesty that is rare even within homogeneous groups. We have truly learned from and about one another. We are all permanently changed by the experience. On the whole, Christians are confirmed in their Christianity and Buddhists in their Buddhism. But the Christianity and Buddhism in question are not quite the same as those that were brought into the encounter.

Masao Abe was born ten years to the day before I was. I take particular pleasure in observing his physical vigor and mental acuity. It gives me hope for my own activity during the next decade. Meanwhile, I join with all others in thanking him for his enormous contribution to the American religious scene and in expressing my hope for his retirement in Japan. I am confident that it will be a productive one and that I can look forward to continuing to see him in this country from time to time.

Even when Abe is no longer active in the Christian-Buddhist dialogue himself, it will continue. It is no longer dependent on a few leaders. It is now an established part of the way religious life and thought take place in North America. It is this fact, that he is no longer necessary, that is the greatest measure of his success.

With respect to the Jewish-Buddhist dialogue, this may not be true. The limited dialogue that has occurred thus far has been chiefly with Abe. It will be incumbent on Christians and Buddhists to make every effort to involve Jews in dialogues with other Buddhists so that this bud, too, will burst into flower.

chapter Eight

INTERPRETATION AS
INTERLOCUTION

William R. LaFleur

IN ALL OUR DEBATES during recent decades about texts and how to deal with them, I have not come across any statement that appeals to me more than that written by Yoshida Kenkō in the fourteenth century in his *Essays in Idleness*: "The pleasantest of all diversions is to sit alone under the lamp, a book spread out before you, and to make friends with people of a distant past you have never known."[1] In this, Kenkō tries to keep alive into a person's mature years the value of an experience that most people, if fortunate enough to be literate, have had in their youth—namely, the sense of being *personally addressed* by the long-dead author of a book spread open before them. That capacity of certain books to seem to leap across time and create a semblance of real conversation between author and reader is an extraordinary one. I suspect that almost all of us who eventually make a career out of reading, teaching, writing about, and analyzing what goes on in text interpretation probably had, at some point in our youth, at least one powerful Kenkō-esque experience of feeling as if we were personally addressed from the pages of a book by a long-dead writer.

It is, both in the elegantly simple statement by Kenkō and in many of our early experiences, a sense of "dialogue" that takes shape. And as such, I would make bold to say that it is not unconnected to what the life-work of Masao Abe has been all about. For in my interaction with him, Abe's consuming passion for dialogue has not been limited to the exchanges between living adherents of major religions but has extended also to his way of reading a text, especially older Buddhist texts or philosophical texts in Chinese or Japanese. In this "man of dialogue" I see a deep connection between what he did in international forums and what he did in the more intimate setting of classrooms and student seminars when reading and interpreting a text. My association with him involved the latter contexts and therefore I write here about them and what I see as the unique style of textual hermeneutics demonstrated there.

My topic is Masao Abe's translation of the dialogic principle into what I have come think of as an impressively unique and important way of "reading" certain texts. Although my brief account will be personal, my aim is to show that the method of text reading exemplified in Abe's actual practice might serve to bring a much-needed corrective to the ways we usually deal with certain texts. The modern West has spent some centuries now discussing and debating the hermeneutics of text interpretation, and during the past two decades these debates have, if anything, exfoliated and intensified. Yet in none of the positions articulated to date—and they are many—do I detect anything exactly like the Abe approach. Perhaps this hints at a certain cultural and intellectual drop-off point on the plateau of possibilities recognized and permitted within the West's discourse about such things. If so, I would suggest that on this level, too, the fact that Abe's approach originates from within a non-Western place exemplifies yet another arena—namely, the debate about texts and readings—within which an energetic propulsion in the direction of deeper intercultural interaction can be detected and encouraged.

For me, it came in the form of a terribly slow, fairly painful, and still muddied recognition that texts such as *The Platform Sūtra of the Sixth Patriarch*, most of the fascicles in Dōgen's *Shōbōgenzō,* and even a modern work such as Nishida's *Zen no kenkyū (An Inquiry into the Good)* deserve—and in some sense demand!—a mode of "reading" that would catch rather than squander the text's potential for placing the reader in a profoundly interactive relationship with "itself." (Scare-quotes seem required by this process that forces the question as to what or who lies on the other side of dialogue into which the readied reader has been propelled—a matter to which this discussion returns later.)

To the extent that I ever grasped this point, it reached me through massive (and I sometimes suspected deliberate) frustrations wrought by

Abe. They started in graduate school because it was while I was working to get a degree at the University of Chicago that I first met him. During the spring quarter of 1969, Abe arrived, through the mediation of Joseph M. Kitagawa, in Chicago to give the Charles Gooding lectures and to conduct a graduate seminar on modern Japanese philosophy. That seminar was, I suspect, the first time I experienced the peculiar mode of forced frustration that seemed, at least in those days, very much a part of the Abe pedagogical style.

I entered the seminar on Japanese philosophy and looked at the syllabus and bibliography—items prepared, as I recall, by Michio Araki, a fellow graduate student and now a professor of religion at Tsukuba National University. To a budding Japan specialist like myself, the course promised to be a historical and philosophical feast. The reading list gave a complete menu of all the big names in modern Japanese philosophy including Kitarō Nishida, Se'ichi Hatano, Hajime Tanabe, Kiyoshi Miki, Tetsurō Watsuji, and Keiji Nishitani. I looked forward to ten weeks, by the end of which, I assumed (if I could get something of a grasp on at least one of these thinkers each week), I would be able to claim some kind of comprehension of the scope and key problematics of modern Japanese philosophy and intellectual life.

It did not work out that way. Just as a map is not the territory, so, too, a syllabus is not the course. Abe was not at all interested in what I now call "*mere* breadth." As I recall, by the end of the term our discussions in class had not gotten very much beyond one portion of one work by Nishida—although in papers we explored other topics. And that did not seem to bother our visiting professor in the least. He not only moved at what seemed a snail's pace through the Nishida text but in the seminar spoke slowly, deliberately, sometimes as if hauling the words forth one by one from some unseen place and waiting for them to resonate in some existential way in the minds of the students.

In honesty I would have to say that I was more frustrated than illuminated by that course in Chicago. I recall writing a naive paper on the ethics of Tetsurō Watsuji. Although that project kindled what later remained an ongoing interest in this figure, Abe, as I recall, found my product merely "interesting" and a "nice start." The weekly sessions with the Nishida text were the truly frustrating aspect of things. At the same time, however, I was fascinated by something in Abe's method that I did not and could not understand. The agonizingly slow pace was, I ever so slowly began to suspect, intimately bound up with the Abe project. The method was meant to be therapeutic—culturally, intellectually, and personally. And that our discussions never began to approximate what the syllabus had promised as point of closure seemed perfectly acceptable to our visiting professor.

Some persons in the seminar, realizing that our common readings would not go beyond the Nishida text, tried to articulate—as politely as possible—a small complaint about there not being much prospect of moving on. Abe seemed nonplused. In his inimitably gentle way, he hinted that trying to get *beyond* Nishida was not something that neophytes like ourselves should be too eager to do. The implication was that it would be a large enough task for us to get close to Nishida; to assume that we would or could get beyond him would be fairly preposterous.

My next engagement with Masao Abe was in 1975 when I spent a year doing research in Kyoto and he was back at home there as well. I contacted him to discuss certain problems I was having in understanding the Buddhism implicit and explicit in the poetry of Saigyō, the twelfth-century Japanese monk I was studying at the time. Abe immediately did two things of great and lasting importance to me. First, he introduced me to Professor Masamichi Kitayama, a scholar of literature who graciously spent much of that year reading Saigyō's verse with me and interpreting it at a level of depth not otherwise then found in Japanese scholarship. Kitayama, like Abe, had been a student of Shin'ichi Hisamatsu; his perspective on how to read a medieval Buddhist poet was exactly what I had been looking for. He has remained a mentor to whom I owe a deep debt.

The second great benefit shown me that year by Abe was an introduction to the community of laypersons who did weekly *zazen* at the Reiun-in, a subtemple of the Myōshin-ji complex. I joined them for sittings on Saturday evenings for most of that year in Kyoto. The group meeting there had been originally organized by Hisamatsu and always seemed to include a number of persons associated with Kyoto University in one way or another. That subtemple had been where Hisamatsu had lived and some of the ashes of Kitarō Nishida were in its cemetery.

The tone of the Saturday sessions had been set by Hisamatsu's insistence that "learning without practice is weak and practice without learning is blind." Thus, those evening sessions were composed of a couple of hours of *zazen* followed by a group reading and discussion of a relevant text. It was Dōgen's *Shōji* (Birth/Death) that was being read and discussed when I took part. Abe encouraged a very open discussion, yet as discussion leader he made sure that we lingered with the text long enough to let Dōgen *address* us. You cannot, after all, expect—in the words of Kenkō—to "make friends with a person of the past" such as Dōgen without letting Dōgen's specific passion for pressing the core question, namely that of life and death, come to the fore.

Abe's method, I slowly began to see, was in harmony with the core problematic of texts such as Dōgen's. While not denying value in what we often call our "modern" and "critical" approaches to texts, he refused to let the intentionality of a writer/interlocutor such as Dōgen get lost in the bramble of textual questions. To Abe, the matter of Dōgen's "intentionality" was itself not so much a textual question as it was—and more properly is—a human and existential one. As pressed forward by the Abe mode of interpretation, the capacity for deep interlocution is still in the text of Dōgen, the author of the *Shōbōgenzō*.[2] It has been Abe's assumption, one totally in keeping with the statement by Kenkō, that the exquisite value of a "book spread out before one" is that through its text, that interlocution can go on and on even after the brain of that book's author has been biologically long dead.

For me, having been for years trained in what I have always taken to be a natural proclivity for dealing with texts historically, there has been no greater challenge than the Abe alternative—the insistence on letting the voice from the great text have *at least* a kind of positional parity with the self as reader. But in all honesty the challenge of the Abe insistence on this point all too often felt like a goad. As things turned out, I felt the discomfort it caused far beyond that year in Kyoto.

For the years 1977–79, during a period when I was a junior member of the Department of Religion at Princeton, I had arranged for Abe to come to Princeton as the Stewart Lecturer. These turned out to be two years during which I was fortunate enough to be able to assist in editing his crucially important essays into the book that became *Zen and Western Thought*,[3] a volume that for the first time put together the component parts of the Abe perspective and dialogic stance for public reading.

Here I want to remain with the topic of Abe's unique way of dealing with texts because at Princeton, too, his unusual style came readily to the fore. One of the things we arranged for him was a reading course focused on the original text of what in English we call *The Platform Sūtra of the Sixth Patriarch*. It was a course for which a small contingent of graduate students was ready and primed—at least, linguistically. What they were not expecting was that Abe would not be satisfied with dealing with the *Platform Sūtra* as a composition of Chinese ideographs or as a complex of textual layers or as something that represents a specific historical phase in the development of Ch'an (Zen) in China or even as a statement into which plays for power among contending monks were infused in a disguised fashion.

The students' shock was quick and tangible. And it was something that I could appreciate also, since in many ways it mirrored what I had myself experienced as a graduate student in Abe's seminar in Chicago. After all, virtually all the things they as graduate students had been taught to think of as the methodological avenues toward what was considered the "sophisticated" grasp of a text were things that Abe refused to accept as sufficient! He wanted more. And the "more" he wanted the students to see was that you have not really understood the *Platform Sūtra* if you have not yourself been brought up excruciatingly close to the question of life and death that is, in his view, the text's *raison d'être* as a Zen classic.

One can do the parsing. One can also see the text as having had a subtle, historical function in a legitimacy dispute. One can raise a host of questions to be addressed to the text. But after that is said and done, there still remains the question of the questions posed *by the text* to the life and mind-state of the reader. The real squirming always starts at that juncture. That is, I venture to say, because the whole panoply of modern "interpretative strategies," however legitimate as far as they go, has at that point come to resemble a set of avoidance strategies. To be shorn of them is to have to see that the life/death question is paramount.

One of the things I noticed during the two years Abe spent at Princeton was that his unusual mode of forcing a far-deeper-than-usual exchange between a student and a text was something to which many bright undergraduates quite readily gravitated—at least, for a while. I could not avoid noticing that, by contrast, graduate students—perhaps especially those envisioning scholarly careers in East Asian studies—were clearly discomfited by the Abe mode. Whereas many undergraduates found excitement and challenge in Abe's way of turning the text into a query that seemed to address each of them personally and existentially, graduate students generally seemed to squirm uncomfortably. Abe's was, some privately told me, a method of textual interpretation that was "out of keeping" with the way things are done at a university—especially on a graduate level!

At the time I found myself in a dilemma, if the truth be told. I was, after all, someone whose own training—at least for the most part—had been in what we call the modern, critical, and historical method of dealing with texts. That method meant a major portion of what I took as my own assumed task as an academic consisted of educating graduate students into the adoption of this stance and the mastery of methods that are its tools. Therefore, when they were unsettled and disturbed by Abe's demand that the text also be allowed to ask difficult questions *of them*, they had the sense that he was not playing by the rules of the expected scholarly game. And, of course, in one way they were right. Something about what Abe was doing was implicitly questioning, if not the appropriateness, then at least the *adequacy* of the game we all had learned to play, the one that consisted of our usual ways of textual criticism and interpretation.

At the time I was frustrated. During the two years we were together at Princeton, Abe and I had long conversations standing at the blackboard even after all the students had left. And then we continued them over dinner. Time after time I tried to get Abe to adjust his method ever so slightly in the direction of the kind of textual study that graduate students had been taught to think of as "normal." And time after time he smiled and gently intimated that what I was requesting was really something rather preposterous. To my mind, it seemed as if I was asking merely for a minor accommodation. However, I later realized that to Abe, my "simple" request really amounted to asking him to be someone he was not—and someone he surely did not want to be!

In the following years I have thought a lot about those struggles with Abe. In fact, they brought into focus one of the most important intellectual and personal questions of my life. I have come to the conclusion that Abe was absolutely right in refusing to bend in the direction I wanted him to move. As I see it now, he *mercifully* rejected my requests out of hand. For if he had not done so, I would never have had a chance during subsequent years to think through what was going on. And then I also would have missed the opportunity to try to articulate my understanding of the matter, something I attempt to do here.

I need to state forthrightly that I do not wish to reject or even to denigrate what we call the "modern" and "critical" approach to texts—including those of the Buddhist tradition. In fact, ever since the late nineteenth century, various types of critical textual analysis, generated within the modern West, have become known and practiced within Japan. They have over the years become normative there, too—so much so that in most areas of scholarship on the texts and history of Buddhism, it is Japanese scholars who are now the leaders in what used to be called the Western modes of analysis. In fact, a good deal of the fine American and European scholarship on Indian, Chinese, and Japanese Buddhism that has appeared in recent decades was stimulated and actually mentored by an unusually generous cadre of Japanese scholars—although the critical stance and methods of these Japanese differed very little from those that originally had been thought of as European or Western.

Therefore, it needs to be said that Abe's way of turning a text around so that the reader feels somehow addressed and even interrogated at the depths of his or her being is scarcely customary or normative within the Japanese scholarly world—at least, as that world is constituted today. Abe's method exemplifies something unique, special, and rare. My own sense—gleaned both from things Abe said to me and from having once seen them together—is that it derives from his direct mentor, the late Shin'ichi Hisamatsu. And as I understand things, Hisamatsu refined a method exemplified by Kitarō Nishida, who in turn seems to have derived it from the long tradition of the *kōan* contexts of Zen temples. It was probably Nishida who insisted that the academic context was also a place where one could carry out the kind of fundamental probing of the question of life and death that goes on in temples when they are functioning as they were meant to. (Hisamatsu was a critic of contemporaneous temples in Japan for their habit of deviating from this core task.) It was Nishida, however, who seems to have first recognized that in modern academic contexts a coping with *the most fundamental questions* needs to be encouraged and faced rather than circumvented and shelved.

Is the fact that this approach is, even in Japan, a statistical rarity reason enough to dismiss it as maverick and inconsequential? I think not. In fact, quite the opposite may be true. This rather extraordinary insistence upon channeling attention toward the life/death question, a question assumed to be at the heart of certain texts, may very well be the *only* approach that gives these texts their due, that allows for a real interaction between the contemporary reader and the text as an interlocutor. This is not to say that the text may not be studied with other methodologies—tools that are likely, for instance, to reveal its historical, intertextual, and ideological dimensions. There is nothing illegitimate or inappropriate about such research.

The only problem is that, at least *in the case of these texts*, these methodologies are incapable of providing any opportunity for the reader to be addressed in any powerful or existential way by the questions that seem central to such texts. Therefore, it is of crucial importance to recognize how different this approach is from the other, usual strategies for text interpretation. They collectively cannot operate without an "objectification" of the text, a procedure essential and correct in terms of their aims. To the extent that they are scientific, such approaches require that a text and its context be investigated as completely *passive objects* of inquiry.

Text interpretation that is modern and critical will, by definition, conceive of the text as the object of a one-way investigation—a process in which all initiative and question formulation arises from the side of the interpreter or decipherer. Of course, as historians of hermeneutics have shown, this insistence upon an objectification of older texts, a hallmark of criticism in the modern world, was itself a reaction to earlier modes of ecclesiastical reading—readings that were premised on the reception and interpretation of texts as scriptural or automatically authoritative. (Much of what we recognize as "fundamentalism" in any religious tradition is, at least in its hermeneutic posture, a wholesale rejection of all modern critical approaches and a professed return to a given scripture as authoritative in this sense. It tries to be premodern.)

What I describe as the Nishida-Hisamatsu-Abe mode of interpretation refuses to be drawn into the belief that these are the only two possibilities. It forcefully resists being captured by the necessity either of totally objectifying a text or of elevating it to a pedestal as scripture. It is important to see that it rejects these as the only available options.

That Abe's method does not run in the bibliolatrous direction is shown by its readiness to accept and grant validity to the results of critical studies. It does not try to immunize even prized texts such as *The Awakening of Faith Attributed to Açvaghosha*, the *Platform Sūtra*, or the *Shōbō genzō* from the sometimes surprising things that have been discovered about their authorship, composition, or ideological matrixing. The fact that many important Buddhist texts had fabricated etiologies and played roles in partisan power games within monastic contexts is not something that this mode of interpretation has any need or desire to deny or suppress.

However, if the interpretative act were to *stop* with the recognition of these things, it would—at least according to what I am calling the Nishida-Hisamatsu-Abe view of things—be a premature and unfortunate termination because it would have stopped before ever getting to the point where the reader/interpreter could be addressed and even interrogated *by the text*. It would then have been, if I may put it so, merely "monologic" discourse. The turnaround would have never been given a chance to take place. The conditions for dialogue—that between the reader of today and the subject within the text—would have never been filled.

Making this observation may even provide us with a much-needed term to designate the mode of text dealing under review. We could, I suggest, call it *dialogic* or *interlocutory* interpretation. Compared with the dialogic mode, all the others—both those that constitute the ordinary critical methods most familiar in the academy and those that cede all authority to the text as "scripture"—are monologic. Critical methods are such, inasmuch as they ask questions of the text but never allow the questioner to be questioned in return. But there is also a decidedly monologic character in the interpretative stance that grants all authority to a scripture and views the activity of the reader/believer to consist of unquestioning assent to the contents of the text.

Dialogue by definition presumes a parity. Therefore, what I am calling the dialogic or interlocutory hermeneutic allows, in contrast to the monologic modes, for a parity between the reader and the text. Thus, if the reader is to question the text, parity requires that he or she be questioned by the text as well. This means, of course, that in some real sense the text out of which an interlocutory engagement with the reader arises must be seen *as a subject*, not as object only.

It is interesting to note that when today we speak of "subjectivity" entering into an interpretive process, we are able to see it only as something happening on the side of the reader/interpreter. During most of the modern era, of course, even this was described as a fault, an indication that scientific objectivity had been compromised. A partial movement away from such a hard position can be seen in what is often called "reader-response theory"—in many ways a context within which the Heisenberg uncertainty principle seems to have filtered down into the realm of interpretation theory and semiotics.[4] In this theory readers are seen as unavoidably conditioning and even in some sense "making" the text in the act of reading. But although this theory leaves open the door to what we might call "subjectivity," it is still only the reader as subject who is given more space for his or her operations.

A dialogic hermeneutic would insist that there is a subject also *on the text side* of the interpretive act. Otherwise, the reader could not be addressed and certainly could not be interrogated on fundamental matters. And this subject on the text side was and *remains* there even after a given text has, for instance, been shown through critical analyses to be the many-layered product of a complex authorship and one in which ideological elements can be demonstrated to exist. That is, in texts such as these, the subject on the text side remains and retains its capacity for interlocution even after the text has been objectified in the process of carrying out the variety of critical procedures. The reason for this continuing capacity for interlocution by a text is that when rightly understood, such a text is not really scripture or even an "authority" of the type whose position as such can be placed in jeopardy by the findings of critical inquiry. (Although there was high respect for the classic texts within the Ch'an/Zen tradition, there was also the antibibliolatrous motif in episodes about *sūtras* intentionally burned or used in the privy.) My point is that the objectification of a text for critical purposes does not in itself destroy the text's capacity to act as an interrogating subject. It is only when it is assumed that historical and critical studies constitute the whole of the interpretative act that something extremely valuable can fall out of sight.

But exactly *who is* this subject that is on the text's side of the dialogic situation? This is both an extremely important and extremely difficult question. And it is here, too, that as I see it, the answer which could be drawn from the Nishida-Hisamatsu-Abe tradition of dealing with classic Zen texts would likely differ from the poetically attractive but simple notion articulated by Kenkō. That is, the "subject" here is not merely some ancient author X who is somehow imagined as still able to be a conversation partner through the book that has carried his or her words down to the present. This notion, while attractive on a naive level, implies that a given author, though long dead, can have a kind of ghostly postmortem presence in his or her text.

Even if hypothetically there were no "critical" reasons for rejecting the notion of the Sixth Patriarch as the origin of the *Platform Sūtra*, from within the perspective of dialogic or interlocutory interpretation, it could not be maintained that he or any putative author is the subject on the text side. When deeply engaged by the existential questions raised by the *Platform Sūtra*, it is not to be thought that a known or unknown "author" lies on the other side of the reading act. Nor is it some kind of perduring "presence" of Dōgen who has a corresponding role when you or I interact on a deep level with the various fascicles of the *Shōbōgenzō*. There may be something pleasantly romantic in the notion of having had a text-mediated chat with Nāgārjuna, with Hui-neng, or with Dōgen, but these are all fully dead men. And it would be to chase an illusion to think of oneself in conversation with any one of them.

If not these, then who possibly can be the subject in question? According to the practitioners of dialogic interpretation, the answer to this question is and must be "our true self."[5] This answer is counterintuitive and also easily misunderstood. If, for instance, it is taken merely as indicating some kind of morally and spiritually improved version of the reader's present self, "our true self" would be no more than yet another ghostly figure impinging on the present—but this time from the future rather than from the past.

However, there is something that at first sight would appear to be a much more serious objection to this answer. Even when qualified by *our* and *true*, the notion that some version of the reader's *self* is *also* on the text's side of the dialogic situation would seem to put the reader on both sides. This would vitiate the very thing that would seem to be the precondition of dialogue, namely, the kind of authentic alterity that has been made much of in recent critical theory.

Parenthetically, it is worth noting here that a charge that the Japanese intellectual tradition as a whole is weak in terms of giving adequate attention to authentic alterity ("the Other") has over the past two decades become the centerpiece of studies of Japan rooted in the perspective of ideological criticism. This weakness leads directly to a tendency to "substantialize the collectivity."[6] I see this argument as valid, at least as a major fault of National Learning and Confucian-based social philosophies of the Tokugawa and modern periods in Japan. The argument is much less convincing when applied to the medieval period, when Buddhism was the major intellectual force. It is important to note that it was to these Buddhist sources that thinkers such as Nishida, Hisamatsu, and Abe returned to articulate their concerns for true subjectivity and what could perhaps be called an alterity that does not substantialize either the collectivity or individual.

The judgment that the interlocutory reading of a text puts the reader as subject on both sides of the action could arise only because the most important implications of dialogue as an activity have not been realized. It needs to be admitted that such a judgment—which is, in fact, a *misjudgment*—could be said to issue quite naturally and justly on the basis of the kind of language that has been used up to this point in this essay. In writing of "the subject on the reader's side" and "the subject on the text's side," I have been portraying a static situation, one in which the text has taken up a position on one side of the polarity and the reader has been given a stance on the other. Even if portrayed as a kind of gulf between the reader and the subject in the text, the situation is basically one that in Japanese is referred to as *tairitsu*, the condition of standing in opposition.[7]

The problem with such a formulation, of course, is that it describes a predialogic situation. Dialogue, by comparison, is an activity that has moved beyond the bipolarity of the two parties envisioned as ultimately separated "stances." Dialogue is not merely something that happens *between* two separated parties but something that happens *to* them. Put starkly, it necessitates the "death" of those two selves conceived of as discrete beings standing against each other. And something of the death of such selves occurs already at the opening moment of the dialogic act.

In this sense, it could be said that the content of dialogue is not so much some "topic" or external "problem" as it is the active/interactive potential of the two subjectivities who have become interlocutors. For want of a better term, Buddhists often called it an "entry into the nondual" because what is being described is not a mere melding or fusion;

it is not that duality is rendered down into a monad—for such a monad would be merely a new, supposedly discrete and stable entity. It is the illusion of an attainable "stability" that is the problem here. My hunch is that it is not, therefore, to prize paradoxes for their own sake, but in order to *preserve descriptive accuracy* that within the Zen tradition this state of affairs is called *jita funi*—literally, "self/other: not two." Any phrase without the dynamic tension allowed within this way of putting things would be less than adequate to describe authentic dialogue.

By suggesting that this view can also inform a way of reading texts—or at least certain texts—I am, I know, running counter to the extensive display of energies put into shoring up the notion that a text is and always must remain an object, the complex but still basically inert thing on the other, opposite side of any reading act. In that sense, I know my interpretation of things—including my hypothesis that dialogic or interlocutory interpretation turns things around on a very basic level—has been shaped and conditioned by the concern to preserve "true subjectivity" that runs through the writings of Nishida, Hisamatsu, and Abe like something that cannot be left alone. And because attention to this subjectivity is either totally absent or sadly inadequate in all the theories of interpretation today, it strikes me as important to give this mode of reading and interpreting the place it seems to deserve.

chapter Nine

A TRIBUTE TO "MR. DIALOGUE"

David W. Chappell

LASTING IMPRESSIONS FROM HAWAII

I FIRST MET MASAO ABE at the First International Buddhist-Christian Conference, held in June 1980, in Hawaii. At that time, he delivered a paper, "The End of World Religion," in response to Paul Tillich and Wilfred Smith.[1] Although his talk was visionary, my most vivid memory of Abe at that conference was *how* he delivered his lecture. Since the podium was built for taller Americans, after coming to the podium Abe could barely be seen. Accordingly, after setting down his notes, he peered over the top of the podium and asked with a wide grin, "Can anyone see me?" His relaxed and gracious humor revealed a humanity that has enabled him to enter into the minds and hearts of many others throughout his lifetime. A few years later, when Abe came to Hawaii as a visiting professor in the philosophy department, he developed a strong and faithful following from his students, again based not only on the richness of his thought but also on his human warmth.

I remember one day when Masao Abe stretched out his hand and said with a smile, "Call me 'Masao.' I am an American now." Although he had not formally become an American citizen, he was indicating his commitment to living and working in America as a new home. It is easy to forget how difficult it is to move from one culture to another. But when I observe Abe's struggle to express some English vowels, I continue to be impressed with the energy and effort that he has expended in overcoming the cultural hurdle in order to facilitate the engagement of East with West. And in spite of his generous invitation, I must admit that his role as *sensei* has always inhibited me from expressing the easy familiarity he invited by asking us to call him "Masao." While feeling a warm friendship and admiration for him, and after knowing him and working with him for many years as a colleague, he still remains a *sensei* as I seek to walk a path he pioneered.

Masatoshi Nagatomi, of Harvard University, recently said that he had received permission from Abe to refer to him as "Mr. *Śūnyatā*." Although this is a revealing title and one that Abe no doubt celebrates, many others throughout Buddhist history could and did claim this name. For me and for many Westerners who have experienced his warmth, humor, and penetrating mind as a Buddhist who enters the heart of Christian theology and earnestly seeks to deepen other religions, we would propose that he is even more deserving of the title "Mr. Dialogue." And in what follows, I will show why this is true.

SIGNIFICANCE OF ABE'S WORK IN THE WEST

As a member of the Kyoto School, Masao Abe has spent his professional career teaching Western philosophy and religion, but unlike his colleagues, he has been unique in journeying to America to challenge Christian and Jewish thought in its own language and on its home turf. Even though it is now thirty years since Abe provoked public dialogue with his essay "Buddhism and Christianity as a Problem of Today," there is still no other Buddhist equally active and penetrating in dialogic insights.

With remarkable consistency Abe has continued to confront Buddhist and Christian thinkers on two fronts: the challenge that they give to one another by making different claims of ultimacy, and the challenge that they face from secular, irreligious critics. Although the issues have shifted somewhat in content and sophistication, and the respondents have had numerous replacements, the drama and the role of Abe as instigator and chief protagonist has remained the same.

Abe has remained center stage in the Buddhist-Christian dialogue because few Buddhist thinkers of his generation have learned Christianity so well, and none of these Buddhists have challenged Christians in so many vital ways. I say "vital ways" because Abe's challenges to Christianity are not just Buddhist rejections but are the application of Buddhist values and views in order to deepen Christianity and make it better. At least among liberal theologians, this challenge has been welcomed like a fresh, water-laden wind blowing across a parched theological field that had lost its vitality since the days of Tillich and Barth. Rather than just opposing Christianity, Abe has tried to show how Christians might find new horizons, hidden resources, and richer meaning in their own tradition. And as Schubert Ogden has attested, this dialogue had become the most refreshing theological engagement of the 1980s.

I can vividly remember a meeting of the Buddhist-Christian Theological Encounter Group (Abe-Cobb group) in which Abe corrected a Christian discussant by applying an important theological principle. In recognition of Abe's insight and correctness, Langdon Gilkey spontaneously responded, "Masao, you are the best theologian in the room." Although perhaps an exaggeration, it certainly showed the esteem of his colleagues and the erudition of Abe, especially since the room also contained such thinkers as John Cobb, David Tracy, John Hick, Schubert Ogden, Gordon Kaufman, Rosemary Ruether, and Hans Küng—a virtual Who's Who of Western theology.

Even if one does not agree with Abe's ideas, it is important to admire and follow the model that he gives for living in this religiously plural age. In spite of the rhetoric of "pluralism," I have observed how easily and commonly religious people become isolated from one another in subgroups so that they fail to engage other religious people in terms of their religious differences. I say this sadly after more than two decades of living in Hawaii, where everyone is an ethnic minority and the theological interchange between different religious groups is almost nil. There is goodwill, yes, but not serious discussion of fundamental religious issues. Accordingly, when I see the challenges and dialogue that Abe has initiated, I cannot but be grateful. Although Abe may not always agree with Christian theology and may not be a leading thinker among Buddhologists in Japan, for thirty years he has been unequaled in being able to bring Buddhist insights to bear on Christian thought and to articulate them in theological terms. In this regard, he stands alone.

QUESTIONS RAISED BY ABE'S CHALLENGES

In taking Masao Abe's challenges seriously, I still have questions about some of his ideas. One such question concerns the use of paradoxical logic, another is the claim of ultimacy for his categories (signaled by the adjective *absolute* or *total*), a third is his claim that his views of *Śūnyatā* are the core of Buddhism, and a fourth is his subordination of ethics to *Śūnyatā*. While all these ways of writing reverberate in the Kyoto School, from Nishida all the way down to Abe, I would propose that they are not as compelling to all Buddhists and that different ways of thinking and writing can be found in other parts of Buddhism. Accordingly, as a way of putting Abe's thought in perspective for his dialogue partners, I shall briefly review these four areas.

Although Zen practitioners have enjoyed the use of paradoxical language, no other tradition of Buddhism has quite matched their enthusiasm for it. Perhaps because Abe is first and last a Zen master, paradoxical language is very meaningful to him. Paradoxical language may be confirming to Zen insiders, but I have noticed that such language can be confounding to other Buddhists or to an outside dialogue partner who is trying to understand. A famous paradox within Mahāyāna is the assertion that "the passions are Enlightenment," which appears on the surface to be contradictory nonsense. However, Abe reworks this phrase as "samsara-as-it-is is nirvana" and explains it with language that may be equally confounding:

> This paradoxical statement is based on the dialectical character of true nirvana which is, logically speaking, the negation of negation (that is, absolute affirmation) or the transcendence of transcendence (that is, absolute immanence).[2]

Abe justifies this kind of paradoxical language by claiming that it reflects the "dialectical character of true nirvana." Although this dialectical method of writing is consistent with the Perfection of Wisdom tradition as seen in such familiar texts as the *Diamond* and *Heart Sūtras*, I am less convinced that it is shared across Buddhism. I may be missing something in Abe's argument, but I do not understand his logic when he claims that the negation of negation is "absolute affirmation." For me to say that a phone is "not not-a-phone" does not mean an absolute affirmation of the object/event; instead, it frees that event/object from my mental categories. That need not be an "absolute affirmation" of the object-as-it-is but merely the removal of my distorting mental projections, which allows the event/object to be seen on its own terms as suchness.

Of course, some of my confusion may just be an unfamiliarity with Abe's shorthand. For example, when explaining the identity of samsara and nirvana to Wolfhart Pannenberg, Abe recently wrote:

> *Now it is clear that "samsara-as-it-is is nirvana" does not indicate an immediate identity of samsara and nirvana, immanence and transcendence, but a dialectical identity through the negation of negation. In Mahayana Buddhism true nirvana is not a static state of transcendence but a dynamic movement between samsara so-called and nirvana so-called without attachment to either.*[3]

Even though this is clear to Abe, it has not always been clear either to Buddhists or to non-Buddhists that "samsara-as-it-is is nirvana" does *not* indicate "an immediate identity of samsara and nirvana, immanence and transcendence." Some Buddhists have gained notoriety by acting immorally in the name of this slogan, whereas such famous Buddhist intellectuals as T'ien-t'ai Chih-i (538–97) and Chan-jan (711–82) have had a very different application of this phrase.[4]

A major contribution by Masao Abe is his application of *Śūnyatā* and nirvana to theological discourse. Nirvana is an experience, but Abe goes beyond this to use nirvana logically and metaphysically. While Abe offers Christians many penetrating insights and questions by using the vantage point of nirvana and *Śūnyatā* some distortion and confusion may arise when he treats statements about nirvana as susceptible to metaphysics and logic in the manner of Abhidharma philosophy because doing so seems to reify nirvana and systematize it, thereby removing it from the dynamics of experience.

Abe's conceptualization of *Śūnyatā* and nirvana is often expressed as a reality at a metalevel that transcends normal dualistic thinking and is signaled by using the adjective *absolute*.[5] An uninformed reader of some of Abe's writings might receive the impression that Abe's Zen sometimes seems dangerously close to being another *one way* fundamentalism that sweeps aside all other distinctions in its *totalism*. Let me hasten to add, however, that Abe's lifelong commitment to dialogue and compassionate engagement and respect for others shows that he is committed to the pluralism of all humanity, even though a certain kind of totalism does appear in his writing:

> *This denial of our life, this death of our ego-self, should not be partial but* total. *Without the* total *negation of our life, or the* complete *death of our ego-self, our new life as a manifestation of the life of Jesus is* impossible. *There can be no* continuity *between the "old person" and the "new person" in the Pauline faith.* . . . *Just as the self-emptying or abnegation of the Son of God must not be partial but* total *and* thoroughgoing *for him to be Christ, the self-denial or death of the human ego-self must* not be partial, *but also* total *and* complete. *Only then can the new person be realized as the* true *and* authentic *self [emphases added].*[6] . . . *Precisely because God is not a self-affirmative God, God is truly a God of love (for through* complete *self-abnegation God is* totally *identical* with *everything* including sinful humans) *[emphases added].*[7]

In this regard, Abe criticizes Karl Rahner for having "traces of dualism," in spite of the fact that Rahner supports Abe's general notion when he writes that "the primary phenomenon given by faith is precisely the self-emptying of God, his becoming, the kenosis and genesis of God himself." For Abe, Rahner's emphasis on kenosis as "primary" is not sufficient, because it allows for secondary aspects. Instead, Abe demands a totalism:

> *The "traces of dualism" must be not only minimized, but also eliminated. God's self-emptying must be understood not as partial*

but as total *to the extent that . . . God's self-emptying is dynamically identical with God's abiding and infinite fullness [emphasis
added].*[8]

Instead of taking Abe's totalistic demands as metaphysically and
logically normative for Buddhism, I suggest that they represent more
clearly an "absolute" in Abe's life when he experienced *Śūnyatā* as an ultimate personal transformation that is the existential foundation from
which he engages in dialogue.[9] However, it is a big step from private experience to public conformity to make the assertion that this is the ultimate
for all Buddhists and the core of all Buddhism. One often has the impression that Abe makes these claims in the spirit of a passionate religious
teacher who has had an experience of ultimacy in his own life. Although
Abe's logical imperatives and claims for an absolute viewpoint express
this personal ultimacy, I suggest that they are less useful when perceived
as theoretical and historical generalizations about what other Buddhists
hold as truth.

To his credit, Abe participates in dialogue through the depths of his
own personal religious experience:

> *In my personal experience the more seriously I tried to do good
> and to avoid evil, the more clearly I realized myself to be far away
> from good and to be involved in evil. The realization of the radical
> evil at the bottom of the struggle between good and evil, and the
> realization of my fundamental ignorance of ultimate truth were
> the outcome of my ethical life. In short, this realization in its
> ultimate form was nothing other than a realization of the death
> of the ego-self. Through this realization of the ego's death, however,
> the "holy" was opened up in me. It is not, however, God as the
> absolute good but God as the absolute nothingness that is neither
> good nor evil and yet both good and evil dynamically. To me, this
> realization of absolute nothingness is the basis of my life and the
> source of my activity. . . . To me, the realization of the spiritual
> death of the ego is essential for a new religious life. It is the radical
> realization of our finitude in both the ethical and ontological senses.
> It is not a pessimistic but a highly realistic event, which provides
> us with a basis for a resurrected, creative life. From this point of*

*view the Holocaust is not the responsibility of the holy/good God
but our responsibility, to be realized through the death of the ego
in the bottomless depths of our existence.*[10]

Abe then takes his personal experience and generalizes it into a universal requirement so that no religion is possible except on the basis that he has experienced:

*All discussion of Christ as the Son of God will be religiously
meaningless if engaged in apart from the problem of human ego,
our own existential problem of the self. The notion of Christ's
kenosis or his self-emptying can be properly understood only
through the realization of our own sinfulness and our own
existential self-denying.*[11]

Similarly, Abe uses his own experience as the norm for true Buddhism by going so far as to say that the "ultimate reality for Buddhism is . . . Sunyata."[12]

There have been various uses of the term *Śūnyatā*, most commonly perhaps as a critical term in Mādhyamika thought to mean simply "the lack of inherent existence." All things and ideas as constructs are emptied of substantial and enduring self-existence and, instead, are interdependent and transient. However, *Śūnyatā* also has positive meanings that Abe outlines in his article "Kenotic God and Dynamic Sunyata."[13] Nevertheless, in spite of these positive values, his longtime friend and collaborator, John Cobb, still has not been able to find *Śūnyatā* dynamic enough to approach the Christian sense of God,[14] and a fellow Buddhist scholar, Kenneth Inada, was moved to substitute the term *tathatā* (suchness, or thusness) in place of *Śūnyatā*.[15]

The two foundational Mahāyāna texts are the *Perfection of Wisdom Scripture in 8,000 Lines* and the *Lotus Sūtra*. Although Abe aligns himself with the Perfection of Wisdom tradition that heralds *Śūnyatā* as the ultimate, the *Lotus Sūtra* celebrates Dharma as the ultimate. Accordingly, because of the influence of Abe in dialogue circles, it is understandable, but inaccurate, when John Cobb or Richard Rubenstein asserts that ultimate reality for Buddhists is *Śūnyatā*, or Emptiness. For many

Buddhists the term *Dharma* is a more accurate expression for their ultimate reality.

The distinction between *Śūnyatā* and Dharma becomes particularly
important in the area of ethics. Western dialogue partners have often
questioned whether Abe's view of *Śūnyatā* offers an adequate foundation
for ethics since Abe argues for a discontinuity between ethics and religion
in the sense that ethics is conditioned and dualistic, whereas the religious
dimension of *Śūnyatā* goes beyond dualism. *Śūnyatā* provides a necessary
ground for moral decisions undistorted by false substantialization but
does not provide concrete guidelines for action. However, Abe does argue
that the experience of *Śūnyatā* naturally gives birth to bodhisattva vows
and moral action.

Lawrence Kohlberg, the former director of the Center for Moral
Development at Harvard University, agrees with Abe that morality and
religion can be differentiated and that they intersect at the highest stage:

> As we would phrase the problem, after attaining a clear awareness
> of universal ethical principles valid against the usual skeptical
> doubts there still remains the loudest skeptical doubt of all: "Why
> be moral? Why be just, in a universe that is largely unjust?" At
> this level, the answer to the question "Why be moral?" entails the
> question "Why live?" and the parallel question, "How face death?"
> Thus, ultimate moral maturity requires a mature solution to the
> question of the meaning of life. This, in turn, we argue, is hardly
> a moral question per se; it is an ontological or a religious one. . . .
> It is also not a question resolvable on purely logical or rational
> grounds.[16]

In reflecting on the kind of religious experience that is necessary to
support a universal ethic beyond the code of particular groups or the general social order, Kohlberg observes that "they involve contemplative
experience of a nondualistic variety."

> In despair we are the self seen from the distance of the cosmic or
> infinite. In the state of mind we have metaphorically termed Stage
> 7 we identify ourselves with the cosmic or infinite perspective

*itself; we value life from its standpoint. At such a time, what is
ordinarily background becomes foreground and the self is no
longer figure to the ground. We sense the unity of the whole and
ourselves as part of that unity. This experience of unity, often mistakenly treated as a mere rush of mystic feelings, is at "Stage 7"
associated with a structure of ontological and moral conviction.*[17]

These remarks are certainly consistent with Abe's view of the role of
Śūnyatā for ethics and must be seen as independent corroboration for
Abe's viewpoint. However, these ideas have not gone unchallenged[18] and
have not been persuasive to many of Abe's dialogue partners. For example, Abe's view removes the edge of particularity from the Holocaust by
interpreting it within the general matrix of karmic retribution. Jürgen
Moltmann raises this point and asserts that "what is said in this manner
about the Holocaust can also be said about every other occurrence."
However, he rejects this view: "As a German and as a Christian I cannot
speak about Auschwitz in this way."[19] Instead, he refers Abe to German
Christians and Japanese Christians who responded to these horrors
through public confession of guilt. Although the Pure Land Buddhist
Hajime Tanabe was deeply affected by his awareness of culpability and
helplessness in the face of World War II,[20] it is not so clear that the Zen
members of the Kyoto School (Abe's teachers) felt similar personal
responsibility.[21] In contrast, the great scholar of T'ien-t'ai Buddhism,
Ryōdō Shioiri, of Taisho University, once remarked to me that he was so
angry at the lack of Buddhist response to the war that he wanted to burn
down every Buddhist temple in Japan. Furthermore, as his own response
he devoted his scholarly career to the study of Buddhist repentance
rituals to highlight the importance and necessity of repentance for
Buddhists.[22]

The various scandals that have rocked the American Zen community have shown that the Kyoto School is not alone among Zen leaders in
neglecting the significance of ethical distinctions. Nor do Zen historical
texts offer a different picture. For example, the *Platform Sūtra* of the Sixth
Zen Patriarch teaches "formless precepts" and "formless repentance"
rather than invoking lists of specific ethical precepts. While not condon-
ing immorality, such an approach leaves the door open to antinomianism
by not emphasizing specific guidelines. In contrast, when T'ien-t'ai

created the category of "formless repentance," it was within the context of also advocating repentance of specific deeds.[23] Although Zen teachers can be as concerned with morality as other Buddhists are, Zen ideology based on Emptiness, inherent Buddha-nature, and sudden Enlightenment discourages discussion of practical measures and ethical gradations.[24]

As a corrective in dialogue I propose that the Buddhist concept of Dharma be used as a term for ultimate reality for Buddhists that would be even more embracing than *Śūnyatā*. Even though Mahāyāna Buddhists have always identified Dharma and *Śūnyatā*, in the experience of Abe, *Śūnyatā* transcends the dualism found in the conflict between good and evil. Accordingly, he has had a major point of disagreement with many Jewish and Christian dialogue partners for whom ethical demands are an expression of the will of God. Similarly, in many parts of the Buddhist community, Dharma not only involves the experience of *Śūnyatā* but also embodies ethical imperatives. *Śūnyatā* as experience is part of the Dharma, but not its total experience. Instead, *Śūnyatā* may be a necessary gate to Enlightenment, but it is not all the Dharma. Equally ultimate and sometimes more ultimate are also the experiences of ethical imperatives expressed as compassion and *upāya*. Indeed, dialogue partners should be alerted to the debate throughout Mahāyāna Buddhism between the idea of sudden and gradual Enlightenment and practice. Abe's viewpoint represents the sudden Enlightenment of traditional Zen, but Zen is not all of Buddhism. Tibetan Buddhists have challenged the Zen emphasis on Emptiness over compassion,[25] and Theravadan Buddhists also can object to the suggestion that *Śūnyatā* has priority over ethics. Instead, ethics is integral to Dharma, as has been argued by Frank Reynolds.[26]

It is true that especially for the Perfection of Wisdom tradition and for Zen, this awareness that all things bear the mark of Emptiness and are unified in this dimension is at the heart of practice. But it isn't all practice, and it certainly is not all Buddhism. From other Buddhist perspectives such as T'ien-t'ai, Emptiness is a partial truth! So we should remember the other early foundation of Mahāyāna, the *Lotus Sūtra*, which celebrates not Emptiness but the Dharma as an ultimate and active reality. It is the Dharma that saves, it is the Dharma that nourishes life and growth in all things, it is the Dharma that is eternal, and it is the Dharma that responds to the needs of beings and takes a myriad of forms in order to save. This emphasis might provide an alternative view of Buddhism for those Christian or Jewish thinkers who are uncomfortable with Abe's emphasis on *Śūnyatā*. However, these Buddhist traditions have yet to find a spokesperson as penetrating, skillful, and dedicated to dialogue as Abe. Accordingly, Abe's own life has become his greatest argument for "dynamic *Śūnyatā*" as manifesting itself in vow and action!

chapter Ten

MASAO ABE AND NISHIDA'S LOGIC OF PLACE

Ashok K. Gangadean

MASAO ABE'S DIALOGICAL WORK IN THE WEST

OVER THE PAST TWENTY YEARS the dialogical encounter of philosophical and religious traditions has flourished dramatically in a global context. This encounter has contributed to a historic change in the hermeneutical landscape of philosophical and religious discourse. It is now more natural to enter religious studies with an interreligious sensitivity and orientation, to engage in philosophical investigations with more awareness of the presence and importance of other traditions. The face of philosophical and religious discourse has been recentering increasingly in an intercultural, intertraditional, intergrammatical context. In this rich and varied encounter, a new global consciousness is emerging to bring into sharper focus certain perennial issues concerning the foundation of dialogical philosophy—the nature of dialogue between worlds, the possibility of intergrammatical conversation and transformations. Masao Abe's appearance and participation in this dialogical encounter, especially over the past fifteen years, is certainly not coincidental. He has played a central and vital role in this historic unfolding. And I welcome this occasion to honor his impressive contributions—to reflect, to appraise, to reconsider, and to assess the historical importance of his dialogical work on the scene of recent Western philosophical and religious discourse.

I first encountered Masao Abe about fifteen years ago. The center of my own work has been the exploration of the universal logic, or grammar of discourse, in a dialogical and global context. At that time I was very active in a range of dialogues in intercultural philosophy, interreligious dialogue, and interdisciplinary discourse. It was remarkable in the late seventies how many contexts for intergrammatical dialogue were emerging: the Society for Asian and Comparative Philosophy, the International Association of Buddhist Studies, and the Working Group for Cross-cultural Philosophy of Religion of the American Academy of Religion, to mention but three. In these various settings, I would regularly find myself participating in dialogues with Abe. Whether in the context of East-West philosophical dialogue or interreligious explorations, I was struck with the consistent eloquence and excellence of his contributions. It was not only that he spoke well for the particular Japanese school of philosophy and religious thought that he "represented," not only that he deepened the dialogues by articulating a certain perspective in Eastern thought, but also that he spoke in a dialogical voice and out of a dialogical mode of discourse. The more I interacted with him in various dialogical contexts, the more it became apparent that Abe was deeply grounded in a religious and philosophical grammar that was itself profoundly dialogical and concerned essentially with performing and making manifest the foundation of dialogical encounter.

This was the period when I was involved with developing the Margaret Gest Center for Cross-Cultural Study of Religions at Haverford College. Through the seventies I worked closely with colleagues at Haverford, especially Paul Desjardins (philosophy) and Wyatt MacGaffey (anthropology), to launch this newly emerging center, which was especially concerned with cultivating interreligious inquiry and dialogue in an intercultural and interdisciplinary context. The center featured an annual lecture series on the unity of religions and an annual interreligious dialogue that brought diverse religious faiths together in the interest of exploring common ground and honoring real diversity among the world religions. I became the first director of this center (1980–83) and was charged with developing a practical philosophy and dialogical strategy for the most creative launching of the activities of the center.

Abe was a natural for the center. And in planning the early dialogues, he played a prominent role. He participated in the 1981 dialogue on the unity of religions, which included John Carman, Tu Wei-ming, Norbert Samuelson, Riffat Hassan, and Rita Gross. It was remarkable to see the dialogical dynamics at work in bringing out the depth and diversity of different faiths in exploring the common ground between religious worlds. I noted over and over how different religious narratives deepened and self-expanded and self-revised in and through this dialogical encounter. I invited Abe back for the 1983 dialogue, "Death and Eternal Life: A Buddhist-Christian Dialogue," which included John Hick, Donald Swearer, and Victor Preller. Here again, Abe's presence helped deepen the dialogue and open space for an authentic encounter of different voices and grammatical perspectives.

The Gest Center at that time also featured a Gest Visiting Professorship. The idea was that one of the best ways to educate and sensitize the community to other religious worlds, religions, and faiths was to have in residence living exemplars of different traditions. One of the original structures of the college—the Woodside Cottage—was converted into a residential and teaching facility and called the Gest Meditation Center. Because of his outstanding performance in the earlier dialogues, I was successful in convincing colleagues and administrators at Haverford to appoint Masao Abe as Gest Visiting Professor for two years (1985–87). Before his arrival we had the good fortune to have three outstanding professors from different cultural and religious traditions—Valentine Mudimbe, Lobsang Lhalungpa, and Lal Mani Joshi. By the time Abe arrived, there was already momentum and high expectations at the Meditation Center. Students were increasingly responsive to the teaching presence of the resident professors, and supporting cultural events became part of the life of the Meditation Center. In addition, Abe gave public lectures to the community and was featured again in the 1986 annual dialogue, "Free Will in Religious Traditions," which included Langdon Gilkey, Norbert Samuelson, and Rajeshwari Pandharipande. Abe set the context for this dialogue with an illuminating paper, "Free Will and Sunyata in Buddhism." His framing of the issues helped bring out a significant dialogical encounter between the diverse religious grammars represented in the dialogue. Abe was most effective in his tenure as the Gest Professor and made a real impact in introducing members of the community to the living reality of Zen thought and practice. He touched the lives of many students, who were most appreciative of their living encounter with the Zen experience.

But for me the most significant and enduring impact of his work at Haverford revolved around the discussions of a distinguished group of philosophers in the Greater Philadelphia area and throughout the Northeast. Abe and I convened an Interreligious Theology Group, which met regularly at the Gest Mediation Center during his two-year residence. This group included thinkers who attended the Sunday seminars on a regular basis—Paul Desjardins, Joan Stambaugh, Douglas Steere, Steven Heine, Kenneth Kraft, Jiten Mohanty, Thomas Dean, Janet Gyatso, Michael Barnhart—some of whom traveled long distances. Some other scholars attended less frequently but nevertheless made important contributions to our discussions—David Dilworth, Richard DeMartino, Donald Swearer, and Edward Casey, among others. Abe led many of these discussions and introduced us to several eminent thinkers in the Kyoto School founded by Kitarō Nishida. The quality of the discussions was high, and it was apparent that Abe embodied a living creative understanding of the rich and deep insights of the Zen tradition.

Masao Abe's book *Zen and Western Thought* had just appeared and provided a further source for our dialogues and inquiry. I should mention in passing that I nominated this book to the American Academy of Religion committee that evaluates new books for its prestigious annual award. Abe's book won the academy's award for the most significant constructive/reflective work in religious studies. The award was another indication of the growing recognition of the importance of Abe's dialogical philosophy for religious studies on the American scene. Abe's grounding in Eastern and Western thought helped bring out the interreligious issues and sparked explorations at the foundation of East-West global discourse. Over the two years, as the group grew more conversant with the Kyoto School, it became apparent that this tradition had powerful resources for deepening interreligious dialogue and East-West comparative philosophical inquiry.

The most exciting aspect of the Sunday dialogues for me was Abe's articulate introduction of Nishida's "logic of *basho*" (logic of place). This

logic became the central focus of our discussions—it was the very foundation of Nishida's lifework and the generative force of the Kyoto School.
It was exciting because I found in Nishida a creative mind of the highest
order whose philosophical life culminated in the attempt to articulate the
foundational logic of the Zen experience. Nishida's recognition and intuition that there is a universal logic of *Śūnyatā* that needed to be excavat-
ed and formulated was deeply akin to my own quest to articulate the universal grammar or logic at the core of existence. It was a thrill to find a
richly developed philosophical tradition deeply grounded in the resources
of Eastern and Western thought moving toward an articulation of a truly
global and universal logic. It was, in effect, an independent experiment
that I could explore in relation to my own efforts to articulate the universal logic at the heart of global discourse.

As Abe introduced the group to Nishida's logic, it became clear that
at the end of his remarkable career, Nishida had reached the foundations
and generative origin of his lifework. The recognition that there is a universal logic of meditative and religious experience—a logic of *Śūnyatā*, or
Absolute Nothingness—is itself an important advance in global philosophical discourse. It became clear to me that such a logic helps account
for the nature and possibility of interreligious dialogue and East-West
comparative inquiry. But it was also apparent that Nishida's logic of *basho*
had to be enacted and performed in the living dialogical encounter that
Masao Abe exhibited so well in his life and teaching. The more I understood the vital pulse of the logic of *basho*, the more I recognized that Abe
was performing this living logic of dialogical encounter in his own teaching practice. While our encounter with the logic of *basho* revealed that for
Nishida the logic of *Śūnyatā* takes us to the core of a living historical
dialectic in the heart of self-consciousness, our encounter with Abe's lifework exhibited and performed this encounter or dialogical hermeneutic
in the unfolding historical scene. Abe's dialogical work, in other words,
was existentially performing and enacting the living logic of *basho* by
deepening the dialogical encounter on the global scene, by helping open
a higher space for a living dialogue between religions and philosophies. In
this respect, the historical drama we are now living through—the emergence of global consciousness through ever deepening dialogical
encounter—is itself the living play of the logic of *basho*. And in this context
Abe's dialogical lifework is the very playing out performatively of this

logical dialectic. So there is a historical consistency between the foundation of Nishida's logic and the living dialogical practice of Abe at this moment of the historical unfolding of a global hermeneutical awareness. This connection between theory and practice is, for me, the significance of Abe's vital work in the West and on the global scene.

So the focal point for me of Abe's lifework of dialogical-encounter philosophy and practice gravitated to understanding the generative logic of *basho* that gave life and foundation to the dialogical philosophy of the Kyoto School. Truly to understand the significance of Abe's work and the teaching of the Kyoto School is to come to terms with the depth of the dialogical encounter—the actual historical deepening of the dialogical space of human life and discourse. And to understand the possibility and depth of this interreligious dialogue and East-West philosophical encounter requires coming to terms with the foundational logic of *basho*. Thus, I present my own understanding of this logic, an understanding based in large part on my extensive notes and reflections from the Sunday seminars in which Abe introduced us to Nishida's philosophy of place (*basho*). I hope that in so doing, the reader can glimpse how Abe presented Nishida's thought to the West as an immensely important Japanese Buddhist contribution to the emergence of intercultural philosophy.

MASAO ABE'S PRESENTATION OF NISHIDA'S LOGIC TO THE WEST

In the full maturity of his career, Nishida gravitated to the articulation of the underlying foundation of his lifework, which he called the logic of place, or the logic of Absolute Nothingness. His life and writings are grounded in the depth of *Śūnyatā*, and perhaps his greatest intuition is that there is a universal logic arising out of *Śūnyatā*, or Absolute Nothingness. At the end of his career, he focused on attempting to bring this logic to articulate expression. Given his deep grounding in the evolution of Western philosophy and logic, he naturally attempted to articulate the logic of *basho* (universal place) in relation to certain great paradigms of logic such as the logics of Aristotle and Hegel. In this respect he attempted to clarify what he took to be the universal logic at the foundation of Eastern and Western thought: a truly global logic. But it is also clear that in attempting to break new ground in excavating the logic of *Śūnyatā*, he faced great challenges in thinking and speaking in the ways of nonduality that is the signature of the dialectics of Absolute Nothingness.

Apparently his attempt to articulate this universal logic of awareness hit great barriers of interpretation and expression, and it is remarkable that in the last thoughts he penned before his death, Nishida stated that his logic had not been understood by the academic world. He begins this remark as follows:

> *As the result of my cogitations over these many long years, I*
> *think I have been able to clarify the form of thinking—that is, the*
> *logic—of the historically formative act from the standpoint of the*
> *historically active self itself. I have endeavored to consider as well,*
> *through my logic, various questions fundamental to the natural*
> *sciences, and to morals and religion. I think moreover, that I have*
> *succeeded in framing questions that have never been properly*
> *framed from the standpoints of previous logics. At least I think*
> *I have been able to indicate the path along which further*
> *clarification can come.*[1]

It is noteworthy here that his logic purports to be grounded in the historically formative act from the standpoint of the historically active self. Moreover, he stresses that he believes himself to have broken new ground in opening this logic in ways that prior logics could not.

> *The reason this path has not been taken is that past logics have*
> *tended to remain without sufficient grounding. From the stand-*
> *point of abstract logic, the concrete cannot even be considered. My*
> *logic, however, has not been understood by the academic world—*
> *indeed, I may say that it has not yet been given the slightest serious*
> *consideration. Not that there hasn't been criticism. But the kind of*
> *criticism it has received has distorted my meaning—merely criti-*
> *cizing by objectifying my standpoint from its own. It has not been*
> *a criticism from within my own standpoint. A criticism from a*

different standpoint which does not truly understand what it is
criticizing cannot be said to be a true criticism. I seek, above all,
an understanding of what I am saying from my own standpoint.[2]

This is a jolting remark. It is shocking and saddening to hear Nishida say at the end of his life that the jewel of his lifework "has not yet been given the slightest serious consideration." He obviously felt that interpreters of his logic had completely misinterpreted his work from external and alien perspectives and had not made a vital transition into the paradigm of logic that he developed. When one looks more closely at his remark, it appears that Nishida thought his standpoint was being objectified by interpreters, that his logic is of the "concrete" and cannot be rightly understood by an "abstract" logic, and that past logics remained without "sufficient grounding."

Another way to express this point is to say that the logic of *Śūnyatā* takes us into the place *(basho)* or field of the most profound existential reality—concrete reality—that is beyond all objectification or dualistic thinking. It is clear in the tradition of *Śūnyatā* that the right-minding of Absolute Nothingness requires the most radical transformation of thinking into the methods of nonduality. And what Nishida is saying is that the logic of the existential immediacy of *Śūnyatā* must be entered from the methods of nondualistic thinking and cannot be accessed through the objectifying ways of dualistic logics. Apparently Nishida is suggesting that prior logics have been lodged in objectification and dualistic thinking that keep them abstract and not sufficiently grounded. He seems to think that logic becomes truly grounded in the ultimate ground of *Śūnyatā* and that only the appropriate method of minding can truly gain access to this concrete historical reality.

There are many assumptions here that need explanation. And it is clear that one main problem concerning Nishida's logic is the problem of right interpretation. One question is, What is the right standpoint for justly interpreting Nishida's logic? If we can satisfactorily make the paradigm shift to interpret Nishida's logic rightly, the next concern is, Does it make sense? Does Nishida's logic qualify as a truly universal logic? Do his innovations make sense? In what sense is the logic of *Śūnyatā* a "concrete logic"? If there is a logic of *Śūnyatā*, what are the scope and the jurisdiction of such a logic—is it truly a universal and global logic? Why does

Nishida think that *Śūnyatā*, or Absolute Nothingness, is the universal and absolute logical ground of all discourse—of all logics, East, West, and other?

Most of all we focus here on the fundamental hermeneutical problem of performing the paradigm shift of moving into the standpoint of rightly minding *Śūnyatā* as the place of concrete historical reality. Of course, this challenge is not unique to Nishida's discourse but has been a perennial challenge in the global quest to enter the place of natural reason, of universal grammar, of right-minding. All traditions have had to struggle with overcoming dualistic thinking and egocentric minding, which have always been stumbling blocks for the nondualistic or unitive essence of reason. Within the evolution of the Buddhist tradition alone we see that the birthing of Buddha's teaching is essentially the attempt to overcome pernicious dualism and the objectifying ways of ego-minding to realize the liberation and flourishing of natural reason. And it is clear that the continuing self-revision and evolution of the Buddhist dialectic, as for example in the logical and dialectical innovations of Nāgārjuna, have been this very attempt to articulate and live the logic of *Śūnyatā*. So we situate Nishida's quest to advance the logic of *Śūnyatā* in the global quest to articulate the universal grammar at the heart of consciousness and the human existential condition. In this respect it is not surprising that Nishida's innovations in excavating the logic of Absolute Nothingness should encounter the hermeneutical barriers it has apparently faced. But I shall suggest that this global quest is the single most important philosophical priority in opening higher space for the cultivation of global discourse and the advancement of natural reason.

Assuming that we can accomplish this profoundly difficult task of performing the paradigm shift and transforming our thinking into the dialectical ways of *Śūnyatā*, there remain a number of problems and difficulties in making sense of Nishida's logic. For in developing his logic of *basho*, Nishida takes as his point of departure the subject-predicate logical space that is the foundation for the evolution of the science of logic from Aristotle through Kant to Hegel. The space of predication as the space of thought, being, and knowledge has been articulated in alternative paradigms through the centuries, and Nishida builds his language of logic in this context. He apparently thinks that despite the paradigm shifts in the space of predication in these major figures of the European

tradition, there has been an ongoing deep pattern of dualism and objectification in these logics. So he attempts to break new ground in the space
of predication, to break through the barriers and limits in the logics of
Aristotle, Kant, and Hegel to resituate logic and predication in the
space—*basho*—of Śūnyatā, or Absolute Nothingness.

In making this radical turn to the allegedly nondualistic universal
ground of logic, Nishida introduces terminology and performs dramatic
innovations in renovating the space of predication. He presses the logical
subject and logical predicate beyond their dualistic limits, all the way to
their transcendental grounding in the universal place of Śūnyatā. He
attempts to break new ground in resituating predication beyond the dualistic and dualizing, or objectifying, logical space of prior logics. He
assumes the model of the "subsumptive judgment," wherein the logical
subject is subsumed logically and ontologically by the logical predicate.
He finds in the logic and ontology of Aristotle the recognition that the
primitive subject—*ousia*, or ontological individual—stands absolutely
beyond the predicate (universal field). This paradigm apparently secures
the absolute irreducibility of the object or existent thing as a ground of
predication. Nishida adopts and exploits this absolute commitment to the
object or being as vital in grounding objectivity.

At the same time, he apparently moves with Hegel in treating the
predicate position as the direction of universality, generality, and consciousness. For him the logical place of the predicate situates the field of
consciousness as the most generic and all-encompassing transcendental
field, which subsumes all subjects or things. So in combining the alter-
paradigms of Aristotle and Hegel, he finds that the place of the logical
subject is the place of the object, while the place of the predicate is the
place of the subject—of consciousness and subjectivity. In this way the
dialectic of subject and object is played out in the inner dialectic of the
logical subject and predicate in the subsumptive judgment. However,
Nishida presses Hegel's position beyond its limits all the way into the
place of Absolute Nothingness. While Hegel places Absolute Spirit
(*Geist*) as the absolute transcendental predicate—the concrete universal—Nishida presses further to inquire into the grounds or place of *Geist*.
He presses the absolute predicate to its absolute ground in Śūnyatā.

By pressing the poles of dualistic predication to their absolute limits
and alleged origin, Nishida attempts to reach the absolute nondualistic or

unitive grounds of predication where the absolute subject and absolute predicate meet and apparently co-arise. By purporting to move beyond Hegel's absolute predicate and *Geist,* Nishida apparently believes that he has overcome the limits of subjectivity by reaching a deeper field of Subjectivity that crosses beyond the dualism of objectivism and subjectivism. Similarly, by pressing to the absolute ground of the logical and ontological subject (object), which cannot be subsumed by any predicate, Nishida believes that he has reached the place of absolute existence—the irreducible impredicable existent. Thus the logic of the absolute subject and absolute predicate meet in the ground *(basho)* of Absolute Nothingness. In a real sense, then, *basho* is the absolute ground or foundation of predication (thought and being) and is thus the universal domain or unified field of the universe of discourse.

By Nishida's situating predication in the nondualistic dialectics of *Śūnyatā,* a radically new method of minding and speaking emerges. Nishida believes he has accomplished the ontological ideal sought by Aristotle in preserving the absolute integrity of the primary subject, the existential individual, in all its singularity and historical specificity. At the same time he believes he has preserved and sublated in a deeper way the ontological ideal and *telos* of Hegel in moving into the truly "concrete universal"— in the field of *basho.* Thus, for Nishida, the absolute ground of *Śūnyatā* is the place of historical existence where the deepest transcendental subjectivity of consciousness (universal) shows itself as the infinitely deep singular and individuated historical being (particular). Apparently what is disclosed as polarized, opposite, and even contradictory in dualized logical space is found to be in a primitive union an identity in the field of *basho.* And Nishida speaks of the principle of "absolutely contradictory identity" as the universal principle of all historical existence revealed in the ground of Absolute Nothingness.

In making this radical turn to the nondualistic foundations of logic, Nishida purports to have discovered and uncovered the true depth of the historically existing individual. In his great last essay, *The Place of Nothingness and the Religious Worldview,* he brilliantly performs the discourse of the logic of place with its paradigm of the historical individual. This paradigm shift to the nondualistic understanding of the individual exhibiting the structure of absolutely contradictory identity is, in my judgment, at once his greatest contribution to the evolution of universal grammar and at the same time the most problematic, puzzling, and difficult breakthrough to comprehend. As he performs, textures, and elucidates this discourse of the historical individual, it is clear that this individual goes beyond the Aristotelian *ousia* (primitive individual substance) to a dynamic interactive process of active historical self-determination.

While Nishida performs articulately the speech and logic of the individual in the place of *Śūnyatā*, many questions remain unarticulated and not theoretically addressed or explicitly thematized and explained. To help focus on these fundamental queries to Nishida's logic, let us take some sample summary remarks from Abe's published presentation of Nishida's logic:

> With this notion of Absolute Nothingness, Nishida transcends the predicative dimension of judgment and stands upon the place of the "transcendent predicate," i.e., upon the place of Absolute Nothingness in contrast to the "transcendent subject" or individual which transcends the dimension of the grammatical subject. Both the direction of the grammatical subject and the direction of the grammatical predicate are transcended, and the one unique individual as "transcendent subject" is subsumed by Absolute Nothingness as the "transcendent predicate." Nishida fully agrees with Aristotle's definition of the individual subject as that which can never become the predicate. But he does not stop at this notion and instead develops the idea of "the predicate that can never become the subject" as the "place" wherein the singular individual exists. The idea of the "transcendent subject" as well as that of the "transcendent predicate" are thoroughly radicalized. Both the transcendent subject and transcendent predicate can be transcendent with respect to each other within the non-abiding place of Absolute Nothingness. Dual transcendence of subject with respect to the predicate and of the predicate with respect to the subject is established through the boundless openness or the uncircumscribable emptiness of Absolute Nothingness. This dual transcendence is characteristic of the subsumption of interactive individuals by Absolute Nothingness. This is not a problem of mere method, but a problem of philosophical principle. We herein make immediate contact [italics in original] with the individual

*for the first time. That is, through the realization of Absolute
Nothingness, the individual is fully known by us in its concrete
immediacy without any conceptualization. Expressed in Nishida's
terms, the individual is realized as "that which lies within"
Absolute Nothingness (i.e., it rests in Absolute Nothingness, its
place), and in Absolute Nothingness determines itself without
being determined from the outside by any other thing. This self-
determination of the individual just as it is, is the self-determination of "place" or Absolute Nothingness and the self-determination
of the world.*[3]

Abe sums up his remarks on Nishida's logic as follows:

*The logic of place is a predicative logic in the radical sense, not a
logic of the grammatical subject. Hence it stands in contrast to all
forms of traditional Western "objective logic" which, strictly speaking, never fully transcend the subject-predicate structure. It is not
a logic about the act of seeing or of knowing nor is it a logic about
that which is seen and known objectively in terms of the grammatical subject; rather it is a logic of "place," which is prior to, and
the source of, both seeing and knowing and that which is seen and
known. It is a subjective or existential logic prior to the opposition
of subject and object, a logic of totally unobjectifiable self-awakening. In comparison with the logic of place, which is Absolute
Nothingness, Aristotle's logic of the grammatical subject, Kant's
highly subjectified transcendental logic, and Hegel's dialectical
logic are all logics of objective consciousness and in this regard do
not escape objective thinking. Consequently, they fall short of the
logic of truly existential self-awakening.*[4]

Finally, Abe stresses that Nishida's logic of this primitive existential
individual moves beyond both subjectivism and objectivism to the Objective ground of the real historical world:

*The logic of place, however, neither confronts objective logic nor
excludes it. Although we term it predicative logic, this does not
signify logic without a subject. As its own self-determination, place*

and its logic grasps all grammatical subjects without marring their uniqueness. Place reflects all individuals and their mutually determining way-of-being within itself and realizes them as its own self-determination. In this regard, the logic of place is the logic of the self-establishment of the objective world and includes objective logic as a necessary factor or moment. The logic of place is not the form of the thinking of the subjective self. Rather, it is the form of the self-expression of true Reality in and through Absolute Nothingness. Since Nishida's philosophy of place is a logic of thoroughgoing subjective and existential self-realization, it is at the same time the logic of the establishment of the objective world. [5]

Returning full circle to our earlier reflections on the dialogical drama we are living through on a global scene, it should now be evident that Abe has played a key role in this drama because of his presentation of Nishida's philosophy to the West. The philosophy of Nishida, and its creative developments by the Kyoto School, play a significant role in the emergence of an intercultural philosophy. I myself have pursued this topic in a recently published book. [6] My own work in this field, like that of many other Western scholars working in related fields, owes much to the pioneering work of Masao Abe.

chapter Eleven

MASAO ABE AS A
ZEN TEACHER IN
THE WEST

Durwood Foster

I

FROM 1988 TO 1991 the Pacific School of Religion (PSR) and the Graduate Theological Union (GTU) enjoyed a qualitative *kairos* of wider ecumenism, and the central figure sparking and validating the wholesome experience was Masao Abe. Those in Berkeley committed to the interaction of religions, and those who sat in his classes and then went forth far and wide, will remain grateful to Abe for instructing and inspiring, charming and challenging us so incisively and so graciously. Mrs. Abe, the effervescent Ikuko, was usually at his side and enhanced his own natural conviviality. In retrospect, it seems the time of the Abes in Berkeley went by all too quickly, and we did not really take due advantage of their presence. We were hardly well enough prepared for a master teacher of Zen who was also probably the world's leading figure, from within Buddhism, of the dialogue with Christianity. This small, humble, courageous man was in spirit and vision miles ahead of his audience, and yet so patient. But if some of the opportunity was not risen to, nevertheless a shining chapter was added to PSR's heritage of global outreach. We can look back to the Abe years as exciting precedent for what, in the study of religion, some of us now more ardently hope will develop widely and permanently. Meanwhile, to Masao Abe we say from head and heart: Thank you! Splendidly done! We miss you!

II

The base of Abe's teaching at PSR began to form in the late 1970s, when prison counselor George Tolson, on learning that he was terminally ill, conveyed his intention to leave a bequest to the school in memory of his father, who had been a professor there. Undecided whether to endow the work of pastoral care (his own field) or "another idea which had come to [me]," Tolson consulted the director of development and the dean (myself), our presidency being in transition then. Pastoral care was, of course, an established element in PSR's program of study as a seminary preparing candidates for Christian ministry. The "other idea" was to underwrite significant exposure in the curriculum to a vital and authentic presentation of non-Western religions like Hinduism and Buddhism. It was Tolson's opinion that such exposure was notably absent from most seminary campuses. We pointed out that the PSR faculty had, in the remote past, included a Jewish scholar as adjunct. But we also acknowledged considerable truth in Walter Kaufman's indictment that "modernity's worst intellectual ghetto" was the theological seminary, precisely in the matter before us. Yet, comparatively, PSR had a fairly good record of commitment to ecumenical and interreligious concerns, and one could therefore believe that openness to other traditions and dialogue with them might flourish here in the future. After further pondering, Tolson came back for more conversation in which he desiderated that not simply occasional lectures but solid blocks of teaching, like semester courses, should be offered in this or that nonchristian faith by a scholarly adherent of it, with the particular tradition rotating from year to year among major world religions. The decision was then formalized, and the Russell Tolson Fund was provided for in the son's will (as the bulk, in fact, of his modest estate). George Tolson passed away in 1982. Without question, he would have been happy to know there was a potential beneficiary of his gift as superbly qualified as Masao Abe to carry out its aim.

Occasionally Abe's name had surfaced at PSR in the 1970s, as in a thesis comparing Tillich and Zen or in an informal forum on current dialogue. I first actually met him at Claremont in the early 1980s at a conference on Christian understandings of Buddhism. The agenda, featuring the positions of Hans Waldenfels, John Cobb, Masatoshi Doi, and Heinrich Ott, was mainly an affair of Christian theologians and philosophers of religion. Abe, who was then teaching at Claremont, may have been the only Buddhist participant. I found myself gravitating to him during mealtimes and was as delighted by his sprightliness as I was impressed by his depth—naturally in Buddhism but surprisingly also in Christianity and Western philosophy. He had been at Union in New York (my alma mater) and had studied Tillich (my chief mentor) penetratingly. His own master had been Shin'ichi Hisamatsu, of whom I was aware as the formidable interlocutor with Tillich in the groundbreaking dialogues they held at Harvard in 1957. So conversation with Abe flowed readily. What really grabbed me in an unprecedented way, among Buddhists I had known, was his élan for reflective inquiry. Here was a learned and profound Buddhist philosopher who was insistently reaching out for dialogue.

In January 1984 the University of Hawai'i hosted, under David Chappell's inspired direction, the pioneering international conference "Paradigm Shifts in Buddhism and Christianity," bringing together a large turnout from both traditions. Within the main format were also held the first sessions of the Buddhist-Christian Theological Encounter as the "Abe-Cobb group." The whole experience—my introductory savoring of focused Buddhist-Christian interaction—was exhilarating. Professor Abe's paper, "Dynamic Sunyata and Christian Kenosis," became thenceforth a thematic marker for the burgeoning discussion, and his contributions in the more intimate encounter group—which dealt with suffering in the two traditions—evoked from Langdon Gilkey the quip, which was significantly more than a quip, that "the best Christian theologian among us was not a Christian." I also became aware during the concomitant socializing that Abe, having taught a year or two at Claremont and then at Hawai'i, would be going to Haverford College on another short-term contract. Apparently there were no tenured positions for his eminent métier of dialogue, in which, I was coming to feel, he was second to none. I tentatively mentioned the Tolson Fund at PSR and found that Abe was cordially interested.

On returning to Berkeley, I inquired about the bequest, strongly recommending Abe as an eventual possibility. The administration responded that the donated estate was still being settled; it might be a while before any money was accessible. Meanwhile, the Institute of Buddhist Studies (IBS), in Berkeley since 1967, was strengthened financially and formally affiliated with the Graduate Theological Union. Seated in Jōdo Shin-shū and training clergy for the Buddhist Churches of America, the IBS also made known its scholarly accountability to the whole Buddhist spectrum, and faculty were engaged with that in mind. Did this tend to obviate the need for PSR to seek a Buddhist, once Tolson funds were in place? Or would it enhance the plausibility in thereby building a varied concentration in Buddhism? Besides the IBS there was the Tibetan Nyingma Institute a few blocks away, and a multifarious Buddhist ambience accented the Bay Area and its outlying regions. The GTU had included from the outset a Center for Jewish Studies as well as a Unitarian-Universalist seminary. An energetic program for investigating the new religious movements had been mounted. And to the broad range of Catholic and Protestant traditions there was added in the mid-1980s an Eastern Orthodox component. The adjoining University of California provided further major resources, so that with academic comity, team teaching, and substantial cross-enrollment, there was materializing in Berkeley a wider ecumenical mix of unusual potency. Still, at the GTU there was as yet no single world-class scholar to galvanize and saliently symbolize what was hopefully taking place. Could Masao Abe, for a few years at least, be that scholar?

Berkeley was chosen as the site for the next (after Hawaii) large International Buddhist-Christian Conference in 1987, and I was asked to be the executive director. This facilitated my entry into the Abe-Cobb group, which met in March 1985 in Vancouver and then at Purdue in 1986. At both gatherings Abe scintillated, and personal interaction with him was sustained. One noted how scrupulously he did his homework. Whether as paper author or respondent, his meticulously written out thoughts gained rapt attention. They were earnest and substantive rather than ever deliberately humorous, and were unerringly centered on the issue at stake. Yet like Tillich, Abe always induced the context of "the human question." It came out that prior to espousing Zen he had identified with Pure Land Buddhism. But the catastrophe of World War II and Japan's defeat had precipitated an existential crisis. Beyond the negation of all meaning, he found through the Kyoto School the way to renewed affirmation. Abe was thus personally experienced in more than a single version of Buddhism as well as in the cultural horizon of twentieth-century nihilism. In Nishida, Nishitani, and Hisamatsu, he found both a basis and model for critical assimilation of Western thought. His own commitment was acted out dialogically in his coming to America to confront the views of Tillich, who asserted Christianity's combination of the "horizontal" and the "vertical" against Buddhism's alleged contentment with the latter alone. For Abe, Buddhist *Śūnyatā* remained the profounder envisagement of the absolute, but he asked as well how it might be construed more dynamically, so as to ground a meaningful history and social ethic. In this concern he was faithfully following the lead of Hisamatsu.

At Houston in 1985, for a meeting of the International Conference on the Unity of the Sciences, I enlisted Abe to do an essay on his master, Hisamatsu, as part of a project, "The Search for a Unifying Global Philosophy." The conference minutes report that "as presented by Masao Abe, Hisamatsu's thought not only resumes the depth of Buddhism and modern Zen in particular" but gives it "an incisive edge" befitting the project's global intention. Clearly Hisamatsu's "F.A.S. perspective is motivated by a creative philosophical ecumenism." The pivot of the "Formless Self (F) opens inwardly for humility and dialogue, the dyadic pole of which is all humanity (A) in mutual historical creativity (S). Christian ego preponderance and Buddhist social recessiveness are reciprocally mitigated in peacefully fruitful affirmation of life." Thus was Abe able to critique constructively both his own and the other tradition, as indeed he chided his fellow Buddhists at the closing Purdue Abe-Cobb session for a lack of dialogic passion. Abe in fact embodied, if anyone did, John Cobb's summons "beyond dialogue" to "mutual transformation."

At the Berkeley conclave, "Buddhism and Christianity: Toward the Human Future," August 10–15, 1987, Abe revved up further his stellar performances with the papers "God and Absolute Nothingness" and "Altizer's Kenotic Christology and Buddhism," along with lively give-and-take in the Abe-Cobb group. Moreover, he was one of five singled out to offer plenary addresses, and his thematization of "a positionless position" called forth some of the week's most intense discussion of openness and commitment. Noteworthily, the first actual use of the Tolson bequest occurred at the same conference. Pacific School of Religion drew upon the fund in responding to the appeal for support that went out to all GTU seminaries and made possible the opening address by Sri Lankan Buddhist sage Walpola Rahula. It was mentioned at the time that the donor had expressed a preference not for single lectures but for regular semester teaching. Accordingly, President Neely McCarter and Dean Barbara Brown Zikmund launched a priority search for the first academic appointment, to be made if possible for the coming spring. Consulting widely, Dean Zikmund became enthusiastically convinced that Abe was the ideal candidate; happily it turned out that he was available from January through May of 1988.

Following the zestful Berkeley conference, Buddhist-Christian interaction seemed to be nearing high tide. Plans were laid for a Society for Buddhist-Christian Studies, and that organization came into being during the American Academy of Religion (AAR) annual meeting in Boston in November 1987. Abe and I were both named to the board. With Ikuko we shared a festive meal—the Abes being definitely "middle way" rather than ascetic about food. We talked of students and courses and smiled in anticipation of the good times ahead.

III

Professor and Mrs. Abe actually arrived in Berkeley during the Christmas week. I was about to fly to Maryland for a few days with my daughter when the phone rang, and it was Masao Abe asking me to recommend a Christian service for the coming Sunday. Clearly, to steep himself for dialogue meant not only textual digging. Ikuko and he vivaciously sought palpable exposures, honing these through a spontaneous talent for socializing. Abe gently lamented being "overbooked." One could believe it, since he never seemed to turn anyone down and was continuously in demand to speak, write, and read various matter foisted upon him. Meanwhile, as went on becoming evident, he held resolutely to his own program of reflective productivity.

Abe's first formal assignment at PSR was to offer a three-session seminar within the matrix of the Pastoral Conference and Earl Lectures Program, the school's big yearly shindig just prior to the spring semester. Addressing the current state of Buddhist-Christian dialogue, it was a spirited start in his role at the school as Tolson Visiting Professor. Many of the dialogically inclined from the Bay Area and northern California attended, some of them adept in Buddhism or Christianity (few in both) and some quite innocent of sophisticated knowledge of either tradition. The Pastoral Conference caters to Christian clergy and educated laity, but neither clerical nor lay education in recent decades had adequately primed the sizable audience in religions other than their own. After all, this was the point of Abe's being there, and he was master of the situation. With patient consideration for the feckless and the reckless, his erudition and resiliency helpfully engaged not only the most advanced but the others, too, wherever they were. As we would gladly see in the months and years ahead, Abe possessed in abundance the "skillful means" of teaching. Charts and bibliographies had been scrupulously prepared along with the finely crafted manuscript, while an ex tempore wit spiced the discussion periods. It was Abe's manner to invite interruption at any time if understanding hung on it, and before a session was over he prompted challenges and listened intently to them. He never seemed threatened, upset, or condescending, no matter how far from the subject or the facts an intervention might be.

Two three-unit courses, the normal full load, were chosen by Abe for the spring semester: "Zen as the Religion of Self-Awakening," and "Creation and Dependent Origination: A Comparative Study of Buddhism and Christianity." Together, these courses covered nicely the scope of his envisaged contribution to the curriculum: depth work in specialized nonchristian subject matter and a dialogically illuminated overview of Buddhist-Christian relations. The latter course also served as an introduction, with a different twist, to both Buddhism and Christianity— remembering that numerous nonchristians (from IBS, the Jewish Center, etc.) take classes in the GTU every term. Both Abe's courses were, for the GTU, well subscribed. For many years in the Berkeley consortium, a surfeit of offerings had resulted in an average enrollment, for courses other than required "basics," of no more than six or seven. Abe's classes usually numbered about a dozen, the limit most professors set for seminars. They came from all over the GTU, including the doctoral areas. Expressions of frustration were heard regarding schedule conflicts or competing requirements, or because Abe's courses had not been well publicized. It was clear that many who would have wanted to hear him did not get to.

George Tolson would have winced. Unquestionably he would have wanted Abe's courses more vigorously promoted by the administration and integrated into the curriculum as more of a forced option.

To enhance awareness of Abe's presence on campus, a special evening address was arranged, as well as a faculty luncheon conversation with him. Abe became a familiar figure at mid-afternoon coffee breaks in the dining hall. He would follow his students over and freely chat for ten or fifteen minutes with anyone who cared to join in. In the wider community, moreover, interfaith groups like West-East Friends sponsored forums in which he participated. One such event that I recall was a conversation at the First Unitarian Church between Abe and myself on creation and dependent origination. Besides affording more opportunity for Abe to be heard, this give-and-take helped me significantly ramify my theological understanding. I hoped it might have had an analogous impact on many of our faculty, but in general colleagues seemed too busy or too fixed on their own agendas to seek serious encounter with the diminutive dynamo from beyond our usual horizons. Huston and Kendra Smith were a shining exception, and one of the best evenings with the Abes, in which Masao Abe gave his personal story, was in their home.

Abe instinctively enjoyed the classroom. His ease with students, combined with a mastery of the subject, got them to relax. There was a good-humored atmosphere as well as keen anticipation. Whatever he treated was simultaneously both factually expounded and thematically charged: for example, "Zen as the Religion of Self-Awakening." One could imbibe a rich spread of the elemental data—dates, names, sources, Japanese terms—but there was always a conceptual torsion, too, that required thinking. The professor, without seeming to try to, radiated authority, while his petite frame and unpresuming attitude removed any tone of authoritarianism. He continually enlisted the class in semantic midwifery, testing English expressions vis-à-vis Sanskrit, Japanese, Greek, or German. Students appeared to love this approach, even if they rarely knew enough to help. They also seemed hugely to enjoy, at comparative junctures, being asked what was the Christian or Jewish, the Catholic or Protestant doctrine. Abe, of course, had pondered these matters long and hard, but he nevertheless imparted openness. A spirit of mutual inquiry was engendered. My teaching assistant, Sharon Burch, a doctoral candidate and pastor who sat in on these classes, found herself boldly reconceiving a lot of her theology.

A device Abe used superbly was the "protocol," whereby an appointed student summarizes what happened at the previous session. I had encountered this technique in Germany and then tried using it in my courses, with only moderate success. Abe's classes took it and ran with it. It would frequently reach several pages, photocopied in advance. The professor would comment, then the class, and a firmer and deeper grasp of the previous week's dialectic would seem to emerge. Consequentially linked would come the new lecture, primed by substantive reading assignments, formulated with precision but punctuated by plenty of ventilating moments when Abe would invite comments or just as frequently query the class himself. The remark was made, just once in my hearing, by a student who had decided not to enroll, that Abe's classroom manner was too deliberate and repetitive, not moving things along or getting anywhere. Heidegger's riposte to the same charge was recalled: he was not aiming to "get anywhere," but rather to circle over and burrow down till a matter might be understood. The students who stayed with Abe's classes beyond the first meeting, which was almost all of them, seemed genuinely to appreciate this.

For several years the PSR administration had been very conscious of course evaluations, the results of which were accorded a lot of weight in faculty review and reappointment. The question had indeed been raised a number of times as the semester progressed whether Abe might be retained for another year or two in the Tolson position. Students had raised this question, applicants for admission had raised it, a varied constituency committed to the wider ecumenism had raised it, and Abe himself had raised it. Since the Tolson appointment was supposed to rotate among religions, an alternative idea was that the GTU should find a place for the distinguished scholar and dialoguer whose recognition worldwide was growing steadily. In this light, the course evaluations at the end of that first semester became critical. To sum them up in a phrase, Abe received from both of his classes a standing ovation. "Excellent, stimulating, exciting, challenging, richly diverse, thoroughly organized, dynamic, effective, clear, and extremely helpful" were typical of the characterizations. A palpably sincere gratitude pervaded the forms. One student wrote that he held Abe in awe, another that he reverently loved him. Altogether the appraisals were outstandingly positive, and both Dean Zikmund of PSR and Dean Judith Berling of the GTU took note. Needless to say, Abe was highly gratified.

However, the evaluations came at the end of the school year, and special appointments had already been completed for 1988–89. It was also reported that the Tolson investments needed time to generate another adequate surplus. Moreover, from Abe's own viewpoint, it seemed convenient to aim for reappointment in 1989–90, since he had a heavy intervening agenda of lecturing and writing. Meanwhile, efforts could go forward to develop a longer-term position for Abe in the GTU. Dean Berling seemed hopeful that such an appointment would be feasible, but funding prospects remained uncertain. Dean Zikmund, even though now quite willing to carry Abe on the Tolson bequest for another academic year, remained convinced that this position should rotate. Some of us at PSR, while acknowledging that in principle the Tolson appointment should rotate, argued that Buddhist-Christian relations were currently important enough, and Abe eminent enough, to justify an exception for two or three years. We lost that argument. Thus, during the summer of 1988, the good news was that Abe would be returning in a year. The bad news was that beyond that year there was no apparent way—yet—to keep him at the GTU. But hope was still sanguine that a way would be found.

Abe and I corresponded over the next year and saw each other at the annual AAR and at an Abe-Cobb gathering at the Hsi Lai Buddhist Temple in Hacienda Heights, California, in March of 1989. In all our contact, we sought earnestly to solve the problem of keeping him in Berkeley for at least two more years, beyond the one that was assured. Efforts were made continually to get help from the development offices of PSR and the GTU. Then at Hacienda Heights a new factor entered the picture—or, to put it as it felt, an angel appeared. In the circle of auditors around the Abe-Cobb discussants, especially when Abe himself was presenting or being responded to, there was a conspicuously intense listener who introduced herself to me as Muriel Pollia. Professionally established in the communications field, she was a student of Buddhism, already knew Abe, and in fact considered herself his disciple. After the concluding session at Hsi Lai Temple, Abe invited me to lunch with a group that included Dr. Pollia. It seemed she might have resources to support our hopes in Berkeley, and she said she would be interested in pursuing the matter. Following up by letter and then a pleasant dinner at Stanford, I described the situation, and Dr. Pollia indicated that she could provide part, though not all, of what it would take to underwrite Abe for one or two years at PSR or the GTU. This was a big boost for our morale and would indeed make the decisive difference a year and a half down the pike.

In the fall semester of 1989 the Abes were welcomed back to PSR, with warm felicitations extended from their side and from that of the school. His title had been slightly altered, to Visiting Professor of Buddhism. The courses offered by Abe in the fall semester were "Philosophy of Absolute Nothingness" and "Kenotic God and Dynamic Sunyata: A Point of Contact between Buddhism and Christianity." Again he made available on the one hand advanced work in Buddhism and on the other a dialogic course. Needless to say, much dialogue went on in both courses, and there were copious insights in both into the two traditions. Students continued to express amazement at how much Abe knew about Western thought and Christian theology. In a curriculum becoming increasingly "practical," it was refreshing to have metaphysical issues unpacked with erudition and seriousness. What an opportunity, exclaimed a doctoral candidate, to have Nishitani's Nothingness expounded by a friend and former student of the sage, and then to have that fundamental concept compared and contrasted with Heidegger's *das Nichts!* On the other hand, in presenting Christianity, Abe impressed his hearers as strikingly more traditional or classical than most GTU systematic theologians. Many of those from a liberal background had never listened before to a painstaking exegesis of historic Christian ideas.

It is necessary to mention now an emerging contextual factor that had nothing to do directly with Abe's activity at PSR and yet beset and beclouded the entire operation of the school—especially the work of the regular faculty—for the following two or three years. As the fall semester of 1989 was fully underway, a turbulent internal political struggle erupted around the deanship. It precipitated conflict and alienation that obsessed the attention of the faculty. Aside from bare-bones teaching, there seemed to be no energy or time for anything else. Concomitantly paralyzed was any new disposition of the Tolson resources. The faculty was polarized in a way that precluded creative planning and that undermined any clear directions for the development office. It is a shame that this rift occurred just as the vision of a wider ecumenism at PSR and the GTU might have been approaching its finest hour. Abe had conveyed to us his amiable inclination to stay in Berkeley, should it be mutually feasible, for the rest of his career; and there were a number of promising possibilities that could have coalesced to undergird and supplement his potential role in the consortium. The fall semester ended, and from the campus grapevine as well as the course evaluations it was clear that Abe's teaching had again been excellent. He seemed to feel good about how things were going, except that he may have wondered why the faculty seemed so preoccupied.

For spring 1990 Abe's two courses were "Zen as the Religion of Self-Awakening," which had been so successful two years previously, and "Religion of Nothingness." Regretfully, because of the bog of acrimony in which the faculty was mired, I was less in touch with the actual teaching of these courses than with anything else Abe did at PSR. However, it was apparent that the students, numbering roughly the same as before, were pedagogically stimulated as well as pleased.

During the semester Muriel Pollia, with her financial consultant Jay Rodriguez, came up twice to the Bay Area to consult and then to fine-tune arrangements for her support. One was struck by her wisdom and sagacity as well as by her generous friendship toward Abe. We agreed that it was unusual for a Buddhist, as she was, to endow a Christian school of theology. But seeing who the teacher was, that might be something for Christians to worry about. I said I taught at the school because it was committed to the truth, period; and therein we found accord. She was a bit nonplussed at the stiffness of the seminary administration—which was balking at appointing Abe unless support money was in hand up front, whereas she could give it only in installments. Such hang-ups were eventually resolved, but it still was not clear how the gap between what Dr. Pollia could give and what was needed might be closed. At the last minute, praise the Lord (both Buddha and Christ!), the San Francisco Zen Center came through with housing for the Abes, plus a small stipend, in exchange for his doing some teaching there. West-East Friends also pitched in to help defray expenses, as did some individuals.

So, 1990–91 was now in orbit, and academically again things went very salutarily. Abe, once more as Visiting Professor of Buddhism, offered one course each semester, since he was also teaching in San Francisco. His listings were, in the fall, "Philosophy of Absolute Nothingness," and in the spring, "Religion and Nothingness." I sat in on several of the sessions and was moved by the intellectual passion with which Nishida and Nishitani were engaged. The students seemed more sophisticated, and one felt all the more poignantly how valuable Abe could be in the GTU doctoral program. I was on the verge of asking him to consider for the following year a joint seminar with me that would adduce Schleiermacher, Dilthey, and Heidegger to interface with the Buddhist masters he was so lucidly exegeting.

Alas, midway through the spring it seemed that funding would again dry up for the following year. The outlook was bleak, as the phone rang one morning and Donald Mitchell at Purdue sensitively felt me out on whether we were legally or morally contracted with Abe beyond the end of that term. If not, there was every prospect of an attractive opportunity materializing for him at Purdue, for two years on a vastly more decent stipend. I gulped, winced, and immediately realized that Providence, of whatever ultimate identity, had happily intervened in Masao's behalf. A call to Dr. Pollia in Los Angeles elicited her total agreement. The main thing—nay, the only thing—was the continuation, under the most optimal circumstances, of Abe's world-class endeavors. So we gave our blessing to Purdue, with pangs, because we had grown fond of our friends and felt there was much unfinished business here, too. But no one could doubt the new situation looked far better for those principally concerned.

IV

Three years then of collegial association with Masao Abe were ending. It had indeed been an auspicious time at PSR. The sterling quality and dignity of Masao Abe, his feisty amiability, and the charm and joie de vivre of both him and Ikuko will long ennoble our memory and inspire our exertions. *Sayonara!*

chapter Twelve

DIALOGUE
AND UNITY

Donald W. Mitchell

DURING THE SUMMER OF 1969, the Philosophy Department at the University of Hawai'i hosted the Fifth East-West Philosophers' Conference. As a graduate student member of the conference staff, I was able to meet a number of the participants, including the two persons who represented the Kyoto School, namely, Keiji Nishitani and Masao Abe. Because of Abe's ability with English, he interacted more with the graduate students, and I remember being impressed by his Zenlike presence and his ability to explain difficult Buddhist ideas by using Western philosophical concepts. This early encounter led me to read as many of Abe's writings as I could after leaving Hawaii to come to Purdue in 1971.

Thirteen years later, I was back in Hawaii attending what has come to be known as the Second International Buddhist-Christian Conference. I noticed Abe's name on the program and made sure that I was present at his major address when he read an early draft of his now-famous essay "Kenotic God and Dynamic Sunyata." I was so impressed with Abe's comparison of Buddhist Emptiness with Christian kenosis that after the presentation I entered into a conversation about it with Abe and Hans Küng. That conversation was the beginning of my personal friendship with both Abe and Küng. At the same conference, John Cobb invited me to be member of what was then called the Abe-Cobb group. This was, and still is, an ongoing theological dialogue group made up of Buddhists and Christian scholars originally chosen by Abe and Cobb.[1]

Some months after returning to Purdue from Hawaii, I was contacted by Cobb and informed that the theme of the 1985 meeting of the theological encounter group would be personal and social transformation. Cobb said that Abe would be giving one of the two Buddhist presentations and that they wanted me to give one of the two Christian responses to Abe's paper. I was to focus on the issue of personal transformation in Zen and Christian spirituality, which was my specialization in the Buddhist-Christian dialogue. As it turned out, at that second meeting of the encounter group, Abe and I were able to spend quite a bit of time with each other, and I was finally able to get to know Abe as not just a scholar but as a person.

At a particular point in one of our conversations, Abe began talking about his personal relationship with his spiritual teacher, Shin'ichi Hisamatsu. Abe told me that when he first met Hisamatsu, he (Abe) was a Pure Land Buddhist with a strong devotion to Amida Buddha. Hisamatsu—the embodiment of nondualistic Zen—challenged Abe's dualistic faith. Abe said that his personal transformation to the nondual religious experience of Zen was an extraordinarily difficult path for him. As he described the steps he took on that path, I was impressed with the totalistic nature of Abe's spiritual transformation under Hisamatsu's guidance. At the end of his story, Abe said that when Hisamatsu was dying, he had made a personal "vow" to his teacher to dedicate his life to the presentation of Zen to the West through dialogue with Western theology and philosophy.

Needless to say, I was moved by Abe's personal revelation. It became evident that Abe's life of dialogue in the West was not just an academic enterprise but a living expression of the deep spiritual transformation he experienced with Hisamatsu. Indeed, Hisamatsu's F.A.S. philosophy stresses the importance of obtaining an awakening to the Formless Self (F) in order to embrace all humankind (A) in a manner that moves history in a truly awakened, or "suprahistorical" (S) direction. From our conversation, I saw that in his life of dialogue, Abe was attempting to do just that. Abe's work as a Zen Buddhist scholar in dialogue with the West was for him a way of living out of the very core of his own spiritual experience. He was a living embodiment of F.A.S.

Abe concluded this conversation of the heart with a very practical matter. He said that given his commitment to his teacher, he was always looking for places to carry out his research and teaching in the United States so that he could remain in the West. It was then that I began to think about the possibility of bringing Abe to Purdue University sometime in the future. This thought became a firm resolve the next year when, in the fall of 1986, we held the third meeting of the Abe-Cobb group at Purdue.[2]

By the time the third meeting of the Abe-Cobb group was held, the idea of Abe being at Purdue was even more attractive to me for a personal reason. After hearing Abe talk about Emptiness and kenosis in 1984, I decided to attempt an in-depth response to his comparison. To prepare for this work, I had taken a sabbatical during the winter and spring of 1986. Part of this time was spent in Japan, where I carried out research and dialogue with such persons as Keiji Nishitani and Nanrei Kobori. I also attended and spoke at a meeting of the F.A.S. Society.[3] During that time, as I studied the ways in which different members of the Kyoto School compared kenosis with Emptiness, I began to realize that to respond adequately to Abe's comparison, I also had to respond to the full range of similar comparisons made by both the Zen and Pure Land sides of the School. In this way, I could place Abe's work in its proper place in the comparative perspective of the Kyoto School.

I also saw that such a response could not be adequately made at just the theological level, it had to be made at the spiritual level as well. Kenosis is not just a theological category, it is also a central aspect of Christian spiritual/mystical life. In a similar way in Buddhism, Emptiness is not just to be contemplated but also lived. And, finally, an adequate comparison would have to explore both individual and communal spirituality to show its relevance to the contemporary postmodern scene. This decision to respond to the Kyoto School's comparison of kenosis with Emptiness on the level of spirituality was confirmed when I traveled from Japan to Rome in the spring of 1986 to meet with some of the Catholic Church's experts on dialogue with Buddhism.[4]

The theme of the Purdue meeting of the Abe-Cobb group in the fall of 1986 was "ultimate reality." Again, one of the major points of discussion was Abe's comparison of Christian kenosis with Buddhist Emptiness. From this discussion, I became confident that I was moving in the right direction with my response to Abe. He and I talked about my ideas, and he gave me a copy of his then unpublished but more fully developed manuscript "Kenotic God and Dynamic Sunyata." We also spoke again about the possibility of his coming to Purdue. Abe and his wife, Ikuko, very much enjoyed the quiet Midwestern environment.

By 1989 it was clear that Abe's essay on Emptiness and kenosis would soon appear in *The Emptying God: A Buddhist-Jewish-Christian Conversation* (Maryknoll, N.Y.: Orbis Books, 1990), and my response would be published as *Spirituality and Emptiness: The Dynamics of Spiritual Life in Buddhism and Christianity* (New York: Paulist Press, 1991). With these publication dates in mind, I approached the Lilly Endowment, Inc., with the idea of bringing Abe to Purdue shortly after our books came out, in order to advance our dialogue, add new voices to it, and present it to a more general audience in a series of public conversations around the state of Indiana. The endowment liked the idea, the books were published, the project was funded, and the Abes arrived at Purdue in the summer of 1991 for a two-year stay.

The Abes took a secluded apartment that was literally on the banks of the Wabash River. During Abe's residence at Purdue, he taught only one course each semester so as to give him more time to work on his research before retiring to Japan in 1993. Each fall he taught "Zen—the Religion of Self-Awakening." In the spring of 1992, he taught a seminar on the Buddhist-Christian dialogue. And in the spring of 1993, he offered a seminar on Nishida's philosophy. All these classes were held in the evening and were open to the public. The classes were very popular, being attended by students, scholars, and leaders in the local religious community.

Besides his classes, Abe participated in four interfaith dialogues around the state of Indiana that were intended to deepen and expand discussion of his comparison of Buddhism and Christianity. The four-part series added new themes and voices to the dialogue and involved a broader public audience.[5] The first conversation was with Marjorie Suchocki at Purdue on November 8, 1991. The topic was the understanding of "peace" in Buddhism and Christianity. Abe presented the Buddhist view that real peace is a deep human reality prior to opposition and conflict. The Buddha did not confront hostile opposition with power but appeased hatred and violence with compassion. Buddhism seeks to enable people to awaken to this inner peace and live compassionate lives from that deep center of their being. For Abe, this compassionate living is an activity that engenders what he calls "nondualistic unity," which celebrates cultural and religious diversity. It is a peaceful harmony that expresses the unity of ultimate reality itself. Suchocki compared Emptiness as the basis of this nondual unity in Buddhism with the "principle of diversity in unity" in trinitarian theology. Both the nondual and trinitarian notions affirm the value of difference in unity in a manner that supports community and peace.

The second dialogue (discussed by Joseph Bracken in Chapter 19, "The Abe-Pannenberg Encounter") was with Wolfhart Pannenberg. It was hosted by the Earlham School of Theology at Earlham College on April 23, 1992. As one can see from Bracken's account, Pannenberg was not especially positive about Abe's presentation of a "kenotic God." In short, Pannenberg sees kenosis as a particular action of the Son out of obedience to the will of the Father. He finds no biblical basis for attributing a kenotic element to the nature of Godself. Abe responded that if Christ is the self-revelation of God, then the kenosis of Christ is revelatory of the very nature of Godself. It was interesting to note that afterward many, if not most, of the Christians in the audience were more inclined to Abe's position than to Pannenberg's. It seems ironic that Christians would prefer a Buddhist's view of their God over a fellow Christian's.

The third dialogue was with Richard Rubenstein (see Chapter 18, "Emptiness, Holy Nothingness, and the Holocaust"). This encounter was hosted by Indiana University–Purdue University at Indianapolis on November 11, 1992. The topic was "The Holocaust, God, and Evil." In an informal setting before the public conversation, Rubenstein told Abe how his own idea of God as Holy Nothingness was confirmed by Abe's work on Absolute Nothingness. Rubenstein enjoyed reading Abe's work on Emptiness and had no quarrel with him on the matter of ultimate reality. He felt that their ideas of the absolute were complementary. However, on the matter of the Holocaust, Rubenstein had a major reservation that they discussed later in the public dialogue.

In that public discussion, Abe stressed that he sees the root cause of evil in the world in general, and the Holocaust in particular, as the "blind will" of human nature. Since we all participate in this general condition of blind willfulness, we are all responsible for its particular results in history, including the Holocaust. The Holocaust calls all humankind to acknowledge this flaw in the human condition and seek a self-awakening that can heal it in individuals and in society. Rubenstein recognized this general "cause" but felt it to be more helpful to clarify the particular psychological, social, historical, economic, and political causes so that one could recognize these forces in the future and intervene to stop them from producing something like the Holocaust from happening again. Abe agreed with Rubenstein that the study of these particular causes is important. But he felt that until humankind faces its blind and selfish nature, it cannot awaken to its true compassionate nature and thereby overcome the tendency to generate evil in the world.

The fourth and final dialogue was hosted by the University of Notre Dame on April 1, 1993. It was with Keith J. Egan and addressed the comparison of Christian and Buddhist forms of meditation. Egan and Abe both traced the historical development of various forms of meditation in their respective traditions. In the context of a very rich dialogue on many issues associated with the spiritual life, Abe noted a basic difference between the two practices. For the Christian, meditation must give way to contemplation where God, rather than the self, is active. This spiritual movement from meditation to contemplation is achieved by the grace of God rather than by any human willfulness. When Christian meditation is perfected, the person finds union with God. Buddhist meditation culminates in wisdom through a process that is similar to grace in that the person cannot produce the wisdom by his or her own efforts. However, what one discovers in the light of this wisdom is not union with a transcendent God but the True Self awakening to itself. While for the Buddhist, wisdom arises from beyond human will, it does so not by the breaking in of the grace of God but by the awakening of the True Self. Egan responded that contemplative grace can also be experienced as an inner process that leads to overcoming unhealthy attachments and the false self.

During Abe's stay at Purdue, I had numerous opportunities to discuss different topics with him. Since my response to his comparison of Emptiness with kenosis was on the level of spirituality, the kinds of issues discussed by Abe and Egan came up frequently, and we shared with each other the experiential bases for our different views. Abe expressed the fundamental Zen experience of ultimate reality in the words of Pseudo-Dionysius: "dazzling darkness." For Abe, the dazzling light of nirvana is totally identified with the world of samsaric darkness. This identity is not a static monism but a dynamic nondualism wherein each is itself in the dynamic identity with its opposite. For him, when this nondual logic is applied to God, the Godhead of infinite light must be seen in its dynamic identity with all of creation. The dynamic of this identity is the kenosis of love that one sees in Jesus crucified and forsaken. This kenosis does not destroy God but affirms the true Godself as full kenotic love.

Abe finds the loving dynamic of this kenotic God in creation since the forms of life are the self-determination of the kenosis itself. He also finds the same kenosis in the Trinity itself where each person is who that person is in a nondual relational kenosis of love and life (*perichoresis*) with the other persons. Now, the problem for me with Abe's view is that he posits the same kenosis in both cases. The dynamic of the inner trinitarian kenosis is the same as the dynamic of the creative kenosis. Or the kenotic *nature* of God in the Trinity is the same as the kenotic *action* of God in creation. As I argued in *Spirituality and Emptiness*, this Buddhist perception of kenosis as always being the same impoverishes the Christian understanding of kenosis. While God creates "according to" his nature, the kenosis between the divine persons is just different in kind from the kenosis between the Creator and creation. And since God is *uniquely* incarnate in Christ, the kenosis of God in Christ is also different in kind from the kenosis of God in the rest of creation.

To fail to make this distinction leads Abe to say that God is just as dependent on creation as creation is on God. For the Christian, it is true that for the Father to be Father in the Trinity, there must be the Son, and vice versa. But it is not true that creation must be necessary for God to be truly a kenotic God. The most one can say is that for the *creative* kenosis of God to function, there must be the things of creation. But God existed as the eternal Trinity before creation began. And God's identity is determined in that eternal inner trinitarian kenosis, not in the kenosis of creation. God's creative kenotic love is necessary for creation, but not vice versa.

It was to maintain this distinction that I referred to Emptiness, in *Spirituality and Emptiness*, as "the creative kenosis *of God*." For me, Emptiness is the creative kenosis of a God whose ultimate triune transcendence is not *fully* emptied out into creation. On the other hand, whenever our discussion touched on the possible transcendence of God, Abe always returned to the nondualism of dazzling darkness—perhaps because of the radical nature of his conversion from the dualistic Pure

Land form of Buddhist spirituality to the radical nondualism of Hisamatsu's Zen spirituality. I do not know. But for me as a Christian, while God is certainly found in all things and all things in God, the Trinity always exists apart from creation, a light without any darkness in which we find an eternal paradise. The Godhead of this Trinity is not beyond the persons of the Trinity. The Godhead just is the dynamic and kenotic love of the persons that is expressed in the kenosis of creation. While this creative kenosis is like Buddhist Emptiness in many ways, it does not mean that the Godhead is dependent on the resulting creation. Again, it is defined within the Trinity itself as love, which in turn defines creation as an expression of love. And it is this intimate and personal triune dimension of God-love that is at the heart of Christian spirituality insofar as we discover and relate to it in Christ.

At the end of our dialogues, it was evident to me that Abe's encounter with Christianity had transformed his thought concerning God but that he had remained a Zen Buddhist, always interpreting the experience of God with a Buddhist nondualistic logic. On the other hand, I had been greatly changed by my encounter with Abe and Buddhism in my own understanding of the kenotic nature and action of God. But I remained a Christian interpreting the experience of God with a Christian trinitarian logic. And as we accepted the similarities and differences between our viewpoints, our dialogue took a new turn. Abe expressed an interest in meeting the spiritual community of which I am a member, namely, the Focolare. This did not surprise me for a number of reasons. First, in any interfaith dialogue there comes a moment when the interlocutors, faced with the similarities as well as the differences between their views, feel a desire to see how these similarities and differences are lived out in daily life. For me, that desire was in part fulfilled in 1986 when I met with Abe's F.A.S. Society in Kyoto.

A second reason for Abe's interest in meeting the Focolare was that from his reading of *Spirituality and Emptiness*, he understood that there are many similarities between the F.A.S. Society and the Focolare.[6] Both emphasize a communal spirituality in which personal and collective kenosis play important roles. In the Focolare, kenotic love helps generate a spiritual atmosphere of unity wherein one can discover a tangible presence of God, making persons one in a manner that reflects the unity of the Trinity. Abe wanted, I think, to see Christian kenosis lived in a community in a manner that fosters the unity of humankind, which is also an ideal of his own F.A.S. spirituality.

A third reason for his interest was the striking similarities between the lives of the founders of both movements, Chiara Lubich and Shin'ichi Hisamatsu. Abe was keenly aware that the founders of spiritualities have very special charismata and was quite impressed with the spiritual depth of Lubich's writings. I had explained to him that although Lubich is a great saint and mystic, she also has the intellectual ability to express her experience in philosophical and theological terms. In fact, I informed Abe that a very important group of Catholic theologians in Europe had formed the Abba School based on Lubich's published and unpublished spiritual and mystical writings.

I should add that Keiji Nishitani once expressed to me his own interest in meeting Lubich. In a letter he said that in Lubich's writings he found a Christian expression of what he himself was trying to say in Buddhist terms. I arranged for him to meet Lubich when she visited Japan in 1985. Unfortunately, the meeting did not take place because the pope asked Lubich to return early from Japan to participate in a synod on the laity. When I met with Nishitani in 1986, he asked Gishin Tokiwa, who was with us, if he knew of Lubich and the Focolare. When Tokiwa answered that he did not, Nishitani went on at some length telling Tokiwa about Lubich and her work.[7] Abe was aware of the planned meeting between Nishitani and Lubich, which would have been her first encounter with the Kyoto School. My own thought was that since Nishitani had died, a meeting between Abe and Lubich would be a historic encounter between the Focolare and the F.A.S. Society as well as between the Abba and Kyoto Schools.

In the spring of 1992 I introduced Abe to members of the Chicago Focolare. I could tell that he was very sensitive to the unity he found there and was happy with the encounter. Then in the summer of 1992 Abe was awarded the Luminosa Prize by the Focolare for his work in interfaith dialogue. To receive this award, Abe traveled to Mariapolis Luminosa, the North American retreat center of the Focolare in Hyde Park, New York. There, he and his wife were quite taken by the spiritual atmosphere of unity. The Focolare was also impressed with Abe's spiritual sensitivity and the depth of his insight into spiritual matters. After these two encounters, more concrete plans began to be made for Abe to travel to Rome to visit the headquarters of the Focolare and to meet with Chiara Lubich.

As this trip to Rome was being discussed, Abe also expressed to me his desire to meet with Cardinal Joseph Ratzinger. It was my impression that Abe was having trouble understanding what "the official Catholic viewpoint" was on the different issues he was discussing in his comparison of Emptiness and kenosis. He was aware that the few Catholic theologians he had read and with whom he was in dialogue, such as Karl Rahner, Hans Küng, and David Tracy, had different views on these issues. So, he questioned whether what he was encountering in their personal theological opinions on the matters under consideration was in accord with the official teachings of the church. Somewhere along the line, Abe had come to believe that if he talked to Cardinal Ratzinger, he would get a precise explanation of what the church actually taught about the theological issues he was exploring in his own dialogical work. I would add that this concern of Abe's is very common in interfaith dialogue. One often wonders, "Am I just encountering the personal views of my interlocutor, or am I actually encountering the authentic tradition for which he or she is a spokesperson?"

In the end, a number of meetings in Rome were arranged for Abe. Masao Abe, Ikuko Abe, and I would travel to Rome in March of 1993 to be hosted by the Center for Interreligious Dialogue of the Focolare Movement. The center would arrange for us to meet with Chiara Lubich and members of the Abba School and would also take us on a tour of Rome, Assisi, Florence, and Loppiano—a little city of the Focolare near Florence where its school of spiritual formation is located. The Pontifical Council for Interreligious Dialogue would entertain us in the Vatican and arrange for us to meet with the pope. We would also visit the Congregation for the Doctrine of the Faith and meet there with Cardinal Ratzinger. The cardinal, who has a personal interest in the work of the Kyoto School, would arrange for some of the theologians of the congregation to spend time answering Abe's questions, which he and I would send in advance.

When March 1993 arrived, I was not able to travel to Rome with the Abes because of ill health. And unfortunately, Chiara Lubich was also not able to be in Rome because she was undergoing medical treatment in Switzerland. However, the Abes were hosted by Enzo Fondi and Natalia Dallapiccola, two of Lubich's early companions in the Focolare and now codirectors of the Focolare's Center for Interreligious Dialogue. There, Masao Abe was able to meet and talk to members of the Abba School. Then after taking the planned tour of Italy, the Abes went to the Congregation for the Doctrine of the Faith, where Masao Abe discussed his philosophical work with two theological collaborators of the congregation: Jacques Servais, S. J., and Piero Coda, who, as it turned out, is also a member of the Abba School.

I would say that this was an extraordinary encounter. When in the history of these two religions has a Buddhist philosopher entered the Vatican for a theological discussion in this most powerful congregation? At one point in this discussion, Servais said that the dialogue between Buddhists and Christians within the broader encounter of East and West is of historic importance. He expressed the view that it will have greater significance than the dialogue between Christian and Greek thought from which Western intellectual history proceeded. Servais quoted Rombach's opinion that East-West dialogue today will lead to a new "planetary unity of people" from which a new global history will proceed. This opinion was directly in line with Abe's own views.

In this discussion, some of the issues that were raised in my own dialogue with Abe were addressed. For example, as for Abe's comparison of kenosis and Emptiness, Servais stated that the Christian view is that divine kenosis is absolute love, not just the boundless openness of the unlimited. In the kenotic dynamic of that love, the personhood of God is never emptied out nor is it ever abolished in the absolute. Coda added that for Balthasar, the kenosis of Christ reveals the absolute love of the *perichoresis* of the Trinity. It is in the kenotic dynamic of this eternal loving relation prior to creation that each person is distinguished. The giving of self in kenotic love does not cancel the selves but leads to the realization of distinction in unity. This for Balthasar is a trinitarian logic, not a dualistic logic. Both Servais and Coda explored with Abe the place of kenosis in trinitarian theology in a manner that greatly impressed Abe. And while admitting both similarities and differences between Christian and Buddhist notions of ultimate reality, both Servais and Coda affirmed Abe's view that because Christ is the self-utterance of God, his kenosis reveals a fundamental kenosis, an *ur-kenosis*, that is of the essence of Godself. For this and other reasons, Abe told me that he found these Vatican theologians to be much more "liberal" than most of the theologians he had encountered in the United States.

At the end of the meeting, Cardinal Ratzinger entered the room. This was a surprise because he had been in Hong Kong and was not expected to return to Rome in time to meet Abe. However, he said that he had realized in Hong Kong even more strongly than ever before the importance of interfaith dialogue for the future of the church. So while he was not able to enter into the conversation, he wanted to come immediately upon his return to Rome to meet Abe to make that point. This confirmation by Cardinal Ratzinger of the historic significance of Abe's interfaith work was very important to Abe. And Abe also saw in his own visit to the congregation a new step in his dialogue with Christianity. He was especially impressed with Coda and continues by correspondence the conversation they began in the congregation. This correspondence also continues Abe's new theological contact with the emerging Abba School in Europe.

The next day the Abes were hosted by the Vatican's Pontifical Council for Interfaith Dialogue. John Shirieda, a member of the council, arranged for a number of scholars of Buddhism in Rome to join him in greeting the Abes and in discussing Buddhism. Then Shirieda took Enzo Fondi and the Abes to meet the pope. At a semiprivate audience, just after the pope's general audience, the pope greeted Masao Abe and encouraged him as "a fellow pilgrim" to continue his work and his "spiritual journey into the truth." He also thanked Abe for his highly significant work in interfaith dialogue. When the pope turned to Mrs. Abe, she told him that his presence gives her hope. He looked deeply into her eyes and said, "Let us carry the Cross together." Both Masao and Ikuko Abe said to me that at that moment, the pope entered the deepest part of their being.

I can say that upon their return to West Lafayette, it was evident that both Masao and Ikuko Abe were deeply moved by their experiences in Rome. I leave it to Masao Abe to express how this was so. It did seem to me that Abe finally felt at peace in his own heart about the relation of his ideas to those of the Catholic tradition. He was very surprised and happy about the degree to which the Vatican engaged his ideas and related them, in a positive way, to some of the deepest insights of its theological and spiritual traditions. In terms of the Focolare, the Abes seemed to find a "spiritual kinship" with the Focolare community, and

Masao Abe now refers to himself as "a Buddhist friend" of the Focolare.

To conclude, at the end of his stay at Purdue, which was the final step on his journey in the West, Abe found in Rome a confirmation of the extraordinary historic value of his life's intellectual work. His important place in the interfaith encounter of Buddhism and Christianity, indeed of East and West, was also recognized by the highest officials of the Roman Catholic Church. And he found a profound personal spiritual unity with the Focolare in that church. Mutual understanding and respect were reached, and a spiritual communion was established. Those are among the most precious goals of true interfaith dialogue! I think that a major reason that Abe returned to Purdue feeling so happy was that this dialogical experience was a concrete sign to him that he had successfully fulfilled his vow to his teacher: he had brought the ideas of the Kyoto School and the ideals of F.A.S. to the West with such intellectual clarity and spiritual force that they were understood and respected. Now he could return to Kyoto at peace.

Part Three

THEOLOGICAL ENCOUNTERS

chapter Thirteen

THE MEANING OF EMPTINESS

John Hick

MY OWN RECOLLECTIONS of Masao Abe's period in the United States come from his time as a colleague for three years in the Department of Religion at the Claremont Graduate School in California, for another year at the neighboring School of Theology at Claremont, and then at various conferences almost every year since. At the Claremont Graduate School he and I jointly taught a couple of seminars, one on the problem of evil in Buddhism and Christianity and the other a comparative study of Buddhism and Christianity—Buddhism meaning on each occasion Zen Buddhism. In these joint seminars, and in many other occasions for discussion, I learned a great deal from Abe. Indeed, he was the first Zen thinker whom I had encountered and the one with whom I have had the most opportunity to explore this—to most of us in the West—very different and therefore strange universe of religious thought and experience.

Among my Claremont memories of Abe are his slow and careful exposition of Zen concepts; his taking a group of us to the Zen meditation center up Mount Baldy, he and his wife dressed in traditional Japanese garb, and our all doing *zazen* there; a splendid Japanese dinner at their house; a long plane flight back together from a conference that we had both attended on the East Coast, during which he once again tried to explain, and I to grasp, the key Zen concept of *Śūnyatā*, Emptiness; and his launching the Buddhist-Christian Theological Encounter Group (the Abe-Cobb group), whose annual meetings have proved so cumulatively fruitful.

My memories of Abe are mainly of the discussions with him through which I have tried to come to understand the basic Zen concepts—or if "understand" is the wrong word, to allow them to function as "skillful means" to draw me into the Zen world of meaning. A secondary interest has been to see whether the clarifying procedures of Western analytical philosophy can be of any help to the formulation and communication of Zen thought. Much of this discussion has centered upon the idea of *Śūnyatā*. I am aware that this notion is somewhat differently understood within different Buddhist schools. But Abe, and it would seem the Kyoto School generally, speaks of *Śūnyatā,* Emptiness, as "the ultimate reality,"[1] meaning this in a profoundly religious sense: "in Mahayana Buddhism Emptiness replaces God."[2] Again, "the ultimate reality for Buddhism is neither Being nor God, but Sunyata."[3] However, Buddhist language about *Śūnyatā,* is—consciously, of course—highly paradoxical. For philosophical analysis, the question is whether the paradox can be resolved by distinguishing different nonconflicting senses of the key terms, or whether paradox and even contradiction are to be embraced for their own sake—or perhaps as "skillful means."

To my Western philosophical eyes, it seems that in Zen discourse *Śūnyatā* has two different but related and not contradictory meanings. It is clear that *Śūnyatā* does not refer to a "thing" of any kind. It is not an entity or substance or person or being itself or any kind of state or process. In one use of the term, *Śūnyatā* is "entirely unobjectifiable, unconceptualizable, and unattainable by reason or will."[4] It lies beyond our entire network of human concepts and is empty of everything that the human mind projects in its activity of awareness. The idea thus indicates "the necessity of going beyond any conceptualization and objectification."[5] In Western terminology, *Śūnyatā,* in this meaning of the term, is absolutely ineffable, outside the scope of our networks of human concepts. Here *Śūnyatā,* as the Buddhist understanding of the ultimate (and parallel in this respect to the Western concept of God), is ineffable, formless, beyond conceptualization—except, of course, in the use of purely formal, logically generated concepts, such as the concept of being beyond conceptualization! *Śūnyatā* in this sense of the term must in the nature of the case be indistinguishable from the totally formless in Indian thought and the totally ineffable (when, rarely, the idea has been understood strictly) in Western thought. Abe himself remarks that "in German mysticism, the Godhead or *Gottheit* is grasped as *Nichts* by Meister Eckhart and as *Ungrund* by Jacob Bohme. Furthermore, in Eckhart and Bohme the essence of God is not the Supreme Good but lies beyond good and evil. This is strikingly similar to the Buddhist understanding of Ultimate Reality."[6]

But there seems to be another use of the term in which *Śūnyatā* has characteristics that can be both experienced and described. Thus, Emptiness "contains the two characteristics of wisdom (*prajna*) and compassion (*karuna*),"[7] and is "a dynamic and creative function of emptying everything and making everything alive."[8] It is "not a nihilistic emptiness but rather a fullness of particular things and individual persons functioning in their full capacity and without mutual impediment."[9] So understood, *Śūnyatā* = nirvana = *pratītya-samutpāda*, the ever changing interdependent universe. These two uses of *Śūnyatā* seem to me to be different and suggest to me a distinction between the ineffable, formless ultimate and the describable forms that it takes within our human thought and experience.

In conversation with Abe, however, I have sometimes come up against the philosophical rebuff that such questions and distinctions and attempts at clarification are inappropriate because they presuppose Western modes of thought, particularly Western "dualism." *Śūnyatā*, as Abe has written, is "very difficult to understand, particularly for the Western mind."[10] I am in fact still uncertain whether or not I have grasped this central Mahāyāna concept at all. There *seems* to me to be a distinction between, on the one hand, the thought of *Śūnyatā* as entirely unconceptualizable, "formless," and empty of all humanly conceivable qualities and, on the other hand, the thought of *Śūnyatā* as having the characteristics of wisdom and compassion, as being the activity of making everything alive, and as being identical with the experienceable state of nirvana and the process of *pratītya-samutpāda*. For these latter appear to me to be ways of conceptualizing or characterizing (even if only partially), *Śūnyatā*.

Assuming that there is a distinction here, an important question for me has been (and is) to what extent the distinction corresponds to one that suggests itself to anyone seeking a religious interpretation of religious plurality. If we reject the naturalistic understanding of religious experience as purely imaginative projection, seeing it instead as a response to, or expression or manifestation of, a transcendent reality (i.e., a reality transcending our ordinary human existence), then we meet the problem constituted by the plurality of different forms of religious experience. Within the monotheistic faiths, the Jewish experience of the Adonai of Israel and the Christian experience of the Heavenly Father and the Muslim experience of Allah differ from one another, and all differ even more radically from the Buddhist and *advaitic* Hindu forms of religious experience. And yet each of these great spiritual traditions seems to be more or less equally effective as a context of the salvific transformation of human beings from self-centeredness to a re-centering in some manifestation of the ultimate. That they apparently produce essentially the same human transformation—though taking varying concrete forms within different religious cultures—suggests that through these traditions the same ultimate transforming reality is affecting us.

But how can this be when the experienced realities are so different? The answer that seems to me most promising is based upon a distinction between the ultimate reality in itself and that reality as humanly, and variously humanly, experienced. For our human experience is always culturally conditioned. The Real, the Ultimate, is experienced in terms of different sets of religious concepts, closely connected with different forms of spiritual practice, developed in different cultural and historical contexts. On this hypothesis, the Real in itself transcends the entire network of human concepts. Thus, the polarities of personal/nonpersonal, substance/process, good/evil, purposive/nonpurposive, conscious/unconscious do not apply. In denying, for example, that the Real is personal, one does not thus affirm that it is nonpersonal but rather, more radically, that this set of concepts does not apply to it. In traditional Western terms, it is ineffable; in traditional Eastern terms, it is formless. But it is nevertheless eternally real and universally present, and it enters into human consciousness in what we call, in the broadest sense of the term, religious experience. And as experienced, it always has qualities of some kind. In the paradoxical words of an ancient Indian text, "Thou art formless; thy only form is our knowledge of Thee."[11]

On the one hand then, *Śūnyatā* as Absolute Nothingness seems to be completely unconceptualizable, unable to be characterized in any way other than as the totally ineffable ultimate reality. But on the other hand, *Śūnyatā* as wisdom and compassion seems to be a form that this ineffable Emptiness takes in relation to conscious beings; and *Śūnyatā* as "suchness" seems to be another such form, namely as the world process when experienced selflessly, without the distortions of the ego point of view.

Such a distinction between the ultimate in itself and the ultimate as humanly known occurs explicitly within the wide range of Buddhist thought. Within the *trikāya* doctrine of the Mahāyāna, the ineffable ultimate is called the *dharmakāya,* the "truth body" of the infinite Buddhanature. And T'an Luan, the first great thinker of the Pure Land tradition within Buddhism, whose writings were used by the medieval monk Shinran, founder of the continuing Japanese form of this tradition, Jōdo Shinshū, distinguished between *dharmakāya*-as-suchness, which "has no form or characteristics, and is beyond conceptualization," and *dharmakāya*-as-compassion, which "possesses form and characteristics, appearing as Amida Buddha."[12] Shinran quotes T'an-Luan: "Among Buddhas and bodhisattvas there are two aspects of dharmakāya: dharmakāya-as-suchness and dharmakāya-as-compassion. Dharmakāya-as-compassion arises out of dharmakāya-as-suchness, and dharmakāya-as-suchness emerges into [human consciousness through] dharmakāya-as-compassion. These two aspects of dharmakāya differ but are not separate; they are one but not identical."[13] Parallel conceptions occur within the Upanishadic tradition in the distinction between *nirguṇa*-Brahman, Brahman without qualities and beyond all conceptualization, and *saguṇa*-Brahman, that same ultimate reality humanly experienced as Īshvara, divine personality; within the mystical strands of Judaism and Islam; and within Christianity, in the distinction between God's infinite self-existent being "before" and independent of creation, and God in relation to the creation, known as Father, Son, and Holy Spirit.

Now the concept of the Real as the ultimate, ineffable, formless reality that is humanly experienced in many different forms, both personal and nonpersonal, sounds remarkably like the concept of Śūnyatā as the ultimate formless reality, empty of all humanly conceivable qualities but manifested within human (and perhaps nonhuman) experience as infinite compassion and wisdom, and as nirvana = *pratītya-samutpāda* = the ordinary world experienced selflessly as "wondrous being." For on the one hand, Śūnyatā as Absolute Nothingness (Shinran's *dharmakāya*-as-suchness) seems to be completely unconceptualizable, unable to be characterized in any way other than as the totally ineffable ultimate reality; on the other hand, Śūnyatā as wisdom and compassion seems to be the form that this ineffable Emptiness takes in relation to the world. Zen's *Śūnyatā* as suchness seems to be the world process experienced selflessly, as it is in itself, without the inevitable distortions of the ego point of view. It appears to me, then, that *Śūnyatā* as the ultimate ineffable formless reality is manifested both in the wisdom and compassion of awakened ones and in the process of the ordinary world as experienced by them. The Formless takes concrete form within our human awakening to it. And if *Śūnyatā,* as the ultimate ineffable reality, is experienced in this way on the path of Zen thought and meditation, may it not at the same time be differently experienced on the paths of theistic thought and worship and of *advaitic* Hindu thought and meditation, and on yet other paths of religious thought and spiritual practice? Thus, *Śūnyatā* has appeared to me as the perfect expression of the key concept that is required for a religious understanding of religious plurality.

However, Abe has, as it has seemed to me, been disinclined to take this view, wanting instead to absolutize the particular manifestation of *Śūnyatā*/the Real that is made available through *zazen.* Instead of seeing this as one manifestation of *Śūnyatā* and acknowledging the monotheistic God figures, the nonpersonal absolutes of *advaitic* Hinduism and of Taoism, and the nirvana of the Theravāda as other manifestations of the ultimate ineffable *Śūnyatā,* he has seemed to me to want to identify one particular manifestation of the ultimately Real—that which is known through his own tradition—exclusively with the Real in itself. Such a move is, of course, familiar in the history of religions. It has indeed normally been made by representatives of each of the great world faiths, thus singling out one's own tradition as uniquely superior to the others. In Buddhist terms it is the claim that the Gods and absolutes experienced within the other great traditions are manifestations of *Śūnyatā* in terms of various human conceptual systems, whereas *pratītya-samutpāda* = nirvana = the universal Buddha-nature is *Śūnyatā* itself directly realized in the awakened human consciousness.

Now I am not in fact sure whether this is Abe's intention, or whether what I have been saying is an accurate and up-to-date account of his thought. He will be able to correct it if necessary in his response and to indicate how he understands the relationship between the ultimates of the different great world religions. For it is, in my view, essential to any viable religious position today to be able to give an account of the fact of religious plurality. It is not enough to expound or proclaim the message of one's own tradition. One must also be able to explain its relationship at least to the other great world religions.

I feel sure that Abe would agree wholeheartedly with the Dalai Lama when he said:

> *I maintain that every major religion of the world—Buddhism, Christianity, Confucianism, Hinduism, Islam, Jainism, Judaism, Sikhism, Taoism, Zoroastrianism—has similar ideas of love, the same goal of benefiting humanity through spiritual practices, and the same effect of making their followers into better human beings. All religions teach moral precepts for perfecting the functions of mind, body, and speech. All teach us not to lie or steal or take others' lives, and so on.*

> *All religions agree upon the necessity to control the undisciplined mind that harbours selfishness and other roots of trouble, and each teaches a path leading to a spiritual state that is peaceful, disciplined, ethical, and wise. It is in this sense that I believe all religions have essentially the same message. Differences of dogma may be ascribed to differences of time and circumstance as well as cultural influences; indeed, there is no end to scholastic argument when we consider the purely metaphysical side of religion. However, it is much more beneficial to try to implement in daily life the shared precepts for goodness taught by all religions rather than to argue about minor differences of approach.*[14]

Would it seem appropriate to Abe to add that this rough salvific parity of the great world faiths arises from their being different human responses to what is ultimately real, in itself formless, ineffable, beyond all (other than purely formal) human conceptuality, but variously referred to in the languages of different traditions as *Śūnyatā*, *dharmakāya*, Tao, Brahman, Godhead? It seems to me that he has gone a long way to granting this in principle when he says, "With full justification, Buddhists regard Jesus as a Buddha or as an Awakened one."[15] For Jesus did not practice *zazen* or any other Buddhist form of meditation and did not experience the ultimate as nirvana/*pratītya-samutpāda*, but as a personal Thou, the heavenly Father. If, then, he had attained the same spiritual goal as a Buddha, he did so by a different spiritual route and consequently experienced the ultimate, *Śūnyatā,* the Real, in a different form.

I now hand this continuing conversation back to Abe, with these questions: How do you understand the relationship between the major different forms of religious experience—the experience of nirvana, of *pratītya-samutpāda,* of God, of Brahman, etc.—if not as different forms of experience of the ultimate formless reality of *Śūnyatā?* Should we not then speak of *Śūnyatā* experienced as Compassion, as *pratītya-samutpāda,* as nirvana; and again as God, as Brahman, et cetera? How can we otherwise account for Jesus' being a Buddha, and yet a Buddha who experienced the ultimate, *Śūnyatā,* as the heavenly Father?

In conclusion, let me say again how much interacting with Abe has meant, and continues to mean, to me, as to very many others. It has been a great blessing to us in the West that he has made it his mission to represent Zen Buddhism among us. He has planted seeds in many hearts. He has opened many minds to another world of religious thought and experience of which we have to take account, and in so doing we are enormously enriched. We look forward to further publications, which I know he has in the pipeline. And so as he now returns to Kyoto after a long period of fruitful work in the United States, we his friends wish him and his wife well, and say both *Sayonara* and thank you.

Chapter Fourteen

KENOSIS AND *ŚŪNYATĀ* IN THE CONTEMPORARY BUDDHIST-CHRISTIAN DIALOGUE

Thomas J. J. Altizer

MASAO ABE WOULD APPEAR to be alone among contemporary Buddhist thinkers in having so fully entered the world of Christian theology, a world wherein he has not only given a powerful Buddhist witness but even more significantly has employed the deepest Christian language and symbolism as a language of Buddhism itself, and in such a way as to open yet another way to a language and a vision that will be Buddhist and Christian at once. Moreover, he has done so in the context of a deeply modern or postmodern thinking, a thinking embodying not only the end of Christendom but the death of God, a death of God that is a dissolution of the transcendence of Being and precisely thereby a realization of a new and total immanence. This is the very immanence that modern Buddhist thinkers have entered as an arena for the realization of *Śūnyatā*. If such an immanence has inevitably been known in the West as a radically new kind, the Buddhist thinker can apprehend it as a primordial totality of Emptiness—a totality that has always been alien to Western thinking (unless it is present in a deeply mystical Western thinking, which is just why the Kyoto School has been so deeply drawn to Meister Eckhart). Now it is not insignificant that both Hegel and Heidegger found a ground for their radically new thinking in Eckhart, just as it is noteworthy that Heideggerian thinking has been so open to Buddhism. If nihilism is now an overwhelming reality in the modern world, it would appear that only Buddhist thinking can purely reverse our nihilism, and reverse it by calling forth the totality of *Śūnyatā*.

One of the most challenging and enlightening dimensions of Abe's presence and language is the very spontaneity with which they can embody a Christianity that is a Buddhist Christianity—and not peripherally, but rather at its innermost center and ground, a ground that is Incarnation itself, and an Incarnation that is a totally kenotic actualization of God. This Incarnation has always been profoundly resisted and opposed by Christian theology, above all so by our Western dogmatics, for even when that seemingly occurs, as in Barth's *Church Dogmatics*, the humiliation and sacrificial death of Christ is inseparable from the exaltation and glorification of Christ, even as the kenotic servanthood of the Son of God is inseparable from the absolute sovereignty of God himself. The simple truth is that Christian dogmatics, whether in East or West, has been unable to accept a totally kenotic Incarnation, unable to accept a crucifixion which is not simultaneously resurrection and glorification, and above all unable to accept or affirm the crucified God. True, this occurs in the early Luther and was a decisive source of the Reformation itself, but even as it was abandoned or disguised by the mature Luther, it virtually disappears in Protestant dogmatics and has never entered Catholic dogmatics, unless in a disguised form, as in Teilhard de Chardin. Thus, when Abe speaks of such an Incarnation, he inevitably shocks his Christian hearer, who has been conditioned by centuries of tradition to disguise or dilute the fullness of the Incarnation. Yet when hearing it from a seemingly alien voice, the Christian can sense the presence of a primal faith that has been lost by that very tradition.

Accordingly, a paradox is present here—and perhaps a deep paradox—for if historical Buddhism is vastly distant from historical Christianity, and seemingly the most distant of all our major religious traditions, it is becoming possible to hear a Christian voice in contemporary

Buddhist language. That voice is possible and real only when it is apparently most distant from and alien to Christianity itself. Above all, it is the virtually infinite distance of Buddhism from the Christian God that is fundamental here, for Buddhism is that horizon most innocent of God, most free of any sense or awareness of an absolute sovereignty and transcendence, and most closed to any horizon of Being itself. Yet Abe can and does speak of God, even as Nishida had done so before him, but these are deeply modern Buddhists who are unaffected by an ancient Christian tradition and have primarily known Christianity by way of Eckhart, Hegel, and Kierkegaard, and even by way of the deeply anti-Christian Nietzsche, so they have known a Christianity that is deeply other than dogmatic Christianity and perhaps most deeply Christian in that very otherness. Certainly that otherness is fundamental to their language about God, which is why they can even speak of God by way of *Śūnyatā;* and yet their very language is most clearly a Christian language, and most decisively so in its evocation of agape, an agape that is purely kenotic and thereby most manifestly Christian.

There is simply nothing comparable in contemporary Christian language about Buddhism, certainly no sense whatsoever of the possibility of a Christian language that could now recover a depth or purity of Buddhism absent from the contemporary Buddhist speaker. Although it may well be true that a deep Buddhism has indeed entered the modern imaginative languages of the West—and done so far more deeply and profoundly than it has done so in modern Eastern art, music, and literature—our modern philosophical and theological language has at best simply been open to Buddhism. Never has it given promise of recovering or renewing a lost or hidden Buddhist ground, unless it has done so in our deepest nihilistic thinking. This possibility may well account for Nietzsche's deep attraction for the Kyoto School, and all too significantly a deeply positive response to Nietzsche occurred in the Japanese thinker before it did so in the Western thinker; and if the Buddhist thinker can know Nietzsche's thinking as a profound reversal both of Western thinking and of Western history itself, that reversal could well be a deep recovery of a primordial horizon, a horizon most purely embodied in Buddhism. And Nietzsche is that thinker who posited the deepest contradiction between Jesus and Christianity itself, who could go far beyond even Kierkegaard in unveiling the Christian tradition as the deep reversal of an original faith, a reversal already occurring in the New Testament itself, and a reversal that is a pure reversal in a uniquely modern Christianity. Thus, Nietzsche could proclaim the death of God as gospel or "good news," and apparently the Buddhist can now know that death as gospel, for it is the dissolution of that God or Being which is most intrinsically "other" than Śūnyatā.

We might well imagine that such an otherness could never be heard or known by the Buddhist. If the Buddhist is finally liberated from the very possibility of an "I" of any kind, certainly comprehending the "I" of God, and most fundamentally so the "I" that is an absolutely solitary "I," an "I" that is only and solely *causa sui,* and thus an "I" that is an absolutely transcendent "I." That is an "I" that transcends any possibility of kenosis, and if the Christian dogma of the Trinity all too gradually came into existence as a way of affirming a sacrificial or kenotic redemption, this dogma became peripheral in modern Christian dogmatics until it was recovered by Barth. But then it could be recovered only by isolating Christian thinking from any thinking that is not purely dogmatic. While that may well be as original a movement as any that has ever occurred in Christian theology, and one that even now is the one firm foundation of Christian dogmatics, it is the most deeply sectarian movement that has ever occurred in theological thinking, and perhaps the one movement making possible a contemporary Christian thinking about God. Yet a contemporary Buddhist such as Abe can speak of God, and even speak of God in the language of self-emptying, a self-emptying that *is* agape but *is* agape only insofar as it is self-emptying. Now even if such agape is Śūnyatā, and therefore is and only could be a purely and totally primordial agape, it does unveil a primordial Godhead that has never been known in the West (unless it was known by Meister Eckhart and his followers) but that does call forth the possibility of a truly new Christian opening to the Godhead, one previously present only in a purely mystical (as opposed to a dogmatic or theological) horizon.

The contemporary Christian theologian can only marvel at the theological language of a Nishida, a Nishitani, or an Abe, for this is a language that is not only at once philosophical and theological but existential and conceptual simultaneously. Not since Heidegger's "turn" has such a language even truly been attempted by a Western thinker, and certainly not by any form of dogmatic theology or by any thinking that is genuinely in continuity with the Christian tradition. Now if *Śūnyatā* makes possible a contemporary Buddhist thinking about God, it is when *Śūnyatā* has been approached from a Western horizon. Just as the Kyoto School was deeply shaped by those modern Western thinkers who have thought most deeply about God, it has thereby been liberated from premodern theological thinking and therefore liberated from the purely transcendent God. Not even Kierkegaard knew and only knew that God, hence the necessity of Barth's renunciation of his earlier discipleship to Kierkegaard so as to make possible his *Church Dogmatics.* Just as Kierkegaard is now wholly alien to a purely dogmatic theology, a dialectical language of any kind is now wholly alien to Christian dogmatics, so that even Kierkegaardian language has become just as distant from our dogmatic theology as is Hegelian or Nietzschean language. But that is a distance from a pure thinking about God, and nothing is more forbidden today than thinking about God—a prohibition that has again and again been violated by Abe, and perhaps that is why he is most treasured by the Christian.

In this perspective, we might well imagine that a truly and fully primordial thinking has never occurred in the West, or insofar as it has occurred, as perhaps in Erigena and Eckhart, it has been condemned and driven underground, only to be reborn in radical and heretical circles. But such rebirths have not occurred in theology itself, at least not in our theological thinking about God. If philosophical thinking has thereby been driven apart from theological thinking in the modern world, and far more so than ever occurred in a premodern theological thinking, it not only distances theological thinking from philosophical thinking but from primal or fundamental thinking itself. Only such a deep thinking can know or realize *Śūnyatā,* and in our world such thinking must inevitably be vastly distant from our given theological thinking, and distant precisely as pure thinking. Yet is it possible that only a thinking of *Śūnyatā* can now think, and purely think, what the Christian knows as God? Is it only an Absolute Emptiness or an Absolute Nothingness that can now give us a horizon in which it is possible to think God? And is it only that Emptiness or that Nothingness which could possibly be a true ground for an absolute kenosis, an absolute kenosis that *is* agape, and thereby is a once-and-for-all and irreversible Incarnation? If traditional Christianity has reversed the Incarnation by its celebration of the resurrection and the ascension of

Christ, is that a reversal which would be impossible within the horizon of *Śūnyatā*, and impossible if only because it is a reversal of self-emptying?

While Buddhism would appear to be closed to the very possibility of a once-and-for-all and irreversible act if totality itself is an Absolute Emptiness, then that totality is what is realized in the Incarnation, and then the Incarnation could be apprehended as a realization of that totality. This view apparently occurs in Abe's theological thinking, and while this view seemingly parallels an Eastern Christian apprehension of the Incarnation as a process of deification, it deeply differs from such Christian affirmations in knowing totality itself not as absolute glory but rather as Absolute Emptiness, an Emptiness that is all in all as Emptiness itself, and therefore an Emptiness that is what an actual kenosis realizes or effects. Thus, if *Śūnyatā* is the true ground of that agape which is Incarnation, the once-and-for-all act of Incarnation could be apprehended as the absolute emptying of that world or actuality in which it occurs, so that it is a once-and-for-all act only insofar as it is an eschatological act, and such an absolutely eschatological act could be an absolutely primordial act. Then a primordial totality of Emptiness could be understood as being coincident with, if not identical to, a total eschatological or apocalyptic fulfillment, and that is a realization of absolute emptying, an Emptiness that could only actually be spoken of as agape, for that is an Emptiness which is a total compassion.

Perhaps what is most disquieting about such apprehensions is that they appear to be all too close to a uniquely Christian gnosticism, one wholly dissolving a true or divine Creator, and one effecting an absolute disjunction between every primal center and everything whatsoever that is manifest or realizable as world. Yet gnosticism is inconceivable apart from a primal ground in Godhead itself, and that is precisely a Godhead wholly absent from Buddhism, unless *Śūnyatā* itself can be apprehended as Godhead, and a Godhead that is absolutely empty of everything whatsoever hearable or speakable, or everything whatsoever that can be known as either Being or beings. Although gnostic mythical language is vastly distant from Mādhyamika or Zen Buddhism, is it really so distant from Tantric Buddhism or even from popular Mahāyāna traditions? Is it even possible that gnosticism was an original Christian movement toward a Buddhist *Śūnyatā* or a Hindu Brahman-Atman? Surely many have thought so, which is surely one reason why gnosticism is so popular today. And if

Christian orthodoxy has continually responded to gnosticism as its deepest internal threat, a threat to the very Godhead of God, that Godhead has been more deeply and more comprehensively dissolved in the Buddhist tradition than in any other tradition. Accordingly, Buddhism may well be a pure embodiment of what a Christian gnosticism only intended; and if such an intention has again and again been assaulted by Christian orthodoxy, is it because this is an original intention of Christianity that cannot finally be erased?

Just as the gnostic *Gospel of Truth* names Christ as the authentic name of that Godhead which it ecstatically proclaims, for here the name of the Father is the name of the Son, could Christ be a Christian name of the Buddha, and of that Buddha who is all in all in everything? While the Buddha is finally unnameable, and certainly could not be a "who" of any kind, is it because the Buddha is absolute compassion and therefore is a totally present immanence without even a shadow of transcendence? We cannot doubt that Buddhism is without everything that Christian orthodoxy has known as the Godhead of God, just as it is wholly closed to everything our Western ontologies have known as the Being of beings, and everything our Western languages have known as the subject or the "I." Hence a contemporary Western deconstruction of our anthropology, our ontology, and our theology appears to many to be a Western opening to a Buddhist ground, and one that was decisively established by Nietzsche himself. From this perspective, our Western nihilism could become or perhaps already is a Buddhist nihilism, a nihilism that is truly a "deconstruction" only insofar as it is an opening to a deeper ground and only insofar as it finally intends an Absolute Nothingness. If that is a Nothingness which Nietzsche named as Eternal Recurrence, is a new Zarathustra's Eternal Recurrence a Western opening to *Śūnyatā*, and one that is inseparable from an absolute reversal of our consciousness and history? Then our apocalypse could be a return to our primordial ground, and an absolute return, a return to an absolutely primordial ground, one that has perhaps been present in our deeper mystical traditions and one that has perhaps been reborn in our most deeply modern or postmodern interior voyages. Perhaps thereby an authentic Christian voyage is being reborn in our time, one whose Omega is Alpha, indeed, and so deeply Alpha as to be a genuinely apocalyptic ending.

And if Alpha is finally *Śūnyatā*, then not only are Alpha and Omega one, but everything "is" or arises or originates with everything else, an "isness" that is "is-notness," and precisely thereby is agape or compassion. Abe can speak the language of compassion, or seemingly so, but he can do so only insofar as his language embodies Emptiness, and compassion can be present only to the degree that Emptiness itself is realized. Yet this is certainly something absent from our Western deconstruction, and most clearly absent from Nietzsche's language, unless No-saying is finally Yes-saying, and a pure and absolute assault a true expression of compassion. Is it possible that Buddhist thinkers are now unveiling such a truth to a Western and Christian world, and unveiling it by their very witness to *Śūnyatā*, a *Śūnyatā* whose purely negative movement is and only can be a purely positive movement, even if it must appear as a negative movement alone to the unenlightened mind? All too significantly God himself underwent an epiphany as the purely alien God when the West discovered a purely negative dialectic, not only in Hegel's understanding of the "Bad Infinite" or "Being-in-itself," but also in Blake's vision of the absolutely transcendent Creator as Satan. Nor were these resurrections of a gnostic vision of the Creator; they could not be, for here the alien God is a necessary expression of a redemptive self-negation or "Self-Annihilation," a self-negation whereby absolute Spirit or "The Eternal Great Humanity Divine" actually realizes itself as its own inherent "other." Just as a deeply Western dualism is truly transcended by Blake and Hegel (and also by Nietzsche himself), this transcendence would appear to be open to Buddhism, and so open if only because Buddhism is that way which is the purest and most comprehensive dissolution of dualism.

This is the very context in which the Buddhist speaks of God today, a God who is the very opposite of a dualistic God and thus a God who is a totally present God or Godhead, but only by way of an absolute emptying, a kenotic emptying that is agape but only insofar as it is *Śūnyatā*. In a Blakean or Hegelian perspective, the God who *is* apart from self-negation is the alien God, but it is precisely the "othering" of God that is a primal ground of a Hegelian actuality or a Blakean "Experience," and it is only the transfiguration of that experience or actuality that is a Blakean or Hegelian theodicy. Is theodicy itself totally absent from Buddhism, an absence inevitable in a purely primordial way, and certainly inevitable if *Śūnyatā* is all in all? Indeed, theodicy would appear to be absent from all twentieth-century thinking; at no other point are we further distant from a Hegel or a Blake, and that distance also seems to open us to Buddhism. Accordingly, a Buddhist can speak of God without any historical intimations whatsoever; thereby, a purity is present that is impossible for the Christian speaker. The Buddhist, unlike the Christian, can speak of God without any negative overtones. Is that a gift now being offered by the Buddhist to the Christian, a gift bestowing a liberation from history, a liberation that is an exit from our Christian and Western history?

Again and again we have heard that the Dharma is coming to the West, and surely it has done so in the work and witness of Masao Abe, perhaps most enticingly so in that quiet joy he embodies. Never have I detected in him a movement of ressentiment, and one could imagine that this is a consequence of his long Zen meditation, a meditation realizing *Śūnyatā,* and realizing a *zazen* in which the "I" disappears. Certainly there could be no ressentiment in the wake of the disappearance of that "bad conscience" which is the center of our interior; and if the West has embodied a unique self-consciousness that is a doubled consciousness, a consciousness in which the "I" is its own inherent "other," such a self-alienated consciousness is the very opposite of a Buddhist consciousness, a consciousness foreclosing the very possibility of a center of consciousness. In the second essay of his *Genealogy of Morals,* Nietzsche unveiled the advent of history as the internalization of a primordial humanity, an internalization occurring through the most total transformation humanity has ever undergone, when an internal consciousness stood forth that was distanced from our primordial energy and life. Then all energy that cannot discharge itself outwardly turns inward, and that internalization expanded and extended itself in the same measure as outward discharge was inhibited or repressed. But that internalization is a return of our free and original energy, yet a return that is necessarily directed against our interior consciousness and that is the origin of the "bad conscience." So the bad conscience in its beginning is an original freedom pushed back and repressed, incarcerated within, and finally able to discharge itself only on and against itself, for all energy that does not discharge itself outwardly turns inward and thus, finally and most deeply, turns against itself.

Such a totally repressed energy and life is a pure No-saying, a No-saying that for Nietzsche is only fully named in the naming of the Christian God, that God and that God alone who is the deification of nothingness, the will to nothingness pronounced holy (*The Antichrist* 18). Accordingly, the death of God is the ending of our history, and therewith the ending of our interior "I," and if that "I" is wholly alien to Buddhism, then so likewise is that ressentiment which is the inevitable consequence of our doubled and self-alienated consciousness. So, too, is our Western historical and temporal consciousness truly absent from Buddhism, an absence that to us could only be the absence or dissolution of history itself—even the absence of everything that we can know as time and space. Insofar as we have approached Buddhism from our own Western perspective, we have inevitably known it as a pure nihilism, a nihilism that many have known as having been resurrected in our uniquely modern realization of the death of God. Now it is in the wake of that death that Abe can speak of God, and can speak of the Christian God as a pure kenosis or agape, a God who *is Śūnyatā,* or pure Emptiness, and perhaps precisely thereby is the will to nothingness pronounced holy! Is that the blessing which Abe is bringing the Christian today?

chapter Fifteen

THE
EXPERIENCE OF
NEIGHBORHOOD

Heinrich Ott

I HAD MY FIRST LONG ENCOUNTER with Masao Abe in October 1978 during a conference on "Heidegger, Mahayana Buddhism and Whitehead: Perspectives on Interfaith Dialogue." Abe spoke on "Substance, Process, and Emptiness." I spoke on "The Beginning Dialogue between Christianity and Buddhism: The Concept of a 'Dialogical Theology' and the Possible Contribution of Heideggerian Thought." Both articles appeared together with others in *Japanese Religions*.[1]

Though the encounter between the world religions reached its paramount importance only after Heidegger's death, his influence on this movement, notwithstanding other quite fruitful theological suggestions during his lifetime, represents perhaps his *deepest* theological influence. To explain Heidegger's significance for the encounter between the world religions, I used in that paper a concept that Heidegger himself developed in his important book *On the Way to Language,* namely, the concept of "neighborhood."[2] Heidegger especially has in mind the neighborhood of poetry and thinking, of the language of the poet and the language of the thinker—the two "eminent ways of saying." He suggested that their neighborhood had until then been neglected and, therefore, that the true essence of language had perhaps been badly understood in general. However, Heidegger's concept of neighborhood can also be used fruitfully in other contexts. (I would really rather talk of a *category*, instead of a *concept*, of neighborhood, for this concept is rather a whole form of thought—though a form of thought that *can be experienced*.)

Heidegger explains what he means by neighborhood in *On the Way to Language* as follows: "Neighborhood is a relationship which emerges from the fact that one person moves into the vicinity *[Nähe]* of the other. Neighborhood is the result . . . of the fact that one settles *vis-à-vis* the other."[3] However, Heidegger says that this cannot be experienced by just measurable distance. Rather, "two lonely farmsteads—insofar as there still exist such things—which lie an hour apart walking across the fields can be neighbors in the most beautiful sense, whereas houses which are across the street from each other or even built together in the city might know no sense of neighborhood."[4] For this reason, it is also true that in "the dominant vis-à-vis-ness each is open for the other, one entrusts itself to the other, and each remains thereby itself."[5]

We can understand this image of neighborhood as a powerful language-symbol for the essential relation of religions to one another as this relationship emerges today and begins to become actual. It leads into an experienceable depth that speaks to our emotions and nourishes thought. And when I say "experienceable," I would like to suggest that I myself have experienced such a neighborhood, that I have been touched in emotion that always precedes and accompanies thought and have thus been inspired to think further. This especially happened to me through Masao Abe's religious thinking. I was also touched by Keiji Nishitani (1900–92), who comes from the same school of thought and spirituality as Abe. I met Nishitani before I did Abe and was deeply impressed by his stature and thinking; I felt enriched and enlightened even if I could not adequately express in my own words what had happened to me. I could at best relate some anecdotes, minute details that I remember, and some words Nishitani had said at several isolated occasions. Yet even through such things our spirit can obtain direction and orientation. When I met Masao Abe, some things became conceptually clearer. It was not that I could simply follow his thinking, appropriate his concepts, and use them as if they were my own. Rather the field of possible future discourse was more precisely delimited, and I could begin to formulate for myself my own ways of asking questions and searching for goals, or at least to determine directions for continuing thought *(Weiterdenken)* within this field. These problems have in no way been solved. They exist as questions that are in the process of being worked out and that develop in accordance with their own laws. On the basis of this still continuing encounter with Abe, I finally obtained much more inner clarity so that I could discuss with my students Nishitani's great work *What is Religion?* in the context of a seminar during a semester in the late eighties.[6]

This encounter appears to be an example of the experience of neighborhood, one on both levels: the encounter with Nishitani and the encounter with Abe. In this experience we did not reach agreements, decisions, or any clear and conscious discovery that we have found "common ground" on which we now work together and with satisfaction. There was only the slightest contact, a presentiment more than knowledge—a presentiment of closeness that can hardly be captured by words but was still inspiring. It led to further thinking in order to formulate the indeterminate presentiment in comprehensible concepts. Yet this determination of further thinking is not a common enterprise. Rather, each one of us who has been touched by the presentiment of the other's nearness undertakes the effort of thinking further on his or her own familiar field. It is like a shyness between those who experience neighborhood, afraid to take one step too far, to distort the secret of the origin of the other by crude words or concepts, by a rash adaptation to one's own thought patterns. Only when the secret of the other remains intact can it make the richness of our inspiration bloom, have an effect on us, and be fruitful for our own thought.

I mean by this experience of the neighborhood one in which "each is open for the other, open in its self-concealing . . . [reaching] out to the other . . . [entrusting] itself to the other, and each [remaining] thereby itself."[7] I believe that I have had this experience again and again with different worlds of partners and in differing degrees of intensity, yet hardly ever with the same intensity as with the Buddhist Kyoto School to which Keiji Nishitani and Masao Abe belong. We Christian theologians consider ourselves champions of the interreligious dialogue and its hermeneutics. And we probably are, on the whole, such champions because of our faith in the Incarnation that determines the entirety of our Christian thinking. Nevertheless, the representatives of the Kyoto School are just as open in their willingness to enter ecumenical dialogue (understood in the widest sense). Indeed, they may in some sense be ahead of us.

THE EXPERIENCE OF NEIGHBORHOOD has become today a paradigm of the theology of religions, and the representatives of the Kyoto School are important witnesses for this paradigm. Perhaps they are the most important, at least they are the best known. They have entered with understanding into Western thought, into Western philosophy, and especially into Christian thinking. Yet though they have appropriated and understood large parts of Western, or Christian, thinking, they have not allowed this to make them abandon their predominantly Buddhist point of view. On the contrary, they were able to develop their own Buddhist religious and intellectual identity more deeply and more convincingly just because they went through this encounter with the West. The paradigm to which I am pointing has already become almost part of the consensus within the discourse of the theology of religions. Many theologians and religious thinkers who are engaged in this discourse act within the framework of this paradigm, even if they are often not yet theologically conscious of it. The notion that the dialogue of religions must be something like a dispute about doctrines about different belief systems seems to be viewed as antiquated by most who are familiar with the subject. Rather, most seem to realize that the coexistence and, hopefully, a certain community between the religions of this one world is inevitable.

Within the field of this experience of neighborhood, we can then observe two characteristic processes. I would like to indicate these two that I have experienced myself.

1.

Masao Abe acquainted me with the following words of a Chinese Zen master (which he often cited, and I myself have since repeatedly cited):

First for me mountains were just mountains and water was just water. When I entrusted myself to the guidance of an experienced master, mountains were no longer mountains, and water no longer water. When I finally reached the abode of enlightenment, mountains became really *mountains, and water* really *water.*

These paradoxical-intuitive words have since then constantly accompanied me. Though I cannot repeat them as an autobiographical witness for myself, they have become for me a theological working tool, as it were. Let me explain. At times, I attempt to close in on a difficult problem that we are confronted with in theology. For example, in the proposed second volume of discussions of Masao Abe's fundamental article "Kenotic God and Dynamic Sunyata," I addressed the Christian problem of faith in the forgiveness of sins. God does not annihilate sin, he does not cause it not to have happened. And yet he does annihilate it in the event of forgiveness. He "forgets" it, as if it had never been. Without both of these aspects, we could not understand the event of forgiveness in its entire depth. To do justice to the theological reality of the topic of the forgiveness of sin, we need the Buddhist-like logic of "No, and therefore precisely yes." This hits into the face of classical Aristotelian logic by which the edifice of Christian doctrine has been erected. Where are the most basic principles, the "principle of identity," and the "principle of contradiction" when "mountains are no longer mountains"? Yet it is just because of this breaking out of Aristotelian logic that we experience true reality: "Mountains are *really* mountains, water is *really* water." From the point of view of our usual Western logic and with regard to its history, we may perhaps come close to understanding this matter if we *(a)* realize that according to the principle of contradiction, something cannot both be and not be *at the same time* and in the same regard and *(b)* expose ourselves to the question of whether in true reality there can be a true simultaneity at all. Perhaps simultaneity in the constant flux of reality is nothing but a fiction. (Aristotle explicitly criticized the "Heracliteans" in the passage in which he argues for the impossibility of a denial of the principle of contradiction.)

A second theological topic that shares this same perspective concerns eschatological transformation and perfection. Are those who are resurrected still genuinely identical with their previous worldly self? If we follow I Corinthians 15:35ff., then apparently identity and nonidentity must also go together here, and do so in a "dynamic" way. For the transformation as new creation is radical. Salvation and transformation of the self cannot be separated.

Yet we cannot take over the way of thinking present in the Buddhist experience of reality in the same way that it is expressed in the witness of the Chinese master. We cannot simply appropriate it as if it could be our own without qualification. However, we can respect it as something that is foreign, keep ourselves open to it; then something might shine through to us from the neighborhood that will inspire us to think further about our very own problems.

2.

I would also like to call attention, though all too briefly, to a second aspect of the experience of neighborhood. *The central Biblical topics of creation and creator* are foreign to Buddhist thought. In the latter, the all-pervasive "Primal Reality" (*Ur-Realität*), whether it be called Dharma or Buddha, is not viewed as a *prima causa*. The Buddha is no "maker," he is not the "Lord of Karma." But our God appears to the Buddhist as just such a lord (as, for instance, in Buddhadāsa's *Christianity and Buddhism*).[8] However, the Buddha as the original power of Enlightenment is all-present, and his clarity penetrates everything from the very beginning.

For us Christians, such an unappreciative rejection of one of our central concepts of faith is at first jarring. Yet how far have we really thought through the concept of creation and realized its mystery? Indeed, the category of causality is insufficient to explain what is here touching us. On the other hand, we find, for instance, in Augustine a passage that sounds as if it could bridge the gap: "Blessed is he who loves You, who loves his friend in You and because of you the enemy as well! He alone loses no-one who is dear to him, since he loves all in the One who can never get lost. It is no-one else but our God, the God who has made heaven and earth and who fills them. In fact: *creating and fulfilling are one and the same*."[9] We must continue to think about all this; and in this sense the question remains open for us.

Here, neighborly closeness is helpful because it inspires us by mis-understanding and rejection to ask still more deeply about the most gen-uine secret of our own faith that we are always seeking. We do not receive any positive signals or substantive hints, but the nearness of the neighbor who has as such become familiar and yet remains "strange" in his or her different identity stimulates and calls us to be ourselves. The presence of the other keeps our seeking and questioning alive.

The theme of neighborhood, in the form in which it was developed by Heidegger as a concept, has not yet been taken up by others who engage in the theological discourse of religions. Yet substantially Heideg-ger's understanding corresponds precisely to what is in fact taking place on a broad front between the different religions in a fashion that is well intentioned and peaceful. In this way, we live beside one another or vis-à-vis one another as neighbors. As we already mentioned, Heidegger obtains his concept especially from the contemplation of the relation of poetry and thinking. They grow beside each other like neighboring trees in the woods, having their roots in the same ground. Their tops approach each other, and yet each remains separate. They can never come togeth-er and become one. The powerful message of this image that Heidegger formed into a concept becomes today an inspiring category in the theol-ogy of religions that enables us to think honestly and realistically about the peculiar way in which we live with those who have a *different* faith, yet who *are faithful*.

chapter Sixteen

A TRIBUTE TO A
"PROPHETIC *RŌSHI*"

Langdon Gilkey

FOR ANYONE WHO HAS KNOWN and worked with Masao Abe over a number of years—our friendship now goes back almost two decades—there are many, many facets of his rich and talented person around which one could well compose a tribute. As a theologian, I have often dialogued with Abe the scholar and have learned a great deal about the "teachings" of Zen Buddhism. However, there was one encounter many years ago during which we spoke very little, but from which I learned much about the "spirit" of the Zen Buddhism from which Abe carried on his dialogue with Christianity. It is the particular facet of Abe's person which I saw in that encounter that I want to present in this tribute—that of a "prophetic *rōshi*." Although "prophetic *rōshi*"may seem an oxymoron, a self-contradictory title, it is not. This was the role in which we first encountered Masao Abe in Kyoto in 1976; and it has been this role that has remained most vivid and most treasured among my many memories of him.

On the advice of Professor Yoshinori Takeuchi, my senior and revered colleague at Kyoto University, Ram Rattan and I visited a session of the F.A.S. Society at the stupendous Zen temple in the northern part of Kyoto. There Professor Abe was "*rōshi*," the guiding spirit of this movement (the F.A.S.), begun a generation before, of which he was now the leader and director. Many of the fifty or so persons of a variety of types and backgrounds seated awkwardly cross-legged on the floor were as amateurish as the two of us; yet the leader was infinitely patient, both with our struggles to do *zazen* (seated meditation) successfully and with our ignorance of Buddhism in general and the Zen tradition in particular. We met once a week for two hours, one hour for *zazen*—how quickly we improved!—and one hour of readings from Dōgen, of commentary from Abe *Rōshi*, and of discussion of the aims of the F.A.S. Society.

This latter subject was to me especially fascinating. A movement begun by Abe's mentor, Shin'ichi Hisamatsu, the F.A.S. Society was dedicated to the "revival" of Buddhism and especially of Zen Buddhism— both suffering from their past association with the "old Japan" prior to the Meiji, Westernizing period. The F.A.S. thus aimed to present an authentic and traditional Zen, but in a quite new guise. The "modern" incarnation, so to speak, now stripped of its older authoritarian elements and its exclusiveness as only for male initiates, sought to develop the inward life of modern men and women through serious meditation, to be open to all who were interested, and, to direct its own energies outward into "engagement" with the social world in a campaign for global understanding, international peace, and domestic justice and equality.

Abe perfectly personified these aims: moral and yet not ascetic, learned and yet not pompous, kind and gentle almost to a fault rather than authoritarian, and deeply concerned for the nurturance of the soul and for the good of the world, he vividly represented for all of us in his person this "prophetic Zen" movement. Whereas the traditional *rōshi* had demanded of his disciples unquestioning obedience and unhesitating assent, and even frequently struck his uncomplaining followers sharply on their bowed shoulders with a wooden staff, this *rōshi* firmly but gently straightened up the sagging backs of his Midwestern aspirants, listened tolerantly to any viewpoints disputing his interpretation of Zen texts, and invited others, less learned and less disciplined, to an open discussion of their common problems as modern people. Here an older and once rigid religious tradition was now made more supple, more flexible, more inclusive, more "other-oriented"; and yet it retained, so it seemed, its intense internal commitment to a deep and healing spirituality combined now with a creative, "progressive" ethic.

The F.A.S. was, so it seemed to me, one of the most impressive of the many efforts in our modern world to bring a strong but partially "frozen" religious tradition successfully and creatively onto the contemporary scene. I have often wondered how it has fared since the late seventies, when Abe, having moved to this country, relinquished its leadership. And I marvel at the number of people—Japanese who were traditional Buddhists or newly interested in meditation, Japanese-Americans seeking their spiritual as well as their cultural roots in Japan, and interested visitors to Japan and to Buddhism like ourselves (some of the latter silly, some serious, some a bit of both)—whom Abe's kind, thoughtful, and deeply dedicated spirit must have touched and quickened. Having since experienced Masao Abe in many other roles—as a firm and unyielding missionary to the West of the Zen viewpoint, as self-disciplined partner in dialogue, and as a teacher of philosophy and of religious studies—I have often felt that his most effective role, where his real intellectual, moral, and spiritual abilities best disclosed themselves, was as a "prophetic *rōshi*." It was in that vocation, as an enlightened and enlightening pastor, that what in our tradition we would call "grace" was most evident.

One more word on Masao Abe's thoughtful kindness. Although his home was in Kyoto, he was, as is well known, a professor at Nara University. After we had been to one or two sessions of *zazen*, he suggested that we come—with our two children—to Nara, a short train ride south of Kyoto, to see under his guidance that earliest of all imperial capitals and hence the first of all Buddhist centers (C.E. late seventh and early eighth centuries). This we did not only once but on three occasions. Each time there were several other visitors to Japan who were invited to share in this rare treat to ourselves. It was a kindness that, clearly frequently repeated, must have been very time-consuming as well as tiring! With never-failing patience and cheerfulness, he showed us the glorious temples, the first Buddhist sculptures, and the artifacts of that earliest capital, explaining each symbol and motif to us and, despite our first-grade questions, never seeming to lose his own interest. Again I wondered how many people from abroad had not this rare man, with great modesty united with great learning, introduced to the beauties of Japanese tradition?

Others, I know, will be writing appreciatively of all Masao Abe has done to explain and expound Zen philosophy and Zen religion, and the great strides that dialogue between Buddhism and Christianity has made because of his leadership from the Buddhist side. Perhaps few others have had the choice good fortune (*karma?* providence?) to have experienced his unparalleled kindness to the strangers who came to Kyoto to wonder and to learn.

chapter Seventeen

MASAO ABE'S CHALLENGE TO MODERN JEWISH THEOLOGY

Eugene B. Borowitz

I HAVE NEVER MET MASAO ABE and have long realized that has been a considerable loss for me. For over many years now he has been a spiritual companion of mine, one whose ideas have given me insight by their direct relevance to my faith, or indirectly by the shock created by our disagreement on certain fundamentals.

We "met" almost two decades ago when I read his article "Non-Being and *Mu*: The Metaphysical Nature of Negativity in the East and the West" (*Religious Studies,* 11, no. 2 [June 1975]: 181–92). What struck me as extraordinarily significant in his argument was that it challenged the very basis of the Western philosophical tradition. Why, even when one was inclined to dismiss much of the development of philosophy as a betrayal of its origins, as was the case with Heidegger, did one still insist on asking, "Why is there anything at all?" Why not, instead, respond fully to the ephemerality of all things—philosophic systems included—and begin one's most serious thinking with the question that has grounded much of the religio-philosophical tradition of the East, "Why is there nothing at all?" To explain why this article made such an impression on me, I need to make a somewhat lengthy digression to explain the particular context in which I, as one of a handful of Jews concerned with "theology," received it.

Since Abe's challenge was issued long before the days when multiculturalism gained a certain normative power, it was still possible for much of the liberal and philosophic establishments to dismiss his argument as "simply not being how one did philosophy." To me, it seemed quite odd—*damning* is closer to the truth but not as euphemistic—that this should be the response of people who proudly called themselves "rationalists." It is obviously not a rationalistic defense to argue that "This is how it is done in the West" or "This is what our guild considers acceptable subject matter and procedures, and if you want to participate in our discussions, you will have to abide by the rules of our language game."

If I put this somewhat crudely today, it is not because the multiculturalists and postmoderns have suddenly empowered me. Rather, I remember quite clearly the similar emotional response I had back then to what seemed to me the unwarranted assumption of authority over all thought, most certainly including religious thinking, that philosophical rationalists claimed for their standards of serious thought. They insisted that any structure of ideas that claimed the earnest attention of reflective people must meet their criteria of cogency. (The early years of *Religious Studies,* though it celebrates the willingness of some philosophers finally being willing to argue religious ideas as serious thought, amply illustrate this cultural situation.) While this self-assertion was most flagrantly displayed in English-speaking philosophical circles, it was similarly found among the remnants of Continental idealism (whose neo-Kantianism still dominated common Jewish discussion) and other more robust intellectual currents. These academic tendencies were socially reinforced by the dominant Western ethos that, impressed by the triumphs of science, took for granted that a naturalistic worldview should provide the context for what remained of religion. Many religionists, it should be noted, had conceded this power to specify the criteria of responsible thought to the rationalists. By and large only the "fundamentalists" resisted the hegemony of the philosophers. But if the choice were between modern and quite traditional religious thought, few academics indeed were then ready to buck what seemed like the inevitable onward movement of the *zeitgeist.*

The problem of intellectual context had particular relevance to me.

I wanted to create a viable—consider the implications of that term—Jewish theology for the changed situation in which the Jewish people found itself in the second half of the twentieth century. Reason had played a critical role in validating and directing the nineteenth-century Jewish Emancipation, the movement from the European ghetto or *shtetl* into those societies that granted them social equality. In some adaptation of German idealism, though regularly more Kantian than Hegelian, rabbis and writers explained the meaning of the radical social transformation taking place. Through the Kantian primacy of ethics and the Hegelian sense of historic progress, they justified their governments' acts of liberation, their own subsequent dedication to good citizenship, and their right to abandon many of the ritual practices of their tradition. Insofar as they remained religious, their faith was typically "liberal": human-centered, science-trusting, God-aspiring, more universal than particular, and with God's revelation reduced to human spiritual discovery. In the works of the great Jewish system-builders early in this century, Hermann Cohen, Leo Baeck and Mordecai Kaplan, this intellectual development received neo-Kantian, Schleiermacherian-Otto-ish, and American naturalistic expression. By mid-century, as my Jewish intellectual search matured, the American Jewish ethos was resolutely rationalistic and thus effectively agnostic, ethically and politically activist, and, where it was not obsessed with social integration, ethnically Jewish.

Even before the community became conscious of the Holocaust, there were minority signs that these older approaches to modern Jewish life were unsatisfactory. At both the Reform and the Conservative seminaries, a new sensibility was making itself felt in experimental practice and, most unexpectedly, by the interest of some few students in working out a contemporary Jewish "theology." As it were, "philosophy" seemed dogmatically rationalistic, with devastating results for Judaism. In short, philosophy, trusting to the primacy of the mind, required atheism, or at least agnosticism, though it could sometimes muster a patronizing tolerance of various nominalistic reinterpretations of the term *God*. For those of us who had sufficient doubts about the ability of human omnicompetence to provide a substantive understanding of God, philosophy thus seemed an inadequate way to understand reality. This attitude also opened up the possibility that the Jewish tradition should no longer be read only to determine where it was in agreement with "the best of modern thought." Rather, it should now be studied to see what it might independently say to us, even though we were not fundamentalists committed to always accept its ideas or follow its dictates.

To some extent, our renewal of involvement with God could also be detected among liberal Christians. But among the Jews, it was intertwined with a strong particularistic thrust. The rationalistic ethos not only negated God but also made dedication to the robust survival of the Jewish people quixotic. The rationalistic philosophies were united in their common assertion that truth is to be found on the universal level and only in a derivative fashion in any particular embodiment. To be sure, the universal truth could not exist in history simply on its own and, as it were, "required" some particular interpretation in order to play a role in history. That was as much validity as could be granted to a particular religion, culture, or institution. But by making all such embodiments essentially inferior in truth and instrumental in value, this validation also justified their abandonment with the appearance of a more effective means to the final end. For a minority such as the Jews, seduced by the lure of the majority culture and burdened with the disabilities of being a Jew in a secularized Christian culture, the instrumental argument for Jewishness seemed only a palliative on the way to assimilation. Even Mordecai Kaplan, who sought to give a rationalistic defense of Jewish particularity, could do so only by making a sociological case for the power and value of ethnicity. But description had no normative effect, so the argument held only as long as Jews retained strong ethnic ties—ones, he acknowledged, that might one day equally be replaced by those of Americanism.

In hindsight it seems clear to me that by the middle of this century, a radical shift in the social agenda had begun to make itself felt among some Jews. Prior generations of emancipated Jews had been passionately devoted to discovering how Jews might best find a place in the general society. For them—and for many Jews today—the underlying drive of their Jewishness is the quest to be more fully universalistic. But the new search took for granted integration into the modern world. That assumption changed the operative question for us, and we wanted to know just what it meant for us moderns to be concerned, caring Jews. We did not propose to give up the strong universalistic commitments that modern

Judaism had by life and thought made convincingly a part of our faith, but we knew these now needed to be balanced by a particularism of equal cogency.

How we came to know that this intuition of the commanding power of a non-fundamentalist Jewish particularity still had sufficient truth to demand our dedication was not clear then, nor is it now. In part, it stemmed from our sense of the hubris of reason and the limitations of science. In part, it arose as a reaction to the anti-Semitism that was so significant a part of Jewish life even in the period before the Holocaust. But if my experience may be taken as reasonably typical, it mostly came from living with reasonable self-acceptance as a modern American Jew and finding in it something ultimately true and compelling, but as yet without proper intellectual expression. Hence was born the seemingly idiosyncratic interest of some few to give culturally acceptable articulation to this fuller view of the truth of Judaism.

For some years existentialism promised to provide an intellectual structure for such a new Jewish theology. Its initial appeal was polemical, for it undercut the rationalistic claim to be self-validating by its argument that existence preceded essence. By focusing on the "I" who was doing the thinking (skeptical or constructive), it made clear that every form of rationality necessarily began from a nonrationalistic ground. If so, more attention should be given to the prerational than to the rational, and any claim that sophisticated reason must be the exclusive arbiter of what was worthy thought and action could be seen as contradicted by its own ground. If, however, the self rather than the mind could be taken as the basis for one's thought—reason as the handmaid of existence—a much broader understanding of the human spirit could reach expression and thus room be made for spirituality. Here the existentialists divided into two groups. Some, like Heidegger and Sartre, had "systems" that ruled out the possibility that existentialist thinking might include a place for God. Others, like Kierkegaard and Buber (in their quite different ways), gave the lived quality of existence more weight than how one thought about it. And for both these religious existentialists, the particular—not the universal—was the place of truth.

In the early 1970s the balance of Jewish intellectual leadership had begun to shift from the rationalists to the existentialists. Masao Abe's article thus came as stunning confirmation of the antirationalism that seemed so critical to the insurgent thinkers. It not only asserted a new basis for denying the normative primacy of rationalism but radically undercut what remained of that notion in the atheistic existentialisms, such as those of Heidegger and Sartre. Yet its polemic was not bought at the cost of obscurantism or the denigration of reason (as in some of the New Age religions of more recent years). Rather, Abe made his case by a carefully argued, thoughtfully stated examination of the nature of reality, one readily accessible to the Western reader but that led in an utterly unexpected direction. The combination was so uncommon and yet so compelling—and in many ways has remained so—that I knew then that I should always benefit by reading his work and, in my own movement from insight to articulation, by following it.

Why did I not then become his follower and explicate Judaism in terms of his Zen understanding of ultimate reality? I put the question this baldly because, in fact, serious interfaith encounter means opening oneself up to the possibility of conversion. But though I took Abe's thought most seriously, I found myself in respectful but unqualified disagreement with him on the ultimacy of Dynamic Nothingness. I was convinced that such a vision would inevitably undercut what I knew to be the ultimate qualitative difference between good and evil—what by that time already had impressed itself upon my consciousness as the incomparable model of the distinction between them, that between the Nazi death camp operators and their Jewish victims.

Our relationship would have remained at this level of my appreciative readership had it not been for the graciousness of John B. Cobb. He had become involved in another of Abe's many efforts to engage in Buddhist-Christian dialogue, one in which a serene irenicism combined with a call to find the more comprehensive religious truth, thus making direct engagement with him a uniquely profound experience. John, assisted by Christopher Ives, was heading up a literary exchange (published by Orbis in 1990 as *The Emptying God*) in which a major essay by Abe would be responded to by a number of oft-published figures. As usual, Abe's lengthy paper was distinguished by a careful, respectful reading of Western literature. But it was a sign of his exceptional openness to other views that his sweeping analysis included a challenge to Jewish theologians. This challenge he based on his reading of some of our leading thinkers seeking to come to terms with the Holocaust. John invited me to respond to this section of Abe's paper and so, honored by the suggestion, I became involved in an active, intense, and enlightening exchange with Abe.

His question to Jewish thinkers may be epitomized this way: Zen Buddhism more comprehensively responds to the critical issue of contemporary Jewish theology than does any present Jewish thought. If the Holocaust reveals God's absence and otherwise overwhelms every effort based on prior thought to come to terms with it, why do not Jewish thinkers carry their experience of absence to its logical conclusion, that the ultimate reality is Dynamic Nothingness? In fact, Richard L. Rubenstein, whose work had sparked a parallel discussion in the Jewish community, had himself used somewhat similar language in seeking to describe his own post-Auschwitz spirituality.

In prior generations those few Jewish thinkers who had touched on Buddhism would have dismissed any suggestion that it might be of religious relevance to them by accusing it of otherworldliness and of lacking an activist, redemptive ethics. In those days these charges were common among self-confident religious liberals. It was another sign of Abe's genuineness in dialogue that he not only knew of these criticisms of his tradition but sought to learn from them. Of course, he did so in terms of his grounding insight into reality; but the result seemed to me an extraordinarily creative interpretation of Zen. Thus, he included in the exposition of his position a section on how the emptying work of Dynamic Nothingness, which affects everything, must therefore also eventually include "itself." The logical effect of a negativity of negativity is a positive, and thus Abe's Zen mandates a far stronger ethics than Westerners had been accustomed to hearing about from Buddhists.

Abe's challenge forced me to think through at least two major aspects of my religious heritage and to ask just how I now felt about them. The first of these was the Jewish understanding of God as, so to speak, Nothing. Offhand, that seems utterly incompatible with the central Jewish affirmation that God is One. Yet even a little reflection indicates that if God is absolutely unique, then nothing can be said in human language that is adequate to God's reality. But to be able to say nothing is to acknowledge that God is, in human language, finally Nothing. While some such notions flitted in and out of biblical and rabbinic Judaism and medieval Jewish philosophy, it was thirteenth-century Jewish mysticism, kabbalah, that gave them more substance. Its theosophy understood God as both the ten *sefirot,* the energy centers of the divine self-manifestation (about which a bewildering plethora of things might be said) and the *En Sof,* the No Bounds, and thus "something" about which nothing might be said. And mysticism asserted that these two understandings of God were, in fact, inextricably one. Through the work of the eighteenth-century Hasidic teacher, Dov Baer of Meseritch, an intensification of the Nothingness of the *En Sof* (and thus of the largely illusory nature of created things) became a major theme in subsequent Hasidic thought. In various transformations, it remains a continuing part of Jewish mysticism. Abe could, as I suggested in my response, probably find his most congenial Jewish dialogue partners among such contemporary Jewish mystics and the more hardheaded people who followed in Rubenstein's path.

I was now led to ponder why most of traditional Judaism from the Middle Ages on found this reinterpretation of Judaism unacceptable, perhaps even suspect. More important, even in today's more spiritually tolerant climate, traditionalists and nontraditionalists have overwhelmingly rejected this response to the Holocaust. I had little doubt that their reason for doing so lay more in the consequences of the theory than in their not having had a mystic experience to confirm it. The hegemony of Nothingness does explain the irremediable awfulness of what transpired. But it does so at a stunning cost: it wipes out the distinction between the murderers and the victims. Within the Nothing there can be no distinctions and because it is the only reality, so even the distinction between good and evil finally is not real. When one truly knows the One through mystic experience in Judaism or Enlightenment in Zen, one learns that evil and good have no true reality but are only appearances. For most post-Holocaust Jews that is far more than they can assert—or bear.

On the theoretical level, the issue now became, What ultimacy did I, did Judaism, did most other Jews, attach to goodness (less inadequately, the good/holy)? Was there a "dimension" in which God transcended the good or was it "part" of God's nature? For me, as for most Jews, there is no such "place" in God or a God-beyond-God. Indeed, that is what makes the Holocaust so heinous, that it violates God's very nature and is thus "diabolic." Without the ultimate standard, whence the outrage at the Holocaust?

This should not be taken to imply that Abe was insensitive to the utter tragedy that had occurred. His discussion shows his sharing in its suffering and, as a result of his positive attitude toward activist ethics, his determination that nothing like it should happen again. But ultimately, what "makes sense" of the Holocaust to him is insight into the reality behind it and all other phenomena, namely, that the only ultimate reality is Dynamic Nothingness.

For me, this philosophy made ethics very important but not essential. To the Jewish spirit, as I understand it, a certain ultimacy attaches to a holy deed. For those who share it, no act of insight or understanding ever takes the place of doing, as valuable as the inner life may be on a secondary level. And to teach people that deed doing is a derivative rather than a primary value is inevitably to lessen the motivation that prompts people to act. Crudely put, most Jews, whether leftist secularists or right-wing pietists, believe there is more genuine holiness in political action to prevent another Holocaust than in any metaphysics.

Abe's response to me in *The Emptying God*—and, in part, to some of the Christian participants who had somewhat similar attitudes toward the ethical—clarified the points at issue between us and restated his views with great cogency. This rich, rewarding exchange might have rested there had two things not then happened. It was now suggested that the participants in the original discussion, perhaps joined by some others, might find it valuable to carry the discussion another step forward. The resulting symposium has now been published in the annual journal *Buddhist-Christian Studies* (VOL. 13, 1993), published by the University of Hawai'i Press.

While this project was in process, I was emboldened by Abe's graciousness in our first exchange to ask him for a personal favor. As publisher and editor of a Jewish journal of ethics, *Sh'ma,* it was my custom to thank contributors to our annual fund campaign by sending them a copy of something I had written. I suggested to Abe that he allow me to publish our two exchanges in a booklet. I also asked permission to include an independent piece of mine on interfaith exchanges between theologians. This piece had resulted not only from what had transpired in our dialogue but by comparison with another dialogue that had gone on at the same time with the well-known Episcopalian theologian Paul van Buren. This study was published as "When Theologians Engage in Interfaith Dialogue" in my collection of papers, *Exploring Jewish Ethics* (Detroit: Wayne

State University Press, 1990). Abe could not have been more cordial about this project, extending himself particularly so as to make the manuscript of his latest rejoinder to me available in time for its private publication by *Sh'ma*. This was, of course, in addition to his generosity in allowing me to utilize his prior statements and suggesting which parts of his lengthy original paper published in *The Emptying God* he thought provided a proper precis of his position. The result was a booklet of sixty-eight pages entitled *A Buddhist-Jewish Dialogue*. (I still have a limited number of copies that I shall gladly send to those requesting one from me at 19 Reid Ave., Port Washington, NY 11050.) I mention it to indicate not only that a self-contained record of this rare instance of direct Buddhist-Jewish dialogue exists but to call further attention to Abe's commitment to interfaith discussion and the genial way in which he carried it through.

In this final exchange we realized that, for the moment, we had come as far as we could. How does one move beyond laying bare the bedrock understanding on which all the rest of one's worldview is built? For Abe it was the realization that beneath all the apparent realities, there is truly only Dynamic Nothingness. For me, it meant the recognition of the Holy One who is beyond creation yet intimately involved with it and the humans in it. As it were, for Abe, the truth comes as that illumination that "this," simply, is the way it is. And in a different context, that is what I know. Only we differ rather significantly on what the "this" is.

One might then ask what value was there in speaking when, as might have been anticipated, we ended up in radical disagreement. At least four answers might be given. I came to understand that Zen has creative possibilities that I would otherwise not have imagined it to possess. Abe's searching challenge, one given added power by his evident spirituality, brought me to understand my own faith in greater depth. The human and spiritual concerns in his activist Buddhism and my postliberal Judaism turned out to have a much greater overlap than I had anticipated. And the exposure to so fine a spirit is a precious human experience indeed. So I am happy to be able to add my words of appreciation to those of the many others who have been the direct beneficiaries of his sojourn in the West.

I must, however, add to this account some final words about the one matter on which we not only disagreed but about which our exchanges seemed only to produce a certain measure of surprise that the other was unable to see what was so plain to each of us. As not infrequently happens, it relates to a matter not central to the discussion but to one only peripheral to it, in this case a citation from Nietzsche's *Beyond Good and Evil*. The great iconoclast, as educed by Abe, divides history into what I characterized as premoral, moral, and postmoral periods. He identified the first stage of history with "primitive religions." Abe then applied this by identifying that period with the time of the Old Testament, reserving the second, "moral" stage for the time of the New Testament and the following Christian era. I bridled at this, seeing it as testimony to the ingrained anti-Semitism of much of Western culture and, believing Abe had inadvertently absorbed this with his immersion in our way of thinking, was appalled that the academic colleagues who had obliged him by a prepublication reading of his paper had not called this matter to his attention. Abe, in turn, was most regretful that any such imputation could be brought against his citation or against his readers since it was the furthest possible thing from his mind to cast aspersions on any religion. To clarify this, Abe then gave his interpretation of the passage, seeing it as concerned with different aspects of sacrifice and not historic sequences of morality (neither Nietzsche nor Abe ever using the term *premoral*). This reading, he believes, was also what his colleagues found in his text.

In my response, I acknowledged that I had introduced the term *premoral* into the discussion, justifying myself by the correct citation, "Then, during the moral epoch of mankind [the time of the New Testament and the succeeding Christian era] . . ." To me, this plainly indicates that a time (of the Old Testament) not yet moral had been succeeded by one that was, hence I remained offended. Abe responded with a more detailed exegesis of his intentions at this point in his argument and felt in this light that his previous explanation of his understanding of the contentious citation should now be clear. And, were there any remaining question, he wholeheartedly agreed with my view that a moral era of civilization had begun at least a thousand years before the time of the New Testament.

Have I been unduly sensitive about a possible remnant of anti-Semitism that has unwittingly found a peripheral place in this noble thinker's paper, and have I overreacted to a possible implication of Nietzsche's phrasing? Or is the deprecation of Jews and Judaism so endemic in our culture that despite our own goodwill we unconsciously transmit the germs of anti-Semitism to anyone who comes to participate in our intellectual life? I must leave those questions to my readers who have all the relevant documents available for their own study and evaluation. This is, I am certain, a somewhat "incorrect" matter to raise as part of a celebration of an uncommon spirit's greatly valued contribution to our continuing religious growth. But I suggest that it would not properly honor Masao Abe if I felt I had to repress a matter of considerable ethical urgency to me and to deny readers here this important if prickly point about interfaith dialogue with Jews.

chapter Eighteen

EMPTINESS, HOLY NOTHINGNESS, AND THE HOLOCAUST

Richard L. Rubenstein

I FIRST BECAME CONSCIOUS of my affinity with Buddhism as a result of an encounter with Masao Abe during a job interview at the University of British Columbia in March 1970. In the Vancouver lectures, I expressed my ideas about the "death of God" explicitly and unambiguously. The next day I met with the religious studies faculty. As was so often the case, the faculty consisted primarily of conservative white Protestant males. Not surprisingly, my ideas made them uncomfortable, especially ideas such as God after the death of God as the Holy Nothingness.

As the faculty questioned me, I noticed a small, thin Japanese scholar seated on the floor in the corner behind me. He became increasingly agitated as the discussion continued. Finally he stood up and said, "I'll have you know, what this man is saying is the essence of Mahāyāna Buddhism." "That's strange," I replied. "I haven't studied Mahāyāna Buddhism." "That proves my point!" was his response.

I was not introduced to Abe on that occasion and left without knowing who the Japanese scholar was. Nevertheless, the memory of the encounter remained vivid. Years later, after I got to know Abe, I wondered whether he was that scholar. Recently I asked him. He replied affirmatively but said that he had a slightly different memory of what had transpired. He told me that in Vancouver he wanted to stress that there was "some affinity" between my thinking and Mahāyāna Buddhism but that they were not the same.[1] Whether his memory or mine is more accurate a quarter century later is less important than the crucial role he played in awakening me to an awareness of the similarity between my ideas about God and Buddhist ideas concerning ultimate reality.

It is not strange that I needed Abe to point out the affinity of my thought with Buddhism. Although I had a degree in the history and philosophy of religion, my interests were exclusively Eurocentric until the 1970s. My interest in religion was initially aroused by the rise of European anti-Semitism and the Holocaust. Moreover, during my graduate years it was possible to concentrate at Harvard on Judaism, Christianity, and Islam while paying only perfunctory attention to Eastern religions. Only as a result of that chance encounter with Abe did Buddhist thought become vital for me.

I was finally introduced to Masao Abe by Thomas J. J. Altizer sometime in the 1970s at an annual meeting of the American Academy of Religion. Although only a few words were exchanged, he made a deep impression. Some of the thinkers who have impressed me most deeply were men like Paul Tillich and Gershom Scholem with whom I did not exchange many words. For example, the most important course I took as a doctoral student at Harvard was Tillich's course "Classical German Philosophy."[2] His lectures on Kant, Fichte, Schelling, and, above all, Hegel confirmed my growing conviction that faith in the traditional biblical God of history and election was intellectually untenable, at least for me. My final break with traditional Jewish theology came as a result of a dramatic encounter with a German clergyman, Dean Heinrich Gruber, in Berlin on August 17, 1961. But Tillich gave me the intellectual tools with which to cope with the break when it came.[3]

In spite of, perhaps because of, his profound influence, I was content to listen to Tillich's lectures and read his books without seeking a closer teacher-student relationship. Similarly, no Jewish historian of religion has had a greater influence on me than Gershom Scholem. He spent a year in Cambridge in 1956–57. I met him once or twice but made no attempt to get to know him. Given their enormous authority as thinkers and scholars, both men would have exerted a very strong influence on me in a normal teacher-student relationship. Unsure of myself intellectually and theologically, I wanted to find my own way.

I had an entirely different reaction when I met Masao Abe. I knew intuitively that he was an important thinker, but one who would in no way threaten my intellectual or spiritual autonomy. On the contrary, were the occasion for closer contact ever to arise, he would encourage and foster it. Unlike many religious thinkers, he had little interest in dissonance reduction to fortify the truth claims of his tradition. Elsewhere, I have argued that theologians are intellectual professionals, one of whose principal functions is to reduce the dissonance between their tradition's claim to accurate and exclusive knowledge of God's will and the disconfirming ideas and events that inevitably confront such claims.[4] This function is especially important in nonmystical Judaism and Christianity, both of which claim that God has acted in history in very specific events, such as the giving of the Torah at Sinai and the election of Israel in Judaism and the Crucifixion and Resurrection of Jesus in Christianity. Abe has no doctrine to teach. He does not resort to dogmatic instruction or theological argument to help others overcome *avidya*. (Abe defines *avidya* as "not recognizing the impermanency of worldly things and tenaciously clinging to them as final realities.")[5] What Abe can do is help men and women awaken to their "suchness," that is, their "primordial naturalness," and their "interpenetration with all things."[6] That is very different than securing their doctrinal or theological conformity. And although there is much room for interpretation and doctrinal flexibility in both Judaism and Christianity, there are certain fundamentals in each tradition that must be affirmed. Thus, there can be no Christian mainstream without the affirmation that Christ is Lord or a Jewish mainstream that rejects the election of Israel. In neither tradition is the awakening of the Enlightened Self the fundamental project as it is for Abe.

Because our professional lives were on very different trajectories, Abe and I had few occasions for personal contact other than an exchange of greetings at AAR annual meetings. Nevertheless, both his simple presence and his writings were important reminders that there are a limited number of religious *alternatives* to theism, the most important being mysticism and Buddhism. In my theological writings, I preferred to use language derived from mysticism and dialectical philosophy. Nevertheless, I had also developed a strong sympathy for the Buddhist understanding of the human condition.

Abe was on target when he identified my views as having an affinity with Buddhism. Elsewhere, I have written of the *experiential basis* of my theological views.[7] My theological position had developed as a result of a *progressive liberation from rabbinic theology, experience and reflection on that experience.* Apart from the formative influences of childhood and the Holocaust, which I experienced with great emotional intensity in spite of the safety of my American domicile, my personal psychoanalysis was crucially important in the development of my religious stance. In some measure, the therapeutic experience enabled me to overcome *avidya.* I came to understand the nonsubstantial, interdependent character of all that exists. Psychoanalytic introspection helped me overcome the illusion of the *substantial self.* Analysis made me aware of the extent to which the ego is a distillate of the personal and collective unconscious, as well as the ego's interactions with others who are themselves links in an unending chain of relationships. Somehow, identity persists but does so without a substantial ground. Psychoanalysis also enabled me to understand that my subordination in prayer and personal behavior to the theistic God of Judaism was for me a self-induced form of false consciousness.

Having turned away from theism, I came to comprehend that Nothingness is the Ground and Source of all that exists, a view not unlike the Buddhist teaching about *Śūnyatā.* The following passages about *Śūnyatā* by Abe exemplify the correspondence in our thinking:

> *The ultimate reality for Buddhism is neither Being nor God,*
> *but Sunyata. Sunyata literally means "emptiness" or "voidness"*
> *and can imply "absolute nothingness." This is because Sunyata*
> *is entirely unobjectifiable, unconceptualizable, and unattainable*
> *by reason or will. As such it cannot be any "something" at all.*
> *Accordingly, if Sunyata is conceived as* somewhere outside of
> *or* beyond *one's self-existence, it is not true Sunyata, for Sunyata*
> *thus conceived outside of or beyond one's existence turns into*
> *something which one represents and calls "Sunyata." True Sunya-*

*ta is not even that which is represented and conceived as "Sunya-
ta.". . . True Sunyata is neither outside nor inside, neither external
nor internal, neither transcendent nor immanent
[emphasis added].*[8]

and

> *In one sense, we are right here, right now, in Sunyata. We are
> always involved in the ceaseless emptying movement of Sunyata,
> for there is nothing outside it. And yet, in another sense, we are
> always totally embracing this ceaseless movement of Sunyata
> within ourselves. We are Sunyata at each and every moment of
> our lives. For true Sunyata is not Sunyata thought by us, but Sun-
> yata lived by us [emphasis added].*[9]

Wherever Śūnyatā appears in these passages, "God as the Holy Nothingness" could be substituted with little, if any, alteration of meaning. While
there is no absolute identity between what Abe means by
Śūnyatā and what I mean by Holy Nothingness, the resemblance is very
close and undoubtedly comes out of somewhat similar personal experience.

Nevertheless, I have some reservations concerning the tendency of
Buddhist thinkers to diminish the significance of the socio-historical
dimension of human existence. Abe and other Buddhist thinkers appear
to view the religious dimension of human existence or Śūnyatā as overwhelming the concrete dimension of worldly affairs and history. Abe, for
example, seems to ascribe a lesser significance to the socio-historical
dimension than to Śūnyatā.[10] Abe concedes that Buddhism has had a limited involvement in the social-historical dimension and, where it has been
involved, has focused more on the arts and literature than on social, political, and economic issues. In this connection, Abe further concedes that
"there are many things for Buddhism to learn from Christianity."[11] By contrast, in spite of my profound involvement in theological questions, the
socio-historical dimension has always been of decisive importance for
me. It was, after all, the historical dimension of Jewish identity, especially twentieth-century Jewish history, that had aroused my interest in
Judaism and had kept me rooted in the Jewish religious community.

Having carried on my own internal dialogue with Buddhism for a number of years, I was pleased to receive a copy of *The Emptying God: A Buddhist-Jewish-Christian Conversation* in the summer of 1991 and to learn that Abe had extended his efforts at dialogue to include Jewish thinkers. I was also somewhat surprised. I had visited Japan and Korea more than a dozen times since 1979. I was often invited to lecture and had many opportunities for dialogue with Japanese thinkers. It was obvious to me that ecumenical dialogue with biblical religion in Japan almost always meant dialogue between Buddhists and Christians. This was hardly surprising. Christians vastly outnumber Jews throughout the world, and much of Judaism's religious influence has been mediated to the world by Christianity. There is a small but significant Christian presence in Japan; the Jewish presence is minuscule. Another reason for the limited interfaith dialogue may have been the decidedly pro-Arab position taken by the Japanese government and media in the aftermath of the oil embargo that followed the Arab-Israeli War of 1973.

Abe's interest in extending the dialogue was thus as welcome as it was unexpected. I was further surprised by Abe's interest in the Holocaust. The Holocaust is not a religious problem for Buddhism as it is for Judaism and Christianity. For Jews and Christians alike, the decisive events of Jewish history are part of *Heilsgeschichte*. As such, they have a religio-mythic significance. Religious Jews interpret these events as confirming the existence of the biblical God of covenant and election; Christians view the same events as confirmation of their faith. For both Judaism and Christianity, the question naturally arises whether the Holocaust, one of the most momentous events in all of Jewish history, constitutes a disconfirming event or further confirmation. No such question arises for Buddhism, because it believes in no such God. In addition, the Holocaust is a remote event for Asians. It did not happen on their continent. They were not directly involved in it as were the Europeans and Americans. Hence, I was very curious concerning how Abe would interpret the Holocaust.

I was also curious about the possibility of dialogue between Abe and Eugene B. Borowitz, the Jewish contributor to *The Emptying God*. Borowitz has had a long and distinguished career as a rabbi and theologian. He is an authoritative spokesman for the Jewish religious mainstream. He is also a man of great gifts whom I have known for fifty-one

years. Nevertheless, I was doubtful concerning the degree to which
Borowitz and Abe could enter into fruitful dialogue, not because of any
want of ability or goodwill on their part but because of the radical dis-
similarity between Abe's understanding of ultimate reality and Borowitz's
theological categories. For example, in response to Abe's question concerning how Jews have coped religiously with the Holocaust, Borowitz
followed Emil L. Fackenheim in replying that "Jews have 'coped' . . . with
the radical rupture of the Holocaust by rededicating themselves to living
in the covenant."[12] Rejecting anything like the notion of *avidya*, Borowitz
argues that Jews believe that *all* people "are not fundamentally ignorant
of how they ought to live *because God has given us instruction (Torah) to
that end and continues to do so [emphasis added].*"[13] Hence, "for Judaism,
the primary human task is creating holiness through righteous living."
This is possible because the God who has given his instruction (Torah) to
humanity is holy and "that means, most closely, that God is good."[14]

Borowitz's reading of the Jewish religious mainstream is accurate
and authoritative. Nevertheless, his exposition and Abe's response make
it clear that Buddhism is the polar opposite of biblical religion. Although
there are quasi-theistic versions of Buddhism, Abe rejects any conception
of a theistic God and certainly finds no credibility in the idea of a
covenant between such a God and a particular human community. As
Abe states," . . . unlike Christianity, which talks about God as the ruler
and the savior, Buddhism does not accept the notions of a transcendent
ruler of the universe or of a savior outside one's self."[15] Indeed, as John
Cobb recognizes, "part of the strength of Abe's approach to Christianity
is his uncompromising rejection of theism."[16] I would add that it is equally an element in the strength of his approach to Judaism.

In addition to rejecting theism, Abe also rejects the idea that ultimate reality can be characterized as good. Abe makes a fundamental distinction between the ethical and the religious dimension. Within the ethical dimension, good and evil are relevant categories, but not within the
ultimate religious dimension. According to Abe, ultimate reality is "trans-
human" and, as such, beyond good and evil.[17] By contrast, Borowitz
asserts that God is both holy and good. Western mystics are in agreement
with Abe's insight. They have expressed themselves with such distinctions as *Deus absconditus*, the absolutely unknowable, inaccessible,

hidden Godhead, and *Deus revelatus,* the God who creates the world and reveals his will to men and women. Ethical categories are relevant to the *Deus revelatus,* but not to the *Deus absconditus.* There is a similar distinction in Jewish mysticism between the *En Sof,* the Godhead, or *Urgrund,* the ultimate ground of all being that is beyond will and intellect, and the domain of the lower *sefirot* or divine emanations that build the "manifest and visible universe."[18]

Borowitz's whole religious stance is that of the Jewish religious mainstream. It requires that God be both holy and good. Without such a God, it would be impossible for Borowitz to deny *avidya* and claim that men and women are not "fundamentally ignorant" of how they ought to live because they have been divinely instructed. In reality, Borowitz would be hard-pressed to find much in either Jewish history or everyday human relations to render credible his assertion that men and women have been instructed concerning how to create "holiness through righteous living." Indeed, the phrase "holiness through righteous living" has a formulaic and incantational quality, as if it could be rendered credible by repetition. In no way does it correspond with ordinary experience, as does Abe's identification of overcoming *avidya* as the fundamental human problem. I wonder where one could find those Jews or non-Jews actively engaged in creating "holiness through righteous living." Even the majority of the clergy and religious thinkers appear to be less interested in creating holiness than in living decent lives and meeting their responsibilities as best they can. Can much more be required of any human being? While I understand the need to overcome *avidya,* I suspect that it would be difficult to relate to people who are trying to create "holiness through righteous living." The formula sounds better on paper than in real life. The Roman Catholic Church may have been on to something when it provided such people with the domain of otherworldly asceticism.

Although Borowitz strongly disagrees with me on theology, he did point out in his essay that my position is very close to Abe's on the issue of theism.[19] He also told Abe that I was the "only . . . Jew who has written extensively on the Holocaust" who has "followed the logic of the problem of evil to the conclusion that God cannot be good."[20] Citing a passage in which I affirm that "in the final analysis, omnipotent Nothingness is Lord of all creation," Borowitz suggested that there is "much" in what I have written that might lead to "fruitful dialogue" between Abe and me.[21]

Borowitz was, of course, correct. There has been fruitful dialogue between Abe and me from the moment that he spoke at the University of British Columbia, when I did not know his name, to this very day. However, the most important opportunities to enter into dialogue came after the publication of *The Emptying God*. As a result of the fruitfulness of the dialogue between Abe and his dialogue partners, Abe invited me to write an essay for a second volume of responses to his major essay "Kenotic God and Dynamic Sunyata."[22]

Abe offered a Buddhist interpretation of the Holocaust in his essay "Kenotic God and Dynamic Sunyata." The title of my essay is "Holocaust, Sunyata and Holy Nothingness: An Essay in Interreligious Dialogue."[23] Writing a response to Abe gave me the most sustained opportunity to grapple with his teachings. The second major occasion for dialogue came when Abe invited me to participate in one of a series of four Buddhist-Christian-Jewish conversations sponsored by the Purdue University Interfaith Project, directed by Donald W. Mitchell. Our subject was "Interfaith Perspectives on the Holocaust, God and Evil." In the face-to-face Purdue dialogue, we presented much of what we had covered in our essays. We were largely in agreement in our understanding of ultimate reality. We were even in agreement on many issues arising out of the Holocaust. In contrast to Borowitz, both Abe and I agreed that the Holocaust was not an absolute evil, although for different reasons. For my part, the Holocaust could have been an absolute evil only if no good had come out of it. While the *unintended consequences* of the Holocaust that can be characterized as good do not remotely outweigh its evil, some good did come out of it, including the birth of the State of Israel. That development gave the Jews of Europe, the Middle East, and North Africa the option of escaping from the ethnic and religious hatred endemic to those regions of the Diaspora. I also agreed with Abe that the Holocaust constitutes a profound, perhaps an insurmountable problem for religious liberals like Borowitz who affirm the existence of the biblical God of covenant and election after their own fashion.[24] I can easily second Abe's rhetorical question "I cannot help but ask how Jewish people understand that the holy/good God ultimately allowed such a uniquely horrible event as the Holocaust to occur."

Abe then made explicit his agreement with me concerning the direction of post-Holocaust:

> *If I understand Borowitz correctly, he suggests two possible*
> *approaches . . . . One is return to the God of the Covenant*
> *through belief in the ultimate commanding power of living in*
> *holy goodness. The other is a shift in the direction of mysticism as*
> *suggested by Richard L. Rubenstein. Borowitz opts for the first . . .*
> *I myself support the second approach.*[25]

Further on, Abe stated, "To me, this realization of absolute nothingness is the basis of my life and the source of my activity. In this sense I find great affinity with Rubenstein, to whom God is 'the Holy Nothingness,' and with Jewish mysticism in general."[26]

The similarity in our views is, I believe, due to the fact that both Abe and I arrived at our understanding of ultimate reality as a result of what Abe has termed "personal existential experience." Speaking from my experience with the Jewish community, I can testify that there is enormous pressure to conform theologically to certain basic ideas such as the belief in the God of covenant and election. There is much room for interpretation, but the penalty for going outside the boundaries is to be treated as an outcast by the community. Understandably, this is not a price most thinkers are willing or able to pay.

There are, however, a number of issues on which Abe and I disagree, especially concerning the Holocaust. For example, I believe that, as a Japanese, Abe takes upon himself far more responsibility for the Holocaust than is warranted by any reading of the event. During World War II the Imperial Japanese Government did more to rescue and protect Jews than many of the Allied governments that were at war with Nazi Germany. Before and during the war, the Imperial Japanese Government repeatedly rejected demands by the German Foreign Office to treat Jews in Japan differently than other foreigners. When SS Colonel Joseph Meisinger, who had served in Warsaw in 1939, demanded that the Japanese exterminate the 20,000 Jewish refugees in occupied Shanghai, the Japanese refused.[27] In spite of this record, Abe asserts that "in the deepest sense I myself participated in the Holocaust."[28] According to Abe, his avowal of responsibility arises from his realization of our collective karma in which "nothing happens in the universe entirely unrelated to us insofar as we realize that everything human is rooted in the fundamental ignorance, *avidya,* innate in human nature."[29]

I find Abe's explanation of his "responsibility" for the Holocaust in terms of karma and *avidya* ahistorical. It is meaningless as an attempt to assert a connection for good or ill with a definite historical event. Since Abe and I were both young adults during World War II, by his logic I and everyone alive at the time share equally in responsibility for the Holocaust. Abe is, of course, correct in asserting the interdependence of all things in the universe. In that sense, all alive at the time were implicated, but that idea trivializes the distinction between the actual perpetrators and the rest of the world, not to mention the victims. To the best of my knowledge, no one has expressed the difficulty in Abe's avowal of responsibility better than John B. Cobb, Jr., in his comment that "a specific event requires a specific explanation" because "original sin and avidya are always with us but events like the Holocaust are fortunately not everyday occurrences."[30]

I also take issue with Abe's notion that it is possible for the victims and the perpetrators of the Holocaust to achieve "solidarity" through the "realization of the collective karma and fundamental ignorance inherent in human beings." It is certainly possible for Jews and non-Nazi Germans to enter into fruitful relationships. Indeed, I have enjoyed such relationships. No such relations are possible between Jews and Nazis or Neo-Nazis, who would gladly repeat Auschwitz if they could, while denying that the Holocaust ever happened. At the ultimate religious level, the "solidarity" Abe posits as possible between Jews and the perpetrators of the Holocaust is so disconnected from concrete experience that I cannot discern any intelligible meaning in it.

My disagreements with Abe may have something to do with our very different life situations. Beginning with *The Cunning of History,* most of my writing, research, and public activities have been concerned with the concrete interrelatedness of religion, politics, and society.[31] Having resolved to my own satisfaction such theological issues as the death of the biblical God of covenant and election and God as Holy Nothingness, I saw no reason to spend the rest of my life defending or further elaborating upon my theological positions. Undoubtedly, my keen interest in seeking to understand the kind of human world in which events like the Holocaust and "ethnic cleansing" are possible greatly influenced my turn toward what Abe calls the socio-historical dimension. By contrast, Abe has chosen to be an interpreter of Zen Buddhism. Hence, the ultimate religious dimension figures more importantly in his work than in mine.

As noted above, Abe is not engaged in the enterprise of dissonance reduction, as are most authoritative Jewish thinkers such as Fackenheim and Borowitz. Their project is mainly an attempt to reduce the dissonance between the Jewish tradition and those ideas and events in the contemporary world that threaten disconfirmation. That is even true of Fackenheim, the most radical of the mainstream thinkers. As theologians, dissonance reduction is their paramount vocational responsibility. If necessary, experience is to be falsified, as when God is proclaimed to be both holy and good, not out of dishonesty, but rather out of motives not unlike those of Dostoyevsky's Grand Inquisitor. Still in the shadow of Auschwitz, a wounded people needs the show of mystery and miracle, if not magic, to make some sense of their terrible experience. And the dissonance reducers give it to them out of loving concern and a resolve that Hitler shall not gain "yet other posthumous victories."[32]

Referring to Borowitz's assertion that Jews are to be holy/good and do holy/good deeds because God is holy/good, Abe comments: "I admire such faith and hope, but my personal existential experience does not allow me to accept this sort of faith and hope as realistic."[33] To repeat, at this point agreement between Abe and me is strongest. As faithful as he is to the Buddhist tradition, Abe is not so much engaged in a dissonance-reduction defense of his tradition as in working out the logic of his personal existential experience. He is supported in this endeavor by the fact that the credibility of Buddhism does not depend on the veracity of its claims concerning the meaning of particular events in history, as is the case in both Judaism and Christianity. Here, the ahistorical character of Buddhism serves thinkers like Abe well.

Similarly, my refusal to engage in dissonance reduction on behalf of the Jewish religious mainstream was not motivated by a spirit of rebellion but by an overwhelming imperative to be faithful to my own experience and to recognize genuinely disconfirming ideas and events for what they truly are. Whenever I see Abe, there is an electric moment of recognition. I rejoice that I am in the presence of a kindred soul.

Part Four

THE BUDDHIST-CHRISTIAN DIALOGUE

chapter Nineteen

THE
ABE-PANNENBERG
ENCOUNTER

Joseph A. Bracken, S.J.
Afterword by Wolfhart Pannenberg

ONE OF MASAO ABE'S KEY POINTS in recent years has been that
contemporary interreligious dialogue must be not only informative but
transformative for the parties to the dialogue. That is, individuals should
not only come to understand one another's religious traditions better but
likewise deepen and widen the reflective grasp of their own religious tradition. Something like this seems to have happened over the years in the
written and verbal exchange between Masao Abe and Wolfhart Pannenberg on issues connected with the Buddhist-Christian dialogue. I shall
briefly try to make clear how Pannenberg's theology has been affected by
contact with Abe's reflections on the relation between Christianity and
Buddhism. At the same time, I shall indicate how Pannenberg remains
opposed to further agreement with Abe on certain key issues. Then by
way of conclusion, I shall suggest possible ways in which further
exchange between them could be facilitated.

In a chapter of a book on Christian spirituality published in the
early 1980s, Pannenberg indicates how reflection on Abe's thought has led
him to a deeper appreciation of the correspondence of Luther's doctrine
of justification (as opposed to that of the medieval scholastics) to the
Buddhist doctrine of the self.[1] In an essay entitled "Man and Nature in

Christianity and Buddhism," Abe had conjectured that Buddhist Awakening and Christian conversion agree "insofar as the death of the human ego is essential to salvation."[2] Pannenberg concurs but points out that medieval scholastics (and indeed many other scholars, even to the present day) misinterpreted Paul's reference to the "inmost self" in Romans 7:22, conceiving it simply as the rational nature within humans that is in ongoing conflict with bodily instincts and desires. Only Luther realized "that in the event of regeneration according to Paul not only some quality of the subject but the subject itself is changed."[3] Accordingly, human beings are helpless to save themselves on their own; only through faith in Christ whereby Christ lives in them and they in Christ can they achieve liberation from bondage to the old self.[4]

Yet Pannenberg carefully points out the residual differences between himself and Abe on this issue. In Abe's mind, the Christian experience of conversion remains dualistic because within it the Christian still relates to Jesus Christ as a savior figure or transcendent reality, whereas a Buddhist in the experience of Awakening has overcome all forms of dualism, even the opposition between nirvana and samsara.[5] In response, Pannenberg once again turns to Luther for an answer. According to Luther, the Christian is *conformed* to Christ so that there exists a dynamic unity between Christ and the believer, although not a unity without differentiation. "As Jesus discriminated himself from the Father in accepting the Father's commission and judgment, so the believer discriminates his or her own person from Jesus in accepting his service and promise. But precisely because of such self-differentiation there is communion between the Son and the Father, and also between the believer and Jesus Christ."[6]

Pannenberg then notes that this correlation between differentiation and unity within Christianity can ultimately be resolved only in terms of ultimate reality. "Christianity can withstand the Buddhist critique of dualism only if the Trinity is not set apart from creation and salvation history but is explained as the Christian answer to the question of how God and the world can be different in such a way that each is nevertheless not separate from the other."[7] Yet differences in perspective still remain. Whereas the Christian thus identifies with Christ in a Trinitarian understanding of the ultimate, the Buddhist identifies not with the Buddha but with Emptiness, which has no existence in and of itself.[8]

Emptiness, of course, implies an ego-transcending experience, not a transcendent object. Indeed, it is "an event of rapture that carries us beyond ourselves, just as Luther envisioned the spiritual event of faith."[9] But even here, both similarities and differences between Christian and Buddhist perspectives come to mind. Whereas the Christian experience of faith "encourages hope for a definitive future of individual existence beyond this transitory state, the hope for a resurrection of the dead and for a renewed heaven and earth,"[10] the Buddhist experience of Emptiness results in "a liberated experience in the midst of the transitory world of Samsara."[11] This difference aside, both experiences are eminently positive and affirmative of a new self that has been liberated from bondage to the anxiety-ridden, ego-centered self of ordinary life. Above all, for a Lutheran Christian, one is thereby liberated from an artificial sense of guilt and sinfulness as the supposed condition of personal salvation. "Sin is the common denominator of everything that resists the spirit of transformation into the glory of God."[12] But while real enough in its own right, sin is a strictly provisional reality, destined to be superseded by the more positive experience of faith in the Divine Promise with its natural affinity to the Buddhist experience of Emptiness.

In brief then, Pannenberg evidently came to a much deeper appreciation of his own faith as a Lutheran Christian in and through careful reflection on Abe's comparison of the conversion experience within Christianity and the experience of Awakening within Buddhism. The second encounter to be documented here was a face-to-face exchange between Abe and Pannenberg at Earlham College in Richmond, Indiana, in 1992. It involved a similar testing of the differences and similarities in perspective between Buddhism and Christianity in terms of the notion of ultimate reality. Antecedent to their meeting at Earlham College in the context of a forum on interfaith dialogue, Abe had published an essay entitled "Kenotic God and Dynamic Sunyata" in which he attempted a new interpretation of Philippians 2:6–11 from the perspective of the Buddhist experience of *Śūnyatā*, or Emptiness.[13] Pannenberg, accordingly, delivered a response to this essay by Abe; and Abe then offered a counter-response.[14]

Pannenberg first takes note of his earlier exchange with Abe in terms of the relation between the conventional ego and the true self but then focuses his attention on what he regards as the much deeper issue, namely, the nature of ultimate reality within Buddhism and Christianity. The first point to be considered is whether *Śūnyatā*, like the God of Christianity, is genuinely transcendent of the reality of this world as well as completely immanent within it. In Pannenberg's mind, Abe does not seem to affirm this kind of transcendence with respect to *Śūnyatā*. Instead, Abe claims, "We are Sunyata in each and every moment of our lives."[15] In this sense, the self and *Śūnyatā* are dynamically one. As Abe explains in his essay, "True Sunyata is nothing but the true self and the true self is nothing but True Sunyata.[16] Thus, *Śūnyatā* has no reality apart from the self and is, accordingly, not transcendent of the self as God is thought to be transcendent of the self within Christianity.

Pannenberg likewise appeals here to Donald Mitchell's analysis of the same text and the latter's conclusion that Abe "posits this world as the locus of ultimate reality."[17] Yet if *Śūnyatā* is thus simply identified with what happens in this world, then it is not strictly comparable with the God of Christianity. Abe, to be sure, frequently uses self-referential language with respect to *Śūnyatā* as though it were some transcendent entity: e.g., "Sunyata is not self-affirmative, but *thoroughly* self-negative. In other words, emptiness not only empties everything else but also empties itself."[18] But, says Pannenberg, it is not clear what is the self to which reference is made, especially since Abe refers to *Śūnyatā* as "agentless spontaneity."[19] It would appear that *Śūnyatā* is simply a name for "the all pervading process of change" and that self-referential language—above all, language that speaks in a personal vein about the wisdom and compassion of *Śūnyatā*—is metaphorical rather than literal.[20]

Within the context of Philippians 2:6–11, on the contrary, Jesus Christ is clearly an agent who empties himself in relation to the Father and thus manifests himself as the Son of God.[21] But, unlike *Śūnyatā* with respect to the human self, the Son of God is not simply identical with Jesus; in other words, the Son does not give up his divinity in becoming human. The unity of the Son with Jesus is a unity in differentiation, as noted above. Furthermore, says Pannenberg, the Father unlike the Son does not participate in this self-emptying activity. "Nowhere [in the New Testament] is it said that the Father emptied himself, nor is it a logical implication of the self-emptying action of the Son. To the contrary, this kenotic action on the part of the Son is described as obedience to the Father and thus presupposes the identity of the Father and of his commission to the Son."[22] Hence, Abe is mistaken in claiming that the kenosis of Christ "inevitably leads" to the idea of a kenosis of God the Father as well.[23]

Pannenberg concedes that many Christian theologians have linked the idea of self-emptying with agape, or self-giving love. Furthermore, the notion of self-giving love is omnipresent in the Christian Bible and certainly applied to the activity of the Father as well as that of the Son with respect to their creatures. But in Pannenberg's judgment, it is a mistake to identify self-abnegation or kenosis with agape. For the kenosis of the Son in Philippians 2:7 "is not connected with love for the world but with obedience to the Father (Philippians 2:8). On the other hand, the love of the Father as mentioned in John and Paul certainly involves an element of sacrifice, but the Father does not surrender himself, but he surrenders his Son. This certainly shows that love can be costly, even for God the Father, but it does not imply his self-abnegation."[24] Indeed, if the Father had emptied himself, he would not have been able to raise Jesus from the dead. Thus, although we may rightly speak about a mutual devotedness of Father, Son, and Spirit toward one another and a mutual dependence on one another, we may not properly speak of a mutual self-emptying toward one another. Only the Son—above all, in the Son's incarnation as Jesus—is self-emptying, that is, fully obedient with respect to the Father.[25]

Pannenberg concludes, therefore, that "the notion of kenosis is of limited value in Buddhist-Christian dialog."[26] The real convergence between Buddhist Emptiness and Christian faith in the Trinitarian God is to be found elsewhere, namely, in "the mutuality of love between the Trinitarian persons which can be conceived of as suprapersonal though becoming manifest only in the Trinitarian persons."[27] What he has in mind here is the divine essence conceived as an all-encompassing "field of perichoretic love" in which the three divine persons exist and are dynamically related to one another.[28] Within this same field of mutual love or mutual indwelling, moreover, the Christian mystic likewise exists "by sharing in the sonship of Jesus and thus in his spiritual relation to the Father."[29] The Buddhist notion of *Śūnyatā*, insofar as it is conceived as the interconnectedness of everything with everything else, is thus "a distant adumbration of the Trinitarian spirit of love, but the latter cannot be reduced to emptiness."[30]

In response to this pointed criticism of his attempt to link the God of Christian theism with "dynamic Sunyata," Masao Abe initially chose to repeat his own understanding of Emptiness or true nirvana and to contrast this with Pannenberg's own understanding of the God-world relationship within Christianity. That is, he emphasized that "true nirvana is not [a] static state of transcendence but a dynamic movement between samsara so-called and nirvana so-called without attachment to either."[31] Hence, true nirvana is equally balanced between nirvana as opposed to samsara and samsara as opposed to nirvana; it exhibits no preference for either side of this logical opposition. Within the God-world relationship as Pannenberg presents it, however, God is clearly more transcendent of the world than immanent within it. Hence, God within this scheme is, from a Buddhist perspective, not truly ultimate because God is still opposed to the world rather than dialectically one with it.[32]

Then, with reference to Pannenberg's insistence that the Son of God in the act of self-emptying did not give up his divinity, Abe reaffirms his conviction that the act of self-emptying must result in the Son of God's becoming totally identified with the man Jesus. For only thus is the Son's self-emptying "brought here to self-fulfillment as the savior."[33] Likewise, with reference to Pannenberg's claim that there is no evidence in the Christian Bible for self-emptying activity on the part of the Father, Abe counterargues that "the kenosis of the Son of God is based on the *will* of God. It is commissioned by God the Father. But, in the case of God the Father, kenosis or self-emptying is implied in the original *nature* of God who is really love."[34] Thus, Abe concedes that the self-emptying activity of the Son is an act of obedience in response to the will of the Father. But he continues to affirm that self-emptying and agape or self-giving love are basically one and the same activity; moreover, this activity constitutes "the dynamism of the innertrinitarian life of the triune God."[35]

Pannenberg, according to Abe, fails to see that Emptiness, or the self-emptying activity within the Trinity, is paradoxically synonymous with fullness (just as in Mahāyāna Buddhism). The self-emptying activity of the Son, for example, results in the fullness of the Godhead being present in Jesus after his resurrection and exaltation. Likewise, God the Father's "total kenosis is God's self-emptying for absolutely 'nothing' other than God's own fulfillment as love."[36] In this way, Abe argues, the nihilism of

Friedrich Nietzsche and other atheistic philosophers is overcome, and a new relationship between Buddhism and Christianity is established. For in both religions the experience of Absolute Nothingness is the basis for the saving experience of unselfish love or compassion. The latter, in turn, is the deeper ground of the spiritual life within both religions.

In trying to assess this second exchange between Pannenberg and Abe, one must bear in mind that Pannenberg's understanding of the Trinity, as set forth in the first volume of his *Systematic Theology*, demands that the three divine persons be defined in their individual self-identity by their distinctive activities vis-à-vis one another. "The Father does not merely beget the Son. He also hands over his kingdom to him and receives it back from him. The Son is not merely begotten of the Father. He is also obedient to him and he thereby glorifies him as the one God. The Spirit is not just breathed. He also fills the Son and glorifies him in his obedience to the Father, thereby glorifying the Father himself."[37] Accordingly, Pannenberg seemingly must resist Abe's proposal that not only the Son but likewise the Father expresses himself through self-emptying love as the expression of their common nature. Yet in reflecting upon Pannenberg's description of the divine intratrinitarian relations, one might well conclude that self-giving love is *generically* characteristic of the activity of the three divine persons toward one another even though it *specifically* takes on a new modality within each person with respect to the other two. In handing over the kingdom to the Son, for example, the Father engages in a form of kenosis, or self-emptying love, even as the Son in turn by his obedience to the Father likewise exercises self-giving love in handing back the kingdom to the Father at the end of the world. "By their work the Son and Spirit serve the monarchy of the Father. Yet the Father does not have his kingdom or monarchy [in effect, his deity] without the Son and Spirit, but only through them."[38] Abe may be right, then, in insisting that within Christianity as within Mahāyāna Buddhism, Absolute Emptiness is paradoxically synonymous with ontological fullness.

The deeper issue, however, has to do with the question of agency, specifically whether *Sunyata* in its relation to the true self can be compared with the Son of God in the latter's relation to Jesus. I believe that Pannenberg is correct in insisting on a lack of parity here. *Sunyata*, after all, is an activity, not an entity; yet only entities are agents in the strict sense. Accordingly, *Śūnyatā* does not correspond to the person of the Son or to the person of the Father; rather, it corresponds to their common nature, the *generic* activity of self-emptying love, as noted above. An activity, to be sure, is indistinguishable from the entity in which it is at work. Thus, Abe is correct in urging that "true Sunyata is nothing but the true self and the true self is nothing but true Sunyata." But one cannot say with equal facility that the Son of God becomes without remainder Jesus of Nazareth and that Jesus of Nazareth is without further qualification a divine being, the Son of God. All that we can affirm is that there is a dynamic unity in differentiation here between two distinct centers of activity, the one divine and the other human, in virtue of the common activity of self-emptying love toward the Father. Neither center of activity can be totally emptied out into the other.

Yet even with this necessary qualification, there may well be in the comments of Abe and Pannenberg cited above the basis for an unexpected accord between Mahāyāna Buddhists and Christians on the nature of ultimate reality. For in different ways both Abe and Pannenberg make basically the same claim. That is, both agree that the nature or essence of God is self-giving love, or agape. Hence, if *Śūnyatā* is, as noted above, the activity of self-emptying love, then *Śūnyatā is* equivalently the divine nature. Accordingly, it is not God—that is, one of the three divine persons; but it is divine in that it is the divine nature, the principle of activity whereby the three divine persons exist and are dynamically related to one another. The operative distinction here is that between *person* and *nature* within the Godhead. The two concepts refer to the same reality but are rationally distinct from each other in that they specify different dimensions of the total reality of God.[39]

If this distinction be granted, then one may reasonably affirm that Buddhist philosophers like Abe and Christian theologians like Pannenberg are quite possibly dealing with the same ultimate reality but from different perspectives or dimensions, so that what is in the foreground of attention for the one is in the background for the other and vice versa. Christian theologians traditionally have focused on the entitative reality of God in terms of three persons dynamically related to one another. As a result, they have tended to leave the underlying nature of God, that which enables the divine persons to exist and to relate to one another, relatively unexplored. To his credit, as noted above, Pannenberg has recently reopened the question of the underlying nature of God by describing it as a force-field or "field of perichoretic love" both for the divine persons and for Christian mystics who conform themselves to Christ in his relationship to the Father.[40] What still has to be explored, of course, is the deeper relationship between this field-oriented understanding of the divine nature within Pannenberg's theology and Buddhist Emptiness.

Abe and other Buddhist philosophers, on the other hand, seem to have focused almost exclusively on the reality of *Śūnyatā* as a never-ending activity and thus to have given insufficient attention to the various "forms" or entitative instantiations of that activity. Admittedly, within a traditional Buddhist perspective, these forms are transitory and thus not worthy of the respect to be accorded to ultimate reality. Yet as the celebrated verse from the *Heart Sūtra* makes clear,[41] Emptiness apart from forms is just as meaningless as forms apart from Emptiness. Hence, more attention should be given by Buddhists to the forms produced by *Śūnyatā*, above all, those representing divine persons as demanded by the Christian understanding of the Trinity. In particular, Abe might then consider abandoning the paradoxical language of "agentless agent" with respect to the self-emptying activity of the Son of God.[42] More precisely, one should say that the Son of God is indeed an agent who remains as such before, during, and after the act of self-emptying. But the Son exercises that agency only in virtue of the divine nature, or what Abe calls *Śūnyatā*. Here, too, therefore, the classical distinction between *person* and *nature* within the Godhead makes clear what remains somewhat confused in Abe's understanding of the kenosis of the Son, valuable as it is in other respects.

Reflection on these two exchanges between a celebrated Buddhist scholar and a noted Christian theologian make clear that much good can be accomplished by interreligious dialogue. The participants effectively test the limits of each other's cherished beliefs. Inevitably, there are subtle presuppositions in the thinking of each individual which go undetected until challenged by the inquiring mind of someone from a different religious tradition. The results may be at first somewhat contentious. But as the second exchange between Abe and Pannenberg seems to indicate, eventually they open up hitherto unexpected possibilities for probing the mystery of ultimate reality to which all religious persons are inexorably drawn.

AFTERWORD: MASAO ABE IN MY ENCOUNTER WITH BUDDHISM
wolfhart Pannenberg

The encounter with Buddhism provides one of the more promising forms of interreligious dialogue for Christian theologians. There is a remarkable correspondence between the two religious views concerning the human predicament—as I became aware of in dialogue with Masao Abe. More specifically, it is the Lutheran criticism of the self-righteousness of the self-affirming ego that corresponds to the Buddhist doctrine on the self. It is only beyond ourselves (*extra nos in Christo*) that we obtain our true self, in the act of faith in Jesus Christ. That relationship with Christ, of course, is a personal one, and there lies the difference with the Śūnyatā doctrine of Buddhists. But even at this point, there might be a possibility of further convergence. This possibility was suggested to me first by Keiji Nishitani's book on religion when he acknowledged that absolute reality does have a personal aspect as well as an impersonal one. While Nishitani assumed that in the Christian conception of God, only the personal aspect is affirmed, it seemed to me that the Christian doctrine on God as trinity involves both, the personal and an impersonal element, because the one "essence" the three persons share is not once more a person in its own right in addition to Father, Son, and Spirit. The one divine essence of Father, Son, and Spirit is supra-personal. It is not separate from the three persons, however, but exists only as it is manifest through Father, Son, and Spirit—more precisely in their mutual relationships with one another, that the classical doctrine described in terms of a mutual *perichoresis*, or indwelling of the three, and that in fact expresses the divine dynamics of love.

Masao Abe, then, seems correct in assuming that there is some correspondence between the Christian conception of God as love and the Buddhist understanding of absolute reality as Śūnyatā. But his way of arguing to this effect with the biblical notion of kenosis (Philippians 2:7) is somewhat unfortunate, as I tried to show at Earlham in 1992. In the

first place, Paul in Philippians refers to a moral attitude of self-abnegation but does not intend the vanishing of the person of Jesus Christ, the
Son of God. Though in his way to the Cross, he is obedient to the Father
unto his own death, he is rescued by the Father and given the title of
highest authority *(kyrios)*. The moral self-abnegation in obedience to the
Father is intended to express the contrast to the first Adam who immod-
erately affirmed himself in disobedience against God. The act of kenosis
does not destroy the person of the Son; on the contrary, it expresses the
very nature of his personality in subordination to the Father. Much less is
it possible (secondly) to attribute the notion of kenosis in the sense of
self-annihilation to the Father. Joseph Bracken, in his account of the
issue, is certainly right in affirming that there is a self-giving relationship
of the Father to the Son as well as in the obedience of the Son in relation
to the Father. But self-giving love is not identical in all particular cases
with kenosis. Only the self-giving love of the Son in his obedience to the
Father is called kenosis by Paul. The fatherly love of God is another matter, though it is in its own way no less an example of self-giving. Even in
transferring his kingdom to the Son, the Father does not "empty" himself,
since it is the very mission of the Son to establish the Father's kingdom
on earth.

Thus, the argument from kenosis seems inconclusive, in spite of a
vague association of the term with Emptiness (*Śūnyatā*). It is only in the
trinitarian doctrine, where the mutuality of love between Father, Son, and
Spirit is taken not only as interpersonal relationship but as the common
essence of the three persons, and thus in a certain sense as prior to their
diversity, that the point of contact with the Buddhist *Śūnyatā* becomes
apparent. But even here one has to be careful to observe that the common essence of the three persons does not have any separate reality prior
to them but exists only in their interrelationship. From a Christian perspective, the Buddhist *Śūnyatā*—precisely concerning its positive meaning as expressing the dynamic nature of absolute reality—appears as
rather vague because it lacks the medium of personal interrelationship.
This appears to be somewhat different in the case of the Pure Land Buddhists. But even there the absolute reality does not seem to be intrinsically constituted by personal interrelation like in the Christian Trinity.

The theses of Masao Abe on kenosis, even when provoking a critical response from Christian theologians, retain the particular merit of

drawing attention to the correspondence between the Christian conception of God as love and the Buddhist *Śūnyatā* doctrine. Undoubtedly, the convergence between the two religious conceptions could further increase if the Buddhist could further explore the manifestations of *Śūnyatā* in *interpersonal relationships,* not in any such relationship, of course, but in a peculiar case of such a relationship that discloses the positive meaning of absolute reality as love.

chapter Twenty

HANS KÜNG QUESTIONS MASAO ABE: ON EMPTINESS AND A GLOBAL ETHIC

Ruben L. F. Habito

AMONG THE MANY HIGHLIGHTS of the 1993 Parliament of the World's Religions held in Chicago was a proposal initiated by Hans Küng, Leonard Swidler, and others, addressed especially to members of various religious traditions, called "Towards a Global Ethic."[1] This declaration is an attempt to lay down a set of common guidelines, drawing from the most fundamental precepts and practices found in the various religious traditions of the world, for ways of living and acting that would respond to the critical situation we are facing as Earth's community.

This essay highlights key points made by Hans Küng, representing a Christian standpoint, in his conversations with Masao Abe on the Buddhist notion of Emptiness. But rather than simply repeating and summarizing Küng's comments made in response to Abe, already available in print elsewhere,[2] I shall venture to "read the mind of Hans Küng," based on a perusal of his other (especially, more recent) writings and focus on a single question he would conceivably pose to Abe. The question is, Can

Emptiness ground a commitment to a global ethic (such as the one proposed by Küng and others at the 1993 Parliament of the World's Religions)?

First, a rough sketch of Küng's recent thinking, as manifested in his writings on interreligious dialogue, especially on the establishment of ecumenical criteria for religious truth, needs to be established. Then the question in the context of Küng's Christian standpoint as he considers the Buddhist notion of Emptiness explained by Masao Abe will be situated. This essay concludes with some reflections on the implications of encounters between Buddhists and Christians with reference to their respective responses to the tasks outlined in "Towards a Global Ethic."

ON ESTABLISHING ECUMENICAL CRITERIA FOR RELIGIOUS TRUTH

As a Roman Catholic who launched his theological career with a major treatise on the theology of Karl Barth (*Justification,* 1957) Hans Küng has been concerned with mutual understanding and dialogue among the various Christian churches. Küng's theological interest has thus been "ecumenical" right from the start as he engaged in conversations aiming at mutual understanding between Christians across denominational lines.

Since the 1980s, Hans Küng has focused his attention on the question of religious plurality and on issues arising in the context of interreligious dialogue. For Küng the word *ecumenical* now comes to be used in a sense closer to its literal meaning (*oikumene*, "the inhabited world"). That is, it is no longer confined only to the relationships among Christian churches but in a more comprehensive way refers to the dialogue taking place among members of the various religious traditions of the world. His writings in this regard call attention to and are themselves inspired by "the awakening of a global ecumenical consciousness."[3] This new consciousness is the basis of his explorations toward a new paradigm for theological reflection.[4]

In this light, a crucial question that Küng has addressed is the one that is inevitably asked by a Christian confronted with the *very fact* of the existence and vitality of other world religious traditions with differing claims to ultimate truth: Is there any theologically responsible way that allows Christians to accept the truth of other religions without giving up the truth of their own religion and, with that, their own identity?[5] Behind this question is Küng's concern to avoid the two extremes of a *conceited absolutism* identified with a standpoint of exclusivity and superiority, on the one hand, and a superficial and *irresponsible relativism* also characterized by an arbitrary pluralism and indifferentism on the other.[6] An underlying issue here is the question of the criterion for truth—specifically, religious truth. Küng addresses this question in an essay entitled "Is There One True Religion?"[7] and proposes a set of "ecumenical criteria" for religious truth. Küng notes first of all that in the context of the religious dimension, what is true *(verum)* and what is good *(bonum)* intersect and overflow into each other: truth and meaningfulness in the context of religion are inseparable from goodness and value. Thus, truth in religion is not simply a matter of describing a state of affairs in a way that one is able to separate such a description from one's personal stance vis-à-vis that state of affairs but is also by its very nature as religious truth, a matter of engagement, commitment, of praxis.[8] With this general principle in the foreground, Küng then goes on in his proposal for the establishment of ecumenical criteria for religious truth by way of "an inward spiral," first outlining a general ethical criterion, then a general religious criterion, and finally a specifically Christian criterion for religious truth.

The general ethical criterion hinges upon the basic question, What is *good* for the human being, in all the dimensions of human existence? In this light, insofar as a religion enhances our humanness as individuals and as social beings and supports and nurtures humans in their search for identity and for a meaningful and fruitful existence, then it is to be considered a true and good religion. Vice versa, whatever leads in the opposite direction and makes humans fail to arrive at a meaningful and fruitful existence is a false (and bad) religion.

The general religious criterion is to be applied in principle to the different religious traditions with regard to the authenticity and canonicity of their respective doctrinal positions and practical rules of conduct. In other words, the particular doctrines and practices of a given religious tradition are to be determined as "true," or to be the contrary, in accordance with their congruence or noncongruence with the original standpoint of that tradition as discernible from its primary sources, including its scriptures and authentic tradition.

The last circle of Küng's "inward spiral" outlining his proposed set of criteria for religious truth is the specifically Christian criterion. Here he makes explicit his own stance as a Christian, presenting it "from within." (See below for further elaboration.) With this, we can take him as extending the invitation, as well as challenge, to adherents of other religions to elucidate their own stance "from within." Küng invites other religions to lay out their own specific criteria for truth based on the religious vision of their own respective traditions. There is an important point to note here: that in the establishment of ecumenical criteria for religious truth, one need not and should not thereby abandon one's commitment to the normativity of one's own tradition. What is required, though, is that first, one be willing to take the test of the general human ethical criteria; that second, one be willing to test the general religious criterion; and that third, one be willing to lay bare the criterion of one's own particular tradition and engage in open dialogue with adherents of other religions with different criteria based on their respective traditions.

To take one's tradition as normative, however, is not the same as to absolutize one's own tradition in a way that excludes others from consideration or regards it as superior. It is simply to acknowledge that one has found what one may rightly call *true religion,* for which one may stake one's all and to which one is able to profess absolute commitment through the mediation of one's tradition. What it does not mean is that the possibility that others may also find *true religion* in their respective traditions is thereby precluded. It is this very possibility that precisely makes interreligious dialogue an imperative for anyone who takes one's own tradition seriously and who is aware of the mere fact of the plurality of religious traditions with their respective claims to ultimate truth.

Thus, the need to establish ecumenical criteria for religious truth arises from the awareness of the concrete global situation that we find ourselves in, a situation wherein religion has often served more as a factor of dissension and conflict than as one of peace and reconciliation among fellow members of Earth's community. Needless to say, this awareness looms large in Küng's initiatives in calling for a global ethic, whose basic idea was spelled out in a 1990 book entitled *Projekt Weltethos.*[9]

QUESTIONING EMPTINESS, FROM A CHRISTIAN STANDPOINT

For the Christian, to take one's tradition as normative means that one has encountered the living God who has sent Jesus Christ as the way, the truth, and the life and is thereby enabled to live in the Holy Spirit, proclaiming the goodness and love of God with one's whole life. It is this encounter that gives the Christian's life its meaning and that grounds involvement in historical tasks (such as those Küng outlines in his proposal for a global ethic) as the Christian's way of living out the implications of this encounter with the God who acts in history and of leading "all things in heaven and all things on earth" toward final completion in Christ (Ephesians 1:3–11).

Here Küng makes the very important distinction that Karl Barth made before him: that Christians believe *not* in the absoluteness of Christianity (i.e., as a religious tradition, with its dogma, rituals, discipline) as such, but in God working in Jesus Christ through the Holy Spirit. Christianity, as a religion among others, is a "highly ambivalent historical phenomenon"[10] and needs to be continually purified, tested against the general ethical criterion, the general religious criterion, and its own specific criterion of fidelity to God manifested in Jesus Christ and working through the Holy Spirit. Insofar as historical Christianity remains a faithful witness to God in Jesus Christ working through the Holy Spirit, and only insofar as it is so, can it be called the true religion.

But as it continues on as a human community rooted in history, Christianity is continually broadened in scope and content, as its adherents live out their historical tasks, responding to their concrete historical situations vivified by the Spirit of God in Christ, and as they engage in dialogue with members of other religious traditions. Christians are thus to be understood as continually on the way to ever greater truth, as they open themselves to the manifold ways of God's self-communication in and through their historical encounters, moving toward the full revelation of the Lord of history.[11]

It would take another extended argument to show that the commitment to a global ethic as Küng and others have outlined is a necessary consequence of being Christian in the world today, given the situation of our global community and the mission of the Christian to be a witness to the message of the Gospel. And as one who, from a Christian standpoint, is committed to the concrete historical tasks that confront us in light of our current global situation, Hans Küng may (conceivably) pose the question to Masao Abe, as a Buddhist dialogue partner, Can Buddhist Emptiness (also) ground a commitment to a global ethic?

We must note that Hans Küng is able to "pose" such a question to Abe not as a hostile adversary or as an indifferent observer but as a sympathetic listener wishing to understand and willing to learn from the Buddhist notion of Emptiness. Hans Küng has undertaken a serious study of the Buddhist tradition,[12] including Abe's works, and shows his deep understanding and sensitivity to the nuances of Abe's thought.[13] From this understanding, he presents the possibility of an Eastern-Western understanding of God coming out of his encounter with Buddhism. In this context, he is led to ask, "Could it be that from this point we can make out a structural similarity between that 'Emptiness' which, for Buddhists, transcends all opposites, and that 'pleroma,' that infinite 'fullness' which embraces all opposites?"[14]

With his sympathetic grasp of Emptiness, Küng is nevertheless also able to mark out the radical difference between his Christian standpoint and the Mahāyāna/Zen position centered on the notion of Emptiness on two counts: on the view of history and on the grounding of an ethic.[15] First, the standpoint of Emptiness is presented as one that subsumes all history into an Eternal Now and thus shows a radical difference from the linear view of history presupposed in Christianity, that is, wherein history is seen as moving from creation to the Eschaton. Second, the standpoint of Emptiness is presented as one that has overcome all distinctions between good and evil, right and wrong, and thereby becomes unable to establish an ethic, which by definition is understood as the principle of doing good and avoiding evil.

These two points constitute the main reasons why it would seem that the standpoint of Emptiness is unable to ground a commitment to a global ethic. In other words, to see everything from the vantage point of an Eternal Now takes away the need for engaging in historical tasks for the transformation of society, since transformation necessarily involves a hope for a "better future," which makes no sense from the standpoint of Emptiness. Further, the collapse of the distinction between good and evil would tend to blunt one's sense of abhorrence for violence, injustice, exploitation, and oppression—realities that we humans continually come up against.

If one takes these to be the consequences of "the standpoint of Emptiness," one who takes such a standpoint would be consigned to being a "dropout" from the world (unconcerned with historical tasks) and a moral failure (no ethical backbone) no less. And for these reasons, the initial answer to the question, Can Emptiness ground commitment to a global ethic? would be *videtur quod non* (it seems not). Küng notes in fairness that Masao Abe himself is aware of the above difficulties in the "traditional Buddhist" (Mahāyāna/Zen) position and that he, Abe, admits the need of "clarification, completion, or correction" with respect to the two points described above.[16]

CONCLUDING REFLECTIONS: TOWARD A BUDDHIST-CHRISTIAN ETHIC OF COMPASSION

Hans Küng's theological project addresses two vital concerns facing the Christian community today. First, how as a Christian does one deal with the fact of religious plurality? Second, in the context of our current global crisis, how can Christians be faithful witnesses to the good news of God's love for the world in Jesus Christ, vis-à-vis the realities of violence, injustice, oppression, and ecological destruction? The first concern has led Küng to consider the establishment of ecumenical criteria for religious truth. The second concern, building upon the first, has led him to take the initiative in proposing "Towards a Global Ethic," which invites the participation of adherents of the various religious traditions of the world to work together toward a more just, more peaceful, and ecologically sustainable Earth community.

It is in light of these two concerns that define his theological project that we have attempted to "read the mind of Küng" and portray him as posing a question addressed to Masao Abe, a Buddhist partner in inter-religious dialogue: Can Emptiness ground commitment to a global ethic? This way of questioning highlights those points in the notion of Emptiness that Abe himself has admitted as needing "clarification, completion, correction." We must note here that Masao Abe himself has undertaken the task of making such clarifications and corrections in some of his recent writings.[17]

First, on the question of how the standpoint of Emptiness relates to history, Abe has explained that it is *compassion,* as an essential aspect of Emptiness, that leads to the very negation of this (ahistorical) Emptiness, whereby it "empties itself into history and becomes history."[18] Second, on the question of how the standpoint of Emptiness grounds ethical action, he has explained that the ethic of Emptiness is one that is no longer based on the distinction of good and evil, right and wrong, but is first and foremost an *ethic of compassion.* In other words, the genuine realization of the standpoint of Emptiness should by no means lead to an abandonment of one's historical tasks or to moral failure, but rather to a standpoint of solidarity with one's fellow sentient beings, grounded in the realization of compassion. The dynamics of Emptiness-Compassion itself is what assures the engagement with history, in the same way as it grounds ethical action.

We can venture to say at this point that it is perhaps Masao Abe's own personal long-term engagement with Christians in interreligious dialogue that has provided the forum for him to continue to clarify and correct his own understanding and presentation of the notion of Emptiness while at the same time challenging Christians in their understanding and presentation of their traditional notions of God, Jesus Christ, the world, and human destiny, from his standpoint of Buddhist Emptiness.[19] From this dialogic context, we can ask two questions, taking a cue from our simulated Küng-Abe conversations with reference to "Towards a Global Ethic." First, what may the Christian learn from the Buddhist standpoint of Emptiness that may enhance one's way of responding to the challenge of this declaration? And second, what may the Buddhist learn from the Christian?

In answer to the first, the standpoint of Emptiness may enlighten the Christian already engaged in his or her historical tasks grounded on a commitment to the Gospel, that the Lord of history is not only to be revealed at the (far) end of (linear) time, but is there *at every step along the way,* as an Eternal Now as well as a Not Yet, encountered as one commits oneself in the struggle against injustice, oppression, exploitation, and the endeavor to stem the tide of ecological destruction. And in answer to the second, the Christian engagement with history and concern with the continual transformation of the world toward the realization of God's reign as a reign of peace, justice, and the harmony of all creation may challenge the Buddhist who can be tempted to remain in the comfort of contemplating Emptiness to come back to the concrete historical realm, where sentient beings continue in different states of suffering, and be enabled to let Emptiness "empty itself out" in compassion, in solidarity with and selfless dedication to one's fellow beings. In other words, the Buddhist and the Christian can mutually enhance each other's way of responding to the tasks that lie ahead in the context of a global ethic, forging together an ethic of compassion from each one's respective religious standpoint.

chapter Twenty-One

FRITZ BURI'S ASSESSMENT OF MASAO ABE'S RELIGIOUS THOUGHT

Harold H. Oliver

I HAD THE PRIVILEGE of being introduced personally to Abe's thought before I met him in person. My introduction was under the guidance of my former Basel mentor, Fritz Buri, who spoke to me about Abe's thought and brought me into closer touch with him after Buri's first visit to Japan in 1968–69, and then again after his second visit in 1978–79. The first work of Abe's I read was his contribution to the Buri *Festschrift* in 1977, entitled "Zen is not a Philosophy, but . . ."[1] I came to a better acquaintance with Abe's thought through the article "The True Self in the Buddhist Philosophy of the Kyoto School," which I translated for Buri's presentation at an American Academy of Religion meeting in the 1980s.[2] But it was Buri's classic work on the Kyoto School and Christianity, *Der Buddha-Christus als der Herr des wahren Selbst* (*The Buddha-Christ as the Lord of the True Self*),[3] that inspired me to enter more deeply into Abe's thought.

Meanwhile, I met Abe and was impressed by his personal qualities and his profound knowledge of Eastern and Western thought. My longest period of contact with Abe occurred at the Fourth International

Buddhist-Christian Conference, held at Boston University in 1992, just a few days after I returned from an extensive visit with Buri in Basel, during which time he and I discussed problems I had encountered in translating his *Buddha-Christ* for publication. Because I have always associated Abe with Buri, I decided in this essay to explore further some aspects of the relationship of their thought.

Since Buri undertook to master the thought of all the major representatives of the Kyoto School, he was constantly tempted to compare and contrast Abe's work with that of his predecessors and with his successor, Shizuteru Ueda. Hence our first subtitle:

BURI'S COMPARATIVE ASSESSMENT OF THE LEGACY OF ABE

In view of Buri's decision in the summary article on the Kyoto School to devote his discussion of Abe solely to the latter's two articles on process metaphysics—a decision influenced by the "general theme of our consultation"[4]—he has little occasion there extensively to compare Abe with his Kyoto colleagues. In introducing his treatment of Abe, however, he does make two comparative remarks: (1) that "among the representatives of the Kyoto School, Abe is the one who has expressly dealt with this theme [i.e., process metaphysics]" and (2) that "Abe has taken over with great pedagogical talent the role of Daisetz Suzuki in the West."[5] There is an inherent connection between these seemingly unrelated remarks: it is because he inherited the role of Suzuki that he would need to deal with process thought, for this philosophy was so central to his colleagues at Claremont who initiated the significant dialogue between process thought and Buddhism. It will be evident only to readers of the book *The Buddha-Christ* why Buri places Abe at the end of the succession, after his younger colleague, Shizuteru Ueda, since insufficient justification for doing so is offered in the article. The reason given is that Abe, rather than Ueda, is the great summarizer of the Kyoto legacy. In fact, Buri introduces the chapter on Abe by referring to the latter's contribution as "A Summa of the Zen Philosophy of the Kyoto School." This claim is two-pronged, for in complimenting Abe in this way, Buri is expressing the judgment that Abe, unlike his Kyoto colleagues, does not "extend," i.e., add to, the Kyoto legacy as did each of the others, including Ueda.

In Buri's volume *The Buddha-Christ,* he points out that in Abe's "lecturing on a world-wide scale and in the great number of publications resulting from it," he "far surpasses his teachers and colleagues—with the exception of Daisetz Suzuki, whose international role he has quite literally assumed."[6] Because of his teaching positions in the States and lectures around the world, Abe—says Buri—"is nevertheless the best known representative of Zen philosophy."[7] On a personal note Buri attributes the high regard in which Abe is held "to the charm of his personality [and] to his gifts as a teacher and his openness to other conceptions with which he represents his conviction about the truth to Zen Buddhism."[8] Buri claims that two features of Abe's essays set them off from those of other representatives of the Kyoto School: (1) "the simplicity and clarity both in the presentation of Buddhist doctrine and in the stand he takes on the positions of Western thinking" and (2) "the interest manifest in every essay in the encounter with Christianity."[9] With respect to the first feature, Buri adds that Abe "is able to illumine much that is dark in [Buddhism] and difficult to follow—without falling into questionable simplifications—and to make it understandable despite its strangeness."[10] Buri expands the second feature by pointing out that in comparison with the other Kyoto philosophers, Abe manifests "a greater openness for certain characteristics of Christianity in comparison with openly conceded deficiencies of Buddhism" and among the Kyoto philosophers presents most impressively "the mutual enrichment and deepening of Christianity and Buddhism."[11] Buri adds that an additional reason for his placing Abe at the end of his seriatim discussion of the Kyoto philosophers is that "the question of the relationship of Zen Buddhism and Christianity which drives us is also his central concern."[12] According to Buri, the question of the relationship of Zen Buddhism to Christianity is "the basic intention of [Abe's] intellectual concerns."[13]

BURI'S ASSESSMENT OF
ABE'S CONTRIBUTION TO
BUDDHIST-CHRISTIAN DIALOGUE

After his initial comparative statement in *The Buddha-Christ,* Buri proceeds diachronically by discussing the great symposium on the theme of

Buddhism and Christianity, inaugurated by Abe in 1963. The symposium solicited responses to Abe from some of the most respected theologians of the West. Buri writes that "Abe has brought about a very meaningful meeting of Buddhism and Christianity, both through the way he fundamentally conceived and carried out this conversation, as well as the substance which he has given it by his expositions so far [1982]."[14] Buri uses the term *impressive* several times to characterize Abe's contribution to the symposium; yet he has some reservations about the details—even to the point of referring to "discrepancies." On Abe's thesis that Buddhism and Christianity are facing a common attack from "anti-religious forces," Buri faults him for failing to ask "whether there are not in the anti-religious phenomena mentioned longings for meaning and actualization of meaning."[15] Buri also faults Abe for applying "the 'existential' interpretation only to Buddhist terms . . . whereas he presents Christianity in its orthodox ossification."[16] Of this early work of Abe, Buri charges that "the main thing that stands out is only the superiority of the Buddhist position over the Christian one, and that it does not become manifest what Buddhism has to learn from such a Christianity about the deficiencies that attach to it."[17] Buri does not hesitate to criticize Abe's derivation of the dualistic, existential understanding of Christianity from the doctrine of *creatio ex nihilo* in its Barthian and Bultmannian versions, which—according to Buri—remains a misunderstanding of both the doctrine of *creatio ex nihilo* and the term *existential*. In a ploy characteristic of Buri, he charges that Abe's arguments about the superiority of Buddhism rest precisely on the "discriminating thinking" that the Buddhist excludes.

After providing a lengthy summary of Abe's Buddhist nondualist "ontology" with its corresponding notion of redemption as "nothing other than awakening to Reality through the death of the ego,"[18] Buri assesses the criticisms addressed to Abe by his respondents in the continuing symposium. When some of the critics cite Abe's lapse into metaphysics, despite the Buddha's injunction, Buri comes to Abe's defense by arguing that "to speak of a self that deals with the realization of the meaning of its existence is not possible without metaphysics."[19] Characteristically, Buri responds by arguing that "there is no knowing without objectivity" and that "we can become aware of nothingness only within [the subject-object schema of our consciousness]"[20]—ideas that Abe, of course, could never accept. Buri then proposes his own version of *creatio ex nihilo,*

which includes the admission that this "symbol for the mystery of being
[is] the absolute boundary of objectifying thinking."[21] By adding that it is
a symbol also "of being destined for responsible personhood and the community that is to be formed in correspondence to it,"[22] Buri introduces his
idiosyncratic thesis: that "for this significance of personal realization of
meaning . . . both the mythology of the Christ and the Bodhisattva figures
can be used."[23] According to Buri, when the former is "extracted from an
illusory eschatology" and the latter from "circular speculation," they can
be "united into a general human redemptive symbol of the Buddha-
Christ."[24]

 Buri seems pleased that Abe finds a "crossing point" between Zen
and Christianity in a discussion of the terms *ontological* and *axiological*:
this crossing point lies in the "ontological understanding of Nothingness"
in Zen and the "axiological emphasis of God's 'ought to'" in Christianity.
Abe concedes that "the strength in Zen is the weakness in Christianity,"
and vice versa.[25] When we recall that Buri routinely defined *symbol* as the
"objectification of what is non-objectifiable," we realize why he can make
no sense of Abe's claim that the question of the meaning of the self
always deals with "an 'objectification of the non-objectifiable,' which for
this reason is nothingness."[26] And even though Abe interprets this "nothingness" as "self-awakening," as "dynamic," and as consisting of "complete
openness and freedom,"[27] Buri oddly remarks that Abe can say nothing
"positive" about it. What Buri means, as is evident in what follows, is that
Abe refuses to interpret it in terms of the kind of "personalism" that Buri
finds in the Christian perspective.

BURI'S ASSESSMENT OF ABE'S
ESSAYS ON WHITEHEAD

Although Buri discusses Abe's two essays on Whitehead both in his book
on the Kyoto School and the article devoted to it, in the latter he limits
his treatment of Abe to these essays. In his book, Buri discounts Abe's
characterization of his own knowledge of Whitehead's philosophy in the
earlier essay as "lay-like," maintaining to the contrary that "at that time
[Abe] had already grasped its essentials."[28] He adds, however, that the
tone of the two essays is different: in the earlier one, Abe concluded that

"Mahayana Buddhist thinkers could learn a great deal from Whitehead's philosophy,"[29] whereas in the later essay, according to Buri, "Whitehead's philosophy here falls completely by the wayside in face of the now perfectly developed Prajna-paramita logic of Nagarjuna's."[30]

In the earlier essay, Abe criticizes the "dipolarity" of Whitehead's view of God as deficient when compared with the "non-duality" of the doctrine of dependent origination. Buri says in his article on the Kyoto School that Abe sees the similarities and differences with a "sharp eye," implying that he agrees with Abe that in Whitehead's system—using Buri's words—"the relationship in which the inner-worldly factors stand to each other has a quite different significance from that of their relationship to the dipolarity of God."[31] Whitehead's exemption of God from temporality leads Abe to maintain the superiority of dependent origination according to which—again, in Buri's idiom—"all 'things' are to be understood as occurring in a mutual co-conditioning and co-suspension that is without beginning or end."[32] Thus, Whitehead's conception of God as dipolar is only "in a way analogous" to the doctrine of dependent origination, a point with which Buri seems to concur.

Whereas Buri's article discusses both of Abe's essays on process philosophy, his book extensively treats only the later essay. Buri's summary—in his article—of the thesis of the later essay is helpful: "Here [Abe] considers Process Philosophy only as an overcoming of the Aristotelian and Christian concept of substance, and he does this for the purpose of unfolding the doctrine of 'dependent co-origination' as the overcoming of both Western ways of thinking, for it alone would be able to satisfy the longing for redemption which lies at the base of both."[33]

In both of his discussions, Buri masterfully summarizes Abe's distinctive interpretation of *pratītya-samutpāda* as a "dependent originatology" and indicates how Abe uses this thesis to exhibit its advantages over Heideggerian and Whiteheadian thought. One has the feeling that in his summary of Abe's criticism of Whitehead, Buri is more sympathetic with the former. But a characteristically Burian slant appears, when in stating Abe's view that "Buddhism is freed from the question of the origin of evil and the problematical attempts at theodicy connected with it in Christianity," Buri asks, "But . . . who is freeing whom and from what, or who is here freed and from what?"[34]

At the conclusion of his article, Buri faults the representatives of the

Kyoto School, including Abe, for claiming "the legitimacy of . . . a demythologized existential interpretation for validating the truth of their Buddhist tradition, while wrongly denying such for the Christian tradition and regarding it instead merely in its dogmatized mythological objectivity."[35]

BURI'S ASSESSMENT OF ABE'S
PREFERENCE FOR ZEN BUDDHISM

According to Buri's chapter on Abe, when Abe speaks of Buddhism in the normative sense, "he always means—like his revered teacher, Hisamatsu—Zen Buddhism."[36] Buri further reminds us that, in his lectures "Zen and Modern Man," Abe "was concerned to show that Zen is the authentic form of Buddhism which alone really corresponds to its historical origin in the enlightenment of the Buddha"[37] and that "Zen alone is useful 'for the realization of human existence common to East and West.'"[38] Buri reports that "for the elucidation and . . . justification of this self-characterization of Zen as an event of immediate enlightenment,"[39] Abe engages upon a critical comparison between the Buddha and the Christ. Unlike the Christian view in which "the title Christ is only assigned to Jesus . . . in Buddhism the Buddha's enlightenment possesses no such once-for-allness that is decisive for the salvation of his devotees."[40]

Buri carefully summarizes Abe's argument that first locates the different conceptions found in Zen and Pure Land Buddhism in their different versions of the *trikāya* doctrine: Zen is "the 'way of holiness' of 'self-redemption' *(jiriki)*" and Pure Land is "the 'way of faith' of 'redemption ab extra' *(tariki)*.[41] Abe then argues—in Buri's words—that "whereas . . . Pure Land Buddhism . . . objectif[ies] the Buddha, that is makes him an object of faith in a salvation event . . . for Zen this event occurs in self-understanding [which is only] a symbolic expression of an event that is essentially non-objectifiable."[42] Buri adds that both Hisamatsu and Abe failed to see in this distinction a way of overcoming "Sutra-dogmatism and Buddhist sutra magic" and "the discussion of the hermeneutical problem in theology," viz. demythologizing.[43]

In *The Buddha-Christ,* Buri then turns to a discussion of Abe's substantial work on Dōgen. A central question to which Abe addresses himself is—in Buri's words—"whether and in what way man still needs

enlightenment for attaining Buddhahood, if according to Buddhist tradition, 'all living beings have the Buddha nature.'"[44] This problematic
prompts Buri to make a comparison with the problem of natural theology in Christianity, that is, to "the question of the relation in which the
image of God given to man by God stands to the New Creation in
Christ." The difference between the Christian and Buddhist anthropolo-
gies of redemption is that the former is "personal," the latter, "impersonal."[45] Dōgen solved the problem by making a "grammatical" shift from
"having-Buddha-nature" to "being-Buddha-nature," in such a way as to
connect the "homocentric" with the "dehomocentric."[46] As Buri reports,
Abe holds that "the connection of these two structures is not possible . . .
in an objective thinking of consciousness and of substance" as is typical in
the West "from Descartes and Spinoza on," but only "in a non-objectifiable existential enlightenment, for which there exists between the
Buddha nature and all beings neither unity nor duality, but 'non-duality.'"[47] Accordingly, Dōgen rejects the distinction between "practice and
enlightenment" by advocating "unintentionally enacted sitting (*shikan-
taza*)" rather than "sitting in immersion (*zazen*)."[48] At this point Buri concedes that, to Westerners, "its enactment seems too difficult to us in
many points," and in the same vein, "for the unenlightened, insights
gained on the basis of enlightenment are also incapable of being understood in many respects."[49] In his own defense, Buri adds that "certain
statements of Christian faith are incapable of being understood by the
unbelievers."[50] This counsel of despair is an unexpected move on the part
of Buri and needs serious reevaluation, for while some "believers" and
some "enlightened" might agree, it raises questions about the ultimate
possibilities of dialogue. Buri does not sufficiently consider the possibility that some Westerners question the duality of the subject-object conceptuality of Western culture as rigorously as do Zen philosophers.

Buri gives considerable attention to Abe's discussion of the well-
known Zen pronouncement: "Before I studied Zen, to me mountains were
mountains and waters were waters. After I got an insight into the truth of
Zen through the instruction of a good master, mountains are to me not
mountains and waters are not waters. But after this, when I really attained
the abode of rest, mountains are really mountains, waters are really
waters."[51] In his masterful answer to the question that follows the *kōan*,
viz. "Do you think that these three understandings are the same or

different?" Abe concludes that in self-awakening, "I am not I, therefore I am you, and yet I am really I. You are not you, therefore you are me, and yet you are really you."[52] Since from the relational perspective that I have presented I fully concur with Abe's conclusion, I have to doubt his claim that this—in Buri's words—is "a matter of Zen enlightenment."[53]

BURI'S ASSESSMENT OF ABE'S COMPARISON OF ZEN AND WESTERN THOUGHT

Although a critique of Western thought runs through all the treatises Buri has reviewed thus far, he thematizes this problem specifically in *The Buddha-Christ,* for which he offers the following summary:

> *What occasions his speaking of the "blind-spot" of all [Western thinking, including the Christian doctrine of the incarnation of the Logos] is identical with what he develops in other connections we have already reviewed, in respect to the non-objectifiability of Being and the self, except that here he all the more applies his principal epistemological-critical point of view to the different formulations of Western philosophy and theology in order to point out that from that perspective their insufficiency compared to "Nagarjuna's view of emptiness," which ultimately represents, in his opinion, the only adequate formulation of the Buddha's doctrine of the "non-I and of dependent origination," and forms as such the basis of Zen and of its claim to be an "independent [spiritual] transmission apart from doctrine or scripture."[54]*

Buri reports that Abe compares the different responses of East and West to the "insufficiency of the world in which one lives and the 'metaphysical' striving to overcome it" by claiming that the West responded—again in Buri's words—"by the erection of a Being that sublates what is lacking in beings, in which use is made of conceptual thinking in one way or another—whether by appealing to natural reason or to a supernatural revelation," whereas the East responded "by an extinction of this thinking that is directed toward Being that is somehow represented objectively."[55]

Against this background, Buri is "surprised" that Abe warns Zen not to let its "'Not-Thinking,' in which it rejects objective thinking for the sake of the non-objectifiability of the self and of Being, lapse into a 'non-thinking as such,' and . . . letting its freedom from 'every kind of moral law and principle' become merely a 'non- or anti-ethic.'"[56] Buri finds it incomprehensible that Abe could conclude his article "Zen and Western Thought" with the claim that Zen must embrace the standpoints of Western "Being" and "ought," for it seems to undermine the case he had been making.[57] I fear that Buri here fails to grasp Abe's intention, which, if rightly grasped, is not to be understood in any sense as an admission of conceptual thinking but as a deepening of Zen "No-thinking."

The point I am making is apparent in another article of Abe's reviewed by Buri, "Non-Being and *Mu:* The Metaphysical Nature of Negativity in the East and West," though Buri seems unable or unwilling to concede it. Buri is unyielding: Abe's

> denial of [the validity of logical conceptuality] presupposes precisely
> what is said to be made inoperative in it. In the supposed sublation
> of the contradictoriness of Being with which conceptual knowledge
> has to do, he still makes use of its aid, just as the "Great Death"
> and "emptiness," Nirvana and "awakening" are conceptual
> designations, even if they point beyond every objectification.[58]

Buri criticizes Abe's equation of "emptying of emptiness" and "existential self-understanding" as "an ontological misunderstanding" of "the thinking of existence."[59]

BURI'S ASSESSMENT OF ABE'S
TREATMENT OF THE PROBLEM
OF ETHICS

Abe's notion of Awakening "to Emptiness prior to the opposition between good and evil" is equally problematic to Buri, whose theology culminates in the Western notion of *Verantwortung.* He agrees with Abe's "de-absolutizing of the conceptuality of objectifying thinking [in ethics], [his] relativizing of the success our moral strivings and [his] de-mystifying of

so-called rites of purification"[60] but counters with the assertion that the
"'ex-istential realization' of 'the Original Purity,' of which he rightly says
that it is 'not an objectively observable state,' is not possible without
conceptual distinctions."[61] Buri makes the point that "if 'existential realization' should only consist in [recognizing that everything is as it is],
then—if it is not merely an 'illusion'—it is different from that which 'is
as it is,' i.e., it consists in a purification of our conceptuality from its abso-
lutizations, but also in a use of our conceptuality in its relativity as the
means to its enactment."[62]

Buri finds Abe's argument that Zen transcends the distinction
between life and death, upon which Christianity is based, to be equally
troubled by the same attempt—to use Buri's phrase—to "think non-
objectively."[63] Abe is aware of the dangers in the Zen position, as Buri
clearly indicates. And in the conclusion to his lengthy chapter on Abe,
Buri sounds a note of appreciation for the possibility of genuine dialogue
between Buddhism and Christianity opened up by Abe's lead in new
directions. Buri's closing words invite citation:

> The summa of the Zen philosophy of the Kyoto School which he
> here offers us represents also a challenge to Christian theology
> which causes us to take up from its side the dialogue with
> Buddhist thinking. For this purpose the critical remarks which
> we have had occasion and opportunity to make in different places
> in our presentation of the individual representatives of the Kyoto
> School, are certainly insufficient.[64]

CONCLUDING REMARKS

In this essay I have briefly reported on the significant contributions to
Buddhist and Christian thought of two scholars, both of whom have
played a unique role in my own thoughts. Personally, I have been closer
to Buri, for our friendship has spanned many years. But these have been
years in which my own philosophical and theological development has
brought me closer to the conclusions of Abe. Even this state of affairs in
my life owes much to Buri, who first drew my attention to the close

connection between my relational philosophy and that of the Kyoto School. In the inscription that Buri penned in my copy of his *Buddha-Christ* volume, he writes of my "Relationalism" that "is so much related to pratitya-samutpada." Just how much I owe to Buri and how much to the Kyoto School, especially in a personal way to both Masao Abe and Shizuteru Ueda, is difficult to sort out. But on this occasion I wish to thank Masao Abe personally for the immeasurable gifts of his friendship and his impeccable understanding of Buddhism.

Chapter Twenty-Two

MASAO ABE AND PAUL TILLICH: A DIALOGUE TOWARD LOVE

Leslie D. Alldritt

WITHOUT QUESTION, MASAO ABE has contributed more of significance to interreligious dialogue in the West than any other Buddhist thinker. However, what I find truly distinctive about Abe is that while many other scholars of Buddhism can speak only from the academic side of the problem (this author among them), Abe speaks from the side of Zen Awakening. Abe noted "of Chao-chou it was said, his Zen shines upon his lips, because the utterances he made were like jewels that sparkled brightly."[1] The same can be said of Masao Abe: "His Zen shines upon his lips."

A recent edition of *The Eastern Buddhist* included an article by Abe entitled "Zen and Buddhism."[2] An important section of this article is "The Affinity between 'Buddha' and 'Christ'." In that section Abe cites Protestant theologian Paul Tillich and Tillich's formulation of Jesus as the Christ. Upon rereading a paper of Abe's, "'Life and Death' and 'Good and Evil' in Buddhism," that he delivered in 1982 at Haverford College, I again found a reference to Tillich's theological position. From my initial introduction to Abe's writing to my reading of his most recent works, the Christian position that I have commonly found articulated is Tillich's. I find my experience mirrored in Abe's list of publications: from his earliest scholarly efforts to the most recent, Tillich—though not the only Christian thinker engaged by Abe—certainly is Abe's primary choice to represent Christian theology.[3]

One way to account for this preferential treatment of Tillich's theology is Abe's early interest in Tillich. Near the beginning of his academic career, Abe was studying and assisting D. T. Suzuki at Columbia University at the same time that Tillich held an appointment at Union Theological Seminary. As Abe wrote about this period in his life:

> *Paul Tillich and Reinhold Niebuhr were two theologians with whom I particularly wanted to study, so when I heard of Dr. Tillich's transfer from Union to Harvard Divinity School that academic year I was disappointed. However while at Union I occasionally visited Harvard to attend his lectures; and during my two years in America I never missed the sermons, lectures and the like that he often delivered in New York.*[4]

Although it cannot be said that Abe was able to study formally under Tillich, it is evident that Abe availed himself of every opportunity to learn from Tillich. He apparently saw Tillich's theology as one that he would have to learn and intellectually engage as a Buddhist teacher in the West, particularly as a scholar interested in interreligious dialogue. Abe had high regard for Tillich's involvement in interreligious dialogue and wrote in a memorial to Tillich that he considered him as "an irreplaceable dialogist."[5]

In his article "Tillich from a Buddhist Point of View"[6] Abe lauds Tillich as "one of the most outstanding Christian theologians and philosophers of religion in the twentieth century."[7] What is it about Tillich's theological position that Abe finds interesting and relatable to his own work? As a provisional attempt to answer a question that perhaps only Abe himself can adequately answer, I offer two propositions. The first is that Abe sees much in Tillich's analysis of the problematic nature of the person that resonates with his Zen view of the ontic plight of the person. The second proposition is that Tillich's and Abe's analyses have found commonality in resolutions that can be characterized as love. A brief exposition of these two propositions follows.

THE PROBLEM OF PERSONAL EXISTENCE

Throughout his many writings, Tillich makes it quite clear that he views human personal existence[8] as problematic: "It is not an exaggeration to say that today man experiences his present situation in terms of disruption, conflict, self-destruction, meaninglessness, and despair in all realms of life."[9] Why the person experiences his or her world as so divisive, in Tillich's view, can be traced to an ontological bifurcation in the self. In defining what a *self* means, Tillich indicates this division more precisely:

> *Being a self means being separated in some way from everything else, having everything else opposite one's self, being able to look at it and act upon it. At the same time, however, this self is aware that it belongs to that at which it looks. The self is "in" it.*[10]

The duality of self-consciousness includes the awareness of being and non-being or, in other words, consciousness of one's finitude. As Tillich avers, "Man is not only finite, as is every creature, but he is also *aware* of his finitude. And this awareness is 'anxiety.'"[11]

Tillich argues that the basic anxiety of finitude—or, as he typifies it in *Courage to Be*, the anxiety of fate and death—is endemic in the ontic structure of the person, regardless of time or place:

> *The human situation is the predicament in which man finds himself whenever he appears under the conditions of existence. What is his predicament? This predicament can be described as estrangement. Man is in the predicament of being estranged from himself. The possibility of contradicting himself is universal actuality. Always and everywhere man is in the state of estrangement.*[12]

By "estranged from himself," Tillich does not believe one is alienated because of an internal bifurcation but rather that one is alienated from the eternal "other," creating this inner anxiety:

> *If love is the drive towards the reunion of the separated, it is hard to speak meaningfully of self-love. For within the unity of self-consciousness there is no real separation, comparable to the separation*

of a self-centered being from all other beings. Certainly the com-
pletely self-centered being, man, is self-centered only because his
self is split into a self which is subject and a self which is object.
But there is neither separation in this structure, nor the desire for
reunion.[13]

Tillich's analysis of the problematic nature of personal existence
provides a basic reason for Abe's interest in his theology. It is consonant
with Abe's view that personal existence is a "predicament"; Abe evokes
Tillich's position of the universality of alienation in asserting that "self-
estrangement and anxiety are *not* something *accidental* to the ego-self,
but are inherent to its structure. To be human is to be a problem to oneself, regardless of one's culture, class, sex, nationality, or the era in which
one lives."[14] This quote evinces the root problem for Abe: one is "cut off
from both one's self and one's world; and to be cut off from one's self and
one's world means to be in constant anxiety."[15] What Abe denotes here is
that the problem manifests itself not only in being unable to encounter
the world fully, because of the limitation of necessarily objectifying the
world but also, for example, when I try to reach for my self (I), I reach
only an objectified self (me), and the subjective self (I) ever regresses
from my grasp:

But how can we grasp this "I"? How can we realize our true Self?
To do so, we may raise the question, "Who is asking, 'who am I?'"
Now another "I" appears as a new subject and converts the entire
situation into the object of still another question.[16]

The inability to truly know oneself is a predicament that besets each
human being in the actualization of self-consciousness. In other words,
in trying to locate the asking "I," it seems incumbent to "step back" from
the duality of the asking "I" and oneself, yet in that very step "backward"
(the direction is illustrative rather than spatial), one *necessarily* creates
another duality between the asking "I" and the new asking "I" that now
asks the question.

Abe clearly posits the problem of duality not only in terms of
self/world or self/God as Tillich does but more concisely in the internal
structure of subjective self/objective self. How this basic direction

manifests itself in coloring one's world adversely—both in suffering and in joy—is essential to fully understand both Abe's and Tillich's positions. However, it is incumbent upon us to examine their respective resolutions to this problem; here the differences become more marked, yet concurrently more intriguing.

RESOLUTIONS TO THE PROBLEM OF PERSONAL EXISTENCE

One must experience the pain of existence, according to Tillich, in order to understand the balm that can alleviate this pain. For "only those who have experienced the shock of transitoriness, the anxiety in which they are aware of their finitude, the threat of nonbeing, can understand what the notion of God means."[17] It is precisely here where the raison d'être is for Tillich: God is the answer to the problem of existence. God is, in Tillich's words, "the answer to the question implied in man's finitude; he is the name for that which concerns man ultimately."[18] As any reader of Tillich knows, "ultimate concern" is Tillich's definition of a religious concern. However, it is imperative to understand that this ultimate concern is not merely an object for one to grasp; its true strength lies in one *"being grasped"* by it.[19] Hence, the problematic self is enabled through a movement of grace to reach a salvific relation with God.

God, for Tillich, is defined as "being-itself":[20] "God is the basic and universal symbol for what concerns us ultimately. As being-itself He is ultimate reality, the really real, the ground and abyss of everything that is real."[21] This being the case, can a finite self approach such a God? Tillich states that God "cannot be called a self, because the concept 'self' implies separation from and contrast to everything which is not self."[22] Moreover, Tillich says that because of the "holiness of God," God cannot be "draw[n] into the context of the ego-world and the subject-object correlation."[23] What recourse has the anxiety-ridden person in light of this ontological difference? The answer to this seemingly insolvable dilemma, in Tillich's theology, is love.

Tillich explains that *"God is love.* And, since God is being-itself, one *must* say that being-itself is love."[24] In *The New Being,* Tillich writes that "God and love are not two realities; they are one. God's Being is the being of love and God's infinite power of Being is the infinite power of love."[25] What this divine love means for the person lies in the dynamic essence of love. In Tillich's theology, every being is separated from that to which it belongs, and every being moves toward reunion with that from which it is separated. For the person, movement toward this reunion is a movement of love toward God. That one can achieve this reunion—albeit fragmentarily—constitutes the Christian resolution for Tillich:

> *Life is being in actuality and love is the moving power of life. In these two sentences the ontological nature of love is expressed. They say that being is not actual without the love which drives everything that is towards everything else that is.*[26]

In one's participation with God, there is an objective and subjective side. That is, one must be receptive (subjective) to the movement (objective) from the "side" of God. This objective movement cannot be coerced or created—it can be received only by grace.

> *In grace something is overcome; grace occurs "in spite of" something; grace occurs in spite of separation and estrangement. Grace is the reunion of life with life, the reconciliation of the self with itself. Grace is the acceptance of that which is rejected. Grace transforms fate into a meaningful destiny; it changes guilt into confidence and courage.*[27]

Grace is the movement of *agape,* or divine love, which acts to heal the alienation in personal existence. As Tillich maintains, "The divine love is the final answer to the questions implied in human existence, including finitude, the threat of disruption, and estrangement."[28]

Jesus as the Christ is the mediating symbol for this movement of agape, as it is through him "by which the self-estrangement of our existence is overcome, a reality of reconciliation and reunion, of creativity, meaning, and hope."[29] Jesus as the Christ, the "New Being" that is also characterized by Tillich as the "Being of Love,"[30] is affirmed in his role as the final revelation since through his death and resurrection, he "negated" himself. In other words, Jesus as the Christ symbolizes the ultimate affirmation-negation of finitude and infinitude.[31] In sum, for Tillich the

Christian resolution is one that results in a personal participation with God; yet it is not a *complete* identification with God—there remains always an "otherness" in the love relationship.

Interestingly, Abe's proffered resolution can be characterized as one of love as well. However, the Zen resolution that Abe presents is not participation with Being itself. Instead, it is the manifestation of a paradoxical identification-participation.[32] This paradox requires further explication.

In Abe's writings, it is clear what the solution to the human predicament is: nirvana, *satori,* or the term of preference herein, Awakening. Faced with the mortal illness of the problematic self, the only cure is radical surgery. The *entire* dualistic consciousness must be uprooted and "replaced" with an Awakened consciousness that is not simply nondualistic but rather a nondualistic-dualistic consciousness, or, more succinctly rendered, a selfless self.[33] Shin'ichi Hisamatsu, one of Abe's teachers, defines this True Self as follows:

> By True Self I mean the Self that is not the ordinary self, the self that has become free, in the true sense of the term, from death and sin, the self that is not limited by time or space, the Formless, Egoless, Self.[34]

Abe has been among a growing number of writers who have opined that Zen Buddhism has been deficient in expressing an idea of justice from the perspective of Awakening. Frequently the effort to remedy this omission has been taken up under the heading of "Zen ethics." While certainly this is an important task for Zen to articulate, what I see Abe as asseverating of equal importance for Zen Buddhists is to speak of the *mahākaruṇā* (Great Compassion) element of this Zen Awakening to the True Self.

In Mahāyāna Buddhism, we see *mahākaruṇā* traditionally emphasized in the description of a bodhisattva: one who upon reaching Awakening forgoes final nirvana *(parinirvāṇa)*and remains in ordinary existence to assist others in coming to nirvana. The bodhisattva acts in ultimate unselfishness because he or she has realized Awakening and has thereby brought about *mahākaruṇā.*

D. T. Suzuki, in an interview article entitled "D.T. Suzuki, Oriental

Thought, and The West,"[35] speaks of how *prajñā*-understanding is identical with the Zen Awakening that "generates" Great Compassion.[36] However, Abe notes that in the view of Suzuki, "the Zen man is apt to seem to make too much of *prajñā*, the Great Wisdom, rather neglecting *karuṇā*, the Great Compassion."[37] Abe goes on to say, "In Zen, properly speaking, *prajñā* and *karuṇā* are not two, but one."[38]

In the Suzuki article mentioned above, Richard DeMartino indicates the relationship of *mahākaruṇā* to love and justice:

> *Yet, compassion—or love—always also entails the duality or differentiation between any one being and every other being, and this differentiation always involves—within the arena of duality—the issue of justice. This means that the relation between karuna, compassion, or love and justice (the relation between non-duality and duality) is, for Buddhism as well, just as constitutive.*[39]

That is to say, for Zen Buddhism to speak on matters of love and justice is an elemental part of Zen Awakening. To characterize Awakening as "Fulfilled Love," a term that DeMartino uses, one is emphasizing the reality of the ontic position "I am I *and* I am not-I," or "I am I *and* I am the Universe (Tao)." This existentially realized assertion represents the ontological reality from which *mahākaruṇā* is expressed and is the only genuine basis for a "Zen ethic"—an ethic that should seek to elucidate the true nature of a person's relationship to other persons and to Nature.

In unparalleled fashion, Masao Abe is taking up the task that his teacher Suzuki left unfinished: to clarify the centrality of the *mahākaruṇā* feature of Zen Awakening and to apply this clarification in shaping a Zen Buddhist response to the concerns of the global community. In his essay "Kenotic God and Dynamic Sunyata," Abe speaks of Śūnyatā as constituting Great Compassion and holds that it is *the* operative principle for Zen Buddhism:

> *In the light of wisdom realized in Sunyata, everything and everyone is realized in its suchness and time is overcome. In the light of compassion also realized in Sunyata, however, time is religiously significant and essential. And the endless process of the com-*

*passionate work of an awakened person trying to awaken others is
no less than the aforementioned process of Sunyata turning itself
into a vow and into act through its self-emptying.*[40]

It is the active, motivating force of Great Compassion in history that
Abe emphasizes here. This force of *Śūnyatā*-Compassion, like Tillich's
God-Love, is a liberative power. Compassion for Abe is the endless work
of the salvific power of *Śūnyatā* bringing to a world what it desperately
requires. In closing his remarkable essay, which calls for Christianity to
explore its understanding of Jesus as the Christ and God as self-emptying (kenotic), Abe penetrates to the heart of where interreligious dialogue
must go, not only between Christians and Buddhists, but so with all spiritual dialogue:

*In this paper I have suggested that in Christianity, the notion
of the kenotic God is essential as the root-source of the kenotic
Christ, if God is truly the God of Love. I also suggested that in
Buddhism, Sunyata must be grasped dynamically not statically,
since Sunyata indicates not only wisdom, but compassion.*[41]

Despite the attending problems that Christianity may have with
Abe's suggestions, Zen Buddhism should have no such problems in
accepting his exhortation. Unless Zen Buddhism begins to focus more on
the *mahākaruṇā* aspect of Awakening, then Abe's hope for a "more profound and creative dialogue" will be negated from the Zen side, regardless of the consolations of the Christian dialogists. If interreligious dialogue is to be *truly* fruitful, perhaps a measure in the shared social concern of the dialogue may be how well it is able to address the question
"What does it do for the lives of children?"[42]

To conclude, I often think of an American Academy of Religion
meeting a few years ago in which a discussion of Abe's thought was
undertaken. I arrived at the meeting room late and was sitting in the very
back. Abe and his wife arrived soon after the discussion had begun and
sat beside me. The moderator noticed Abe and asked him to move forward, whereupon Abe somewhat reluctantly moved about halfway closer
to the podium. This seemingly insignificant event struck me, a graduate
student at the time, as indicative of Abe's spiritual humbleness and has

come to exemplify a sense I receive from Abe every time I encounter him: Abe truly is striving to bring the ethos of Zen Awakening to the world through his words and actions. Perhaps the aforementioned event is additionally a metaphor for Abe's academic life: he may prefer to sit in the back, but the world requires him to move at least halfway toward it as we contemplate his work in a public fashion. We are fortunate that he has given so unselfishly in accordance with *mahākaruṇā*. There is reason to hope that Abe's philosophic contribution to the Western history of ideas will continue to transcend academia and move inexorably into the greater public discourse. This must happen if the dramatic change Abe envisions is to occur, and occur it must for the good of us all.

chapter Twenty-Three

MASAO ABE AND KARL RAHNER: ON TRACES OF DUALISM AND MONISM

James L. Fredericks

I CAN REMEMBER LISTENING to Masao Abe speak at a banquet closing one of the meetings of the Abe-Cobb dialogue group. A few minutes before, he had slipped me a sheet of paper with comments written in English that he had asked me to edit. Now he was criticizing his Buddhist colleagues in the group for not being as daring as the Christians had been in experimenting with their tradition. This story notwithstanding, Abe himself has generally been more creative in his revisions of Christianity than with his presentation of Zen. I say this not to accuse Abe of failing to practice what he preaches. Many of us involved in interreligious dialogue can say the same thing about ourselves. Rather, it is to emphasize the importance of what Abe has stated repeatedly: the great sign of authentic dialogue is the *mutual* transformation of traditions. Thus, as a token of what Masao Abe has taught me over the years, I offer here a critique of his exposition of Zen and a suggestion as to how he might develop as a Buddhist in the hope of contributing to the transformation of Buddhism so dear to Abe's heart. Let me start with a kind of *mondo*.

I had the good fortune of having many long conversations with Abe in the fall of 1987 while he was lecturing at the University of Chicago. That was the time when he was formulating the essay that was to become "Kenotic God and Dynamic Sunyata."[1] After reading a handwritten draft, I had suggested that Abe read some of the fundamental theology of Karl Rahner, whose notion of Being itself as "unobjectifiable mystery" directly addressed Abe's interest in the problem of metaphysical dualism in the Christian understanding of God. One cold evening, sitting together in his office, Abe brought up Rahner. He agreed Rahner was deeply aware of the problem of dualism, but Rahner's association of "mystery" with Being itself suffers from what Abe called "traces of dualism." Abe paused for a moment before asking me what I thought. I agreed with him in his criticism of Rahner, which surprised more than pleased him. Then somewhat boldly, I went on to say that Abe's exposition of Zen suffers from "traces of monism." At this, Abe laughed.

Abe's critique of the Christian notion of God for its dualism is well known. There is no need to rehash it in detail here. Christianity consistently honors being over non-being in looking to the triumph of life over death, good over evil. This tendency is apparent in the Christian doctrine of creation. The absolute transcendence of God from the world generates a distinction between Creator and creation that the immanence of God in Jesus Christ does not fully overcome. For this reason, the relationship between God and creation is not governed by the logic of Absolute Nothingness, and faith in the Christian God cannot realize true selfhood as Zen understands it.

Abe, as I mentioned above, is well versed in the work of theologians such as Rahner in whose theology Being itself is understood nondualistically as "mystery." This more nuanced understanding of Being, nevertheless, is still not Absolute Nothingness in Abe's view. It is still founded on the positive pole of every duality (being versus non-being; good versus evil), and thus Being itself remains somewhat objectified. For this reason, Abe detects "traces of dualism" in Rahner.

As I said in the *mondo,* Abe is correct in his criticism of these "traces of dualism." Christian theology seeks to objectify in conceptual language religious truths that exist first in the overarching first-order language of its own narratives and metaphors. These narratives and metaphors speak of God's creative fiat and intervening action within history and even of God's worldly presence as a particular human being. That Christianity should have to resist an inevitable tendency to decay into a dualistic understanding of God and creation (which, Rahner states, is "basically very unreligious")[2] should come as no surprise. Nor should it surprise us that Christianity has also developed doctrinal strategies for resisting these tendencies.

If dualism is a constitutive danger for Christianity, arguably Zen struggles with the parallel danger of monism. Zen (and perhaps Japanese religions more generally) seeks to cultivate a living sense of participation in the whole. Thus, in Zen we find not only logical strategies for breaking down distinction and differences but also the affirmation of immediacy. Also parallel to Christianity, Japanese Zen has had to develop doctrinal correctives of considerable sophistication in order to resist this tendency to decay into a naive monism.[3] If I understand correctly, monistic Zen cannot be considered authentic. Awakening to Emptiness decays into a mere aestheticism of "wondrous being." The freedom and spontaneity of the "true person of no status" is reduced to a passive and quietistic caricature of itself. I also think that by surrendering to its monistic tendencies, Zen has at times succeeded in denying its own capacity for social criticism.

It must be stated without qualification that Abe well understands that Zen is neither monistic nor dualistic. He has, in fact, written expressly on this theme.[4] I think it is also the case that over the years, his appreciation of the problem of monism for Zen has only deepened. Compare, for example, the exposition of Emptiness in his very early article (in English) "Buddhism and Christianity as a Problem for Today: Part II" (1963) with his extensive discussion of Emptiness in *Zen and Western Thought* (1985) and finally the above-mentioned essay "Kenotic God and Dynamic Sunyata" (1990).[5] In the earliest work the focus is on Zen's uncompromising nondualism. The Christian doctrine of creation is criticized as dualism with no concern over the possibility that *jinen* or *Śūnyatā* might be misconstrued as a metaphysical monism. Thus, Abe writes with relative innocence of "the One Self in which all things including oneself and other selves are one."[6] In *Zen and Western Thought,* the affirmations of wholeness and even totality that accompany Abe's characterizations of Emptiness are more qualified, suggesting an increased awareness of the problem of monism. Emptiness is "boundless and limitless" and "expands endlessly into all directions throughout the universe" so that "Nothing can be outside this endless and all-dimensional 'expanse' of Emptiness." It is "the unrestricted dynamic whole, in which you, I and everything else in the universe is included and realized equally just as it is in its suchness." However, in this same passage, Abe qualifies this nondualism by telling us that "everything in the universe retains its individuality because each thing is neither supported nor limited by any 'something' whatsoever."[7] In the essay "Kenotic God and Dynamic Sunyata," there is much more of a sense for the deconstructive strategies of the Mādhyamika and *Prajñāpāramitā* literature in Abe's exposition of Emptiness and, it seems, less prominence given to Zen's affinity with Japanese *hongaku* thought. This essay is significant in that Abe emphasizes the "dynamic" character of Emptiness not only as a way of relating Mahāyāna metaphysics to Christian thought but also as a doctrinal corrective to any monistic misunderstanding of Zen. As true Emptiness is in no way substantial (monistic), neither does it form a metaphysical substratum as the basis for undifferentiated totality. Instead, the identity of all things with nonsubstantial oneness is "dynamic."[8]

In contrasting "dynamic Sunyata" with "kenotic God" Abe shows more creativity and daring in his reworking of Christian doctrine than he does with Buddhist doctrine. The experiment, however, should not be abandoned. Instead, we need to ask how it can become as challenging to Abe's Buddhism as it is for Christianity. In pursuing this question, I suggest that we hold in reserve our interest in "dynamic Sunyata" as a model for understanding the Christian God and explore more deeply "dynamic Sunyata" as a critique of monism.

More concretely, Abe himself might deepen his experiment by looking to possible connections between a dynamic interpretation of Emptiness and the meaning of alterity ("otherness") for Buddhism. One possible way for Abe to appropriate a more nuanced sense of "the other" in his investigations of *Śūnyatā's* dynamism would be for him to look less to the Zen tradition and more to Jōdo Shin-shū (the Pure Land School of Japanese Buddhism). Jōdo Shin-shū may prove to be important in that it offers what may be the most sophisticated example of "dynamic Sunyata" known in Japanese Buddhism—and for this reason, it also offers what is perhaps the best critique of Japanese Buddhism's monistic tendencies. Jōdo Shin-shū's basic metaphor for Emptiness is "other power" (*tariki*).

With this metaphor, Jōdo Shin-shū believers affirm *Śūnyatā* as non-monistic ("other") and as dynamic ("power"). At the same time, Jōdo Shin-shū also has been required to develop impressive doctrinal strategies for defending the compatibility of this "otherness" with Mahāyāna Buddhism's insistence on strict nondualism.

Let me offer two comments. First, in some ways, a turn to Jōdo Shin-shū would not be an easy task for Abe to carry out. As a young man, Abe took the costly step of leaving the Jōdo Shin-shū faith of his youth to adopt the Zen of Shin'ichi Hisamatsu. Abe comments on this time in his life in an account of one of his first encounters with D. T. Suzuki.

> In those days I knew nothing about Zen. Or it would probably be
> more accurate to say that I viewed Zen through my own subjective
> reactions and prejudices. I was sticking hardheadedly to the path
> of Pure Land Buddhism and made no move to yield to anyone on
> religious matters.[9]

At great personal cost and by means of an impressive personal transformation, Abe's religious outlook was reshaped by the Zen movement. Experimenting intellectually with Jōdo Shin-shū would require him to move away from the familiar (the classic texts of Zen and the Kyoto School) and begin to experiment with the less familiar and, for Abe, the more dangerous language of grace and alterity that we find in Shinran's *Kyōgyōshinshō*.[10] However, in other ways, this departure may not be as radical as it would seem at first. D. T. Suzuki, who continues to serve as a model for Abe in his engagement of Western thought, remained an exponent of Pure Land Buddhism throughout his long life. Nor do I mean to imply that Abe has ever rejected Jōdo Shin-shū. Still, it would be of great interest to see Abe engage, in his senior years, the Buddhism of his youth, but now as a mature scholar.[11]

My second comment has to do with the impact a new encounter between Abe and Jōdo Shin-shū might have on his dialogue with Christianity. Jan van Bragt has suggested we look to Jōdo Shin-shū as a bridge between Christianity and other forms of Buddhism.[12] As Zen and Christianity look to the problem of "the other" in their respective struggles with monism and dualism, perhaps the dynamism of *Śūnyatā*, manifest as "otherness" yet understood entirely in terms of the Mahāyāna critique of dualism as we find in Jōdo Shin-shū, might lead to a deeper basis for the mutual transformation of Buddhism and Christianity. At the very least, Masao Abe's contribution to interreligious understanding has led us far in this direction.

Part Five

COMPARATIVE PHILOSOPHY

Chapter Twenty-Four

MASAO ABE
AS D. T. SUZUKI'S
PHILOSOPHICAL
SUCCESSOR

Thomas P. Kasulis

AS IS PROBABLY TRUE with many other contributors, it is difficult for me to separate the writings of Masao Abe from the man I know and who has meant much to me in my career of studying Japanese philosophy. Appropriately enough, I first met Abe within the first few days of my very first visit to Japan in 1972. As an East-West Center student fresh from my course work at the University of Hawai'i, I was trying to set up in Kyoto, where I would be spending six months in further language training and in an introduction to Zen Buddhist practice. Armed with a list of contacts in Japan, I began with the man who had kindly offered by letter to help me find a place to live in Kyoto. When I reached the Reverend Sōhaku Ogata's home at Shōkoku-ji, a Zen temple in central Kyoto, I was shocked to learn that he had just recently died. Mrs. Ogata, who was extraordinarily kind under such distressing circumstances, invited me for tea and asked whether I had the name of any other contacts in the area. When I mentioned Masao Abe's name, she immediately went to the phone and called him. The next day he found me a temporary home in Kyoto. Over the years he has helped me find a more permanent home in Japanese philosophy. In so helping, he has influenced me both by his written work and by our personal conversations.

In considering Abe's contribution to the field of Japanese philosophy over the two decades I have known him, a few key points bear mentioning. Let us consider first his cotranslations (with Norman Waddell) of Dōgen's writings in *The Eastern Buddhist*. In those translations Abe made available to the West the ideas of one of Japan's most fascinating premodern philosophers. The significance of this enterprise is best understood when we consider the perspective taken by one of Abe's teachers, D. T. Suzuki. The West owes a profound debt to D. T. Suzuki for introducing Zen Buddhism. Yet, it is important to note that Suzuki was often an apologist for the Rinzai against the Sōtō tradition of Zen. In fact, on several public occasions in America when Suzuki was asked about Dōgen, he boldly asserted that Dōgen was not enlightened; therefore, we need not study his writings seriously. In so doing, Suzuki had rejected out of hand a representative of the Zen tradition who might have been of great interest to Western philosophers. Suzuki would undoubtedly have known about this potential interest since he had made his anti-Sōtō and anti-Dōgen comments in the 1960s. By then Dōgen had already become a topic of deep interest among such Kyoto School philosophers as Hajime Tanabe and Tetsurō Watsuji. This suggests that Suzuki had not only an anti-Sōtō but also an antiphilosophical stance. (Or as Suzuki sometimes put it, an "ante-rational" or "ante-scientific" standpoint.)

In this respect, Abe's cotranslation of Dōgen's writings was a major breakthrough, especially since it was carried out by a former disciple of Suzuki. Abe had the insight to realize that as effective as Suzuki had been in the West, the impact of Zen *philosophy* had been artificially restricted by Suzuki's perspective. By bringing the Dōgen translations to the West, and by supplementing them with his own philosophical commentary, Abe successfully served as a corrective to any misconceptions that the West might have had about the relation between Zen and philosophy. This is also the case with his interest in the Kyoto School.

Again, the relation between Suzuki and the Kyoto School fit the anti- or ante-philosophical pattern mentioned in relation to Dōgen. From childhood days, Suzuki was a lifelong friend of Kitarō Nishida, yet Suzuki did very little to introduce the ideas of this most prominent of modern Japanese philosophers to the West. The only significant exception was

Suzuki's essay attached to the first English translation of *Zen no kenkyū* (translated as *A Study of Good*, by Valdo H. Viglielmo, Tokyo, 1960). It is noteworthy that the translation was done under the auspices of UNESCO, and the book, published in Japan, had limited circulation in the West. Suzuki apparently did not use his excellent connections with Western publishers or his own reputation to push for a wider readership of this book among Western readers. So, again, as much as Suzuki opened a new vista to the West, that vista was not really a philosophical one. Abe is a study in contrast. Not only did he cotranslate (with Christopher Ives) a new English version of that same work but he has written numerous essays on major figures of the Kyoto School—in addition to Nishida, most notably, Nishitani, Tanabe, and Shin'ichi Hisamatsu.

To sum up, one of Abe's distinctive contributions to the West has been his service as a successor to D. T. Suzuki. As Suzuki's disciple, Abe is deeply entrenched in the Zen tradition and the way Suzuki presented it to the West. Yet Abe is also a philosopher, a disciple of the Kyoto School as represented by both his teachers: Nishitani and, more intimately, Hisamatsu. Therefore, Abe has brought a new dimension to Western Zen studies. He carried on the tradition of Suzuki and brought to it a new, distinctively philosophical, element. Furthermore, by drawing inspiration from the writings of Dōgen, the founder of Japanese Sōtō Zen, he has brought a less sectarian perspective to the West's understanding of Zen Buddhism.

Abe's other major contribution as a historical figure in East-West interaction has been his personal, active engagement with Western thinkers, especially Christian theologians. Through that engagement he has brought a Kyoto School and Zen Buddhist perspective directly into the forums of Western theology's pluralistic conversations. Buddhist-Christian dialogue has become one of the most active enterprises of inter-religious discourse, and the prominence of that dialogue is directly linked to Abe's own efforts and concerns. Because of his training in the Kyoto School philosophy, Abe knows the Western tradition in some detail and has been able to engage Western theology in its philosophical presuppositions. By presenting a more philosophical insight into the meaning of Zen, Abe has been able to establish a more fruitful level of discourse with Christian theologians. In the past ten or fifteen years, there has been a series of works by Kyoto School philosophers translated into English. It is fair to say that Abe was instrumental in preparing the Western ground for the introduction of those texts. In this respect, Abe has had a profound effect on the climate of interreligious discussion, especially on a philosophical plane.

By keeping in mind Abe's historical role as mediator between Western and Japanese philosophy, we can now undertake a brief evaluation of his philosophical contributions. As has been suggested, Abe has consciously directed his philosophical energies to engage with the West. He is the only philosopher trained in the Kyoto School to have done so on such a scale. No commitment is without its price, however. In formulating his own ideas, he has often adapted his thinking to the needs of his Western audience. This does not mean that Abe's work is totally unknown or unappreciated in his own country. It does mean, however, that the problematic he has assumed has often been more immediately applicable to the Western than to the Japanese intellectual condition. In turning to answer his Western interlocutors, he has sometimes had to turn away from issues most interesting to philosophers and Buddhist scholars within his home culture. Yet unless he made that turn, the face-to-face encounter with the West would have been ineffective.

Let us briefly consider one specific example of the general point just raised: Abe's interpretation of Dōgen. Abe does not present us with a profile of Dōgen that we would find in much contemporary Japanese buddhological scholarship. Abe's Dōgen is somewhat abstracted from his historical and sectarian contexts, for example. Abe is not concerned with Dōgen as the founder of a particular sect frequently engaged in sectarian dogmatics. Nor is Abe's Dōgen primarily a historical product of a particular mind-set formulated in Kamakura Japan. Nor is Abe's Dōgen a fallible individual who was undergoing personal anguish and changes of mind. Nor is Abe's Dōgen a text explicable only by a closed tradition of commentary or explicable only insofar as we bring to him our own presuppositions as modern readers. All these perspectives might be found in a number of more mainstream scholarly readings of Dōgen in either Japan or the West. What Abe presents as Dōgen is fundamentally different, however. In Abe's writings, Dōgen is posed more as a philosophical position, a set of interrelated ideas emergent from the experience of *satori*.

Why does Abe take this view of Dōgen? Probably because it is the one he believes most relevant to his interface with the West today.

Because the West had fallen into the pattern of thinking of "Zen philosophy" as an oxymoron, Abe brought the philosophical Dōgen into his conversations with the West. Even if subtleties about Dōgen's social and historical context might be muted by this approach, Abe has been willing to make that concession in favor of presenting a Zen view that, Abe believes, would be beneficial to Western philosophy and theology. Hence, Abe's Dōgen is primarily an idea or position Abe argues for and defends, not a mere historical thinker subject to evaluation, criticism, and at least partial rejection. Abe's reading of Dōgen cannot be separated from the audience for whom Abe is making his reading.

In some ways, Abe's was a choice like Suzuki's. Suzuki could have been a traditional scholar of Buddhism in Japan. If he had turned all his efforts in that direction, his contributions to, and influence on, pure buddhology might have been enormous. But the West would still today probably know little about Zen. Not only would the number of Western scholars of Buddhism be much smaller but even American literature, poetry, arts, and theology would probably have a slightly different cast.

In a similar way, Abe has taken himself somewhat out of the closed circuit of philosophy and Buddhist studies in Japan. By so doing, he has come to ask different questions and to give a different approach in his answers from many of his Japanese colleagues. In this respect, he has broken out of the constrictive boundaries of his own tradition: it is misleading to continue to identify him as simply a "representative" of the Kyoto School or of Zen Buddhism.

Certainly there is no denying Abe's roots in those traditions, but as his problematics have evolved through his contact with the West, he is no longer simply "representative" of those Japanese traditions. He now stands for his own particular orientation within the Kyoto School and within the Zen tradition, an orientation that looks more pointedly toward the West as his foil and as his conversation partner. That orientation is steeped in Suzuki and, to a much lesser extent, Hisamatsu, but it is in the end really Abe's own. By bridging the gap between the intellectual worlds of Japan and the West, he is no longer simply one or the other; nor is he both. Rather, he is a philosopher in his own right, and through the stance he takes, communicative lines between Japan and the West have been established.

Because of the importance of Abe's distinctive stance, I prefer not to evaluate his work in terms of whether I agree with his interpretations of Dōgen, Nishitani, or Nishida. On many technical points I suspect we would disagree. Would we really expect otherwise from two philosophers' interpretations of other philosophers? Such a discussion might be valuable in certain contexts, but when I think of Abe's overall contribution, it is in terms of what he has done with the ideas of those philosophers, how he has used them to develop his own philosophical viewpoint with its own personal insights. In short, we may miss the significance of Abe's contribution if we focus too much on the scholar who interprets other thinkers. Rather, I prefer to see Abe as a philosopher who uses the ideas of others to promote his own philosophical agenda. To dwell inordinately on Abe's readings of Dōgen, Nishitani, or Nishida would be like dwelling on Heidegger's reading of the Presocratics. Certainly, there are points we could make in either case, but to reduce Heidegger to his reading of the Presocratics or Abe to his reading of the Japanese philosophers would be to ignore the simple fact that their real contribution is as philosophers, not as scholars or historians of ideas.

When I examine Abe's own philosophical position, a position that runs through his analyses of other Japanese philosophers as well as through his own substantive philosophical essays, one emphasis is particularly striking. Namely, Abe's view emerges from an emphasis on the immediate and mystical experience of Emptiness *(Śūnyatā)*. This experience is immediate insofar as it occurs outside the normal processes of conceptualization. It is mystical in the technical sense that it cannot be expressed in language directly (that is, without contradiction, metaphor, analogy, etc.). Put in simpler terms, Abe's philosophy emerges from the standpoint of *satori*. In this regard we can, I think, see the strong influence of Suzuki and Hisamatsu. The assumption is that without the clarity of that experience, philosophical thinking runs into unavoidable obstacles. Philosophical problems may be solved in normal philosophical discourse, but their solution inevitably leads to further philosophical problems. Only in *satori* can philosophical problems be truly resolved (and, in a sense, dissolved).

This is why at certain critical points in his argument, Abe often resorts to paradox and apparent contradiction. At such points his argument typically takes the form of "*A* as not-*A*" with the *A* determined by the issue at hand—for example, "the personal as impersonal," or "self as no-self." It is not that Abe is *solving* the philosophical issue with such a locution but rather that he is pointing to the limitation of the conceptual web in which the issue has been posed. We might even say that he is transcending the philosophical discourse entirely.

On this point we can find a nuance of difference between Abe and some of the other members of the Kyoto School. The so-called logic of *soku* expressed in the "A as not-A" rhetoric can be interpreted in different ways. For Nishitani, for example, it is more a structure within his epistemology than a transcendence of epistemology. Like Nishida, Nishitani wanted to *explain* the *soku* logic, not merely *use* it. In this respect, by the very fact that they are trying to explain this notion, both Nishida and Nishitani tend to avoid references to the *satori* experience as a foundation for their philosophies. To overstate the contrast with Abe, for Nishida and Nishitani *satori* is something to be explained philosophically, not something that explains (away) the problems of philosophy. It is not surprising, therefore, that in his *Inquiry into the Good,* Nishida avoids direct references to the "Zen experience" and instead talks about Mozart's composing musical pieces all at once, Goethe's composing of a poem in a dream, and even the analysis of a judgment like "the horse runs." Similarly, Nishitani's analysis of Emptiness in *Religion and Nothingness* was framed as a response to modernity's experience of nihilism and nihility. In discussing his perspective on the mind as body, the external as internal, Tetsurō Watsuji used the example in his preface to *Climates* of the everyday experience of "cold." In his *Philosophy as Metanoetics,* Hajime Tanabe used his version of the *soku* logic to argue for an internal deconstructive dialectic that would undermine any assertion of ultimate truth, personal insight, and uncritical authority.

As I have noted already, I have intentionally overdrawn the contrast between Suzuki/Hisamatsu/Abe and Nishida/Nishitani/Watsuji/Tanabe. Certainly all these thinkers, each in his own distinctive way, treasures the importance of Emptiness and our possible experience of it. There is no fundamental disagreement on that point. The difference, however, is in how that experience of Emptiness enters into their respective philosophical discussions. In broad terms, the first group advocates that experience as beneficial to the resolution of philosophical problems. For the second group, however, the experience needs to be explained and located in relation to more mundane, more secular, more everyday types of experiences.

Why do these two groups take such a different approach? Again, I think audience is important.

Nishida, Nishitani, Watsuji, and Tanabe primarily wrote for Japanese. The reality and importance of the Buddhist experience was not, therefore, questioned. The issue for them was more often the problem of what that experience could mean in an increasingly Westernized context. How could that experience enrich Western philosophy with new and useful categories? For all of them, in one way or another, this was ultimately an issue of logic, the way concepts can be said to entail one another.

In the case of Hisamatsu, on the other hand, there was an unusually powerful emphasis on the spiritual-aesthetic dimension of life. Personally involved with the traditional arts of Japan, Hisamatsu advocated and articulated the *satori* experience as the ground of creativity. According to his analysis, one could not grasp the essence of tea ceremony or flower arranging unless one first came to grips with the experience of Emptiness. In other words, compared with other members of the Kyoto School, Hisamatsu was less interested in developing a comprehensive epistemology. Instead, he was more involved in fathoming the spiritual basis of creativity and showing us how to capture it.

Suzuki and Abe's audience has been typically more Western than Japanese. For that audience, the nature and importance of the Buddhist experience of *satori* cannot be taken for granted. Inevitably, therefore, the issue of how to locate *satori* in everyday life and its ramifications for epistemology and logic could not be their main concern. Instead, Suzuki and Abe found that they had to point to the importance of the experience itself. Rather than locate *satori* within the everyday, they had to show how there was something *beyond* the everyday as it has been normally understood in Western thinking, at least Western secular thinking. Furthermore, to the extent the West has recognized a spiritual dimension beyond the everyday, Suzuki and Abe have had to show that the nature of that spiritual dimension is not the same in Christianity and the West. In this respect, Suzuki and Abe have both had to approach their Western conversational partners as "other," at least initially.

With this fix on the historical and cultural context of Abe's position, we can better understand why his influence has been so broad and his work so engaging. In his reading of other Japanese thinkers, both traditional and modern, he keeps his focus on the importance of Emptiness as an experiential reality in their works. In his interactions with Christianity, he sees Christianity as constructive in its emphasis on the spiritual dimension but also importantly different from Buddhism in the way that spirituality is philosophically articulated. Ultimately Abe's philosophical goal is primarily edification rather than analysis. That is, he strives to point us beyond where we ordinarily look so that we see and experience something more than the everyday. He strives to show us the limitations of our philosophies even while engaging us in them. In this edifying dimension he is more akin to Socrates than Aristotle, more to Kierkegaard than Hegel. Most of all, though, he is akin to his teacher, D. T. Suzuki.

chapter Twenty-Five

KITARŌ NISHIDA, WILLIAM JAMES, AND MASAO ABE: SOME COMMENTS ON PHILOSOPHY EAST AND WEST

John E. Smith

MORE THAN ANY OTHER Japanese philosopher, Masao Abe has been responsible for introducing the Western philosophical community to the immensely creative and highly significant comparative work of Kitarō Nishida. Nishida was Japan's foremost philosophical thinker of the twentieth century. And during Abe's tenure here in the West, he did much to draw our attention to Nishida's philosophy through his many seminars, lectures, articles, and books.

In the introduction to his English translation of Nishida's *Inquiry into the Good*,[1] Masao Abe makes two illuminating contributions to the continuing dialogue between the traditions of European and Anglo-American reflective thinking and that body of ancient insights stemming from India, China, and Japan. In the first place, Abe underlines the basic differences between the two traditions while not losing sight of the presence in each of thinkers who, so to speak, cross over to the other side. In the second place, he seeks to show how Nishida's thought represents not so much a "synthesis" of the dominant features of philosophy East and West as the presentation of a third alternative "which is neither Eastern nor Western" but is in reality "a new world philosophy."² The originality of Nishida's effort and Abe's interpretation is found in the way in which major insights from each tradition are brought into play in the formation of a new outlook that transcends both. In his introduction, Abe traces the entire development of Nishida's thought; here I shall confine attention to the *Inquiry* alone since, as Abe writes in summing up the significance of the book:

> Nishida transformed Zen into philosophy for the first time in
> the history of this religious tradition and, also I for the first time,
> transformed Western philosophy into a Zen-oriented philosophy.
> In Nishida, then, the East-West encounter took a most remarkable
> form.³

Abe finds the Eastern and Western ways of thinking to be qualitatively different from each other in that Western philosophy as represented by Descartes, Kant, or Hegel aims at a purely rational and theoretical system controlled by logic and precise language, while Eastern thought—Zen is the extreme case—is indirect, suggestive, symbolic, intuitive, and not dependent on either language or demonstrative argument. Abe takes note, however, of the exceptions to these patterns in both traditions and cites Augustine, Schopenhauer, and Kierkegaard as examples from the West, and Kūkai, Shinran, and Dōgen as counterparts from the side of Japanese thought. It is interesting that Dōgen, who introduced the Sōtō sect of Zen, is often depicted as a kind of Japanese Kant because of his emphasis on the temporal character of the phenomenal world and his idea that Enlightenment is a precondition (*a priori*) of practice.

The second difference between the two traditions, according to Abe, has to do with the relation between philosophy and religion. As he rightly points out, the two are closely interwoven if not indistinguishable in the writings of Indian, Chinese, and Japanese thinkers, whereas in the West philosophy and religion came to be distinguished from each other and were often opposed except when they enjoyed a creative interchange in the philosophical theologies that flourished in Christianity, Judaism,

262 John E. Smith

and Islam up to the end of the Middle Ages. This difference is important because one of the aims of Nishida was to provide a central place for religion in his reconstruction of a philosophy expressive of the Eastern way of thinking and mode of life.

With regard to Nishida's view of Western thought vis-à-vis his own tradition, Abe calls attention to three points. First, Nishida valued the universality of Western philosophy and logic and sought to learn from it but at the same time saw it as an instance of what he called the self-formation of life that is not free from the particularity of Western experience. Second, he believed that the Eastern way of thinking is also a mode of self-formation but that it is in need of a "logical foundation" so it can be expressed as a *philosophy*. As Abe says, this was a central problem for Nishida because that foundation cannot come from a Western "objective" logic. Third, in view of the divergence of the two ways of thinking, Nishida had to search for a "truly universal logic" adequate for his purpose.

Mention has already been made of Abe's judgment about the importance of Nishida's having transformed Zen into philosophy and the consequent impact on philosophy of that change. One of Abe's signal contributions is his insightful account of how Nishida sought to resolve the problem. Nishida had practiced Zen, and according to Abe, it had a great influence on his thought despite the fact that it is not mentioned in the *Inquiry*. Since the book is thoroughly discursive in its aim of answering the philosophical question "What is ultimate reality?" Nishida's outlook cannot be "based" on Zen in any ordinary sense, because of his rejection of words and doctrinal thinking. But in Abe's view, that does not mean Nishida could not proceed in the direction of Zen, but by transforming its character—which is in fact what Nishida did. For Nishida to have a *philosophical* answer to the question about ultimate reality, Abe writes, "he had to engage in philosophical thinking, he had to transform Zen experience into a philosophical answer."[4] Abe sees two aspects to the development: first, the practice of philosophy demands a logical expression of Zen experience, which means breaking through Zen's rejection of discursive thought, and second, Zen practice requires a transformation of philosophy and its primacy of rationality in order to allow for a receptiveness to ultimate reality.

Abe seeks to throw further light on the meaning of Nishida's achievement by recounting the philosophical situation he faced in 1911, at the time of the *Inquiry*. The aftermath of Hegel took the form of an opposition between two basic philosophical outlooks. On one side stood positivism, empiricism in the vein of Hume, and materialism old (Feuerbach) and new (Marx) in which the prevailing attitude was antimetaphysical, prompted by the belief in some cases that natural science would come to replace philosophy, and often atheistic. On the other side and opposed to scientism and the rejection of metaphysics and religion stood Schopenhauer, Nietzsche, Dilthey, and Bergson, whose position was called *Lebensphilosophie* because of its emphasis on human life, the central place of will and ideals, and the value of individual personality. They were joined in their opposition to materialism and atheism by the philosophers of Existenz—Kierkegaard, Unamuno, Berdyaev, and others—who sought to recover the role of religious faith by forcing each individual to confront the question of the ultimate meaning of existence.

Abe rightly calls attention to a third position that was then emerging, which was motivated by the attempt to grasp the *phenomena of consciousness* as a matter of presented fact. He associates this position with Wilhelm Wundt, William James, Gustav Fechner, and Ernst Mach and at the same time notes its dependence on *psychology*. The point is important because Nishida was greatly attracted to this position but sought to go beyond this psychological dependence because of his interest in a philosophy that would allow for metaphysics. The problem of "psychologism" implicit in this new turn to find the ingredients of "pure experience" is well focused by a thinker Abe does not mention, namely, Edmund Husserl, the founder of the Phenomenological movement. Husserl's aim was akin to that of James in the quest for pure experience, but he inveighed against "psychologism" in the belief that the phenomena of consciousness could be recovered directly as veridical meaning contents without the need to bring them under the rubric of "psychology," which at the time meant "subjective" states of individual consciousness. It is of the utmost importance as well that James, whose earlier attempts to describe the "stream of thought" that appeared as the basis of the analysis in his *Principles of Psychology,* was later to move to a metaphysical position when he developed "radical empiricism" at the center of what he called "a world of pure experience."

As Abe makes clear, it is impossible to overestimate the extent of

Nishida's attraction to the idea of a philosophy based on pure experience, and he cites his assertion in the preface to the *Inquiry*: "For many years I wanted to explain all things on the basis of pure experience as the sole reality."[5] Nishida was well acquainted with the works of Wundt and James, and there can be no question that he was thoroughly sympathetic to the philosophical approach through pure experience. But he had at least two reservations about it and in grappling with them Nishida was led to develop his own original version of the nature of pure experience. I am not convinced that Nishida's criticisms of James's position are entirely justified, but except for the light that might be thrown on Nishida's own view by joining the issue, it is wiser to concentrate on that view itself, especially since it is at the center of his position and since Abe very skillfully presents Nishida's modifications. First, however, must be seen what view of James there was to modify. I am confining the discussion to James because his view is not open to Nishida's objection that Wundt's "pure" experience must conform to Kant's forms of intuition and categories.

To begin with, James's fundamental idea of "pure experience" is the present awareness of a content—the things resting on my desk, for example—in which there is no awareness whatever of a duality between objects and a subject, between things apprehended and one who apprehends them. In this sense, pure experience is prior to any such distinction, or as James puts it, the distinction between subject and object well known to common sense and to many philosophical theories comes by way of *addition* to a primordial experience in which it is not to be found. The second characteristic feature of pure experience for James is that it includes relations, conjunctions, transitions, tendencies, and continuities, in contrast to classical empiricism, in which all the emphasis was on distinctions and disjunctions so that, in effect, fixed and static things (terms) took precedence over continuities and connections (relations), with the result that the dynamic of experience was lost.

According to Abe, Nishida developed three objections to the Western philosophical conception of pure experience. First, it is assumed that such experience is *individual* in character, which constitutes an addition of a dogmatic sort. Second, the West sees pure experience only from *without,* by which Nishida means that the concreteness of pure experience is lost in the process of analyzing it into psychological elements—perception, feeling, etc.—that are then reconstructed. It is important to notice that Nishida sees this shortcoming as the "generalization" of what was originally living, "individual" experience. Third, there is the problem that Western thinkers miss what Nishida calls "direct experience" because they view pure experience itself in terms of an observing-and-observed consciousness and thus fail to grasp it prior to the separation of subject and object.

Some comments about the consistency of these objections are in order, but I shall postpone them until after we have set forth what Abe rightly sees as Nishida's new and original depiction of "direct experience" that is to serve as the avenue to a new metaphysics. My comments will be more understandable in the light of Nishida's new insight. Abe singles out the passage from the *Inquiry* that I take to express the crucial distinction Nishida wants to make. Nishida writes:

> It is not that experience exists because there is an individual, but that an individual exists because there is experience. I thus arrived at the idea that experience is more fundamental than individual differences, and in this way I was able to avoid solipsism.[6]

Nishida is clearly arguing against the view—attributed both by Nishida and his interpreter to common sense and much Western thought—that there is "first" an individual who experiences things so that the experienced thing and the experiencing self are distinguished. Abe sees an insuperable obstacle in this way of describing the situation, namely, that the attainment of any universal truth becomes possible only by transcending individual consciousness, usually in the direction of a transempirical realm. Against this whole approach, Nishida claims that it is not the case that the self first exists and then experiences things as objects, but that in actual experience the self is also experienced and he concludes that experience is more fundamental than the individual, which is the reason why he insists that an individual exists because there is experience.

I believe that Nishida and Abe are right in attacking the idea—it can be found in Descartes, in Hume, and in a less obvious sense in Kant—that there is "first" an individual who as a subject experiences and comes to know objects in some incorrigible way that is ultimately confined to that individual alone so that the problem becomes that of "transcending" this individuality to reach an intersubjective truth. I should add that both James and, in an even more pointed way, Peirce were making the same attack as Nishida proposes; but there are problems to be considered that bring me to my postponed comments.

The first is that James did not start with a full-blown individual but rather with the "stream of thought" that, as he says, "tends toward personal form," by which he means that the person *experiences* the self as having an interest in or concern for what is experienced in the stream and which *in time* leads to a consciousness of being a self. There is, moreover, no initial reference to an individual in the two papers of 1904—"Does Consciousness Exist?" and "A World of Pure Experience"—in which James set forth the basic ideas behind both pure experience and radical empiricism. The first of these papers declares that "consciousness" does not exist as an individual *substance* but is rather a *function* or "an affair of relations." In rejecting the idea that we have an immediate consciousness of consciousness itself and hence are aware of it by subtracting the content, James makes the following conclusive statement:

> Experience, I believe, has no such inner duplicity; and the separation of it into consciousness and content comes, not by way of subtraction but by way of addition.[7]

In short, for James any distinction between subject and object is always consequent and not primordial. Referring to "pure experience," James writes that "in its pure state . . . there is no self-splitting of it into consciousness and what the consciousness is 'of' . . . 'pure' experience . . . is only virtually or potentially either subject or object."[8] From these and similar passages it is clear that James did not think of an individual consciousness or self coming "first" to be succeeded by a world of objects, and the point is reenforced by his speaking of a "world" of pure experience and by his description of the radical empiricism that follows from the idea of pure experience as a *Weltanschauung*.[9]

In light of the foregoing, it is reasonable to conclude that Nishida and Abe are mistaken in the claim that James *assumes* pure experience to be individual at the outset. In fact, we might turn the tables—this is my second comment—and point out that Nishida, in his charge that Western thinkers see pure experience only from without and "generalize" it through abstractions, is the one who assumes that such experience is *individual* from the outset; otherwise, what would there be to generalize? And, of course, in regarding this generalized experience as "abstract" and therefore no longer pure experience, Nishida is contrasting it with, in Abe's words, "living individual experience."[10] I understand Nishida's concern that the admission of individual experience not lead to encapsulation within the individual with no possibility of reaching what is transindividual, but there is no reason why both aspects should not exist together. One does not have to deny the reality of the individual in order to reach what transcends the individual. Indeed, I believe that all three thinkers hold this view and that they stand together against that mistaken idea of individual consciousness as closed, completed, certain, and so separated from the rest of existence that only a move away from experience to an Absolute could overcome the subjectivity. Abe's summary of the three characteristics that attach to Nishida's view of pure experience confirms the belief that in pure experience individuality and transindividuality can go together.

According to Abe, pure experience for Nishida is realized prior to the distinction between subject and object by virtue of the fact that both the self and things are experienced equally within the undivided complex called "direct experience." The seeing of a color, the hearing of a sound is prior to any thought of an object that is colored or that is the source of the sound. In the second place, direct experience, in contrast to the old empiricism in which experience is passive and static, is active and constructive. It is a system of consciousness that is self-developing and that, in Nishida's words, "manifests its wholeness through the orderly, differentiated development of a certain unifying reality."[11]

The third feature of direct experience is that in it knowledge, feeling, and volition are undifferentiated so that ultimate reality is a matter not only of theoretical knowledge but of practical and affective character. The last feature becomes clearer when Nishida goes on to speak of the good in the direction of human self-development. Pure experience tells us that it is neither "consciousness" nor "matter" that is ultimate, but a self-sufficient, *pure* activity—"the unifying power at the basis of our thinking and volition"—which is also the unifying power of the universe. It is from this vantage point that Nishida interprets the nature and significance of morality and religion. Personality is now seen as an infinite

268 John E. Smith

power of unity to be realized by "forgetting" the subjective self. The good is beyond both duty and utility and consists in fulfilling one's deepest nature, which is at the same time the realization of the universe. In a passage describing the good that Abe says is "deeply rooted in the Asian tradition,"[12] Nishida writes: "We reach the quintessence of good conduct only when subject and object merge, self and things forget each other, and all that exists is the activity of the sole reality of the universe."[13]

For Nishida, the religious demand is one that concerns the self as a whole; it aims at the transformation of the self and the reformation of life and is thus the deepest demand for the ultimate unity of the self and the universe. God is the basis of that ultimate unity, an insight Nishida regarded not as a matter of speculation but of pure experience. "Our consciousness," he writes, "is one part of God's consciousness and its unity comes from God's unity."[14] The religious consciousness finds this unity in pure experience, but in characteristic Oriental fashion, Nishida declares that "as long as one has even the slightest idea of believing in the finite self, one has yet to acquire a true religious spirit."[15]

Abe rightly finds problems with the idea of pure experience—especially the matter of meaning and content and the equation of experience and knowing—and he traces Nishida's further efforts to deal with them. I shall not attempt to follow him there; I would, however, strongly support Abe's appraisal of Nishida's *Inquiry into the Good* as a point at which the East-West encounter took on a most remarkable form. There is a true interchange involved with a resulting transformation on both sides.

chapter Twenty-Six

MASAO ABE'S
ZEN PHILOSOPHY
OF DIALOGUE:
A WESTERN RESPONSE

Thomas Dean

IN THE SECOND HALF of the twentieth century, the Japanese thinker most responsible for building bridges between Zen Buddhism and Western thought has been Masao Abe. It was my good fortune to have attended a discussion group led by Abe from 1985 to 1987 at Haverford College on the Kyoto School of philosophy and its implications for comparative and cross-cultural thought, Asian and Western. I came away from that experience with a deep sense of indebtedness to Abe not only for the intellectual feast he laid before us but also for his openness to each of us participants, no matter what our sophistication or lack thereof on the subjects under discussion. His personal magnanimity and gentle humor were matched only by the seriousness and thoughtfulness with which he responded to each of our questions, doubts, or criticisms. As a teacher, he was the embodiment of intellectual integrity, personal warmth, and spiritual life-wisdom.

It is a privilege, therefore, to enter into this discussion with Masao Abe. In exercise of this responsibility, I shall focus on some questions that arise concerning Abe's approach to Asian-Western dialogue in philosophy as set forth in his major work, *Zen and Western Thought*.[1] In our colloquium Abe continually encouraged us to engage him in dialogue on the topics we were considering. It follows that in essays honoring his own work in dialogue, he would not have us do any less. It is only by taking such philosophical work as that of Masao Abe with the utmost serious-ness and entering into the most strenuous dialogue with it that this late-twentieth-century project of constructive global philosophy, for which Masao Abe above all has shown the way, can go forward.

Masao Abe's book *Zen and Western Thought* represents the mature fruits of his decades-long effort at cross-cultural bridge building. In this book he enters into a profound dialogue with Western philosophy and theology from the standpoint of a Zen philosophy. In responding to Abe's Zen thought from a Western standpoint, I shall raise a number of ques-tions about his understanding of the nature, goal, and resources available for cross-cultural encounter in philosophy. I shall draw in part on Heidegger, another twentieth-century thinker who reflected, though more briefly, on the nature of Asian-Western dialogue in the realm of philosophical thought. The questions I shall be asking arise against the background of Abe's insistence that such dialogue must not compromise the irreducible differences between various philosophical ways of think-ing. Such differences, says Abe, are "not of degree or extent but rather of quality and structure."[2] They are "systematic,"[3] "structural,"[4] and "deeply rooted."[5]

I

My first question is whether Abe conceives of dialogue as a matter sim-ply of describing these differences or whether it also involves evaluating which way of thinking is superior. If the latter, from whose standpoint and by what criteria are such normative claims to be made? Abe seems to be of two minds on this issue. On the one hand, he insists that his stress on the differences between Buddhism and Christianity is not meant as "a rejection or exclusion of Christianity from a Zen point of view, or as a pre-sumption of the superiority of Zen to Christianity."[6] He says, "My empha-sis on difference does not intend to judge which one is better."[7] It is rather an invitation to further dialogue "beyond the essential differences."[8] Critical questioning of another's tradition "will not destroy but rather deepen" that tradition.⁹ Further, he admits that his criticisms of Christianity may be based on an understanding of Western thought that is "insufficient and limited." Thus, he invites correction, his own analyses, he says, being "completely open to your criticism."¹⁰

On the other hand, Abe reminds us that persons can enter into dialogue only from the standpoint of their respective traditions. Abe acknowledges that one of his commitments is "to promot[e] a dialogue between Christianity and Buddhism from the side of Buddhism."¹¹ Here he draws attention to an important requirement for dialogue. Although we do share common existential concerns, our response to those concerns will always proceed from some particular standpoint embodying the presuppositions of one tradition or another. There are only two ways of "overcoming" or "bridging" the structural differences between two systems of thought, and that is by building such bridges from one side or the other. There is no universal or external standpoint, common or neutral to both.

This requirement returns us to our question. Approaching the task of comparison and bridge building from one side or the other would seem to entail that the resulting judgments will not be simply descriptive but normative as well. To refer to a "point of view" is to refer to certain criteria or standards of comparison and judgment. As Abe grants, "I have tried to clarify the differences of the thought structures of the two systems by using the conceptions of Mahayana Buddhism as the standard and by trying to see how closely [Western] philosophy approaches Mahayana Buddhism."¹²

It should be noted that while Abe admits to doing his work of comparison and bridge building "from the side of Buddhism," he expects Western thinkers to approach such dialogue and make such judgments similarly from their point of view using their criteria and standards. "I do not," says Abe, "exclude the opposite approach of using [Western] philosophy as the standard and then taking a look as to how close Mahayana Buddhism comes to it."¹³

However, it must be pointed out that Abe's proposal to use the categories of one side as the standard or criteria for describing and assessing the other involves, of necessity, judging how the other side does in answering a common set of questions not by a set of common criteria but by criteria specific to only one of the parties to the dialogue. This means that Abe is committed to judging the adequacy of the other tradition's answers solely in terms of how nearly they approximate his own. From this it is an easy step to the conclusion that to the extent the Western tradition does not approximate the Zen answer, it, not the Zen tradition, must reexamine its basic assumptions and presuppositions.

The problem this poses for Abe's effort is that there would seem to be a logical inconsistency between maintaining that one is not engaged in judging which system is superior while noting that one's judgments are being made from the standpoint of one's own tradition, particularly with reference to the criterion of how closely that other tradition approximates one's own presumably normative answers. Is this an inconsistency in his project, or is there an underlying rationale for what on the surface seems to be an effort that goes off in two different directions? Or as a third possibility, does this apparent inconsistency point to an unavoidable but not necessarily fatal "circularity" in any such second-order project of comparative philosophy or interreligious dialogue?

Just so we are clear that there is a potential problem here, Abe does in fact make normative claims about the superiority of Zen philosophy to Western thought based on the irreducible difference between the Buddhist category of Absolute Nothingness and Western notions of Being and God. I shall simply note several of these claims as evidence of this problem without going into the first-order details.

First, from a Buddhist perspective, Abe states that "the priority of (u) being over (mu) non-being is not *ontologically* justifiable."[14] Second, from a Zen perspective there remains a dualism between "subject and object, transcendence and immanence, being and non-being," "God and Creation," in the Christian concept of God.[15] Because Christian thought fails to answer the question of the origin of this duality, of the more original ground from which even God must emerge, it represents, says Abe, a doctrine that "must be thoroughly overcome."[16] Third, from a Zen perspective one cannot appeal to the divine aseity. For "how is God's self-existence possible? What is the *ground* of God's self-existence?"[17] The idea of "a self-sustaining God" that is the ground of its own self-existence is not only unjustifiable but unintelligible on Buddhist grounds, because, says Abe, the very notion of Being (and the ontological priority of Being as self-existence, *svabhāva*) is what is called into question and "overcome" by the Buddhist doctrine of Absolute Nothingness.

Thus, while Abe does allow that Zen needs to learn from Western thought, this admission apparently changes nothing in the essentials. Abe's approach to dialogue is so formulated as not to call into question the fundamentals of the Zen tradition. While Western thought is "forced to a basic reexamination" of its fundamental ontological categories and presuppositions, Zen is asked only to "internally embrace the standpoints of Western 'Being' and 'Ought' which have been foreign to itself."[18] In so doing it may "grasp again and renew its own standpoint of 'Nothingness'" without having to change anything in its own fundamentals.[19]

While there is nothing wrong and indeed much that is good in the idea that dialogue might lead to the incorporation of ideas previously viewed as "other" and to the further development of one's tradition in a more global direction, it does seem that the burden of Abe's critique is one-way. Further, it is simply assumed that the category of Nothingness will be able to "internally embrace" "foreign" categories that we have earlier been told are "irreducible" to one another.

II

My next set of questions about Abe's approach to the dialogue between Zen and Western thought has to do with one of his goals for such dialogue: that it provide "a spiritual foundation for future humanity in a global age."[20] In common with other members of the Kyoto School, he has in mind constructing, through a "creative synthesis between Western thought and the Mahayana tradition,"[21] a global or "world" philosophy capable of bridging and drawing East and West together on a common spiritual foundation. This project is more ambitious than the usual program of "comparative philosophy, East and West." Comparative philosophy does not necessarily envision or lead to such an all-embracing spiritual goal. The kind of dialogue Abe has in mind, on the other hand, does have a constructive, global ambition.

My questions are, What ontological assumption underlies Abe's vision of this global spiritual horizon? and Why in particular is it that the philosophy of Zen Buddhism and the dialogue between Buddhism and Christianity are especially well suited for achieving this new spiritual foundation?

Abe's assumption is that there is a position-transcending position from which we can properly evaluate all other positions. This assumption contains the answer to our first question. What makes the goal of a spiritual horizon for a unified world possible is that a corresponding ontology already exists and that it has been historically actualized in Zen Buddhism. The Buddhist position, founded in an ontology of Absolute Nothingness, "is a 'positionless position' in that, being itself empty, it lets every other position stand and work just as it is."[22] It does not evaluate other philosophies or religions as false but recognizes the relative truth they contain. On the basis of this Buddhist acknowledgment of the relative truth of other positions, the possibility of "productive dialogue and cooperation" is affirmed.[23] The ontological category of Absolute Nothingness, in short, "may provide a spiritual foundation for the formation of the rapidly approaching One World in which the co-existence of a variety of contrasting value systems, ways of life, and ways of thinking will be indispensable."[24]

There are limits to Abe's second-order strategy of affirming the relative truth of other traditions. Should a particular tradition resist the relativizing of its first-order truth-claims, it would be judged false or illusory. According to Abe, "in Buddhism, mutual relativity or inter-dependency is the ultimate truth, and doctrines of absolute truth which exclude other views of truth as false are similarly considered illusory."[25] Clearly, there is a second-order ontological criterion at work here. Only some ways of thinking about the truth of one's own or other traditions will pass the test. And given the assumption of a "positionless position" that relativizes the absolute truth-claims of all other positions and that does not consider the doctrine of Absolute Nothingness as a "position" in its own right, Abe can, without inconsistency, claim "on the basis of such a metaphysical standpoint, to bring under one purview the philosophical thought of the West and East, representing the latter by Buddhist thought in particular."[26]

The obvious question we must ask, from a Western perspective made sensitive by Heidegger and others to such notions as the "hermeneutical circle" and the "theory-laden" nature of all discourse, is whether such a clear separation between second-order ontological criteria and first-order ontological doctrines is in fact possible, and if not, whether Abe's second-order "positionless position" is not itself implicated in and in fact derived from a first-order "position" as well. If so, what does this do to his goal of achieving, through dialogue between different positions, a spiritual horizon common to them all? If we remove the ontological presupposition of a second-order "positionless position," if we insist, as do Heidegger and Gadamer, that such second-order proposals are themselves hermeneutical reflections of corresponding first-order positions, on what basis can Abe's global dialogue proceed?

Abe's second assumption is that Buddhism and Christianity are the closest world-historical approximations to this global horizon in the East and West, respectively. Abe argues from a quasi-Hegelian or developmental view of the history of religions as advancing from an earlier stage of "nature" or "primitive" religions to an intermediate stage of "ethnic" or "national" religions (examples: Judaism, Hinduism, Shinto), arriving at last at world or universal religions (examples: Buddhism, Islam, Christianity), which represent "the most advanced stage of human consciousness."[27] Christianity and Buddhism, which, according to Abe, are already universal in their "structure" or "inner essence" despite their "occidental" or "oriental" origins, are best qualified to achieve a truly global spiritual horizon through dialogue. Through such dialogue, they will become universal in their "outer" cultural forms as well.[28]

I have already indicated a difficulty in Abe's first presupposition, namely, the impossibility of establishing in a noncircular manner a second-order ontological criterion that is theory-neutral as to all first-order participants in a global dialogue. The consequences of that impossibility, when disregarded, become clearer when we see its implications for first-order traditions such as Judaism or Hinduism. These religions are apparently disqualified from coshaping the universal horizon of the future because of the irreducible particularity not of their cultural form but of their spiritual essence. I submit, on the contrary, that Abe's theory of the quasi-historical development of the essential forms of religious consciousness, grounded in a corresponding development in the stages of human consciousness and motivated by an underlying ontological agenda, is not only historically and philosophically questionable but, more important for his project, religiously unjustifiable as well. From the perspective of late-twentieth-century dialogue between Jews and Christians, at least, the spiritual validity of Judaism, both in its form and its content, must be absolutely affirmed by Christian thinkers against any attempt to relegate Judaism to second rank in an otherwise laudable effort to shape a more global, interreligious future.

An additional reason that Abe assigns Buddhism and Christianity a privileged position in this dialogue is that they constitute the two poles of a global spiritual horizon. Though Buddhism and Christianity are irreducibly different, they are not incompatible, because between them they embrace a fundamental polarity in the typology of world religions—the polarity between the ontological, represented in Zen by the doctrine of Absolute Nothingness, and the axiological, represented in Christianity by the doctrine of God as a personal moral being—Being as Ought. Abe's distinction is an interesting one and while not, I believe, ultimately defensible, it does shed light on a question that troubled us earlier. Given that Abe is relatively critical of the ontological foundations of Christianity from a Zen point of view, how can he also maintain, without falling into inconsistency, that Zen is in profound need of something from Christianity? The answer lies in his account of the "polar" relation of the two traditions.

For Christianity, the concept of God "should not be understood merely ontologically, but also axiologically." Christianity's chief religious concern is with the problem of good and evil, which, says Abe, "is not simply an ontological issue, but rather an *axiological* issue."[29] For Christians, the most significant issue is not God as Being but God as Ought. In Zen, on the other hand, the central religious issue is the problem of being and non-being. The idea of justice (the Ought) is relatively secondary, in fact, says Abe, "rather lacking, or at least very weak."[30] Abe therefore contrasts "Zen and its ontological understanding of Nothingness [and] Christian faith with its axiological emphasis on God's 'ought.'" Zen is radically critical of Christianity, but on ontological grounds. It finds Christianity's doctrine of God ontologically unjustifiable. But, says Abe, "Zen's criticism of the Christian view of the one God . . . does not necessarily hit the core of, or do justice to, the essence of Christianity," for the core or essence of the Christian concept of God has only secondarily to do with the concept of Being, whereas it has everything to do with the concept of the Ought. Therefore, he concludes, "the strength of Zen is the weakness of Christianity and vice versa. Based on this recognition of these mutual strengths and weaknesses, we must enter into dialogue."[31]

There are several problems with this formulation. First, as Abe himself notes, in both Zen and Christianity "ontological and axiological aspects are inseparably connected."[32] The fact that one aspect is allegedly "more central" to one tradition, while the other is "more strongly emphasized" by the other, does not therefore mean that one aspect represents the "strength" of one tradition and the "weakness" of the other. More important, since in each tradition these two "aspects" are "inseparably connected," that is, have an internal, systematic connection to each other, one cannot simply lift the axiological aspect out of the Christian context and set it in the ontological context of Buddhism. Nor, conversely, can one simply import the Buddhist concept of Absolute Nothingness into the Christian doctrinal scheme to provide an alternative ontological foundation for the distinctively Christian axiology. For as Abe himself has already told us, the metaphysical categories of Nothingness, Being, and Ought are irreducibly different.

III

My last set of questions is addressed to Abe's use of Western philosophical terms and the Western notion of philosophy as systematic thought to articulate the concepts and structure of his dialogue.

First, what are the implications of using a Western vocabulary to help clarify the "essence" of Zen "philosophy"? What are the implications of translating Buddhist terms into Western concepts or of trying at least to find "correspondences" between Buddhist and Western terms? If such translation is not possible without distortion, or at least interpretation, taking place, what does this mean for the translinguistic, transcultural ontology presupposed by Abe's project?

I have already raised a question about the "trans-lation" of concepts from one system of thought to another in the discussion of importing an axiology of justice from a Christian context into an ontology of Nothingness in a Zen context. But what happens when the process of translation takes place not between two different conceptual systems but between systems located in two radically different cultural "worlds," the worlds of Europe and East Asia? I am not suggesting that cross-cultural translation and dialogue are impossible, but can they proceed in the way Abe's project seems to suppose?

For another, more cautious—if not contrary—perspective on cross-cultural dialogue, let us look at Heidegger's conversation with a Japanese professor (and translator) of German literature, recorded in his essay "A Dialogue on Language between a Japanese and an Inquirer."[33]

In the discussion of a Japanese term conducted in a European language, Heidegger observes that

> the languages of the dialogue shifted everything into European. Yet the dialogue tried to say the essential nature of East Asian art and poetry. . . . The language of the dialogue constantly destroyed the possibility of saying what the dialogue was about.[34]

Why? Because, says Heidegger,

> if man by virtue of his language dwells within the claim and call of Being, then we Europeans presumably dwell in an entirely different house than East Asian man. Assuming that the languages of the two are not merely different but other in nature, and radically so. And so, a dialogue from house to house remains nearly impossible.[35]

Despite this difference, Japanese thinkers in the Kyoto School have tried translating Zen Buddhist terms into a conceptuality that might help Western and Asian thinkers alike to better understand the Zen tradition. But, Heidegger asks, do you really need Western philosophical "concepts" to articulate the spiritual experience of Zen? The Japanese professor replies, "Presumably yes, because since the encounter with European thinking, there has come to light a certain incapacity in our language." Heidegger says, "Here you are touching on a controversial question . . . the question whether it is necessary and rightful for East Asians to chase after the European conceptual systems."[36]

The problem Heidegger raises proceeds on at least two levels. First, are the "languages" in which Westerners and East Asians dwell not just different but radically other? Second, are "concepts," a feature distinctive of Western languages, inappropriate for expressing what the Japanese language says? If so, how, asks Heidegger, can we have any "assurance that European-Western saying and East-Asian saying will enter into dialogue such that in it there sings something that wells up from a single source?"[37] And if we can have no such assurance, where does that leave the prospects for dialogue?

Heidegger's answer is a great deal more tentative, perhaps even uncertain, than Abe's:

> J: *As you may have surmised, I see more clearly as soon as I think in terms of our Japanese experience. But I am not certain whether you have your eye on the same.*
>
> I: *That could prove itself in our dialogue.*
>
> J: *We Japanese do not think it strange if a dialogue leaves undefined what is really intended, or even restores it back to the keeping of the undefinable.*
>
> I: *That is part, I believe, of every dialogue that has turned out well between thinking beings. As if of its own accord, it can take care that that undefinable something not only does not slip away, but displays its gathering force ever more luminously in the course of the dialogue.*[38]

In other words, for Heidegger dialogue continues, but how and why it is possible and where it might lead—these are issues that remain to be pondered.

With this counter-example from Heidegger before us, let us look at Abe's treatment of this question of language. Abe is sensitive to the difficulty of finding concepts in Western philosophical vocabulary that correspond to, let alone adequately translate, the meaning of key Buddhist terms. The most fundamental problem of translation concerns the Japanese terms for Nothingness and Being, *mu* and *u*. Abe says this is because of a conceptual bias of the Western metaphysical tradition that subscribes to "the priority of Being over non-being." This bias he attributes to the fact that the Western tradition does not take the fundamental human experience of negativity as deeply or seriously as does the

Buddhist tradition. Because of this lack of common ground in thought or experience, *mu* and *u* have no exact equivalent in Western philosophical terminology and, in fact, are completely foreign to Western ways of thinking. Hence, such terms cannot be adequately translated.

Abe's conclusion, which would appear to be in accord with Heidegger, is particularly worrisome, however, because the concept of Nothingness is the fundamental term in Abe's account of the structural difference between Buddhist and Western ways of thinking and his critique of it. It is of crucial importance for a dialogue between Zen Buddhism and Western thought to be able to translate the Japanese term for Absolute Nothingness, *mu,* into philosophical terms that, from traditional Western categories, can nevertheless be understood. If no equivalent Western terms can be found, the effort at translation will founder and the enterprise of dialogue, as Abe conceives it, will be rendered problematic. We are thus confronted with a dilemma. To the extent that the translation of *mu* into alien Western terms succeeds—and every translation is an interpretation—will it be at the cost of no longer saying what, in its original setting, it really says? Must it be, as Heidegger seems to suggest, that "the language of the dialogue constantly destroys the possibility of saying what the dialogue was about," namely, the Japanese experience of *mu?*

One possible conclusion from these observations, which seem to make the idea of a philosophical dialogue between Zen and Western thought "nearly impossible" (Heidegger), is that the attempt to clarify the essence of Zen Buddhism with the help of Western philosophical concepts (Abe's other major goal in these essays) cannot succeed, that such an effort runs too great a risk of distorting both the Zen experience and the Western understanding of Zen as well.

My second question is whether, by shaping his concept of dialogue in terms of a Western concept of philosophy, Abe compromises his ability to remain faithful to the Zen side of the dialogue. Given that philosophy in the Japanese academic setting is primarily Western philosophy, it is not strange that Abe should formulate a Zen "philosophy" along Western lines of a structured system of thought. But this means that Abe's approach to dialogue is problematic from the outset. For by seeing his Zen "philosophy" in a Western way, Abe is forced to construe dialogue as a critical encounter, even a polemic struggle, between irreducibly different and alternative systems of thought.

My question is whether this sort of dialogue is appropriate to the Zen position he represents. Is not the model of comparative philosophy or dialogue as an encounter between irreducibly different systems of thought itself a typically Western, rather than Asian, model for understanding interreligious encounter? While such a model might be appropriate coming from a Western philosopher of dialogue, is it not surrendering a bit too much to Western modes of thought for an Asian thinker to adopt such a model? On the surface, at least, this model of dialogue seems quite different from the traditional model of interreligious encounter found in the East Asian experience—for example, in the interweaving of Buddhism, Taoism, Confucianism, or Shintoism in China or Japan. By adopting a Western rather than an Eastern model of dialogue, Abe's Zen "dialogue" with Western thought may be over before it starts—and it is not clear that Abe or Zen comes out the "winner." Perhaps the tentative conclusion of Heidegger's conversation with the Japanese professor more closely approximates the spirit if not the substance of a Zen approach to dialogue.

My question, therefore, is whether, in formulating his Zen philosophy in Western metaphysical concepts and in the Western form of a structured system of thought, Abe has compromised the possibility "of saying what the dialogue was about," of "saying the essential nature" of the Zen experience. I agree with Abe that Zen experience needs a Zen philosophy. However, it is only by keeping close to its "root-source" in Zen experience that Zen philosophy will find language that enables it to "say" that experience. It is this root-source, rather than Western philosophical concepts and structures, on which Zen philosophy must draw in its dialogue with the West. Remaining close to this root-source is of particular importance since, as Abe himself contends, it is Zen as religion that is the source of the fundamental differences between Zen as philosophy and Western thought. As Abe states, "The difference between Western intellectual traditions and Buddhism in their understanding of *negativity* in human life involves not only an ontological issue but also an existential and soteriological one."[39]

Therefore, the dialogue between Zen philosophy and Western

thought must not proceed simply on the level of comparative ontology but requires a step back to the fundamental "experiences of Being" (and Nothingness) that underlie their respective ontologies. It is in service of this task, I have suggested, that Heidegger offers an important corrective to Abe's approach to dialogue. By taking a fresh phenomenological and hermeneutical, even "deconstructive" look at those experiences and the ways in which they have been traditionally expressed, perhaps Zen thinking on Nothingness and Western thinking on Being will discover new linguistic terms and structures for bringing to language what ultimately remains an "indefinable" source or mystery.

chapter Twenty-Seven

MASAO ABE ON NEGATIVITY IN THE EAST AND THE WEST

Joel R. Smith

IN 1984 I PARTICIPATED in the N.E.H. Institute for Comparative Philosophy at the University of Hawai'i at Manoa. This was my formal introduction to comparative philosophy, and the faculty in the institute stimulated me to change my teaching and research toward doing comparative philosophy. Masao Abe was one of the teachers whom I encountered at the institute. What I remember is not so much his lectures but a personal encounter I had with him in the hallway one day. I was just beginning my study of Keiji Nishitani then and had asked Abe something about Nishitani's criticism of Nietzsche. At a certain point Abe turned to me and asked, "What *does* Nietzsche mean by the Will to Power?" In the context of our conversation, the way Abe asked the question unsettled my previous interpretation of Nietzsche and provoked me to begin thinking about Nietzsche from a very different angle. As I continued my research comparing Western existential philosophers (especially Nietzsche) and Mahāyāna Buddhism, Abe's writings and lectures have often had this same effect. Abe almost always unsettles my previous interpretations of Western and Buddhist ideas so that I can see them in a new light. I am deeply indebted to him for unsettling me so often!

Abe's depth and breadth of knowledge about both Western and

Asian philosophy allow him to make insightful comparisons of a general nature that avoid some of the pitfalls involved when one paints in broad strokes. One of Abe's most stimulating comparisons occurs in an article titled "Non-Being and *Mu*—the Metaphysical Nature of Negativity in the East and the West."[1] I think this is an important article that deserves serious discussion by philosophers. I will offer a brief analysis of Abe's article by arguing that while Abe correctly shows that Buddhism helps us see a dogmatic ontological bias in Western thought in favor of positivity over negativity, he fails to show that Buddhism avoids a complementary ontological bias in favor of negativity over positivity. Abe has succeeded in clarifying the respective ontological commitments and biases of Buddhism and Western thought, but he has not succeeded in showing that the former resolves the antinomy between negativity and positivity any better than the latter does.

Using ancient Greek and Christian thought as his primary examples,[2] Abe claims the following about Western thought:

> *That being has priority over, is somehow superior to, and more fundamental than, non-being, had been assumed, perhaps uncritically . . . for quite some time by the West in general.*[3]

The West's assertion of the ontological priority of being over non-being is dogmatic because

> *in reality there is no ontological ground on which being has priority over non-being. It is assumed that being embraces both itself and non-being. But the very basis on which both being and non-being are embraced must not be "Being" but "that which is neither being nor non-being."*[4]

> *The priority of u (being) over mu (non-being) is not ontologically justifiable with regard to things in general and humans in particular. This is the position held by Buddhism. Herein, we see the essential difference in understanding the negativity of beings, including human existence, between the West and the East, especially as exemplified in Buddhism.*[5]

While certain Christian mystics such as Eckhart and Bohme and Western philosophers such as Nietzsche and Heidegger begin to overcome this ontological bias,[6] it is only Taoism and Buddhism that truly provide an alternative ontology.

Abe holds that the crucial difference between the Western and Buddhist ontologies lies in

> *whether or not relative* mu *(non-being) is understood as completely equal and reciprocal to relative* u *(being). The negativity of human life is felt more seriously and deeply in Buddhism than among the followers of Western intellectual traditions. This is true to such an extent that it is not considered inferior but equal to positivity.*[7]

Abe elaborates:

> *Only when the positive and negative principles have equal force and are mutually negating is the dialectical structure of* Sunyata *possible. . . . Unlike Western ideas of being and non-being . . .* u *[being] and* mu *[non-being] are of completely equal force in relation to one another. They are entirely relative, complementary, and reciprocal, one being impossible without the other. In other words,* mu *is not one-sidedly derived through negation of* u. Mu *is the negation of* u *and vice versa. One has no logical or ontological priority to the other. Being the complete counter-concept to* u, mu *is more than a privation of* u, *a stronger form of negativity than "non-being" as understood in the West. Further,* u *and* mu *are completely antagonistic principles and therefore inseparable from one another, and thus constitute an antinomy.*[8]

Negativity in the West is a mere privation, while in Buddhism it is ontologically equal to positivity:

> *Negativity in this [Western] view is no more than something to be overcome by positivity. On the contrary, [in Buddhism] when positivity (or* u) *and negativity* (mu) *are equal and reciprocal, it is the*

286 Joel R. Smith

antinomic and contradictory tension between positivity and negativity that is to be overcome. Then, as in Buddhism, liberation is
realized in Emptiness as the emancipation from this existential
antinomy.[9]

The Mahāyāna idea of Emptiness, or Śūnyatā, provides the alternative ontology for Abe:

> Now, mu is not a negative form of u (being) and is not, like me
> on or non-being, one-sidedly derived through a negation of u.
> Being the complete counter-concept to u, mu is a more powerful
> form of negation than "non-being." . . . In other words, mu is on
> equal footing with and is reciprocal to u. . . . But if mu is absolu-
> tized in principle, it can transcend and embrace within itself both
> u and mu in their relative senses. The Buddhist idea of Emptiness
> may be taken as Mu in this absolute sense.[10]

Nāgārjuna's Middle Path is "the Way which transcends every possible
duality including that of being and non-being, affirmation and negation."[11]
Śūnyatā is not nihilistic and is not simply identical with non-being.[12] It is
a negation of a negation, "not a relative negation but an absolute negation,"[13] and so an affirmation:

> Yet, it is not a mere and immediate affirmation. It is an affirma-
> tion which is realized only through double negation, i.e., absolute
> negation. Thus we may say that absolute negation is absolute affir-
> mation and absolute affirmation is absolute negation.[14]

If Śūnyatā is conceived as a third category in relation to u and mu,
then it is not true Emptiness, because it is still a kind of something.[15] True
Emptiness (Absolute Mu) must empty itself of all vestiges of being, and
when it does it allows being and non-being to appear as they are:

> Absolute Mu or true Sunyata is existentially realized as such
> through overcoming Mu or Sunyata as a third category standing
> beyond relative u and mu, and through returning to and affirming
> relative u and mu as they are.[16]

When Emptiness is emptied, so it is not a third category beyond being and non-being, then Emptiness is not different from Being:

> *Thus true Emptiness is wondrous Being, absolute* U, *the fullness and suchness of everything, or* tathata; *it is ultimate Reality which, being beyond* u *and* mu, *lets both* u *and* mu *stand and work just as they are in their reciprocal relationship.*[17]

When Emptiness is emptied, it is an emptiness that is fullness:

> *Emptiness as* Sunyata *transcends and embraces both emptiness and fullness. . . . This is why, for Nāgārjuna, true Emptiness is wondrous Being.*[18]

However, Abe carefully contrasts the Buddhist and the Western notion of Being:

> *The Buddhist idea of wondrous Being is clearly different from the idea of "Being" understood as ultimate Reality in the West. In the West, "Being" is neither non-dualistic (unlike absolute Nothingness) nor realized through the realization of Emptiness. It is not considered to be beyond the antinomy of being and non-being.*[19]

Western thought, for Abe, has been ontologically biased in giving priority to being over non-being, so it cannot resolve the antinomy between them. This bias is not merely ontological but is also soteriological and existential. It is soteriological because, as Abe puts it in another essay, "attachment to something means *substantializing* that thing."[20] In giving primacy to being and positivity, the West gives existential priority to life over death and to good over evil. In contrast, Buddhism does not give priority to life over death, or good over evil.[21] Buddhism sees these as equal and reciprocal, a real antinomy, that can only be resolved through the realization of Emptiness.

Such is Abe's basic position. However, if we listen closely to his summary statement in the last section of his article, we can discern something problematic:

> To sum up, in the West such positive principles as being, life, and
> the good have ontological priority over negative principles such as
> non-being, death, and evil. By contrast, in the East, especially in
> Taoism and Buddhism, negative principles are not secondary but
> co-equal to the positive principles and even may be said to be
> primary and central [emphasis added]. . . . In short, the ultimate
> which is beyond the opposition between positive and negative is
> realized in the East in terms of negativity [emphasis added] and
> in the West in terms of positivity.[22]

One might wish that Abe did not identify "the East" so closely with
Taoism and Buddhism, especially since earlier he had held that Confucian philosophy[23] and Upanishadic philosophy[24] have understood positivity much like the West. But the crucial point here is that in the passage
just cited, Abe concedes, perhaps unintentionally, a point he had denied
earlier. The whole thrust of his argument has been to assert that the positive and negative principles are coequal so that Buddhism is not ontologically biased toward either positivity or negativity. But in the preceding
passage, Abe acknowledges that in Buddhism negative principles are not
only coequal to positive principles but "even may be said to be primary
and central."[25] He explicitly says that the ultimate is "realized in the East
in terms of negativity and in the West in terms of positivity."[26] Abe seems
to contradict himself, claiming both that Buddhism does not give priority to negativity and that it does give priority to negativity. What are we to
make of this?

Abe pointed out earlier that what embraces both being and non-
being must be that which is neither being nor non-being.[27] As we have
seen, Abe claims that Śūnyatā is neither being nor non-being but transcends and embraces both without becoming a third category. He also
claims that when Emptiness is emptied, it is Fullness, so that Śūnyatā
embraces both emptiness and fullness and is an absolute affirmation as
well as an absolute negation. But it is significant that Mahāyāna's initial
and basic characterization of Śūnyatā is negative in connotation. Why
is this? As a soteriological and ontological concept, Śūnyatā functions
to deny the substantiality that we, in our ignorance, tend to impute. It
is negative in that it negates ignorance and egoism to realize Anātman,

or No-Self. Of course, ontologically we need not negate form because reality already is nonsubstantial. It is only philosophically and soteriologically that we must negate our mistaken imputation of substantiality.

The *Heart Sūtra's* assertion that form is empty[28] articulates how we must see form as lacking inherent, substantial existence. But *Śūnyatā* also has no inherent existence, so phenomena continue to function but as dependently co-arising *(pratītya-samutpāda)*, not as inherently existing. Indeed, inherent existence would obstruct dependent co-arising, so *Śūnyatā*, as the lack of inherent existence, is what allows phenomena to occur as dependently co-arising. *Śūnyatā* is not some reality beyond form; rather it is nothing else than dependently co-arising form. Not only, then, is form empty but, as the *Heart Sūtra* says, Emptiness is also form. There is no difference between form and Emptiness, between samsara and nirvana.[29] Form and samsara, properly realized as nonsubstantial, are no different from Emptiness and nirvana, properly realized as nonsubstantial. Nāgārjuna, as Abe cites, expresses this key Mahāyāna insight in the lovely phrase "True Emptiness, Wondrous Being." *Being* here does not refer to any substantial reality but to dependently co-arising form, things as they are in their interconnected transiency.

Buddhism emphasizes negativity, then, in order to counter our ignorant emphasis on positivity when we mistakenly impute inherent, substantial existence. It emphasizes negativity again when it empties Emptiness to ensure that we do not impute some sort of inherent existence to Emptiness. This double negation allows us to see phenomena as they are, not as inherently existing but as dependently co-arising. Buddhism emphasizes negativity in negating inherent existence (both of phenomena and of Emptiness), but it emphasizes positivity in how this double negation allows us to see phenomena functioning positively as dependently co-arising, which is their true reality. The negativity of emptying is not different from the positivity of dependent co-arising. They are two ways of making the same point. This expresses the Buddhist Middle Way between eternalism and annihilationism, between being as substance and non-being as the void. *Śūnyatā* is neither being nor non-being, but dependent co-arising.

We might summarize this view by saying, "Empty. Empty. Just as it is." The first *empty* negates the inherent existence of form. The second *empty* empties Emptiness to negate any subtle inherent existence we might impute to Emptiness. *Just as it is* points to phenomena positively functioning as dependently co-arising when no inherent existence is imputed. In this positive sense, Śūnyatā is suchness *(tathatā).* As Abe says in another essay,

> *I think that "everything is empty" may be more adequately ren-*
> *dered in this way: "Everything is just as it is." . . . While every-*
> *thing and everyone retain their uniqueness and particularity . . .*
> *they have no self-nature.*[30]

This seems to be the meaning of the well-known saying of Ch'ing-yuan,[31] which might be paraphrased as "First there were mountains, then there were no mountains, then there were mountains." When we first see mountains, we impute inherent existence to them. When we realize Emptiness and negate the mountains' substantiality, we may think that they cease to exist. But when we further empty Emptiness to realize true Emptiness, we again see mountains but now in their true form as noninherent and dependently co-arising. As the Chinese poem says, "I went there and returned. . . . It was nothing special."[32]

Although Abe does not discuss Mahāyāna's doctrine of the Two Truths in his article, we can now understand the point of this doctrine. To use Geshe Rabten's language in his commentary on the *Heart Sūtra,* ultimate truth *(paramārtha-satya)* refers to how form is "void of inherent existence," while conventional or relative truth *(samvṛti-satya)* refers to how "conventionally form appears and functions."[33] Wisdom *(prajñā)* relates primarily to ultimate truth, while method *(upāya)* relates primarily to conventional truth.[34] Affirming the Two Truths affirms the Middle Way and avoids the two extremes of permanence and annihilation. Ultimate truth empties form and denies inherent existence, thus avoiding the permanence of eternalism. Conventional truth affirms dependent co-arising, the appearance and functioning of form in a noninherent way, and so avoids annihilation.[35] Both express reality as it is in its dependent co-arising, so ultimate truth and conventional truth are essentially identical,[36] but each counteracts a different mistake we tend to make. Note how the doctrine prevents us from overemphasizing either positivity or negativity.

Abe is correct, I think, that Western thought tends to be ontologically biased toward being and positivity over non-being and negativity and that Buddhism takes negativity more seriously. Abe is certainly correct that *Śūnyatā* is ultimately not simply negative in character and in some sense transcends and embraces both positive and negative. However, has Buddhism avoided ontological bias? If we think of the issue in terms of Being and Becoming rather than being and non-being, we see that most Western thought gives priority to Being or substance while Buddhist thought gives priority to Becoming or dependent co-arising. While the West may not have justified its ontological commitment to Being, neither has Buddhism justified its ontological commitment to Becoming. Each is a mirror image of the other reflecting a complementary ontological bias.

Let us examine Abe's view more closely to see why this is the case. Buddhism does seem to take negativity more seriously than most Western thought does. We have seen Abe claim that Mahāyāna sees non-being as more than merely derived from being in that they are equal and reciprocal. This equality and reciprocity extends to life and death, good and evil, so that Buddhists do not assume that "one overcomes death with the power of life" or that "good is strong enough to overcome evil."[37] In the existential and soteriological cases of death and evil, one can understand Abe's point in that there is no guarantee that life and good will conquer death and evil to defeat the threat of meaninglessness that they pose. But Abe, and Mahāyāna in general, does not offer an account of what relative *mu* is ontologically if it is more than the West's privation of being. Abe discusses *u* and *mu* as abstract principles that are equal, but what is relative *mu* if it isn't a privation of *u*? We can understand the ontological nature of *u*, but what is the ontological nature of *mu* such that it is not merely the privation of *u* but is a dynamic power that is reciprocally equal to the dynamic power of *u*? Mahāyāna takes negativity more seriously than the West, but without providing an adequate ontological account of relative *mu*.

Abe further claims, as we have seen, that Emptiness transcends and embraces being and non-being in a way that the Western idea of Being does not. But without having established the equality of *u* and *mu*, Abe's argument fails. He argues that in the West being and non-being are not equal (since non-being is a privation of being), so their opposition is "resolved" in the direction of Being, which is more on the side of being than non-being. He diagrams the Western conceptual terrain as follows:[38]

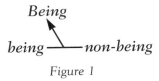

Figure 1

Abe does *not* diagram the Mahāyāna view in a complementary way, with the opposition resolved in the direction of Śūnyatā, which is more on the side of non-being than being:

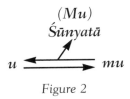

Figure 2

Instead, he diagrams Śūnyatā as not slanted in the direction of either being or non-being, as follows:[39]

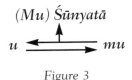

Figure 3

After Abe develops his claim that Śūnyatā is not some third category beyond *u* and *mu*, Śūnyatā is diagrammed as follows:[40]

Figure 4

Note that Abe does distinguish (relative?) being from (Absolute?) Being in figure 1 by the use of a capital letter, and in his text he also does so by speaking of "Being with a capital 'B.'"[41] As we saw earlier, Abe contends that Western Being is not beyond the antinomy of being and non-being the way *Śūnyatā* is. But Being is beyond being in that it does not simply oppose non-being but transcends and embraces being and non-being, although its embrace gives priority to being. It seems that Abe should diagram Buddhist ontology as in figure 2 rather than as he does in figure 3, because *Śūnyatā* transcends and embraces *u* and *mu*, but so that its embrace gives priority to *mu*. Just as Buddhism distinguishes between relative *mu* and Absolute *Mu*, the West must and does distinguish between relative being and Absolute Being. (Consider the Being of platonic forms compared with the being of appearances, or the Being of the Western God compared to the being of the created world.) If figure 2 is the correct diagram for Buddhism, then Western and Buddhist thought are mirror images of each other, reflecting complementary ontological biases. Indeed, the problematic passages cited earlier say as much:

> In Buddhism . . . negative principles . . . even may be said to be primary and central. . . . In short, the ultimate which is beyond the opposition between positive and negative is realized in the East in terms of negativity and in the West in terms of positivity.[42]

So in addition to not having given an account of *mu* that renders it equal to *u*, Abe also stands charged with not doing justice to how the West distinguishes relative being from Absolute Being in a way that parallels the Mahāyāna distinction between relative *mu* and Absolute *Mu*. Further, although Abe claims that *Śūnyatā* is not simply relative *mu* but is Absolute *Mu*, he does not provide an account of how relative *mu* is "absolutized in principle" (to use his phrase quoted earlier) so that relative *mu* becomes Absolute *Mu* and embraces both *u* and *mu* in their relative senses. Surely this is as mysterious as how Western Being embraces both being and non-being. Since it is relative *mu*, not relative *u*, that is absolutized, *Śūnyatā* still bears some of the negative connotations of *mu*. Indeed, as discussed earlier, the negative connotation of *Śūnyatā* is crucial because it is its empty character (or rather, lack of character) that allows dependent co-arising to occur.

While Abe does speak, as we have seen, of *Śūnyatā* as suchness (*tathatā*), Fullness, Wondrous Being, and Absolute *U*, he does not speak of absolutizing relative *u* to attain *Śūnyatā*. *Śūnyatā* is the absolutizing of relative *mu,* so it retains negative connotations even as it transcends relative *mu* in order to allow both relative *u* and relative *mu* to function as dependent co-arising. So, Abe has not shown adequately that *Śūnyatā* completely transcends the being/non-being antinomy any better than Western Being does. One must grant that neither view resolves the antinomy adequately, because one still gives subtle priority to being while the other still gives subtle priority to non-being. Or one must grant that if Mahāyāna can adequately resolve the antinomy by absolutizing relative *mu,* then by parity of reasoning the West can do so in the complementary way of absolutizing relative being. Whether one prefers that the antinomy be resolved through Being or Emptiness simply reveals one's ontological bias.

In conclusion, we have taken issue with four points in Abe's discussion of the metaphysical nature of negativity. First, Abe argued that Mahāyāna Buddhism takes negativity more seriously than does Western thought by understanding relative *mu* as equal and reciprocal to *u.* We agree that Buddhism takes negativity more seriously, but Abe has not given an adequate account of the ontological nature of relative *mu* to show how it can be more than a privation of *u.* Until he provides this ontological account of relative *mu,* his entire position is weak.

Second, Abe argued that what was truly beyond being and non-being must be what is neither being nor non-being. Abe argued that the Western idea of Being is not truly beyond them and so is not truly nondualistic because it is slanted toward being. We agree that Absolute Being is obviously slanted toward relative being, but Absolute Being also transcends relative being and non-being to embrace them both. Absolute Being is not the simple opposition to non-being that being is. Abe tacitly recognized this point by distinguishing Being from being, but he did not develop the distinction adequately. Developing it would bring out how Western Being does, in some ways, embrace relative being and non-being.

Third, Abe argued that Absolute *Mu* is neither being nor non-being and so is truly nondualistic and beyond them. We agree that Absolute *Mu* is not identical to relative *mu,* so it does transcend and embrace relative *u* and *mu,* in some ways. But Absolute *Mu* still bears traces of negativity in that it is relative *mu,* not *u,* that is absolutized in principle, and this negative quality of Emptiness is necessary to allow dependent co-arising to occur.

Fourth, in light of how Western Being transcends relative being and non-being more than Abe recognizes, and how *Śūnyatā* transcends them less than he recognizes, because it retains connotations of negativity, we claim that each view exhibits a complementary ontological bias.

We are grateful to Abe for helping us see how Buddhism reveals a dogmatic ontological bias in Western thought toward positivity over negativity. We appreciate Abe's thoughtful attempt to argue that Buddhism avoids a complementary bias in favor of negativity over positivity. But we conclude that *Śūnyatā* remains ontologically biased toward negativity more than toward positivity, even as it transcends them to some extent. Buddhism and Western thought articulate complementary ontological biases. We must underscore Abe's own concluding statement, which contradicts the thrust of the rest of his article, that the ultimate is realized in Buddhism in terms of negativity and in the West in terms of positivity. Hence, Buddhism does not resolve the antinomy between positivity and negativity any better than the West does. One of the tasks that remains for comparative philosophy is to show which commitment is more valid, or to develop from within either position or as some third position an ontology that truly transcends any bias toward positivity or negativity in order to embrace both fully.

chapter Twenty-Eight

MASAO ABE
AND
MARTIN HEIDEGGER

Joan Stambaugh

I HAVE KNOWN MASAO ABE for approximately fifteen years. I had
studied his translations of Dōgen, prepared together with Norman
Waddell, in *The Eastern Buddhist*. As I recall, I first attended an undergraduate seminar that Abe gave at Princeton University on Buddhism
about 1978. After the seminar I had the opportunity to speak with him
briefly about his future plans, for I hoped to be able to work with him
further.

Since that short meeting, it has been difficult to keep track of
Abe's itinerant life. In 1984–85 he was in Hawaii, a bit too far away for
me, even when on sabbatical. But during the last months of that sabbatical, in the fall of 1985, I returned from a summer in Maine to commute as often as possible to Haverford College to attend most of his
undergraduate lectures and seminars. Then in 1986, when I returned to
teaching, I continued to commute to his Sunday-afternoon seminars on
international religion. These seminars were composed of faculty members and graduate students from the New York–Philadelphia area. The
seminars on the Kyoto School centered primarily on Kitarō Nishida,
with some brief excursions into Hajime Tanabe, Keiji Nishitani, and
Shin'ichi Hisamatsu. However, during the last two seminars we

ventured into Dōgen, a particular interest of mine. I must say that these seminars were of invaluable help to me. Abe went to a great deal of trouble to photocopy and hand out materials otherwise unavailable to most of us. In addition, Abe's profound and benign presence in the room simply gave one a good feeling. In November of 1986 I also attended his lecture "Kenotic God and Dynamic Sunyata" at Union Theological Seminary.

I learned a great deal from intensive study of his book *Zen and Western Thought*. With difficult and demanding material, it is a distinct advantage to have it in print and to be able to go back over it several times. In particular, I found the section "Dōgen on Buddha-Nature" extremely helpful. When Abe edited *A Zen Life: D. T. Suzuki Remembered*, he asked me to review it for *The Eastern Buddhist*. As a graduate student in philosophy at Columbia University in the spring of 1955, I had attended a seminar of Suzuki's. Abe's book contained numerous personal reminiscences plus beautiful photographs of that great man by Francis Haar. Finally, in the summer of 1991, the State University of New York Press asked if I would be a reader for Abe's manuscript *A Study of Dōgen*. With great anticipation, I replied yes. I took the manuscript with me to an inn in New Hampshire, requested the quietest room they had, and settled in to read. Improbable as it may seem, an Agatha Christie mystery could not have fascinated me more. (Actually, I have never read an Agatha Christie mystery.) In addition to chapters on Dōgen, the book included the chapter "Time in Heidegger and Dōgen" and two chapters on the problem of death in Dōgen and Shinran. Of course, I was able to recommend the book most enthusiastically for publication, and after it came out, I reviewed it for *The Eastern Buddhist*.

To get away from anecdotal reminiscences, I should like to briefly approach the more substantive issues that Abe raises about Martin Heidegger in *A Study of Dōgen*. I shall discuss some of the criticisms Abe raises in an effort to push Heidegger's views a little closer to Dōgen's. First of all, let me remark that Abe is quite generous in acknowledging the degree to which Heidegger succeeds in getting out of metaphysics and, to a lesser extent, out of anthropomorphism. I am fundamentally in agreement with Abe's criticisms; I simply want to slightly raise the degree to which Heidegger succeeds in these enterprises. Abe's criticisms that I shall discuss are (1) the degree of transanthropomorphism, involving a discussion of thinking; (2) the ontological difference; and (3) the priority of time over being.

I

Concerning transanthropomorphism and thinking, Abe says:

> Accordingly, Heidegger's thinking is an essentially new way of thinking that is beyond "metaphysical" thinking, and is a thinking of this other origin (des anderen Anfangs), that is, the ground of metaphysics. In Heidegger, however, this other origin of thinking is encountered as the unthinkable from the side of thinking. . . . Consequently, despite their close resemblance, Heidegger's thinking is categorically different from Dōgen's notion of thinking of nonthinking, because the former does not reach the unthinkable as the true origin of thinking, whereas the latter is a thinking that is a self-realization of the unthinkable origin of thinking itself.[1]

Now I am not trying to assert that Heidegger practiced any form of "meditation" (even though one of his new kinds of thinking, *Besinnung*, has been translated as "meditative thinking"), nor that he ever experienced or even wanted to experience anything that corresponded to *satori*. Heidegger remains an unmistakably Western thinker. But his whole life long, beginning with *Being and Time*, he was highly critical of substantializing things as *Vorhandenheit*, as objective presence. Accordingly, his thinking did not have to do with objectifying or substantializing of any sort. The question is, Apart from his analyses and deconstruction of the history of metaphysics, what *did* his thinking have to do with?

I start with quotations from a small volume entitled *Out of the Experience of Thinking (Aus der Erfahrung des Denkens)*.

> The Saying of thinking would only be appeased in its essence when it became incapable of saying that which must remain unspoken. Such an incapability would bring thinking before its matter.[2]

Thinking for Heidegger was essentially *experience,* experience not in the sense of *Erlebnis,* or a kind of thrill-seeking that he abhorred, but in the sense of *Erfahrung,* of literally *going through* something.

> *Meditative thinking requires at times a higher effort. It demands a longer procedure of practice. It needs an even finer care than any other genuine craft. But it also must be able to wait like the farmer, to see whether the seed will come up and ripen.*[3]

Heidegger would not call his thinking "meditation," but it definitely was a kind of "practice." The thinking that he sought to cultivate was *experiential,* not conceptual. I turn now to the small volume entitled *Gelassenheit,* available in English as *Discourse on Thinking:* "Yet releasement toward things and openness for the mystery never befall us automatically. They are nothing accidental. Both thrive only out of an unceasing, heartfelt thinking."[4] Releasement toward things and openness for the mystery are never matters we can take for granted. They do not just happen to us. We must unceasingly practice this kind of thinking that comes from the heart, not from calculative planning.

These quotations are from a memorial address for the German composer Conradin Kreutzer. What follows in the volume is a conversation on a field path between a scientist, a teacher, and a scholar. The discussion begins with statements to the effect that releasement requires relinquishing the will.

> TEACHER: *If only I had the right releasement, then I would soon not need to relinquish (the will).*
>
> SCHOLAR: *So far as we can at least give up willing, we help to awaken releasement.*
>
> TEACHER: *Rather, remain awake for releasement.*
>
> SCHOLAR: *Why not awakening?*
>
> TEACHER: *Because on our own, we do not awaken releasement in ourselves.*[5]

It is abundantly clear from this dialogue that Heidegger realizes that the most we can do to attain releasement is to remain awake; we cannot awaken releasement in ourselves. It comes to us, if it comes at all.

SCHOLAR: *But if the reigning essence of thinking up to now has been transcendental-horizontal representing from which releasement, because of its belonging to that which regions, releases itself; then thinking is transformed in releasement from such a representing to waiting for that which regions.*

TEACHER: *The essence of this waiting, however, is releasement to that which regions. But because it is that which regions which lets releasement belong to it, because it lets releasement rest in it, the essence of thinking lies, if I may say so, in the fact that that which regions regions releasement within itself.*

SCHOLAR: *Thinking is releasement to that which regions because its essence lies in the regioning of releasement.*

TEACHER: *But by this you are saying that the essence of thinking is not determined through thinking, and thus not through waiting as such; but through the Other to itself, that is, through which the region presences by regioning.*[6]

This sounds more convoluted in English than it does in German. But the basic point is clear. What allows thinking to enter "that which regions," is not thinking's waiting (which is already released from any kind of willing, calculation, and representation), but what is Other to thinking. This Other is simply "that which regions." Abe might want to object that what is Other to thinking constitutes a duality, perhaps akin to the duality of thinking and not-thinking, and thinking is thus "outside" of what is Other to thinking. This objection could possibly have some merit. Heidegger never discovered the apt and felicitous term *non-thinking,* and he probably would not have trusted such a term anyhow, since one of his main concerns in this work and elsewhere is that ours is precisely a time of thoughtlessness. Thus, to say that thinking is allowed to enter, is admitted into *(eingelassen)* that which regions, is as far as he goes. My contention is that the thinking that has been described here is not anthropomorphic. A Buddhist might well not want to call an awakened state of awareness "thinking," but he or she surely would not want to characterize it as a totally blank stupor, either. Some kind of *awareness* is there. After all, one does not awaken to a totally blank stupor.

In other words and far more prevalently, Heidegger's terms for noncalculative, nonobjectifying, nonreifying, nonsubstantializing, *non-conceptualizing* thinking are *Besinnung* and *Andenken*. I have dealt with these terms elsewhere;[7] thus, my treatment here is extremely brief. *Besinnung*, often translated as "meditative thinking," is not a technical philosophical term. It is a common, everyday term with a rich variety of meanings. It has roots in both the mental and the physical sphere. The root noun *Sinn* has both significations of "meaning" and of "sense," as in the senses (*die Sinne*). Thus *Besinnung* is really a kind of "sensing" that includes the whole being, body and mind. It is never merely cerebral and has nothing to do with conceptuality. *Andenken*, usually translated as "remembrance" or "recollection," is perhaps best described as a kind of approaching, moving *toward* something. Appealing to the older, impersonal use of *ahnen*, whose root is the preposition *an* (toward) in *Andenken*, in the constructions *es anet mir* and *es anet mich*, Heidegger distances the idea that *I* think toward something by reversing the direction: *it* comes *to* me, comes over me. Any "subjective" element—which, after all, is a feature of representational thinking—is excluded.

With these remarks on thinking, I am by no means suggesting that Heidegger had or even wanted to have anything akin to Dōgen's experience of Awakening. I am merely suggesting that what he says is truly close to the following passage in Dōgen: "To practice and confirm all things by conveying one's self to them is illusion: for all things to advance forward and practice and confirm the self is enlightenment."[8]

II

Abe states that "only when the Heideggerian idea of *ontologische Differenz* is overcome can Dōgen's idea of 'whole-being is the Buddha-nature' be truly understood."[9] I should just like to quote a passage from *Vier Seminare*, a volume that has not received the attention it deserves and of which Abe may not be aware:

> It will not be possible to think Appropriation with concepts of
> being and history; nor with the help of the Greeks (which must be
> "gone beyond"). When being disappears, the ontological difference
> does also. Anticipating, one would have to also see the continuous

reference to the ontological difference from 1927 to 1936 as a nec-essary Holzweg (*dead end*).[10]

III

The last point I wish to touch upon is Abe's oft-repeated assertion that time has priority over being, that one can say being is time but not that time is being. One passage he refers to from *On Time and Being* to sup-port his contention I read in a different way: "Secondly, it is precisely a matter of seeing that being, by coming to view as Appropriation, disap-pears as being."[11] I understand this to mean not the priority of time over being, but rather that the term *being* is being relinquished as too bur-dened with traditional connotations in favor of *Appropriation* as the belonging-together of what Heidegger calls being *and* time. In other words, strictly speaking, one can ultimately not speak of either being or time in isolation but rather must think their unity. However, this does not refute Abe's objection. It is, of course, tied up with his reservation about anthropomorphism. I believe that with this objection, Abe is getting at something that has some validity, and I would appreciate his response to this issue at some length. I would simply add that, after all, even in Bud-dhism, it is difficult to know that trees, animals, mountains, and streams are Buddha-nature without some realization on the part of a human being.

Returning to the mode of reminiscence, in conclusion, I should like to say that it is a rare privilege to know a person of such absolute integri-ty, intellectual or otherwise, as Masao Abe. Intellectually he strikes a fine balance between mediating his own independent thought and faithfully explicating other thinkers of the Kyoto School. D. T. Suzuki "brought" Zen to this country. Masao Abe, who penetrated Western philosophy and theology much further than Suzuki could or wanted to, has instigated the first serious *dialogue* between Eastern and Western thought in general and between Buddhism and Christianity in particular. One next step, should it ever be able to come about, would be to engage the philosophers in this dialogue as well. Abe has at least opened the door to this possibil-ity. And given the state of Western philosophy today, this could prove to be most therapeutic.

chapter Twenty-Nine

DIAGRAMMING THE ULTIMATE: CONVERSATIONS WITH MASAO ABE

Robert E. Carter

WHAT I MOST WANT TO SAY about Masao Abe is that he has inspired a generation of scholars to explore the richness of Zen Buddhism and the Kyoto School; in my case, he has both encouraged and cautioned me in my pursuit of a philosophical understanding of the importance of the elusive Nothingness that is so central to much of East Asian thought. Abe has been at the forefront of that increasingly substantial dialogue between Buddhism (particularly Zen Buddhism) and other faiths. He is at the forefront in interpreting the Kyoto School to the Western world, and he is a first-rate comparativist, as his *Zen and Western Thought* demonstrates. In the midst of these vitally important scholarly contributions, he has been a tireless teacher and a faithful supporter of others, at many career levels, who have come to him for assistance in researching and writing about matters of mutual interest. Of one of the most profound Zen scholars and writers, Dōgen (1200–1253), Abe writes that "we find [in him] a rare combination of religious insight and philosophical ability."[1] This reflection could apply to Masao Abe as well. Those who have encountered him are aware of the presence of a robust religiosity as well as a seasoned philosophical mind. He provides an embodiment of what many would take to be an identity of self-contradiction: spiritual intensity and philosophic analysis!

In saying what I want to say about Masao Abe, I must attempt to say something—no doubt, too much—about the place of Nothingness, or Emptiness, in Zen Buddhist thought. Let me begin with an autobiographical recollection. I journeyed to Japan for the first time in 1976 to research Zen Buddhism, in particular the thought of Kitarō Nishida. I visited and spoke with many scholars and Zen Buddhist practitioners, but nothing was more helpful than the dialogue that took place upon meeting Masao Abe for the first time. I arrived at his home in Kyoto in the early afternoon, and Abe greeted me warmly, leading me into his home. We sat in his living room, a small room in his inviting but unpretentious Japanese-style home, sipping green tea and getting to know each other by discussing Zen Buddhism, and in particular the Zen notion of ultimate reality. Rather than specifying particular passages of text to examine together, working out the details and ambiguities, my questions had something of a more diffuse cosmic focus. Like so many before me, I was struggling to "understand" the meaning of the Buddhist notion of Nothingness, and Nishida's insistence on a distinction between Absolute Nothingness and relative nothingness only made things more obscure. Abe was not only willing to talk about Nothingness; he had actually begun to diagram it!

He spoke convincingly, knowing his Nishida extremely well, and peppered his interpretation with anecdotes about Nishida the man. We spoke increasingly abstractly for several minutes, and then he resorted to sketching a diagram to make as clear as he could what it was that he thought about this incredible notion. He sketched before me, on the tea table between us, explaining as he went why the circles indicating levels and kinds of reality were placed as they were. I looked at his diagram and quickly found an ambiguity in the drawing. I drew a revised and, I thought, improved second diagram and handed it across the table. He glanced at it, accepted my criticism with modestly evident pleasure, as though we were in the midst of a platonic dialogue set in East Asia, and then quickly set about drawing a third sketch to modify the obvious shortcomings of my version, patiently explaining what was lacking and detailing the improvement that he sought to express. We talked all the while, reaching for concepts to carry our mutual exploration forward, until there were nearly a dozen diagrams strewn about on the table, each a variation on those that had gone before, yet each achieving a corrective improvement at the expense of revealing yet another defect occasioned by the revision.

When Abe finished the last diagram, now quite complex, he began to laugh; and his laughter increased steadily in intensity. I sensed what was happening, and laughter overcame me as well as I reflected back on our joint undertaking. The laughter continued until tears rolled down our cheeks in shared delight at the presumption that the ultimate could not only be conceptualized and intellectualized but actually be diagrammed. My learned friend actually lightly brushed his thigh beneath his dark Zen robe, in delight. He shook his head in merriment and then blurted out, "Forgive me. I am sorry, but somehow this always happens to me when I try to talk about ultimate reality."

In the years since my first visit, Abe has been a constant contributor to Nishida and Dōgen studies and an original and steadfast interpreter of the Buddhist notion of Nothingness, from whom I have learned much. He has often supplied me with drafts of articles, with offprints, and with advice about my work. He has always been willing to write yet another letter of recommendation for some pressing reason in my academic life.

Like Nishida and Keiji Nishitani, Masao Abe is a comparativist. Not only is he thoroughly versed in Buddhist studies, and in Japanese philosophical and cultural ideas generally, but he is unusually accurate and probing in his understanding of Western thought, from the pre-Socratics to Paul Tillich and Karl Rahner. His evident prominence in the Buddhist-Christian encounter is beyond question. A focal part of that debate has been the comparison of God and *Śūnyatā*, Being and Nothingness, and the various synonyms and related concepts that serve to define or point toward ultimate reality in those two traditions (and in others as well). Abe makes it clear that "ultimate reality for Buddhism is neither Being nor God, but Sunyata."[2] *Śūnyatā* is "entirely unobjectifiable, unconceptualizable, and unattainable by reason or will. As such it cannot be any 'something' at all."[3] Thus, Nothingness, or *Śūnyatā,* is not to be understood as somehow existing "out there," beyond one's own existence as a self, in an independent realm separate from us. *Śūnyatā* is not a something, which explains why it is impossible to represent and to intellectualize *Śūnyatā* in the first place. Thus, "Sunyata is non-Sunyata (*asunyata*): therefore it is ultimate Sunyata (*atyanta-Sunyata*)."⁴ In Christian terms, this results in God not being God, and "precisely because of this, God is truly God."⁵ Yet this "true God" is now not a thing, not a something, and even more curiously, not an emptiness or a nothingness, either, if these terms contrast with somethingness. Therefore, "just as the attachment to being must be overcome, the attachment to emptiness must also be surmounted."⁶

The mountains are, are not, and therefore are: God is, is not, and therefore is; and *Śūnyatā* follows exactly the same pattern. This is the linguistic formulation of ultimate reality, as undiagrammatic and laughable as it may seem. Abe has made it abundantly clear that Buddhism and Zen Buddhism are not intellectual or strictly philosophical schools of thought.⁷ Zen is practice, and Zen is immediate experience. Therefore, "when thinking is taken as the basis, Zen loses its authentic ground and degenerates into mere conceptualism and abstract verbiage."⁸ Indeed, Zen *kōans, zazen* meditation, and the ordinary life of practice of the Zen Buddhist strive to break the iron grip of conceptualizing, abstracting, thinking, and intellectualizing. Zen is not thinking, whatever else it may be. And, of course, it is not not-thinking, either. It is *non-thinking*.

Experience is reality as it presents itself to us. By contrast, conception halts the flow of pure experience, isolates one or more aspects of it, abstracts these from the whole for practical purposes, and thereby harnesses reality. However, these selective abstractions "must never be taken as the full equivalent of reality,"⁹ partly because they are partial selections from the whole and partly because they are static fixations of a reality that is always and everywhere a flux, a changing flow. William James, who was a decisive influence on Nishida and who contributed the phrase "pure experience," maintains that concepts "form an essentially discontinuous system, and translate the process of our perceptual experience, which is naturally a flux into a set of stagnant and petrified terms."¹⁰

Dōgen, the thirteenth-century Zen master, is considered to be one of Japan's most outstanding philosophers and possibly its most creative thinker. One of Abe's latest books is a collection of essays about this great early thinker, who argued that impermanence is reality and that reality is impermanence. Basing his conclusion or insight on the Buddhist doctrine of Emptiness, he saw that objects of the world are nonsubstantial, as were subjects (egos); hence, they were nothing more than nodules of temporary cohesive integration, persisting for a time. Abe observes that "this may sound surprising to the ear of one who holds to a stereotyped understanding of Buddhism, according to which the task of Buddhism is to emancipate oneself from impermanence or samsara and to enter nirvana by realizing the Buddha-nature."[11] The correct understanding of this seemingly paradoxical claim—another instance of apparent self-contradiction—is that "true nirvana is attained only by emancipating oneself even from nirvana as transcendence of impermanence. In other words, it is realized by a complete return from nirvana to the world of impermanence through liberating oneself from both impermanence and permanence, from both samsara so-called and nirvana so-called."[12] The result of this rejection of both impermanence and permanence as the correct view of the nature of the ultimate is that "genuine nirvana is nothing but realization of impermanence as impermanence."[13] Thus, it is in the moment, the *nikon*, of "reality appearing fully right-here-now," that we should dwell, as participants rather than as observers. We, too, are a part of the flux, and the only wise outlook on the reality of change is to step into the flux and to flow with it in the recognition that one is a participant in it.

It is little wonder that in Buddhism, and in Zen Buddhism in particular, we often find such aphorisms as "If you see the Buddha walking down the street, kill him" and "The Buddha is improving: when will he be finished?" The Buddha symbolizes the flow of things that is itself ultimate. For it not to change would be for it not to be. Reality is change. Similarly, to see the Buddha "in the flesh," as it were, is to fix one's conception of reality, to stop the flow. In so doing, it is you who have killed the Buddha, for the Buddha is impermanence itself. To catch sight of him too clearly is to lose him, to succumb to idolatry, or to anthropocentric hubris. Every conception must change, just as the Buddha must be said to be changing every instant. To know reality is to know change, and to know change is to throw oneself into the flux—to swim with the change, observing what one can along the way. The markers we find will be sources of meaning, but even they must not be clung to, turned into permanent markers. Reality is a process, and our understanding of it is an unending process. As Abe writes, "true Emptiness 'empties' itself," for it is "not a static state which is objectively observable but a dynamic activity of *emptying* in which everyone and everything are involved. Indeed, there exists nothing whatsoever outside of this dynamic whole of *emptying*."[14] The emptying is "self-contradictorily identical"[15] in that Emptiness must empty itself, thereby becoming fullness, and fullness itself had already been emptied, yielding Emptiness. But is all of this clear and distinct, an adequate guide for those of us who wish to glimpse what it is that Emptiness, or Nothingness, adds to our understanding of ultimate reality, its nature and activity?

If one is to use words, and to think about Zen, then paradoxicality is the best form of linguistic expression with which to point toward ultimate reality. Zen is not thinking; and so to think about Zen is not to do Zen. Yet systematic thinking may be applied to anything at all. It is utterly useless only if thinking is taken as the subject matter itself rather than as the method by means of which understanding of that subject matter is, at least partially, achieved. Zen and thinking stand in opposition only if the one is confused with the other: "Although intellectual understanding cannot be a substitute for Zen's awakening, practice without a proper and legitimate form of intellectual understanding is often misleading. An intellectual understanding without practice is certainly powerless, but practice without learning is apt to be blind."[16]

Paradoxical expression is a technique that inhibits substantializing thought activity. A thing is what it is, and yet it cannot be just that, for a static formulation robs reality of its changeability, its flow. On the other hand, to speak only of the flow is to find nothing on which to fix, and one is thus thrust back into saying both yes and no at the same time. Paradoxicality rids fixation of its substantiality: it empties substance of its substantiality. And even Nothingness itself must be emptied, nonsubstantialized. We must empty Emptiness itself and keep everything nonsubstantial and in the flow of movement in being-time. We must also empty being-time so that it points to the going on of events and then empty the event of any fixity or substance. Nothingness is the empty, or the emptying, or the filling and emptying, or the empty as full, or the emptied as filling, and the filled as emptying—for it is the *process* that one is to focus on and come to grasp. In Abe's words, "in order to attain true Emptiness, Emptiness must 'empty' itself; Emptiness must become non-Emptiness."[17] The Emptiness beyond emptiness is not "Wondrous Being." It indicates the dynamic structure or process of being (*u*) and emptiness (*mu*) being emptied. Being becomes empty, and emptiness becomes being; and yet being is being and emptiness is emptiness, because even this reciprocal emptying is also emptied. True Emptiness is "paradoxically and self-contradictorily identical."[18]

How else can any of this be said, except paradoxically? Not to speak paradoxically is to fix the focus, to stop the flow, to carve out a discrete time and event, and to privilege oneself or something as the center from which all else is distinguished and located. One is, of course, privileged in being the place where all arises, but now one must empty even this self-place-substance. To grasp Absolute Nothingness is to comprehend the "coincidence of ceaseless negation and straightforward affirmation."[19] The self, the I, is never "there," but is at each moment in the process of transformation, now losing every trace of itself in Nothingness, now blooming selflessly with the flowers and like one of them.

We meet others and encounter the natural world in the "place" (*basho*), the space, the betweenness, that separates on the one hand and allows for union on the other. This is the "place-as-nothingness," where two meet and become one. Yet in order to be one, the one had to be two. Hence, neither the one nor the two is the point, but rather the one-as-two and the two-as-one as a continuous flow back and forth. Thus, we have the "nothingness of nothingness," as the process of desubstantializing all permanence, all fixity, all boundaries, all egos, all concepts, and all distinctions altogether. Then, as though to fill the nothingness of nothingness, each thing is now just-as-it-is, *thus (tathatā)!* The mountains are mountains again, and I am I. As a reflex, each of us now qualifies the above, and instantly we add, "And so the mountains are not mountains, and I am not I, and yet I am I and not-I, and the mountains are mountains and not mountains." Paradoxicality is the form of expression that most nearly captures the process and, when unpacked, forces us to deny, affirm, deny, affirm, without ceasing.

All of this is said so crisply by Abe when he writes,

> In the realization of Sunyata in the light of suchness, both distinction and equality, distinctiveness and sameness, are fully realized. For example, in the locus of Sunyata you are thoroughly you as you are and I am thoroughly I as I am—with our distinctive individuality and without ending in a single ultimate principle—and yet you and I are equally sharing the sameness in that both you and I are equally realized in terms of being-as-we-are. This is true

not only of you and me, but also of the self and any other, the self
and nature, and self and the divine. The self is the self, nature is
nature, and God is God, and with their distinctiveness, and yet
they are all equal in terms of "each is as each is" or "as it is."
Accordingly, in the realization of suchness, there is no difference
between human beings and nonhuman beings.[20]

By moving beyond dualistic thinking and a static ontology, and by
affirming an identity of self-contradiction, the various anthropocentrisms
of "ego and power" can be lessened or eliminated altogether. Nature is not
nonhuman or antihuman, nor are people "other." When we awaken to
Śūnyatā, or Nothingness, we see that these differences are embraced by
a *cosmological* vision of interconnectedness. Self-awakening embraces
everything in the universe,[21] and Abe urges us toward such realization as
a transcending of distinctions between races and between people. Self-
realization is, paradoxically, self-negation, for as Dōgen taught, to find the
self is to have lost the self. Thus it is, to continue Dōgen's teaching, that
we are open to being enlightened by all things, for the expanse of Self-
awakening is emptied. Self-awakening is now written with a capital S to
indicate that this is not the unenlightened egoic self that is then lost, but
the Self regained when the self and the not-self are emptied.

The Self-awakened no longer considers "such things as land, water,
air, the sun, and all kinds of energy only as the common resources of
mankind but considers them as the common blessings on behalf of the
myriad phenomena of the universe."[22] Our point of reference is no longer
that of the individual, nor of the state, nor even of the earth: we have
moved from an anthropological fixation to a cosmological vision of the
interconnectedness of things, which, nonetheless, are wonderfully distinctive and unique in their suchness. The unity is not just a oneness of
mush, a cosmological porridge of undifferentiation, but an identity that
preserves both the oneness of interconnection and the suchness of
unique diversity. Anthropocentrism is overcome, but not at the expense
of differentiation, but only by rejecting a differentiation that is unable to
empty its foreground fixation by comprehending, at the same time, the
background-of-the-whole that enlivens and connects the unique particulars into a cosmic whole.

Ecological sensitivity, like aesthetic feeling, is selfless awareness of a nondual sort such that whatever is perceived is taken as arising from the Emptiness, the Nothingness, underlying all subsequently discernible things. Just as aesthetic awareness is awareness as an activity of the Formless Self, so a tree or a tea bowl "is no ordinary" tree or bowl, but a "wonder-full" tree or bowl "seen as the self-expression of the formless self."[23] In other words, all things take on a depth, a *meaning* that they did not previously have for us, for they are now seen in their *suchness*, as "divine" expressions or manifestations arising out of the heretofore undifferentiated source of things. It comes as no surprise that the point is often made in poetic form: "this means that the colors of the mountain are those of the Buddha, and that the murmuring of the mountain stream is his voice."[24]

Nothingness-as-divine is found underfoot, as it were, as the ground, figuratively and literally, of everything in the world. In Zen terms, nirvana (the divine, sacred) is samsara (the things of the ordinary world), and samsara is nirvana. Nothingness, or the divine, or the sacred is only knowable in the phenomenal world of experience *as* every *thing.* Each and every *thing* is an expression of (a manifestation of) Nothingness itself. The phenomenally real of experience is not a creation separate from the creator, nor is it simply made in the image of the absolute. Rather, it *is* the absolute, expressed as the absolute expresses itself, i.e., phenomenally: "If one is really overwhelmed by the consciousness of absolute Nothingness, there is neither 'Me' nor 'God'; but just because there is absolute Nothingness, the mountain is mountain, and the water is water, and the being is as it is."[25] The function of the concept of Emptiness, or Nothingness, is to shatter the ordinary and habitual way of looking at things. Shatter the habits of language, of anticipatory seeing, and of your own purposes and preferences, and the object of consciousness will likely appear in a new and more ample light. Anticipations strip down what is before you to an expected cluster of properties. Empty-mindedness, or "no-mindedness," affords a fresh glimpse at the richness of experience prior to the anticipatory structuring and impoverishment of what is "there" to be experienced.

Nishida refers to nothingness as a "field," or "place" (*basho*), in which distinctions arise. The enlightened, sensitive, true-seeing individual, for Nishida, is one who has attained nondualistic consciousness and yet, of course, is dualistically able to operate in the everyday world of distinctions. This twofold awareness yields stereoscopic vision; you see the richness of differentiation, but now things stand out against the background of the formless, of Nothingness, of the vision of the greatest whole as creative source. You must learn to look at things, savoring every detail, and at the same time look through things, toward the not-yet thinged richness beneath the habitually seen surface that things present.

In contrasting Whitehead's philosophy with that of Mahāyāna Buddhism, Abe writes:

> Mahayana Buddhism is based on non-duality by rejecting all possible dualisms. . . . Although "becoming" rather than "being," "process" rather than "substance," "flux" rather than unchanging "permanence" are stressed in Mahayana Buddhism, they are at every point supported in one's existential realization by the realization of the absolute Nothingness. . . . Thus, becoming is not simply becoming but Being in any moment; process is not merely process but always the beginning and the end at the same time; flux is not just flux but permanence at any point.[26]

So, there is no resting place outside of or beyond the everyday, for it is in the midst of suffering and impermanence that nirvana is to be realized and manifested.[27] Our freedom is the freedom to plunge into this impermanent and inexhaustible profundity that leads beneath the surface of things, beneath the expected, beyond the merely separate, into the full realization that "all beings are absolutely all beings,"[28] which realization is a prime source of genuine meaning for us.

Have I now got it right! Am I as close as the language and thinking of paradoxicality can take me to an expression of a finger pointing toward the moon of ultimate reality? I can hear the laughter beginning, softly at first, and then growing to a roar that shakes even the moon! In my blushing imagination, Abe patiently sits down at his table, sipping green tea, and draws a diagram improving on my attempt to grasp the ungraspable, giving form to the formless, voice to the voiceless. No doubt he will mail it to me. But no sooner will the diagram arrive at my home, be read several times, and then filed away in my folder on "ultimate reality" than another envelope will arrive from Abe: and this one will be empty. . . .

Part Six

INTERFAITH
RELATIONS

chapter Thirty

BUDDHISM AND
HUMAN RIGHTS

William Theodore de Bary

IN ASSOCIATION WITH the late Ryusaku Tsunoda and Horace Friess at Columbia, I joined in extending the original invitation to Daisetz Suzuki to lecture at Columbia in the early 1950s and subsequently arranged for invitations to Yoshinori Takeuchi and Masao Abe to lecture in the early 1960s. The reflections contained in this essay arose in significant part from this early exposure to the work and thinking of these Buddhist scholars. The immediate occasion that precipitated my own writing on the subject of Buddhism and human rights was a convocation held at Columbia on October 7 and 8, 1984, on the occasion of a visit by the Dalai Lama. As one primarily devoted to the study of China, yet also mindful of the plight of Tibetan Buddhism in the hands of a repressive Chinese government, and also as provost instrumental in setting up a major Human Rights Center at Columbia, it was natural that I should have used the occasion to express some of my concerns on this subject. What follows is based on that lecture as it relates to Masao Abe's work.

The subject of Buddhism and human rights—quite obviously a relevant subject when we hosted an exiled religious leader whose very person embodies the principle of freedom of conscience—is one on which my thoughts and feelings are still somewhat unsettled. Yet this is not because I have only just begun to think about it. The matter has been much on my mind for years. In fact, my involvement with it goes back to when, as part of Columbia's Bicentennial Celebration in 1954, I was asked to organize a convocation on the theme of "Man's Right to Knowledge and the Free Use Thereof." Not long before that, as mentioned above, I had a part, along with Professor Horace Friess and Ryusaku Tsunoda, in arranging for Daisetz Suzuki to lecture at Columbia on Zen Buddhism—a series of lectures that proved to be of historic significance.

By a happy coincidence I had also, not long before, had discussions, first in Peking and then in New York, with Hu Shih, the Chinese scholar, student of John Dewey, and prominent spokesman for Western liberalism in modern China. Hu Shih was a skeptic in regard to many of the claims for Zen Buddhism made by Suzuki, and so when each of them agreed to speak at this convocation, it was to have been expected that there should be a striking juxtaposition of radically different views.

Hu, though in his younger days a sharp critic of Confucianism, on this occasion argued that the Confucian tradition positively affirmed the value of learning, scholarly inquiry, and the right of all people, regardless of class or social position, to share in that knowledge—typified by Confucius in his professed love of learning and in his assertion, recorded in the *Analects* (XV:38), that in education there should be no class distinctions; learning and knowledge should be open to all. Suzuki, by contrast, upheld the view that people's "right to knowledge" was almost valueless, if it were not indeed a meaningless abstraction. The only significant freedom, he held, was freedom from illusion; apart from the experience of Enlightenment, *satori,* such a right had no real importance. So he proceeded to talk about an "enlightenment" that went beyond all cognitive learning or scholarly knowledge.

In such an academic setting, with many, if not most, of his hearers disposed to accept the value of learning and the importance of human rights, this frank debunking of all that most scholars held sacred in the name of academic freedom was, to say the least, disconcerting. One could conclude from Suzuki's remarks that Zen Buddhism simply has nothing to contribute to the discussion of human rights. Yet when Masao Abe later came to Columbia, he proposed that Buddhism could make important contributions to building a more united and peaceful world where such rights are respected. But is Abe's claim compatible with Buddhist tradition and history? It is this question that I wish to address at some length.

It is my own view that when Suzuki presented his shocking ideas, he stood on very traditional ground in Mahāyāna Buddhism (whether or not it can be called "solid" ground is perhaps arguable, but not to be argued here). If I may cite the *Vimalakīrti Sūtra,* a central text of the Mahāyāna, in the translation by Robert Thurman, the following passage speaks in much the same terms as Suzuki concerning freedom from illusion:

> *What is bondage? And what is liberation? To indulge in liberation from the world without employing liberative technique is bondage for the bodhisattva. To engage in life with full employment of liberative technique is liberation for the bodhisattva. To experience the taste of contemplation, meditation and concentration without skill in liberative technique is not liberation, but wisdom integrated with liberative technique is liberation. Liberative technique not integrated with wisdom is bondage, but liberative technique integrated with wisdom is liberation.*[1]

Here the key terms are *wisdom* and what Thurman renders as *liberative technique* (Sanskrit *upāya,* Chinese *fang-pien,* and Japanese *hōben*), a term more commonly rendered as "accommodation," "adaptation," "expedient means," and by Lamotte, "salvific means" (*moyens salvifiques*). Wisdom, of course, is not to be confused with much learning or erudition. It is the higher insight attained as the passage indicates, by "contemplation, meditation and concentration," and scripturally speaking, Suzuki is warranted in distinguishing this from all cognitive learning of the kind we understand by "knowledge." Such wisdom is attained, as the *Vimalakīrti* says, by "concentration on voidness, signlessness and wishlessness."[2] It is the understanding that cures the sickness of object-perception. "Insofar as objects are perceived, they are the basis of sickness. What things are perceived as objects? The three realms of existence are perceived as objects. What is the thorough understanding of the basic apparent object? It is its non-perception, as no objects exist ultimately. What is its non-perception? The internal subject and external object are not perceived dualistically. Therefore it is called non-perception."[3]

To cure this sickness, says the *Vimalakīrti,* one should tell oneself, "Just as my sickness is unreal and non-existent, so the sicknesses of all living beings are unreal and non-existent. Through such considerations, he arouses the great compassion toward all living beings without falling into sentimental compassion. The great compassion that strives to eliminate the accidental compassions does not conceive of any life in living beings."[4] And elsewhere this wisdom is spoken of as "the consideration of body, mind and sickness as impermanent, miserable, empty and selfless [i.e., nonsubstantial]."[5] This view of things does not, of course, exclude the pursuit of ordinary knowledge once one has attained the higher wisdom, but it does see objective knowledge or scholarly learning as tending to illusion, sickness, and suffering in the absence of such insight. As a matter of human priorities, intellectual and scholarly pursuits are not, in themselves, given very high standing.

One cannot, however, arrive at a proper estimation of the matter without considering the liberative technique that the *Vimalakīrti* insists upon as the necessary complement of the higher wisdom. This is the adaptive or expedient means through which the higher wisdom and compassion are expressed, i.e., adjusted to the level on which, or the manner in which, others may comprehend it. As one of the most fundamental principles of Mahāyāna Buddhism, it has a wide application on both the discursive and nondiscursive levels, for it posits that there is a "salvific means" appropriate to all beings on any moral or intellectual level or of any affective nature. In other words, it is ready to meet, and come to terms with, human belief of any kind on any level. It is altogether flexible, exhibits unlimited adaptability, and is universally available to all. Another way of putting it is that it accepts all states and stages of consciousness as relatively true and none as irremediably false or totally unredeemable.

In this respect, Buddhism offers a basis for religious tolerance, and historically it has shown itself able to coexist with, as well as adapt to, the religious coloration of many different peoples and cultures. To the extent that Mahāyāna Buddhism stands on any determinate principles at all, its doctrine of the potential for Buddhahood in all beings, of compassion for all beings afflicted by illusion and suffering, of an enlightenment that accepts people as they are and not only as we wish them to be can serve as the ultimate ground for an implicit doctrine of human rights in matters of religious conscience.

A difficulty has often attached, however, to making explicit what is implicit. Partly this difficulty is one shared with all great religions in their translation of belief into practice. Like Christian peoples in their frequent failure to achieve in action the charity and love they profess for all of God's creatures, Buddhist people, too, have historically not always been able to avoid the violence and sectarian strife that stands in painful contrast to their ideal of universal compassion.

Yet there are further difficulties, it seems to me, in the way of rendering this implicit belief in the freedom of conscience into an explicit doctrine of human rights. One is the problem of deriving defined principles, with the force of a moral imperative, from a view of truth as essentially transcending the moral and rational sphere. Once one had denied the validity, for instance, of "man's right to knowledge," it is a question of how one can ever re-establish that right unqualifiedly. By this I do not mean that Buddhists are precluded from recognizing and accepting such a right as a matter of salvific means, assuming that the right is already accepted as a given in an existential situation; the question is, rather, whether they could derive that right from their own basic premises or feel any more imperative need to assert it than did Suzuki.

A second difficulty is closely related to the first: How, on the same premises, could one deal with conflicting claims among such rights? The problem is somewhat like the difficulty of modern liberalism in responding to the radical critique of unlimited toleration, that is, what tolerance can be shown to be evil? Should we tolerate the abuse of human rights? Christians, or at least some of them, attempt to deal with this problem by distinguishing between the act and the agent. Evil actions are to be condemned and resisted, but it is only God, not persons, who can render final judgment on the sinner. Such a tolerant view must, of course, be prepared to run the risk that evil people, given the benefit of the doubt, may take advantage of this opportunity to work incalculable harm on others, a prospect that certainly puts ultimate values to the test.

In the Buddhist case, I should like to cite two instances, one historical and the other contemporary, to illustrate the problem, and then finally I would like to suggest in what direction one might look for its resolution. The historical instance is that of the Chinese monk Hui-yüan, who is sometimes cited as an advocate of the freedom of religious conscience. Hui-yüan argued the case before his ruler that a monk need not bow down before a king, or in other words, that ultimate religious claims transcend secular authority. Symbolically the issue was expressed in terms appropriate to the Confucian tradition, for what we today call "rights" were often expressed in terms of the forms of social respect Confucians called "rites" (reflecting incidentally the basis they found for forms of human respect as deriving from acts of religious reverence and sacrifice). Symbolically prostrating oneself before the king acknowledged his supreme authority, and Hui-yüan insisted that those committed to the religious life owed allegiance only to the higher value of a transcendental Enlightenment.

Hui-yüan put it this way:

> If one examines the broad essentials of what the teachings of the Buddha preach, one will see that they distinguish between those who leave the household life and those who remain in it. . . . Those who revere the Buddhist law but remain in their homes are subjects who obey the transforming power (of temporal rulers). Their feelings have not changed from the customary and their course of conduct conforms to the secular world. . . . [On the other hand] he who has left the household life is a lodger beyond the earthly [secular] world and his ways are cut off from those of other beings. . . . Although those who take up the religious life do not occupy the positions of kings and princes, yet fully in harmony with the imperial ultimate, they let the people be.[6]

In the interests of brevity I have shortened Hui-yüan's argument considerably, but I think I have not done violence to his essential point. Much of what I have deleted here is concerned with reassuring the ruler that Hui-yüan does not mean to challenge the ruler's rightful authority over other people and that the Buddhist monks intend to let this stand, or as he puts it, "let the people be," obedient to imperial authority.

It does not take much discernment to see that this is something less than a full claim for the freedom of religious conscience. What Hui-yüan actually asserts is something more like an immunity or exemption from the obedience exacted of most people. True, even that claim has a significance in the history of Chinese Buddhism because of its unique assertion of a religious law higher than temporal authority and its implicit claim for the autonomy of the religious community—a claim conspicuous by its absence in China.[7] Even in the later history of East Asian Buddhism, when lay Buddhism predominated over the monastic or clerical types, I know of no such general claim being put forward for the freedom of religious conscience in general. This, it seems to me, is most probably a reflection of the very policy of accommodation Hui-yüan himself exemplifies: it rendered unto Caesar a considerable part of the autonomy that in Europe the church would have claimed as properly reserved for God. Thus, in the larger perspective of world history, the doctrine of "accommodation" or "expedient means" may have entailed substantial costs as well as benefits.

To bring the issue closer to our own time and place, I would like to cite a recent report, "Buddhism in China Today," written by someone who identifies himself as the leader of a delegation of American Buddhists to the People's Republic.[8] This report runs true to the generality of reports by visitors to mainland China today, with heavy emphasis on the deplorable state of affairs before and during the Cultural Revolution, as compared with the more enlightened policies that have prevailed under the current leadership. It quotes eminent Buddhist prelates to the effect that, as one put it, "we have forgotten the past and are acting solely for the future."[9] It also cites approvingly the guarantee of religious freedom in Article 35 of the present, revised Constitution.

And after describing the extensive rebuilding of temples that is going on, the report states, "With the policy of restoring temples, the Chinese government realized that monks and nuns were required to care for these temples. For this reason monks and nuns are now honored citizens in China. The monks cooperate with the state, but maintain the Buddhist heritage."[10] Further on it quotes one of these new monks, at the famed White Horse Temple, near Loyang, who says, "I worked in a factory until several years ago, but in considering the present situation, I decided to devote myself to Buddhism to make China a better country." He was then asked, "Is there a contradiction between Communism and Buddhism?" He replied, "No, there is no contradiction. Buddhism is a teaching that promotes the welfare of the people and that is also a goal of Communism."[11]

As I have suggested, the tone of the article is not untypical of the euphoric accounts these days by the recipients of traditional Chinese hospitality, and there is nothing remarkable in that. One cannot reasonably ask what some American liberals seem to demand in such situations: that such visitors should in all conscience immediately present to their hosts a catalogue of human-rights violations and a list of human-rights demands. But since in this case the writer himself raised the issue of the freedom of religion, and even cited the regime's current patronage of Lamaism, one cannot help wondering why he failed to indicate in any way his awareness that there is a different side to this story. Certainly the Dalai Lama and his followers would have reason to question whether their human rights are being adequately guaranteed. Apparently, here as in innumerable historic instances, the policy of accommodation (*upāya*) prevails and the concern for human rights is muted.

Now, having raised the issue in this way, and having posed it for myself as much as for anyone else, I am going to suggest in conclusion a possible way to resolve it. By that I mean not a final solution, but a direction in which to look for it. And for this I turn in what may seem a surprising direction: back to the seventh century in Japan, to the so-called Constitution of Prince Shōtoku. The authorship and date of this document are still in some dispute, but whether it is a century earlier or later is of no consequence to us here. To me, its significance lies in that, as far as I know, it is the only political document, the only "constitution," inspired at least in part by Buddhism. Many of its provisions, admittedly, owe nothing at all to Buddhism, and one could well argue that except for the direct reference in the second of the seventeen articles to taking refuge in the Three Treasures or Three Precious Things (*sampō*), it owes more to the political traditions of Confucian China than to any Buddhist political tradition (if such indeed exists).

But repeatedly in these articles the question is raised as to where ultimate wisdom and authority lie. Alongside of passages that assert the authority of the ruler and the state, in terms not dissimilar from those found in Hui-yüan's case, there are other passages that give expression to a profound contradiction: on the one hand the need for great wisdom if the business of government is to be properly conducted, and on the other the extreme rarity of finding such wisdom. Let me cite a few of the relevant passages:

> When wise men are entrusted with office, the sound of praise
> arises. If unprincipled men hold office, disasters and tumults

*abound. In this world few are born with knowledge; wisdom is the
product of earnest meditation. . . . [Article 7]*

*Let us cease from wrath and refrain from angry looks. Nor let us be
resentful when others differ from us. For all men have hearts and
each heart has its own leanings. Their right is our wrong, and our
right is their wrong. . . . We [speaking for rulers] are not unquestionably sages, nor are others unquestionably fools. Both of us are
simply ordinary men. How can anyone lay down a rule by which to
distinguish right from wrong? For we are all, one with another, wise
and foolish, like a ring which has no end. Therefore, though others
give way to anger, let us on the contrary dread our own faults, let
us follow the multitude and act like them. [Article 10]*[12]

Such language is altogether extraordinary in the dynastic history of
East Asia. One can, it is true, find in the *Analects* disclaimers by Confucius that he has any final claim to certain knowledge as well as repeated
disavowals that he possesses sage wisdom, but such language is hardly
typical of Chinese sovereigns when they are enunciating imperial prerog-
atives (their ritual professions of humility are another thing, not analogous to this case). We know, however, that in Prince Shōtoku's time a very
strong influence was felt from Buddhist thought in the skeptical vein of
the *Vimalakīrti Sūtra*, and we have reason to believe that Shōtoku was
profoundly touched by it. Yet that does not constitute the whole story.
Article 14 goes on to pose the dilemma that follows from this admission:

*Therefore it is not until after a lapse of five hundred years that we
at last meet with a wise man, and even in a thousand years we
hardly obtain one sage. But if we do not find wise men and sages,
wherewith is the country to be governed?*[13]

The answer is to be found, according to the next article, in public-spirit-
ed persons and such as can act harmoniously with others: "If one fails to
act harmoniously with others, he will assuredly sacrifice the public interest to private feelings. . . . Therefore in the first article it was said that
superiors and inferiors should agree together. . . ."

Here, then, is repeated a theme introduced at the beginning of the

Constitution: "When those above are harmonious and those below friend-ly, and there is concord in the discussion of business, right views of things spontaneously gain acceptance. Then what is there that cannot be accomplished?"[14] The last article returns to this theme:

> Decisions on important matters should not be made by one person
> alone. They should be discussed with many. But small matters are
> of less consequence. It is unnecessary to consult a number of peo-
> ple. It is only in the case of the discussion of weighty affairs, when
> there is a suspicion that they may miscarry, that one should
> arrange matters in concert with others, so as to arrive at the right
> conclusion.

In these disarmingly simple statements, we find a singular synthe-sis of Buddhist, Confucian, and native Japanese views: the need for social harmony and public spiritedness from Confucianism; the contrasting Buddhist skepticism concerning people's ability to attain true wisdom and certainty in judging human rights and wrongs; and, in the absence of fixed or final rights and wrongs, the resolution of the dilemma in the Japanese instinct for consultation and consensus. What is right will become known only through the public process of dialogue and a sharing of views.

I realize that this kind of "constitution" in the seventh century is still far from providing the specification of human rights that we look for in a modern constitution, but it seems to me it does provide a basic outlook and process conducive to the formulation of human rights. That these precise formulations emerged only with the advent of Western concep-tions of constitutional law suggests that there were still some ingredients needed—some enlargement of the process of sharing others' views—to improve on what had been articulated earlier. But the fact that such guar-antees have become widely established and observed since Japan's open-ing to the West, and especially in the fifty years of Japanese postwar his-tory, suggests that, contrary to predictions made in the forties that Japan would have the greatest difficulty in shaking off its authoritarian past, in fact democratic attitudes and human-rights concepts proved not all that incompatible with native traditions. These traditions derive from this ear-lier confluence of cultures and fusion of divergent views, by which

Buddhist skepticism, adaptability, and tolerance found their appropriate complement in values, identifiably Confucian and Japanese, that Buddhism by itself did not supply.

To conclude, then, Masao Abe wishes to see Buddhism making a significant contribution to building a more just and peaceful world community. However, as he himself has said, to do so, Buddhism must overcome certain traditional skeptical attitudes toward social engagement. I have suggested that one way of doing so is through public conversation and interfaith/intercultural dialogue. Buddhism in Japan has used this process successfully in the past with Confucianism to contribute to a more positive social climate. Perhaps Masao Abe's dialogue with Christianity in the West can be seen as initiating a similar process by which Buddhism can appropriate complementary ideals concerning such things as human rights in order to meet what has become a shared global responsibility.

chapter Thirty-One

A CHRYSANTHEMUM WITH A LOTUS STALK: REMINISCENCES FROM A HINDU PERSPECTIVE

Arvind Sharma

I

AT THE TIME I WAS TEACHING in Sydney, Australia, but was spending the year at Temple University on an exchange program. I was enjoying the hospitality of my colleague, Patrick Burke, a philosopher of religion, when the conversation took an unexpected turn.

"What do you make of the Buddhist doctrine of Emptiness?" he asked unexpectedly.

"I don't quite understand it," I replied.

"Come on now," he said, clearing his throat on purpose as if I was affecting modesty. "Is it some kind of reverse snobbery that we Westerners can't ever understand the profound Orient?" He made the word *profound* come out of hidden guttural depths as he said it. I think he still rued the occasion when he had asked me, "What is Brahman?" And I had begun by saying, "As a concession to Western empirical modes of thought, let us . . ."

"Honestly I don't know," I insisted. "I can teach it but I don't understand it," I elaborated. "In fact, I even once landed a job offer by giving a lecture on it!"

Patrick Burke, however, was not to be deterred. So, more or less to appease him, I said, "I think I understand its soteriological intent though not its doctrinal content."

"How is that?" asked Pat, putting his cup on the table.

"Well," I said, "The root cause of involvement in samsara according to Buddhism is desire."

I looked at Pat and he nodded in assent.

"Well, then," I continued, "desire requires three elements in order to exist: someone who desires, something which is desired, and some relationship between the two." Pat nodded again.

Thus encouraged, I continued, "If everything is empty then there is no one to desire and nothing to be desired and no relationship between the nonentities. Hence, if one really accepted the doctrine, it axes desire at its root."

"Not bad," Pat murmured, "not bad. Now what about the philosophical exposition?"

I rehearsed the stock arguments but said limply, "This is what I tell my class. To tell you the truth, I don't know," just as Bodhidharma had told the Chinese emperor. But he spoke from a state of knowledge; I was speaking from a state of ignorance.

"Have you heard of Masao Abe?" Pat then said tentatively.

"Now I have. Why?"

"You might wish to talk to him about it. Of all the people I know, I find him its most credible interpreter."

It was 1982. The name stuck: Masao Abe. There was something in the way Patrick Burke mentioned his name that involuntarily made me think of D. T. Suzuki. Here, then, was someone I had to see when I could. How many people are there of whom it can be said that one can discuss Emptiness with them and not return empty-handed?

II

It was a wise person who said that all things come to them that can wait. I did not have to wait for too long, only until 1986. Abe had just made a presentation at the annual meeting of the American Academy of Religion. People wishing to have a word with him had formed a queue. I found myself in that line right behind Dean Gamwell of the Chicago Divinity School, who was apparently there to invite Abe to teach at the University of Chicago as a visiting professor. The arrangement was quickly and easily finalized, leaving Abe free to talk to me. I introduced myself and was amazed that a scholar of his international standing could be so totally devoid of any visible trace of ego. As our conversation commenced, however, Abe suddenly recalled an appointment for which he was late. I prepared to leave. Sometimes, however, an initial setback, in a Taoist sort of way, results in an even greater gain, for as I was turning away from the aborted interview he asked, "What are you doing for dinner?" The words were spoken slowly, softly, and one might even say, serenely. When I told him I wasn't doing anything in particular, he reflected for a moment and then said, "If you are free, then why don't you join us? I am meeting a Japanese scholar, but you are welcome to join us."

We often hear of the East meeting the West. It was about time the East started meeting the East. I gladly accepted the invitation. Abe broke into a smile. I still remember it vividly because it had a compelling ineffable quality about it. It was so totally unencumbered. It seemed curiously and totally detached from the environment, a happening complete in itself, with a childlike simplicity beguiling in its guilelessness. When his face assumed its normal expression, one was left with the feeling of something very precious—found fleetingly and then lost irretrievably—until he smiled again. I was to marvel at it later all the more when in the midst of a deep philosophical discussion, all of a sudden Abe would smile for no apparent reason except that as he beheld the universe, "it was very good." It must have possessed anabolic properties, for I still remember my astonished bewilderment when I learned that he was close to seventy!

The dinner was a very pleasant experience. It was then that I met Mrs. Abe for the first time, whose benign presence enhanced the occasion. My attempt to contribute to its expense was turned down with polite firmness. I wanted to talk about Zen, but courtesy came first;

philosophy had to wait. However, the serene deportment of Abe throughout the meeting, occasionally bordering on the sublime, left me wondering if the medium might not be the message. As I took leave I still wonder why the following lines flashed in my mind:

> *The moon is reflected deep*
> *inside the lake*
> *But the water shows no*
> *signs of penetration.*[1]

III

My next encounter with Abe was one in which I barely met him, and yet
it is among the most memorable, for a single remark opened many doors
and even vistas. What is even more remarkable is the fact that the remark
was not even addressed to me. Furthermore, it was made in response to
an utterance that either I did not hear or could not follow. However, in
the course of his response, he uttered the following sentence: "It is in us
but we are not in it." He made the statement in answer to a question at
the end of a plenary session at the 1987 International Buddhist-Christian
Conference at Berkeley.

This sentence has followed me ever since and keeps surprising me
with the versatility of its application and how it could be enlarged with
the spiritual dimension of virtually any tradition. It can be applied with
equal ease to absolutism and theism. We can say of God that he is in us
but we are not in him—that he hides himself by being too close to us! It
can be applied to Hindu absolutism as represented by *nirguṇa*-Brahman:
it is in us but we are not in it. It can, of course, apply to the doctrine
of Emptiness, perhaps the context in which Abe originally used it. In fact,
it can be extended to even secular situations to offer an excellent sum-
mation of it, as when one might say that life is in us but we are not in it.

Once launched, such aphorisms take on a life of their own. I have
since faced situations, intellectual as well as existential, to which the
statement applies in a delectably dialectical way: we are in it but it is not
in us. For instance, one could be physically present in a country but one's
emotional commitments or intellectual interests could well lie outside it,

as could happen easily in the case of a landed immigrant. I could, for instance, be in Canada and yet Canada not be in me, in the sense that what is happening in India could still tug at the strings of the heart much more, at least initially, than what might be happening in Canada. The illustration of Canada is not entirely capricious. At the time I heard the aphorism, I was en route to Montreal to take up a position in the Faculty of Religious Studies at McGill University.

IV

My most sustained meeting with Abe took place in San Francisco in April 1990 at the San Francisco Zen Center (where else?). Through his kindness, my stay had been arranged for and it was with great pleasure that I stayed in the quiet and gentle surroundings of the center. Once, in my adolescence, I had been "stranded" in a Hindu temple for six months. Since then, I had never doubted the elevating impact of one's environment on one's psyche. My stay at the Zen Center once again confirmed this.

It was in his study, after we had glanced at some of his recent books, one of which had just been published by the Yale University Press,[2] that Abe asked me, in his quiet and gentle manner: "What do the Hindus think of the Buddhists?" It took me some time even to comprehend the question, for modern Hindus barely differentiate between the two. Certainly I was not brought up to do so. One of earliest verses in my mother-tongue I remember is the following:

> *Sujātā awaits you with a bowl,*
> *Lord of Compassion, descend again!*

In my adolescence, on a trip to Anuradhapura in Sri Lanka, I even plucked a leaf from the Bodhi tree as a memento. And in my youth when I was asked to specify my chosen deity as a Hindu, I always specified it as the Buddha. In fact, the domestic fire ritual I was taught to perform as a child specifies that it is being performed in the "division of the Rose-Apple continent called Bhārata, in the country of the Aryas, during the period of the incarnation of the Buddha" (*jambūdvipe bharatakhaṇḍe āryāvarte buddhāvatare*). When recently my sister asked Swami Chimayananda, who had initiated my mother into Advaita Vedānta, what he thought of Zen, he declared: "It is the quintessence of the Upanishads."

Abe must have thought his gentle voice had dissolved into inaudibility before reaching my ears, for he softly repeated the question. That broke my reverie, and I pondered for a moment how to reconcile history with biography without sacrificing factuality or integrity. Then I said:

> Hinduism has historically been characterized by two approaches toward Buddhism: a positive one and a negative one. The positive one emphasized the compassion of the Buddha and the greatness of his mission. The negative one disapproved of his criticism of the Vedas and his renouncing the world while still a youth, etc. In classical Hinduism both strands are present, but the negative one is often prominent. By contrast, in modern Hinduism the ratio is reversed. The Buddha's role has been reassessed positively to the point where it now dominates to such an extent that modern Hindus consider the difference between Hinduism and Buddhism no more significant than between two Hindu schools or sects.[3]

This reminds me of a thesis that was presented by Professor Frits Staal at the Second International Buddhist-Christian Conference at Hawaii in 1984. He stated how in the course of teaching Indian philosophy, he described the Hindu Brahman as free from all distinctions and devoid of any distinguishing characteristics. Without quite realizing it, he described Śūnyatā (Emptiness) in a similar way while teaching the Buddhist component of Indian philosophy. Thereupon, a Chinese student got up and raised the following question: "If Brahman is without distinctions and distinguishing attributes and if Śūnyatā is also without distinctions and distinguishing attributes then how is one to distinguish one from the other?" Professor Staal thereupon concluded that they are identical.[4] The similarity between the two doctrines has not gone unnoticed, and much as it would please the irenic Hindus and Buddhists, I could not help feeling uncomfortable about the identification thus established. I was haunted by its possible glibness. The point seemed to have been finessed philosophically, and it was only some years later that I was able to articulate my objection: indistinguishability had been confused with identity. The fact that two things are indistinguishable does not necessarily mean that they are identical as had been supposed. It would be interesting to have Abe's thoughts on this question.

It was on this visit to San Francisco that Professor and Mrs. Abe decided to take me out for a Japanese meal. The meal itself was a novelty in richness and delicacy, for someone like me who subsists on sandwiches. But the intellectual repast surpassed it. I ventured to say, as the taxi went over one of the undulations that are so much a part of the landscape of San Francisco, that "Zen involves a transformation of consciousness." Abe provisionally agreed.

"The question then is," I ventured further, "if this altered state of consciousness can still be called consciousness in our usual sense. When driving the car we change gears. However, although we use the expression 'neutral gear' when the car is in neutral gear in fact no gear is actually engaged so that a car, when in 'neutral gear' is in a qualitatively different state than when it is in first, second or third gear."

"That is a good example," Abe commented, and supplemented it with that of fire which "burns but cannot burn itself," implying thereby, I surmise, that the characteristic state of normal consciousness in a sense cannot be applied to consciousness itself.

Discussions with Abe often had this quality, that they were more in the nature of sharing a position or a point of view than anything else. They were enriching rather than conclusive and had the nature of an ongoing dialogue. It also made one feel uneasy at times with the realization that it is so easy to be sophisticated without being mature in academia.

After the meal we strolled into a bookshop to follow through on our eating with some browsing. And as I headed for the shelf on religion and philosophy, I was greeted by no fewer than three books by my host Abe himself!

V

Abe is justly credited with introducing the philosophy of the Kyoto School, especially as represented by Kitarō Nishida, to the West. In my own case, however, although I have greatly profited from his contribution in this respect, it is my encounter with Abe as a partner in dialogue to which I must give precedence. There have been those moments, doubtless experienced by others, when a slight correction by Abe has rescued one from a major pitfall. I was at the time grappling with the question of the identity of nirvana and samsara in Mahāyāna Buddhism when I offered the following illustration to Abe for his comment. "I have just finished teaching a class and as I step out of the building I see three people being chased and shot. I am terrified but not petrified and turn to run and call the police. As I turn, however, I espy a camera crew perched on top of the building and it suddenly dawns on me that what I am witnessing is not an actual case of murder but a take for a film. What was so terrifying a moment ago in a flash turns into something entertaining. The outward activities are still the same and identical with the goings-on before but they are now transformed: samsara has become nirvana. They are one." Abe listened to the example quietly and then commented with frugal understated elegance: "Samsara in your example becomes nirvana; in Buddhism it *is* nirvana!"

Masao Abe's role as a partner is not merely the negative one of saving us from our own ignorance; it is a far more positive one as well. At the annual meeting of the American Academy of Religion in Boston in 1987, Thomas Dean and I organized a panel on "Buddhist-Christian Dialogue: Its Effects on the Participants." I have long been interested in the question of how our self-understanding of our own tradition is affected by engaging in dialogue. Abe's paper entitled "The Impact of Dialogue with Christianity on My Self-Understanding as a Buddhist" captured the spirit of the issue as elegantly as one could have wished. For the point I wish to make, however, we must go further afield. In his chapter on Confucianism in the book *Our Religions* (1993), Tu Wei-ming raises the intriguing issue that while in accordance with the spirit of Confucianism, one can assert that Confucius would have gone on seeking perfection had he lived longer,[5] could the same be said of the Buddha once he had already attained nirvana when he was thirty-five? I cannot speak for the Buddha, but having had the privilege of knowing Masao Abe for a decade, I can perhaps speak for a Buddhist, especially a Buddhist who engages in dialogue. And I hope it will not be considered impertinent of me when I say that on the basis of having known Abe and the openness and willingness with which he engages in dialogue, he will continue to be positively affected by dialogue and to continually affect people positively through dialogue as long as life continues and perhaps even beyond.

BETWEEN ZEN AND THE WEST, ZEN AND ZEN, AND ZEN AND PURE LAND: ON MASAO ABE'S SENSE OF INTER- AND INTRAFAITH DIALOGUE

Steven Heine

ON INTER- AND INTRAFAITH DIALOGUE

MASAO ABE'S SENSE OF INTERFAITH DIALOGUE between Zen and Western philosophy and religion has been singularly dynamic, open-ended, and progressive. It is dynamic in its vigorous commitment to articulating and establishing the modern significance of Zen by synthesizing the best of traditional and contemporary perspectives from Rinzai and Dōgen to Nishida and Nishitani on a wide range of issues involving metaphysics, psychology, soteriology, and ethics. Its open-endedness lies in Abe's willingness to encounter profoundly and ongoingly the preeminent minds of Western thought, past and present, from classical Greek and biblical writings to existentialism and phenomenology. In particular, Abe

has engaged in continuing dialogue with Paul Tillich, John Cobb, Hans
Küng, Langdon Gilkey, David Tracy, and Eugene Borowitz, among many
other leading representatives of Christian and Jewish as well as feminist,
liberation, process, and ecological theologies. Finally, Abe's dialogue is
progressive in that his outlook is not insistent or dogmatic but reflects a
genuine concern with the future development of society at this critical
turning point in human history. As Abe has often explained, he believes
that the mission of Kyoto School thought, and of the F.A.S. Society in
particular, for which he has been the primary spokesperson in the West,
is to help highlight and unify the most constructive elements of thought,
East or West, Buddhist or Christian. As at other major turning points in
human history, it is necessary to come to terms creatively and critically
with diverse competing and conflicting viewpoints in order to rectify the
world in an era that Abe's Kyoto School senior colleague Hajime Tanabe
has referred to as the "age of death" because of the threat of nuclear holocaust and other humanly fabricated dangers. Like his mentor Keiji
Nishitani, Abe seems to see Zen as a "self-surpassing" (*kōjō*) viewpoint
that stands not only as an addition to other perspectives functioning in
dialogue but as the very basis of the dialogical process that is unfolding.

   While Abe is probably most widely known for his contribution to
the East-West philosophical encounter, a crucial aspect of his effort to
establish interfaith dialogue has been the undertaking of a multifaceted
intrafaith dialogue involving various factions of Buddhist thought, especially Zen and Pure Land as well as, within the context of Zen, the Rinzai
and Sōtō sects. The two dimensions of dialogue—interfaith and
intrafaith—complement, reinforce, and enhance each other. The base of
Abe's overall dialogic project is Zen thought. But before (in an ontological rather than chronological sense) he turns to examining other traditions, he clarifies the meaning of his own tradition. Therefore, intrafaith
dialogue is the necessary building block that makes possible the construction of the larger interfaith edifice, or the micro-element needed for
the macro-structure. Or to use a naturalist metaphor favored by a host of
Eastern thinkers, it represents the roots that allow the growth of the
branches.

   As just indicated, Abe's involvement with intrafaith dialogue divides
into two main levels, which are themselves intertwined with interfaith

concerns. The first level, which exists on the borderline between inter- and intrafaith dialogue, deals with dialogue between Zen and its apparent ideological opposite within Buddhism, the Pure Land school. This intrafaith dialogue particularly involves Dōgen, the founder of Sōtō Zen Buddhism in Japan, and his contemporary in the Kamakura era, Shinran, the founder of the Jōdo Shin-shū sect of Pure Land Buddhism. Zen is known as the path of self power, and Pure Land is the path of other power. Zen stresses an inner, contemplative realization of the unborn moment in this life, while Pure Land emphasizes attainment through humility and faith in Amida Buddha of rebirth in the next life. Yet in the respective approaches to such issues as naturalism and causality Abe shows underlying similarities between Zen and Pure Land, which both derive their philosophies from the Mahāyāna doctrines of the universality of the Buddha-nature and original Enlightenment. He also demonstrates how and why the two schools of thought should dispense with polemics and creatively encounter each other in a modern context on the issues of human nature as well as the potentials and obstacles for soteriological fulfillment in relation to the primordial potentiality of Buddha-nature in order to reach a higher degree of self-understanding. In comparing Dōgen and Shinran, Abe's methodology stresses that although contemporary reason allows us to set up a critical contrast, "we cannot help but confront the issues . . . when we subjectively inquire into the religious attainment of the two thinkers in terms of our own existential realization rather than objectively compare them by putting ourself outside of their experiences."[1] That is, Abe's approach is never merely comparative in an abstract speculative sense, but drawing on the critical approach of objective scholarship, he incorporates into the dialogue the dimension of Zen subjectivity with its deeply existential awareness of identity and difference to creatively empathize with alternative viewpoints.

The second level of intrafaith dialogue is between Zen and Zen, that is, between the two main branches of Japanese Zen, Rinzai and Sōtō. These schools have been traditionally divided in terms of methods of practice, with Rinzai tending to favor the use of *kōan* riddles to realize sudden Enlightenment and Sōtō espousing the use of *zazen* meditation to attain a continuing state of Enlightenment. Abe, an heir to the Kyoto School's comparative philosophical methodology primarily influenced by

Rinzai Zen as well as by Western existentialism and mysticism, offers a philosophical analysis of the theories of Zen practice of Dōgen. Most modern scholarship on Dōgen, especially within the Sōtō sect itself, has been predominantly informed by textual historical studies. Abe fuses an interfaith method involving comparisons with Heidegger and other Western thinkers, including Spinoza, Kant, and Hegel, with the most basic intrafaith concern of clarifying Sōtō in light of Rinzai Zen. Another aspect of Abe's intrafaith dialogue related to the above is his extensive analysis of other figures in or connected with the Kyoto School, which is itself divided into Zen (Nishida-Nishitani-Ueda) and Pure Land (Tanabe-Takeuchi) streams. This has resulted in the volume Abe co-edited, *D. T Suzuki: A Zen Life Remembered,* and will lead to another volume of Abe's essays on Kyoto School thinkers to be edited by James Fredericks, one of several collections currently in preparation.

Both of these main levels of intrafaith dialogue are also amply expressed in a number of other sources. These sources include Abe's essays edited in 1985 by William R. LaFleur, *Zen and Western Thought;* a two-volume sequel to this collection that I have edited, *Buddhism and Interfaith Dialogue* (1995) and *Zen and Comparative Studies* (1996); the translations of Dōgen that Abe produced with Norman Waddell in *The Eastern Buddhist* during the 1970s, which will be appearing in a book edited by Waddell; and the 1992 collection of Abe's essays, *A Study of Dōgen: His Philosophy and Religion,* which I also had the opportunity to edit and to translate in part. During the course of the translating process, while Abe corrected and revised my work, he not only paid careful attention to the renderings into English but also significantly rewrote portions of the original text. Thus, the two essays on Dōgen and Shinran at the end of *A Study of Dōgen,* originally written in the early 1960s in Japanese, were updated for the English version thirty years later. The concluding section of the second essay, which sets up a philosophical encounter between the two seemingly antithetical Japanese Buddhist thinkers, was added at this stage. I believe that it stands as the high point of the entire book and contributes greatly to Abe's overall inter/intrafaith dialogical methodology.

In this article I first highlight and evaluate Abe's contributions to the dialogue between Zen and Zen, particularly in the area of Dōgen studies, because that is the more fundamental of the intrafaith building blocks. Then I discuss Abe's contribution to the dialogue between Zen and Pure Land, especially the encounter he sets up between Dōgen and Shinran, which has broader implications in terms of clarifying the relation between the intra- and interfaith dimensions of dialogue.

BETWEEN ZEN AND ZEN

While several of Abe's essays on Dōgen were written in Japanese before being rendered and published in English, one of his main contributions to intrafaith studies of Zen since the early 1970s has been as a translator and interpreter of Dōgen for the West. Since the first translation of a Dōgen text in 1958, there have been many prominent translations, especially of his main philosophical work, the *Shōbōgenzō*. However, the series of Abe/Waddell translations has set a remarkably high standard not only for Dōgen studies, but for East Asian studies as a whole. These translations are at once accurate in terms of capturing the allusions and references to other Buddhist works scattered throughout Dōgen's writings, complete in following every word of the text without resorting to paraphrase or a shortcut technique, and philosophically thought-provoking in conveying the full range of subtleties and nuances expressed by Dōgen's use of paradoxical language and philosophical wordplay. Coupled with Abe's 1971 essay in *The Eastern Buddhist,* "Dōgen on Buddha Nature," the first main philosophical study of Dōgen in English, these works have greatly helped stimulate and develop Western studies in the field.

Abe's interpretations of Dōgen display the comparative philosophical bent of the Kyoto School combined with a mastery of textual scholarship. Unlike Nishitani, Abe does not cite Dōgen as part of the construction of his own speculative philosophy. Yet at the same time, unlike Zen scholars such as Seizan Yanagida and Genryū Kagamishima, his concerns are not strictly historical. Abe is not interested merely in comparing Dōgen's thought with the Rinzai school or in allowing scholarly distance to infect his studies with unwarranted skepticism. Rather, Abe provides an interpretation that highlights both Dōgen's consistency with other approaches to Mahāyāna and Zen thought and the distinctiveness and uniqueness of his writings. Abe's scholarly apparatus is relatively sparse; he sticks to the text at hand while drawing out the existential implications that illustrate Dōgen's significance as a world philosopher who in some ways surpasses the more limited metaphysical concerns of leading Western thinkers. What Abe does provide is a deftly probing analysis that penetrates to the core of Dōgen's philosophy and religion. He offers a consistent and coherent portrait of Dōgen's fundamental doctrines of the "oneness of practice and attainment" (shushō-ittō) as the resolution of his doubt concerning Tendai "original Awakening thought" (hongaku shisō), the "casting off of body-mind" (shinjin datsuraku) as the Awakening he attained under the guidance of the Chinese master Ju-ching, and "impermanence-Buddha-nature" (mujō-busshō) as the experience of the eternal now, or reconciliation of time and eternity.

Based on an interpretation of the origin and solution of Dōgen's formative "doubt," Abe's essays explore the profundity of the Zen master's philosophy of time, death, Buddha-nature, enlightenment, and morality in comparison with Buddhist and Western thinkers such as Hui-neng, Shinran, Spinoza, Kant, Hegel, Kierkegaard, and Heidegger. Abe shows how the doctrine of the oneness of practice and attainment is the crux of Dōgen's unique approach to the Buddhist Middle Way of nonduality in his handling and overcoming of the conventionally presumed polarities of life and death, space and time, self and world, beings and Buddha-nature, and illusion and realization. Reading Abe on Dōgen, to cite a traditional Mahāyāna metaphor, is like entering a great ocean with waves rippling in multiple directions. For Abe, a Dōgen quotation concerning death becomes an opportunity for comparison with Shinran, which in turn leads to reflection on the different conceptions of life and afterlife in Christianity and Buddhism. His comparative analysis of Dōgen and Heidegger is thoroughly grounded in an understanding of both thinkers and always retains its critical edge so that the broader similarities and finer contrasts come into focus in an appropriate and compelling manner.

The importance of the doctrine of the oneness of practice and attainment highlighted by Abe must be seen in the context of Dōgen's criticism of Tendai's original Awakening thought, which played a dominant role in the late Heian/early Kamakura era of Japanese religion. The notion of original Awakening was initially found in *The Awakening of Faith in Mahāyāna Buddhism*. It was refined in the Japanese Tendai school as an extension of Mahāyāna nonduality by accepting and affirming the concrete phenomenal world as coterminous with absolute reality. Abe shows that according to the traditional biographies, Dōgen deeply questioned during his early monkhood why it was necessary to practice meditation at all if Awakening was already provided as an original endowment, as the Tendai doctrine suggests. After his Awakening, Dōgen went on to criticize severely some tendencies in the Tendai teaching of original Awakening as leaning toward a non-Buddhist position by at once hypostatizing an eternal, *a priori* mental nature in contrast to ephemeral phenomena and affirming the natural world in a way that obviated the need for sustained commitment to religious training.

Yet Dōgen's relation to Tendai is rather ambivalent and complex for several reasons.[2] First, Dōgen, like other leading thinkers of his day, was greatly influenced by Tendai thought. Although he avoided the notion of *hongaku,* or "original Awakening," he used similar terms—*honshō,* or "original Realization," and *honrai no memmoku,* or "original face"—in the *Bendōwa* fascicle. He also praised Chih-i, founder of the sect in China, and cited the central Tendai scripture, the *Lotus Sūtra,* more than fifty times in his writings, endorsing many of its main tenets, such as *shohō-jissō* (all *dharmas* are true form). On the other hand, Dōgen was certainly not alone in his criticisms, but was joined by other reformers of the "new" Kamakura Buddhism, including Hōnen, Shinran, and Nichiren. Nor was Dōgen the first to raise the issue of practice. An earlier Tendai monk, Shō shin, criticized the *hongaku* mainstream for many of the same reasons and tended to stress the notion of *genjō* (spontaneous Realization), which was a central topic in Dōgen's writing. Abe makes it clear that fundamentally Dōgen affirms the notion of original Awakening by giving a new interpretation of the oneness of practice and attainment as expressed in the *Bendōwa* fascicle: "In the Buddha Dharma practice and attainment are identical. Because one's present practice is practice in attainment, one's initial negotiation of the Way in itself is the whole of original attainment."[3] To Dōgen, "practicing Buddha (*gyōbutsu*) is . . . neither *shikaku* [acquired Awakening] nor *hongaku* [original Awakening]"[4] in the usual sense but is based on original Awakening in the above or *genjō*-oriented sense. That is, Dōgen did not try to maneuver from original Awakening as one extreme to the opposite extreme of acquired Awakening (*shikaku*), which is equally problematic. Rather, while uncompromisingly embracing nonduality, he also thoroughly stressed the differences and distinctiveness of each and every phenomenon that can only be fully realized at each and every moment through continuous, unceasing practice.

This issue of the overcoming of doubt is also crucial for understanding Dōgen's relation to other Zen thinkers. He stands in basic accord with the doctrine of sudden Awakening that was the hallmark of the early Southern School associated with sixth patriarch Hui-neng. This doctrine became the defining mark of Zen as a whole, although sometimes Rinzai and Sōtō are distinguished with the former representing suddenness and the latter a gradualist approach. However, a close examination of Dōgen's writings indicates that despite an occasional sectarian polemic, he is careful to avoid the extreme positions of sudden versus gradual approaches, or of *kōan* versus *zazen* practices. Rather, he emphasizes the continuity of meditative training that embraces spontaneity and simultaneity. For Abe, Dōgen's willingness to criticize other Zen thinkers in China, including Hui-neng and Rinzai, in addition to Tendai thought, qualifies him not only as a leading existential philosopher in Japan but in the Buddhist tradition as a whole.

Abe also makes clear how the key to Dōgen's breaking through his spiritual impasse concerning original Awakening is a clarification of the meaning of time, death, and Buddha-nature. Dōgen realized that the true nature of time is beyond the polarities of now and then, before and after, means and end, potentiality and actuality, and reversibility and irreversibility. Therefore, Enlightenment cannot be considered to occur either prior to practice, as an innate potentiality from the past awaiting actualization, or at the conclusion of practice, as a teleological goal to be reached in the future. Dōgen overcame any subtle inclination to hypostatize or conceptualize either practice or attainment as a static occurrence rather than to realize their dynamic unity as a ceaselessly unfolding event fully integrated with all aspects of temporality. True time encompasses the simultaneity and particularity of past, present, and future as well as the spontaneity of the moment and fullness of continuity. From this standpoint, life at once contains death and yet is complete unto itself as a manifestation of absolute reality, and death at once contains life and yet is complete unto itself as a manifestation of absolute reality.

Dōgen's understanding of the nondualities of practice and attainment, life and death, and beings and Buddha-nature fulfills the Buddhist transanthropocentric, nonsubstantive, and cosmological approach. Dōgen grasps the world of Absolute Nothingness unbound by humanly fabricated deceptions or presuppositions, but at the same time he is eminently concerned with the concrete, personal issue of authenticity or attainment. That is, the human dimension is only realized by transcending it, and vice versa. Furthermore, Abe shows that Dōgen's philosophical vantage point of being and nothingness, based on the religious experience of the casting off of body-mind, is the basis of the underlying differences between the Zen master and Martin Heidegger. Among Western thinkers Heidegger appears closest to Dōgen in stressing temporality as the key to unlocking the question of Being. Like Dōgen, Heidegger penetrates to the inseparability of life and death and the three tenses of ecstatic temporality from a nonsubstantive philosophical perspective. Yet even though Heidegger's insights are revolutionary in Western thought, he remains bound to an anthropocentrism that values thinking over non-thinking, beings over nothingness, or the future over the eternal now. Therefore, Heidegger never fully resolves the religious quest for self-Awakening.

BETWEEN ZEN AND PURE LAND

The Kyoto School, although primarily oriented around Zen thought, has been interested and involved from its inception in Shinran's Jōdo Shinshū approach to Buddhist theory and practice in several ways. First, Nishida frequently cites Shinran, particularly his saying "If even good people can be saved, how much more so the sinner," and he suggests a parallel with Kierkegaard's existential theology based on a radical acceptance of faith. Suzuki has written a short but important work on *Shin Buddhism*. Tanabe, Nishida's junior colleague and critic, stresses the importance of repentance (*zangedō*) as the basis of philosophy, especially in the postwar period. Takeuchi, following Tanabe's Pure Land stream of thought, also uses Nishitani's distinction between transcendence and "trans-descendence" to clarify the role of other power in relation to self power. He writes, "Transcendence entails a sense of 'from . . . to' that involves not only a transcendence from the hither shore to the yonder shore, but no less a transcendent 'ad-vent' (*Zu-kunft*) [or trans-descendence] from the yonder shore to the hither shore."[5] According to Takeuchi, the two aspects—of transcending upward through one's own effort toward the Dharma and trans-descending downward through the grace of the formless form of Amida Buddha from the Dharma—can be seen as complementary and ultimately reconcilable in terms of the basic Buddhist doctrine of dependent origination. They are, then, not contradictory or invariably in conflict.

While Abe seems to agree with Takeuchi's synthetic approach, he also emphasizes that it is necessary to clarify the differences and oppositions between Dōgen and Shinran as a necessary stage in coming to a sense of their reconcilability. Abe writes, "I explore the possible overcoming of the fundamental differences between these dimensions in Buddhism and suggest the need for an awakening to the most authentic Dharma, which is beyond the opposition between Buddha and Mara (demon)."[6] Māra, symbolizing temptation in Pali texts as well as in Rinzai's recorded sayings, is the source of delusion who continues to stalk the Buddha and his disciples even long after their Enlightenment. He represents a sense of extreme "otherness" or antithesis that must be integrated and encompassed in Mahāyāna nonduality.

Therefore, Abe shows (1) the basic affinity between Dōgen and Shinran in that they express and exemplify the Buddhist Dharma, (2) the crucial differences between them, and then (3) the possibilities for going beyond these discrepancies. The affinities are based on the fact that both thinkers seek to overcome anthropocentrism or humanism through a realization that liberates one from all attachments to the realms of human, sentient, and existent beings. As opposed to Christianity, which sees humans as privileged beings who must die and will reach salvation only in the afterlife, Buddhism sees humans as "undergoing" life and death with all other manifestations of being and nothingness in each present moment. However, the main difference between the thinkers is that Dōgen realizes nirvana in the unborn and undying moment, whereas Shinran's sense of bottomless sin and the hopelessness of human endeavor means that realization comes only through the gift of Amida Buddha. That is, Dōgen's self-power understanding of the identity-in-difference of life-and-death realized through the sustained exertion of meditative effort stands in marked contrast to Shinran's other-power, Pure-Land view that there is no possibility whatsoever, no matter how hard one tries, of liberation from life and death without the transformative grace of Amida's compassionate vow. Also, Dōgen asserts the potential for the realization of the true Dharma (*shōbō*) by each person while Shinran emphasizes how people are spiritually incapacitated by their sense of sinfulness and evil in the age of degenerate law (*mappō*). In addition, Dōgen maintains the absolute identity and reciprocality of faith, practice, and realization as three selfsame though provisionally distinguishable aspects of the Dharma, while Shinran sees these three elements as inherently separate and unidentifiable for even faith is a gift to people delivered by Amida Buddha.

One of the key aspects of this intrafaith dialogue is that each participant would likely view the other as representing a fundamentally misguided and deluded viewpoint, a kind of bad faith that is an example of Māra masquerading under the guise of authentic Buddhism, or a view that "unconsciously lapses into Māra in the name of Buddha and yet believes itself to be practicing Buddha."[7] Dōgen must refute Shinran's extreme reluctance to exert himself as an example of unfulfilled Dharma, and Shinran must refute Dōgen's assertion of meditative power as an example of self-deception. Yet from the standpoint of the Dharma itself, even the contradiction between Buddha and Māra must be overcome, not by escaping from or facilely erasing it but only by at once encompassing and breaking though the distinction. As Rinzai writes, "But if [the enlightened one] cannot distinguish Mara from Buddha, then he has only left one home to enter another. He may be dubbed a karma-creating sentient being, but he cannot be called a true renouncer of home."[8]

On the one hand, there are some important similarities that become apparent through the dialogical process, especially in the way both thinkers emphasize the goal of effortless naturalness realized in and of itself as opposed to conditioned naturalness or a false sense of immediacy reached through calculation. Shinran's view of rebirth is not the typical Pure Land idea of something that occurs at death, but a demythologization so that being reborn is continually taking place within life. From the standpoint of the Dharma itself, as Takeuchi suggests, these thinkers to some extent represent two complementary approaches to the same experience. On the other hand, even the notion of naturalness is attained from opposite angles and with antithetical motives. For Abe, the opposition between Dōgen and Shinran never disappears. But when each thinker is seen in light of the other thinker, it becomes apparent that there is a certain naïveté that each expresses. Dōgen, for his part, according to Abe, must acknowledge the "paradoxical contradiction that fundamentally accompanies our *practice,* that the more one concentrates on practice, one cannot help but increasingly see that the self is not in accord with the Dharma." On some level, even Dōgen must see that he is not always and in every case in absolute correspondence with the Dharma.[9] To be faithful to existential experience, he must recognize a sense of frustration and futility that accompanies training. For Shinran, there is always a mutual separation and opposition of practice and realization, and yet he speaks of a return to the city of Dharma-nature, which is a body of naturalness, emptiness, or boundlessness. On some level, even Shinran must see that if he is to be returning to the Dharma, then he must already be in accord with it. His feelings of hopelessness and anguish must be accompanied by a sense of confidence and trust in the power of Amida's vow to prevail over karma-strickenness.

Thus, dialoguing is crucial, according to Abe, for "if we consider only Dōgen's own view or only Shinran's own view, the issue[s] discussed above cannot arise."[10] In order to existentially encounter and come to terms with the opposition between Dōgen and Shinran, Abe makes a fascinating and important distinction that raises crucial questions for other forms of dialogue, including Buddhist-Christian dialogue, concerning the relation between self power and other power. In borrowing yet modifying Nishida's terminology Abe refers to Dōgen's self-power view as "true correspondence to the Dharma" and he refers to Shinran's other-power view as "inverse correspondence to the Dharma." According to Mahāyāna holistic metaphysics, both views are encompassed by the true Dharma, or the Dharma in and of itself prior to human construction of these polarities of self and other, true and inverse. To paraphrase a famous passage in the *Diamond Sūtra,* the Dharma is no-Dharma; therefore it is Dharma. By insisting that the polarities be indexed to the standpoint of no-polarity that is manifest through polarities, Abe shows that Dōgen and Shinran must ideologically confront and engage each other as necessary philosophical opposites and that this encounter allows for the completion of their respective doctrinal standpoints. That is, they must come to recognize their own limitations and see the unconscious lapsing into the self-deceptive inauthenticity of Māra not only in antithetical viewpoints they refute but in their own views, which at times or on some level may have left themselves closed off to and incapable of encompassing the apparently antithetical views.

Abe deliberately avoids coming to a firm and fast conclusion regarding the relation between Dōgen and Shinran. That would defeat the whole point of intrafaith dialogue. But he does evoke other intrafaith factors, such as Rinzai's thought or Nishida's philosophy, to shed light on the notion of dialogue as a process of becoming fully cognizant and empathetic to underlying affinities and similarities while also being fully aware and sensitive to basic differences and oppositions and also being aware of breaking down unconscious barriers so that Māra is seen as Māra and yet as not-Māra. From the multiple perspectives of this intrafaith dialogue, he has laid the groundwork of the constructively critical yet self-surpassing attitude necessary for various kinds of East-West interfaith dialogue. Yet another intrafaith direction in which Abe's dialogical approach could be extended is the ideological encounter between intellectual and popular religious traditions, in particular, between Zen and folk religions in China and Japan. This approach could be used, for example, in exploring how the greatly iconoclastic first patriarch Bodhidharma becomes an icon of good fortune and prosperity in contemporary popular Japanese religiosity. Although Abe has not dealt with such an issue in his studies, he makes it possible to view this as a matter of intrafaith dialogue involving the question of the philosophical viability of the respective viewpoints, rather than in a purely functional way as an example of social-historical syncretism or indigenization. It seems clear that Abe's dialogical interests and methodology will continue to be explored and expanded upon as the unconscious barriers between and within traditions are overcome by creative, critical communication.

chapter Thirty-Three

MASAO ABE AND HIS DIALOGICAL MISSION

christopher Ives

WITHOUT DOUBT, THE MOST ACTIVE Buddhist participant in North American interfaith dialogue over the past four decades has been Masao Abe. Rooted in his own religious quest and Zen experience, he has worked tirelessly to introduce Zen Buddhist thought to Western students and colleagues through his teaching, writing, and conference participation. In many respects, these efforts have been informed by what appears to be his life's mission: to strive through dialogue to find a religio-philosophical ground on which a peaceful postmodern world can be constructed.

I first met Abe in 1978, when he returned to Kyoto for the summer between his two academic years at Princeton and I was studying and practicing Zen with the F.A.S. Society at Myōshin-ji. He asked me to translate into English an essay entitled "On the Establishment of a Self-Awakened Cosmology." So, for several months I met with him repeatedly at his home in northern Kyoto. This project led to further translations, and over the next few years we spent many evenings huddled over a low table in his Japanese-style living room.

Although our primary focus was translating some of his articles, our exchange extended far beyond discussion of how to render philosophical terms or difficult passages into English. With the translation work as a catalyst, we talked at length about his ideas, and he patiently indulged me along lines of questioning about such topics as Awakening, Emptiness, karma, ethics, time, and history.

What stands out prominently as I reflect on my contact with Abe during those years in Kyoto and after I left Japan in 1981 to follow him to Claremont Graduate School is his calmness, warmth, and great patience as a teacher. My sense is that others who have known Abe have been struck by these parts of his personality. It seems that in interreligious dialogue, often the character of one's dialogue partner makes a more lasting impression than the person's particular religious worldview. This seems to hold not only for more formal, official dialogue of conferences and university classrooms but for the informal and much more prevalent yet often overlooked "dialogue" in living rooms and on streets around the world.

Mediated by his personality, Abe's work outside Japan has been built upon overlapping religious, ethical, and philosophical bases. His professional path began in a personal religious crisis while working for a Japanese company in the midst of World War II. Facing great internal anguish, he quit his job and turned to studies at Kyoto University and to Zen practice. This early existential crisis has colored his life's work, as reflected by his frequent treatment of the problem of the human ego in his writings, including those on such metaphysical topics as *Śūnyatā* or Nishida's "logic of place." His underlying religious concern also found expression in his taking students to such Buddhist sites as Mount Baldy Zen Center. In his own way, Abe has striven to practice what his main teacher, Shin'ichi Hisamatsu, termed "the unity of study and practice" (*gakugyo-ichinyo*). Thus, he has distinguished himself from many other scholars of Buddhism, who for better or for worse do not engage in Buddhist religious practice and perhaps even reject religious engagement as contrary to the critical distancing necessary for proper scholarship.

Abe's grounding in the Zen tradition has generated other creative points of tension with his fellow scholars and dialogue partners outside Japan. He has held fast to central truth claims of certain Zen traditions, including the necessity of the One Great Death of the human ego entangled in dualism and the possibility of "pure" or "direct" experience opened up through that "death." This leitmotif of self-negation has prompted challenges from feminist theologians and social ethicists, and his statements about "pure" experience fly in the face of prevailing epistemologies since Kant as well as current theories of social constructivism.

Philosophical and ethical dimensions of Abe's efforts in Europe and North America emerge in his attempt to uncover (create?) through dialogue a common ground on which people can live religiously in their respective traditions while maintaining a recognition of commonality conducive to world peace. Abe's writings and talks refer repeatedly to compassion, world peace, and environmental preservation. On the other hand, in certain circles influenced by what might be referred to generally as poststructuralist critiques, his attempt to clarify and build upon a common metaphysical ground might appear naive, Buddhistically ideological (in that his appeal usually is to Śūnyatā as the ultimate Ultimate), and oriented toward a false, "totalizing" universal.

The ethical dimension of Abe's work found expression several years ago when he was making housing arrangements in conjunction with his position at the Pacific School of Religion in Berkeley. While exploring possibilities, he was asked by the San Francisco Zen Center to reside in one of their nearby apartments as a teacher/scholar in residence. This invitation came soon after a series of crises caused by two leaders of that Zen community. So, I asked Abe whether he knew about the problems and had considered whether affiliation with the Center would hurt his reputation and by extension his efforts as a representative of the Zen tradition in North America. He responded that he was well aware of the problems, and as we talked it became clear that he greeted residence there not as a liability but as an opportunity to provide constructive guidance to an embryonic Zen community in trouble. This response may reflect less of an ethical concern than a sense of missionary calling, but, suffice it to say, his efforts over the years have not been merely philosophical or academic.

Acknowledging Abe's character and the various dimensions of his work outside Japan, one can highlight several general points about his contribution to interfaith and cross-cultural dialogue. The first is the nature of the "Buddhism" or "Zen" about which Abe speaks. Appearing in such essays as "Kenotic God and Dynamic Sunyata" are a cluster of ideas that constitute the core of his presentation of Buddhism—Śūnyatā, ignorance, karma, Awakening, wisdom, compassion, vows, and reversible time. When analyzed across his many writings and talks, his "Buddhism" in certain respects appears to be a philosophical composite of his own making, combining elements of various Buddhist traditions—especially Zen and Pure Land—at a high level of abstraction. In addition to this observation, one might wonder about the extent to which his presentation of "Buddhism" is shaped both by his awareness of, or responses to, ideas advanced by his Christian dialogue partners and, more generally, by the overall arena of interfaith dialogue in which he is usually presenting the Buddhist "other" to his Christian hosts. (This question connects to the larger issue of the risk of monolithic reification when Abe and many of his partners continue to speak in terms of "the West" and "the East" in their dialogue.) In short, to what extent is Abe's "Buddhism" an abstract composite, a construct created for—and by—a specific dialogical context?

More specifically, Abe's "Zen," though usually set forth along the lines of actual Zen ideas, is largely ahistorical and at times idealized. His portrayal of "Zen" fails to encompass many of the beliefs, rituals, and institutions experienced by the majority of Zen Buddhists in Japan. His presentation usually does not acknowledge the various "Zens" that have existed over time and hence seems to assume an essence to "Zen" even though historical study soon reveals a complex, multifaceted, and ever-changing tradition (or, more precisely, an array of traditions). Further, idealization enters into his portrayal of Zen when he speaks of how a Zen Buddhist acts wisely and compassionately on the basis of Awakening (*satori*) and bodhisattva-style vows, even though many of the socio-political stances taken by Zen Buddhists in Japanese history seem clearly divorced from Abe's bodhisattva ideal.

Perhaps these observations about his presentation of Buddhism and Zen go beyond Abe and hold for the overall interreligious dialogue in which he and many contributors to this book have been participating. First, most of the dialogue has been theological and philosophical, in effect privileging theory over ritual praxis and institutional history. One might safely argue that most Buddhist and Christian experience is ritualistic or liturgical. The majority of Zen Buddhists in Japan have no interest in the nature of Emptiness or the sticky epistemological issues that arise when we engage in dialogue about the nature of Enlightenment as opposed to grace. Their religious attention more often than not focuses on funerals and rites for ancestral spirits. Second, much of our ongoing dialogue is idealistic, as we, for example, compare Jesus' love ethic with the compassionate vows of a bodhisattva or compare rarefied formulations of kenosis with the self-emptying seen in Zen meditation or the kabbalah. Would it not be fruitful to balance this with more discussion, for example, of the full range of *actual* beliefs and practices of ordinary Buddhists and Christians, inclusive of such issues as intolerance and exclusivism? In this regard, a comparison of Pat Robertson and Daisaku Ikeda might prove far more illuminating and productive than comparisons of Eckhart and Hakuin.

Moreover, much of our dialogue is indeed ahistorical. Is there not a tendency to lift our respective heroes, whether Dōgen or Luther, out of their historical contexts and portray them as universal thinkers? One sees this especially on the Buddhist side, which often offers up retrospectively constructed and largely sanitized images of figures like Dōgen and Shinran as being universal thinkers free from such popular religious practices as divination, exorcism, ancestor worship, or prayers to the local *kami*. This holds for the Christian side as well, where in dialogue one will hear about Luther's notions of justification but little about his denunciation of peasant uprisings in the 1520s or his tirades against Judaism in the 1530s, both of which reveal the historical contextualization of his thought. As a corrective to this generally ahistorical nature of our dialogue, perhaps we could benefit from a conference on German Christians and Japanese Buddhists in the 1930s. This is not to say that we should turn interfaith dialogue into a masochistic act of confession and repentance in which we display our dirty laundry to each other, but dialogue does usually portray the participating traditions as a bit cleaner than they actually are.

Given these comments about Abe and the dialogue in which he has been participating, how might we assess his legacy? Although he has written and spoken in a range of contexts with a range of audiences, he might best be seen as a Japanese philosopher of religion indebted to the Kyoto School of philosophy and its interaction with various forms of Buddhism, Christian mysticism and theology, German idealism, American pragmatism, and strands of existentialism and nihilism. This perspective on Abe promotes a further recognition of the hybrid and creative nature of his thought and enables his audience—especially those going to him to learn about "Zen"—to avoid viewing Abe's statements as *the* Zen view, or his "Zen" as the actual Zen experienced by the average Zen Buddhist in Japan.

In short, we have had a wonderful opportunity to hear from Masao Abe, a sincere and profound thinker who has highlighted aspects of Buddhism in dialogue and has offered philosophical statements variously determined by his personal background, strands of Buddhist thought, the Kyoto School's way of philosophizing, Christian theology, and such thinkers as Plato, Hegel, and Whitehead. Unfortunately, because so much of his writings have been occasional in the sense of responding to specific requests, he has yet to produce a systematic statement of his own religious philosophy. Back in Japan with more time for uninterrupted writing, he may now write such a work. Recent conversations with him have indicated that he hopes to begin a systematic statement of his views in the form of a "Sunyatology." This endeavor will serve to clarify that it has not necessarily been "Zen" or "Buddhism" with which many of us have been in dialogue but the creative and stimulating thought of Masao Abe, which will finally gain the systematic clarification and recognition it deserves as an important contribution to cross-cultural understanding in the twentieth century.

chapter Thirty-Four

A ZEN PRESENCE IN AMERICA: DIALOGUE AS RELIGIOUS PRACTICE

Stephen C. Rowe

THE SECOND TIME I MET MASAO ABE was on a snowy early April evening in South Bend, Indiana. I arrived with my colleague Peimin Ni in the late afternoon, with plenty of time to walk the University of Notre Dame campus before the evening program: "The Interfaith Encounter of Zen and Christian Contemplation: A Buddhist-Christian Conversation Between Masao Abe and Keith J. Egan." This program was part of the Interfaith Dialogue Series sponsored by the Religious Studies Program of Purdue University.

Professor Ni and I walked, talked about great universities East and West, specifically this one and Fudan University in China. In the midst of our conversation and touring, we heard familiar voices from around a corner in a billiard room and encountered a small group of our students. They had made the journey from Michigan because we were reading Abe's work in our senior seminar in philosophy. Embodiment had emerged in our inquiry as an issue, the relationship between philosophical work and life, such that seeing and hearing Abe in person became important for them.

In our touring we also came upon an impressive art gallery, and exploration led us to the discovery of several Buddha heads in this collection. Peimin remarked that Eastern art and devotional collections, as a result of the Western head-hunting, contain many headless Buddhas. Multiply this situation many times to account for the many collections like the one at Notre Dame, then envision the manner in which those heads were acquired, and we have an opening onto the background of the current "meeting of East and West."

At the evening program, Abe read from a prepared statement, responding to a paper of Professor Egan's and to the issue of meditation practice in Christianity and Buddhism. Abe emphasized that, in contrast to the ways in which "Christians meditate day and night on the Law of the Lord,"[1] Buddhist meditation *(dhyāna)* "must issue in *prajñā* (wisdom) and *karuṇā* (compassion). It must develop into seeing the world as it really is and acting to save the suffering world."[2] This mutual dependence and even identity of meditation and action to save others is what distinguished original Buddhism from the rest of Indian teaching: "This was the reason why the Buddha was dissatisfied with the teaching of his teachers. And it is why after attaining enlightenment, he did not stay in meditation but left the seat of enlightenment to begin preaching to save sentient beings for his entire remaining years."[3]

Abe also said that this crucial relationship between meditation and saving others, one that "is most clearly realized and most strongly emphasized in Zen,"[4] arises only out of the Great Doubt: "In the Great Doubt what is being doubted is the very doubter himself. The doubter and the doubted are not two but one. When this Great Doubt, often called 'great-doubting-mass,' is overcome, the bottom of man is broken through and the True Self is awakened."[5]

Back in Michigan, I struggled with my students to find the full significance of Abe's presentation. One student's response in particular was very interesting to me. He proclaimed that reading Abe's *Zen and Western Thought* and then seeing Abe at Notre Dame had changed his life. What became clear to him, he said, was that " 'saving others' is the only non-relative value," the only value that cannot be eliminated by accounting for it in terms of something else—like a psychological state or self-interest. My student insisted that through meeting Abe in person he had come to this as a deep existential realization, not just an intellectual proposition. I found myself marveling at how Abe had worked such a creative stopping-short of Western philosophy in my student. I also wondered about the depth and extent of my student's realization and even about its genuineness (whether Abe was being used as a subtle way out of the rigors and frustrations of Western philosophy and liberal education at this time).

Another student responded by saying that Abe's influence was such as to enable her to appropriate the Western tradition in a different, deeper way. Out of my previous correspondence with Abe, he had sent his essay "Education in Zen." Here Abe points to affinity between Zen practice and the "midwife's art" of Socrates, especially in the centrality of "*aporia*" or position with no way out,"[6] the realization on the part of the students that they do not know what they think they know, a realization that is necessary preparation for genuine knowing. Abe says, "In a similar way a Zen master tries to make his disciple face himself, to get him to return to the root-source of his being, by showing him a kind of *'aporia'* in which his analytical reason and intelligence come to a deadlock that can be overcome only by the awakening of his original nature."[7]

We had read the Platonic dialogue *The Apology* earlier in the semester, and it now became possible to understand the "examined life" of Socrates more deeply, the necessity of the aporetic experience in order to have access to one's "inner voice" or "prophetic voice," and the sense in which "discussing goodness and all the other subjects about which you hear me talking is really the very best thing a person can do." However, Abe points out in his essay that though there is similarity and affinity between Socrates and a Zen master, Socrates is limited; the Zen master does "more severely" what Socrates did and in a way that is more fully existential, not "largely colored by intellectualism."[8]

While my student reveled in her newfound enthusiasm for Western culture, as she moved from Abe's Socrates essay to his newer exploration of Christianity in "Kenotic God and Dynamic Sunyata,"[9] I found myself wondering if, for Abe, Zen is always superior. I had wondered this first in 1986, at the Third North-American Buddhist-Christian Theological Encounter, held at Purdue University.[10] There Abe stressed, as he has elsewhere, the challenges to all religions that are presented by the religion-negating ideologies of scientism, Marxism, traditional Freudian psychoanalytic thought, and nihilism. Abe made it clear that he values dialogue as a way toward meeting these challenges, and he proposed two necessary aspects of effective dialogue between world religions: (1) seeking clarification of the views peculiar to one's own tradition and allowing the different views between traditions to confront one another and (2) being "free from the peculiarity of our own traditions in order to scrutinize the notion of ultimate reality itself most fitting to our contemporary human predicament and the future of humanity." The second aspect needs to involve "a very creative and penetrating discussion in which we must be radically critical of our own tradition so that we can re-examine and regrasp the essence of our religion from the more universal and more fundamental position" and hence "find out the truly ultimate reality for the future of humanity."

Evaluating the meeting of Christianity and Buddhism in the contemporary situation, Abe distinguished between a "religion of faith," grouping Christianity with Judaism, Islam, and Hinduism, and a "religion of Awakening," citing the original form of Buddhism and Zen. Religions of faith are based on "an unquestioned belief in God or the divine which includes complete trust, confidence and reliance." Buddhism, as a religion of Awakening, involves two necessarily simultaneous realizations: (1) of True Self, which is no-self or the death of the ego sense of self, and (2) of Dharma, the true nature of reality.

Abe further developed the distinction between the two traditions in relation to the specific ways in which Christianity and Buddhism address the contemporary situation. The essence of the contemporary situation, characterized by the strength of religion-negating ideologies, was presented in terms of Nietzsche's philosophy, as perspectivism—or relativism. Abe argued that Nietzsche moved from the insistence "that everything related to us in one way or another is false, utterly devoid of truth, because everything is a construction through our interpretation based on our particular perspective," to the assertion of "the will to power as the most basic cosmological principle—admitting that even this is an artificial construct, a self-deception."

Abe said that the challenge represented by Nietzsche does not affect Buddhism because Buddhism is based on a "completely perspectiveless perspective." By this he means that Buddhism is based on an Awakening that is beyond the inherent limitations of *any* perspective. Thus, Buddhism comprehends and embraces Nietzsche's relativism and goes beyond it in a direction that is very different from that taken by Nietzsche. Abe suggested that Nietzsche remained attached to philosophical and ontological concepts—or to their absence or ineffectuality—and was not radical *enough* in his grasp of Emptiness. Had he been more radical, he might have come to the spiritual (not merely conceptual) Awakening that is the Buddhist realization of wisdom and compassion. Instead, Nietzsche drew back from Nothingness, into the groundless assertion of "the will to power." Abe cited the silence of the Buddha on metaphysical questions and the ability to empty even the concept of Emptiness as the crucial marks of going beyond the nihilistic or indifferent way of life (as well as Nietzsche's way of desperate assertion) and into the "perspectiveless perspective" or "positionless position."

According to Abe, although Buddhism and Zen are able to meet the challenge of relativity and nihilism in this way, Christianity and the other world religions have not been able to do so. Other religions remain *perspectives* and thus are susceptible to Nietzsche's proclamation that "God is a sacred lie." Only Buddhism, and especially Zen, is founded on and faithful to Śūnyatā, Nothingness, radical or Absolute Nothingness. Hence, Zen is quite at home in the homelessness that is integral to contemporary life.

Yet for Abe, it seems, the superiority of Zen does not mean that other religions are inferior. For some time, in the East-West dialogue to which he has contributed so much, Abe has acknowledged the limitations of Zen and the complementarity between Eastern and Western views. The East has been strong in the ontological dimension, in its relationship to Being itself, but weak in the axiological, in matters of value and justice. The West, in the historical period, has displayed just the opposite strengths and weaknesses. Thus each side of the East-West dialogue can address the limitations of the other, as Abe indicates also in terms of gender distinction:

> We can be no more satisfied with mere paternalistic Christianity
> as an occidental form of world religion, than with mere maternal-
> istic Buddhism as an oriental form of world religion. Both father

and mother are needed to provide a real "home" for us. Yet this
should not be seen as only a mixture of Christianity and
Buddhism. Christianity, we can see from its mystical tradition,
is not totally lacking in the maternal, receptive aspect, nor is
Buddhism, judging from Nichiren, entirely alien to the paternal
and justice-oriented aspect. However, neither in Christianity nor
in Buddhism have these two essential aspects been thoroughly and
harmoniously realized. But, to cope with the radically changing
meaning of the "world," and the resultant human predicament,
Christianity and Buddhism must break through their respective
occidental-paternal, oriental-maternal structures. Each must
develop and deepen itself to achieve a universal form of world
religion.[11]

Abe, then, is not recommending a mere blend, an exchange, or dialogue as only "mutual understanding." Rather, he has been willing to go
beyond the "superiority" of Zen, into what John B. Cobb, Jr., has referred
to as the "mutual transformation" that occurs through full dialogue.[12]
Given "the contemporary confrontation between religion and irreligion,"
Abe's position is that "both religions must fundamentally transform themselves such that their prevailing basic assumptions are drastically
changed and a new paradigm or model of understanding can emerge."[13]

Abe joins his longtime dialogue partner John Cobb in the suggestion that the new paradigm we search for lies in the direction of radicalization and mutual transformation. Radicalization of what? What is radicalized first, for Abe, is religion itself, as opposed to the prevailing reli-
gion-denying ideologies. And "spiritual death" seems to be the center of
religion: "Both St. Paul and the great Buddhists clearly saw this as an
essential element of true religion."[14] Perhaps for Western people like me,
it is Abe's repeated citation of Saint Paul in Galatians 2:20 that makes this
point most dramatically: "I have been crucified with Christ; it is no longer
I who live, but Christ who lives in me; and the life I now live in the flesh
I live by faith in the Son of God."[15]

In Buddhist terms this means radicalization of Emptiness, *Śūnyatā*.
We must go beyond the intermediate, "mystical" stage of Emptiness and
negate even that experience. This entails the "double negation," "negation of negation," or "absolute negation" that is, in fact, an affirmation—

the absolute affirmation of Wondrous Being! "Emptiness as Sunyata transcends and embraces both emptiness and fullness."[16]

Radicalization of *Śūnyatā* means radicalization of compassion. This is so in that "in Zen, properly speaking, *prajna* and *karuna* are not two but one . . . the great wisdom is rooted in the great compassion and the great compassion is rooted in the great wisdom."[17] But here is a point at which Abe has been willing to accept the need for further radicalization that has been revealed through dialogue. Responding to John Cobb's criticism that in Buddhism compassion has not generally been applied to ethics and history,[18] Abe has agreed "that we should interpret compassion in ways broader than helping others to awaken."[19]

Finally, to state the obvious, radicalization is a form of religious practice. And since this radicalization is taking place through dialogue, dialogue itself is a form of religious practice. Clearly this is so for Abe.[20] And yet I know of nowhere in his writings where he addresses directly and on its own terms this form of practice to which he has contributed to so greatly. I would invite him to reflect back on his years of dialogue here in the West and address this matter from his new (or returned) location in Kyoto. Meanwhile, many of us will continue to practice dialogue with him in both words and listening.

chapter Thirty-Five

THE ROAR OF A LION: REFLECTIONS ON A LIFE DEDICATED TO WHAT IS ULTIMATELY REAL

Stephen Morris

MASAO ABE'S PRESENCE IN THIS HEMISPHERE is a gift. It stems from a selflessness, almost uncanny in its completeness, that seems to mark the truly religious life. In fact, Abe's three decades of service in the West, which this book purports to celebrate, have flowed from this single origin. Tirelessly over the years he has immersed himself in one task after another, writing article after article, teaching class after class, attending conference after conference. And the irony is that this ceaseless work, which he seems thoroughly to enjoy and at which he is so obviously expert, was never his original intention, nor even his main interest. He himself has said that in order to become a scholar, it was necessary to "kill" his own life. Yet he continues to labor at his calling with unflagging devotion. To watch him go about his business, day in and day out, is to be reminded of Mother Teresa, and to see acted out the meaning of an old Zen saying:

The accomplished hermit
hides in the town;
The immature hermit
hides in the mountains.[1]

Abe himself operates out of an inveterate, inner calm, yet he never fails to create a stir. Reactions are often strong to what he has to say, and discussion always lively. But this is inevitable, that his remarks should prove jolting, because the intellect has always been puzzled to consider spiritual profundity; and what we have here is a case of a spiritual adept haunting the academic world. No one questions Abe's stature as a scholar. Westerners consider him an authority on Buddhist philosophy, and they are at the same time deeply respectful of the immense range of his knowledge of Western thought. Certainly in terms of philosophy and theology, his command is firm. Still, it must be clear that the real force of Abe's position lies not in the breadth of his thought but in its depth.

Someplace along the line, rather early on, Masao Abe embarked on the religious journey. For some people, the issue of what is ultimately real becomes the sole concern of their life, the only true business. So fervently do they pine for what Emerson called "that deep force, the last fact behind which analysis cannot go,"[2] that they will stop at nothing short of wholly penetrating the mystery. It is not that such a way of life is comfortable, or that the undertaking is not hazardous, but that the alternative, of not knowing the core of one's own being, of getting to the end of life without ever having burrowed to its very source, is absolutely unthinkable. And as time is short and the stakes high, postponement is out of the question.

Abe's own search took him to Kyoto. While most men were going off to battle, he went to the university. Skipping out on the war effort in a time of national crisis, for the purpose of pursuing philosophical interests, must have entailed a sizable, personal risk. But such is the nature and gravity of the deep conflict Abe felt impelled to resolve, that it looms large enough to swallow every other consideration.

And resolve it he did. I don't know the details, only that he had the benefit of an outstanding teacher, Shin'ichi Hisamatsu, and that ultimately Abe found himself in the world of Zen, a sphere wherein he discovered simultaneously his own unqualified freedom and his undying commitment to humanity. His every effort since has been a direct result of the successful outcome of that severe and bitter inner struggle. Indeed, related to this are two characteristics, both instructive, which seem to typify not only Abe but the Kyoto School philosophers generally. In the first place, while they wisely utilize philosophy as a tool, they tend to refrain from putting forth their own, that is, from philosophizing, until *after* the existential matter has been positively settled,

> One encounter:
> once for all.[3]

Thus, they teach and write with unmistakable authority. Second, they persistently remind us what is all too convenient to forget, that religion is primarily a personal affair, not a communal event but an individual quest. And neither is it a never-ending one. Someone like Abe demonstrates, therefore, exactly what the Buddha showed, that there is all the difference in the world between seeking and having found. The former teacher may customarily address scholars, but he also, like the latter, speaks even more fundamentally to anyone alive to the religious call and determined to overcome their basic existential dilemma.

In any case, this is how I see things, and why I find the man's work so compelling. I met Abe in the fall of 1990 while he was a visiting professor at the Pacific School of Religion, also serving at the California Institute of Integral Studies, where for a year he taught courses in Zen Buddhism and Buddhist-Christian dialogue. It was there, in an environment where East-West comparative studies are encouraged, as well as attempts to integrate body, mind, and spirit, that I was afforded the honor of coming to know Masao Abe. It is a rare occasion to meet a man who actually embodies the philosophy he espouses.

Committed myself to neither the Buddhist nor the Christian perspective, I am, frankly, less interested in religions per se than in the spirituality they hope to foster. Yet right here is where a consideration of Abe's own outlook proves electrifying. Buddhists practice the discipline of living wholly in the present moment, forever dying to the past and greeting each moment anew. And for those who are "awake," there is no time that is not holy, no space that is not sacred, no act not potentially divine. It is a fundamentally different mode of existence. D. T. Suzuki once suggestively remarked:

Again, you and I sip a cup of tea. The act is apparently alike, but who can tell what a wide gap there is subjectively between you and me. In your drinking there may be no Zen, while mine is brim full of it.[4]

What begins as a discipline turns later into an art. Abe takes his tea the same way. Displaying outwardly a personality of patience, humility, and humor, who knows from what bottomless depths, or what he himself calls "boundless openness," his activities flow?

It is, of course, precisely this mode out of which he functions wherein is rooted Abe's philosophy and theology. What he refers to philosophically as the Absolute Present not only defines his existential stance but provides both the pivot and the focus of his formal position. Indeed, from within the Zen perspective, it might be more accurate to suggest that Abe's scholarship is itself an expression of the Absolute Present, inevitably directing, moreover, all inquiries and so-called problems back to itself. Thus, as wide-ranging as his pen is, though he is able to traverse several disciplines to treat a variety of topics, all of Abe's written work could be viewed as a lone, multifaceted gem. The luster shoots off in many directions, but it is all the light of a single jewel. And the more closely you study it, the more it is turned over and carefully examined, the more precious it appears and its value is discovered.

This is particularly noticeable when we consider Abe's contribution in religion. He has invested considerable time and energy in the interfaith dialogue, in effect, both confronting Christianity from the outside and challenging it from within. Abe places substantial weight on such interaction, and for good reason. In his hands it serves as a process of crystallization. Abe consistently highlights the very raison d'être of religion and clarifies the spiritual project. His input is a boon, since, in Christianity at least, both of these vital elements tend to get covered over.

On the surface, Buddhism poses a distinct contrast to Christianity. The former is rather bare compared to the latter, which is sometimes presented as a somewhat extravagant package. Zen, certainly, appears very simple and flexible. It rests on Nothingness, considers Buddha one of us, and understands the *sūtras* as genuine but imperfect spiritual teachings—all of which is reasonable enough. But Christianity, on the other hand, proposes a Supreme Being, whom it invests with both human and superhuman attributes and powers; insists, still, that Jesus was his only Son; and views the Bible, an ancient and admittedly highly complex document, as "the word of God," and so incontestable. This state of affairs alone has produced an elaborate system, debating the fine points of which has been the preoccupation of its innumerable great thinkers.

Over and against the intricate web of Christian doctrine, Abe, in his role as a Zen philosopher, holds up a rather simple model: one reality, this very world, including everything and everybody, only seen from a different point of view.

> *Emptiness is boundless and limitless. It is expanding endlessly into all directions throughout the universe. Nothing can be outside of this endless and all-dimensional "expanse" of Emptiness. Although it is opened up through "my" subjective realization of no-self it extends endlessly and objectively beyond "me." It is the unrestricted dynamic whole, in which you, I, and everything else in the universe is included and realized equally just as it is in its suchness.*[5]

Abe's description here is just that—description. He is not engaging in speculation, discussing mere abstractions that sound good in theory. His explanation is, rather, an account of the world in which he lives. We'll remember that the key to Abe's presentation is his existential orientation in the Absolute Present, a stance about which at least two things can be said. In the first place, it is clearly an absolute unity, wherein each single thing maintains its uniqueness but participates fully and immeasurably in the universal, is simultaneously both the part and the whole. *Here any and all duality is overcome.* Abe's own remarks, therefore, should be viewed not so much as philosophical analysis, made objectively from without, but as *phenomenological description,* offered from within.

Second, life lived within, or rather *as,* the Absolute Present is apparently completely inconsistent with life as we normally experience it. Always elusive to the mind, it cannot be penetrated intellectually but requires a "radical and fundamental change of the basic mode of being of the self."[6] Transcendent to the ego, the organism knows it as buoyancy.

Effecting this radical shift is what Abe sees as the whole purpose of religion. Thus, in his work as a Buddhist encountering a different religion,

Abe's laser-beam focus on this crucial issue of transformation acts some-what as a chisel in the hands of a sculptor. By chipping away at what is extraneous to it, Abe seeks to reveal Christianity's essential form. And oddly enough, when the complex creeds give way and the simple practice emerges, the product thus fashioned does not appear particularly "Bud-dhist," or even "Eastern." Emerson argued similarly and presented a com-parable spirituality a century and a half ago. He felt that by constantly surrendering our footing, we could break through to the miraculous world Jesus lived in, just as we walk under the same sun and breathe the same air. Emerson, too, saw the problem as sleep rather than sin, and when awake found eternity in the present moment.[7]

Besides sculpting, Abe attempts the same kind of removal from the inside—in fact, from very deep inside. At the very heart of Christian spiri-tuality a fierce intensity seethes, and it is from this molten core that Abe proffers his theology. Thus, what is superfluous in the tradition he melts off from within. And as for his theology, though couched in the most sophisti-cated language, it is elemental, and its purport could be summed up in two of the sayings attributed to Jesus: (1) "He who finds his life will lose it, and he who loses his life for my sake will find it."[8] (2) "The kingdom of God is not coming with signs to be observed; nor will they say, 'Lo, here it is!' or 'There!' for behold, the kingdom of God is in the midst of you."[9]

Abe has discovered an account of his own spiritual practice tucked inside Christian scripture, and the message he finds glaring at him there, though absolutely astounding because inconceivable to the traditionalist, is the very one he has always striven to instill. It is that we are already where we are going, and that with our own negation a wholly *new* world opens up. "There can be no continuity between the 'old person' and the 'new person' in the Pauline faith."[10] Abe builds on Saint Paul, the crux of whose message was equally radical, in presenting his understanding of the *fully* "Emptying God," which is not an event of the past or a hope for the future but a fact of the present. It is, for him, description, not analysis. Abe at the same time makes it clear that this version of ultimate reality can be grasped only by undergoing the very same process of self-emptying:

> *Only when the ego-self negates itself completely does it come to understand who the kenotic God is and what God's total self-emp-tying means to the self.*[11]

Abe is here, as always, on target. It is the ego that has, or rather is the problem, and its emptying out lands one in the Absolute Present, where no answers are provided because none are called for. There are no questions.

All of this sends shock waves throughout theological circles, but Christianity has felt the same tremors before. Self-kenosis is unquestionably the single hinge upon which Eckhartian spirituality hangs. And Eckhart's "barren Godhead" abolishes, like Abe's Emptying God, as I have argued elsewhere,[12] any opportunity to conceptualize or objectify ultimate reality, and always and only directs us to what is right underfoot. If anyone ever was unhampered in their work, it was Meister Eckhart, who spoke and wrote freely out of the Eternal Now. His directness and simplicity confounded the orthodox, and he was controversial because he was taken seriously. His strength he drew from deep within himself, and his voice, though it still baffles, continues to thunder:

> One roar
> of a lion
> Cracks the brains
> of a hundred beasts.[13]

Eckhart and Abe are, to borrow an analogy, like two mirrors reflecting each other. There is nothing there in either case; and it is difficult to distinguish between two transparencies. Moreover, they are united in their stance, *not in spite* of the fact that they rely on their experience, *but because they do.* And this is precisely what, when he takes his place on the world religious stage today, sets Abe apart from so many of the other players.

And where he sets himself apart is exactly where Abe issues his stinging challenge. Abe is dissatisfied with current religious formulations and disappointed with the interfaith dialogue, complaining that "in most cases dialogue has been theologically oriented, not spiritually oriented." He argues that "both Buddhism and Christianity must give more serious attention to their spiritualities and their relation to theology."[14] Abe is less interested in philosophical concepts than in spiritual substance, and required to get at that is an existential commitment:

> *In respect to the Buddhist-Christian dialogue in which we are now engaged, what is needed is not a detailed discussion of . . .*

doctrine . . . but . . . that each participant in the Buddhist-Christ-
ian dialogue represent his or her own religion, not merely intellec-
tually or as based on doctrine, but existentially as well. By doing
so, each participant may spiritually clarify the essence of his/her
religion through a personal existential commitment. Without
speaking from such an existential commitment, the interfaith dia-
logue may apt to be merely conceptual and superficial.[15]

By making such a plea, Abe is here cutting to the quick. It is as vital to him as to the objective observer to ascertain where any person gets her or his information. The events of two thousand years ago, or before, may be of interest, but they can also be a diversion. Proclamations about the past, and certainly the future, constitute hearsay and guesswork, neither of which packs any potency. By insisting simply on a more authentic theology, with a solid, indissoluble bond between the theology and the theologian, Abe is calling into question the way we usually go about such business. At the same time, it seems to me, he is directing us to some very fertile ground, and not as a missionary either, but as a gadfly.

Abe is a Buddhist from Japan, but the crowning achievement of his scholarship is that it demonstrates what his heart knows full well—that *the essence of religion goes beyond religion itself.* It is rooted in a spirituality so fundamental, so ever present and alive, and so inherent in the organism, that it is virtually independent of any cultural expression. Rarely realized, it is nevertheless universal.

Thus, it would be a grave error, and a costly one, to view engaging with Abe as an encounter with a different religion, or as a collision in thinking between East and West. Such a casual appraisal would be a surefire way of missing the true significance of his work and skipping over his challenge; for although time and place are weighty circumstances that can exert a seemingly inescapable influence, Abe's stance is not confined by such limitations or cognizant of any boundaries. What he ultimately represents is far more basic, far more profound, and far more unnerving. The magnetism of his position draws us back to ourselves, terribly far inside, whence his call issues. *Genuinely to confront Abe, then, is to face oneself;* it is not to glance outward, as at some novel set of ideas, but to peer directly into the fathomless depths of one's own being alone, where the absence of a horizon strips one of any beliefs at all.

*There is alienation from nature, from family, from community,
from the world, and from oneself. In reality, all forms of alienation
originate in self-alienation, i.e., alienation from oneself through
self-consciousness.*[16]

It always boils down, for Abe, to the problem of the ego. That conditioned, false sense of self is the prison in which we are caged, and it is by breaking through *that* barrier that the individual is released into an infinite expanse and gains the absolute freedom of timelessness. Thus the pith of Abe's philosophy and theology is acutely relevant to any person who, at this very moment, still feels even the least bit shackled. If the age-old questions Who am I? or Why am I here? continue to gnaw, if a shred of wonder (Does God exist? Is there a heaven?) can manage to surface, if an iota of doubt about what is ultimately real is able to seep in, then the issue remains unresolved. It is the *isolated* self that fidgets so.

*Insofar as one is a human being, he or she cannot escape this basic
anxiety. In fact, strictly speaking, it is not that one has this anxiety,
but rather that one is this anxiety.*[17]

Abe goes on here to confirm that to "overcome this fundamental restlessness . . . is the *raison d'être* and essential task of religion."[18]

And so it is, but of religion only? The light Masao Abe has shed on this entire subject opens a brand-new door. To take full stock of the import of his work could launch us into a most exciting (and long overdue) exploration. If the idea is to alter the *mode* of our existence, then the truest spirituality, in the final analysis, might have little to do with repeating ancient formulas; but it has absolutely everything to do with *how* we brush our teeth and tie our shoestrings.

If a fundamental spirituality can be developed outside of religion, then, as we enter the twenty-first century, isn't it time education took the bull by the horns? It is no longer a matter, with respect to Abe's *currently* radical position, of waiting for, and relying on, religion(s) to catch up. It is a question now, instead, of whether we have a *right* to so wait and to so rely. It is through the educational process that we endeavor to develop people intellectually and socially in the soundest way, offering classes designed to provide the necessary information and practical know-how so that, by acting responsibly, they can continue to live physically healthy lives. But in a culture committed to educating the "whole person," the spiritual dimension has been sadly neglected, leaving a tragic void that is all too painfully obvious. Yet is not an individual's psycho-spiritual well-being integral to human health and happiness?

No one is suggesting here that the depth of spiritual freedom some-one like Abe enjoys can be institutionalized; but if we cannot deliver it to our children in a capsule, can we not at least slip them a compass? Sure-ly they can learn, in twelve years of schooling, that their spiritual growth requires daily attention and that just as they know that personal hygiene, diet, and regular exercise all bear on their physical welfare, so can real steps be taken to enhance this precious aspect of their lives. Such an enterprise would be innovative, but one must seriously wonder if in the long run widespread spiritual change will trickle from the top down or sprout from the bottom up. And what is advanced here is all in keeping with Abe's own vision of supplying a spiritual ground for the modern world; his very participation in the philosophical religious process is an attempt to push the highest good within reach of the greatest number of people. *Everyone* deserves to be provided the wherewithal to retrieve the pearl.

A RESPONSE

Masao Abe

IT IS INDEED A GREAT PLEASURE and honor for me to receive so many heartfelt tributes from friends and colleagues around the world on the occasion of my eightieth birthday. All of them are deeply rooted in the genuine friendship and critical encounter we have shared over the years, and I feel greatly encouraged as I turn to new horizons in my work and life.

I had originally intended to respond to each essay in full, but I came to realize that because of limitations of time and energy, I must forgo writing full responses to all of the rather substantial essays contained herein. Given this situation, I have tried, in the following pages, to respond to crucial issues in the best way possible and to further develop the ongoing dialogue as deeply as possible. Even so, the results achieved here can never be fully satisfactory, as they treat only limited aspects of each essay.

Before I proceed further, I would like to express my deepest gratitude and sincere appreciation to all the contributors. Special thanks go to Donald W. Mitchell for the great pains and meticulous care he took to plan and edit this volume. Without his efforts, this work would never have been realized.

CHAPTERS 1 & 2:
Jeff M. Shore, "The True Buddha Is Formless: Masao Abe's Religious Quest," and Steven Antinoff, "The Fire in the Lotus"

With different insights and sensibilities, Jeff M. Shore and Steven Antinoff present their accounts of meeting me during the period when my inner turmoil and religious quest were at their peak. Reading their impressions of and stories about me, I often felt as if the man they describe were a third person. At the same time, the inner struggle of that period came to life vividly in my present being. Thus, I confirmed that the religious quest of my younger days is still the driving force and creative source of my life now.

CHAPTER 3:
Valdo H. Viglielmo, "My Encounters with Masao Abe in Japan and the West"

Valdo H. Viglielmo confesses that he experienced a trancelike state of mind during the intensive sitting at Myōshin-ji Temple in Kyoto. Insofar as I understand from his writing, this was his first experience of *kensho* (seeing one's original nature). One may say that Viglielmo passed through the first barrier of Zen experience. But *satori* in Zen is not a special state of mind, however lofty it may be. *Satori* is "the body-mind falling off."

Toward the end of his essay, Viglielmo discusses the Kyoto School, especially Kitarō Nishida and the problem of nationalism. According to Viglielmo, initially he thought the imperial institution was of minimal importance to understanding the writings of the Kyoto School. But then he "became convinced that it was not only important but *critically* important to an understanding of the writings of . . . Nishida during the last fifteen years of his life." With this special problematic as background, Viglielmo proceeds to raise the question of how I assess "Nishida's writings on the imperial institution and other aspects of the 'national polity' (*kokutai* in Japanese) and how [I view] the Japanese imperial institution, both in the prewar period and today." With deep appreciation for Viglielmo's serious concern over this issue, I will try to respond fully to his questions.

To begin with, regarding Viglielmo's strong emphasis on the problem of the imperial institution, it is not perfectly clear to me why the imperial institution is so important to Viglielmo—not only important but *critically* important—in understanding Nishida's writings. Nishida's stance toward the emperor may be most clearly perceived in his phrase "The imperial family is a self-identity of contradictories, a being of non-being" (*Nishida Kitarō Zenshū* 12, p. 336). As Shizuteru Ueda astutely points out, however, Nishida never refers to the imperial family as an "*absolute* self-identity of contradictories" but only as a simple "self-identity of contradictories." This means that Nishida regarded the imperial family as a historical reality of self-identity of contradictories—*without absolutizing it*. Thus, Nishida did grasp the imperial family as being free from imperialism, ultranationalism, and fanatic Japanism.

For philosophy to be authentic, it has to be not only metaphysical but also metahistorical. Just as philosophy transcends the physical world, it transcends the historical world. In the case of Nishida, his fundamental philosophical principle, "the place of Absolute Nothingness," is not only not delimited by any being or non-being, but also by any historical or nationalistic phenomena. However, it is only natural that Nishida, as a philosopher, would also involve himself with the problems of nationalism. But as Michiko Yusa makes clear in her essay, "Nishida and the Question of Nationalism" (*Monumenta Nipponica* 46, no. 2), Nishida was strongly opposed to nationalism. In his letter to Nagayo Yoshiro on March 14, 1945, Nishida wrote, "I think that it was a fundamental mistake [for the nation's leaders] to have identified the national polity with military power." Nishida went on to criticize Japanese nationalism for its lack of universality and global-historical perspective.

Finally, during the war Nishida was attacked as an antinationalist by nationalistic ideologists. After the war he was attacked as a promoter of the "Japanese spirit" by left-wing ideologists. But throughout the prewar, war, and postwar times, Nishida constantly remained the philosopher who perceived world affairs from a world-historical perspective. So I think we should view Nishida and his philosophy from this same world-historical perspective.

CHAPTER 4:
Felix E. Prieto, "The F.A.S. Acronym in Masao Abe's Life Trajectory"

Felix E. Prieto describes my life beautifully with the scheme of development traced by Shin'ichi Hisamatsu's notion of F.A.S. His analysis and evaluation of my life trajectory into three dimensions of depth, width, and length of human existence are appropriate and thoroughgoing. As such, his essay is not only very helpful for readers but also very encouraging to me.

CHAPTER 5:
Richard J. DeMartino, "The Zen Roots of Masao Abe's Thought"

Richard J. DeMartino tries to trace the "roots" of my thought to my direct teachers: D. T. Suzuki, Kitarō Nishida, Shin'ichi Hisamatsu, and others. He further goes back through Suzuki to Suzuki's teacher, Shaku Sōen, a pioneering Zen master who first introduced Zen Buddhism to the West on the occasion of the Parliament of the World's Religions held in Chicago in 1893.

DeMartino elucidates that even in that early period when Buddhism was first being introduced to the West, much care was taken to explain the pivotal Buddhist notion of *Śūnyatā,* or Emptiness, so as to prevent people from falling into a dualistic or exclusively one-sided negative or nihilistic misunderstanding of Buddhism. The non-nihilistic and nondualistic nature of Emptiness was also treated by Suzuki in his early works *Açvaghosha's Discourse on the Awakening of Faith in the Mahayana* (1900) and *Outlines of Mahayana Buddhism* (1907). It is also true that Suzuki goes even further to emphasize that Emptiness itself is empty—"*sunyata-sunyata.*" Even Emptiness is empty, and so Emptiness and suchness are synonymous: Emptiness is in truth no less than the concrete manifestation of reality itself. From this realization, DeMartino clarifies Suzuki's influence on Nishida's notions of "the identity of absolute contradiction" and "the logic of *soku hi*" ("is" and "is not"). Finally, following this line of thought and quoting my essay "Kenotic God and Dynamic Sunyata," DeMartino seems to accept my statement that "God is not God, and precisely because God is not a self-affirmative God, God is truly God."

Toward the end of his essay, DeMartino asks my reaction to his proposal that a central focus in Zen should be given to *jinen,* or "Nature-in-itself." DeMartino's exposition is very complicated and difficult to grasp, but as far as I understand his discussion, I agree with him on the following two points. First, Zen can indeed be understood in terms of *jinen,* or Nature-in-itself, instead of more traditional notions such as Buddha-nature. Second, *jinen* must be understood as a dynamic and ongoing process of simultaneous self-generation, self-extinction, and self-regeneration.

CHAPTER 6:
Hans Waldenfels, "Masao Abe's Intellectual Journey to the West: A Personal Reflection"

Hans Waldenfels points out that in my attempt at interfaith dialogue "the Japanese as well as the larger Asian side was rather missing" and goes on to suggest that Asian thinkers should be invited to the roundtable discussion. This is good advice. I shall seriously take it into consideration in the future.

Clearly realizing that "Buddhist thought aims at overcoming all kinds of dichotomies and dualisms," Waldenfels raises a question: "How can a nondualism beyond good and evil strengthen human responsibility?" As Waldenfels knows well, nondualism in Buddhism does not indicate a mere nondualism as the absence or negation of dualism. Mere nondualism must be overcome in order to attain true nondualism. True nondualism is dynamic because it is beyond both dualism and nondualism and yet includes both. Therefore, in this true nondualism the distinction between good and evil is *reaffirmed* and *regrasped* in the new light of Emptiness; and it is here that ethical responsibility is clearly realized.

CHAPTER 7:
John B. Cobb, Jr., "Masao Abe, Process Theology, and Buddhist-Christian-Jewish Dialogue"

John Cobb vividly describes his encounter and mutual exchange with me. According to him, one of the main points of contention between us was the Buddhist notion of codependent origination and Whitehead's concrescence. In Whitehead, the present's relation to the past differs from its relation to the future. Hence, reflection on and in the immediacy of the moment does not eliminate temporality. The Buddhist understanding of the issue is, however, quite different. The Buddhist view, based on full immersion in the depth of the moment, is that there is no difference between past and future. The temporal distinction belongs to the observer's perspective on the horizontal and historical plane. In the vertical or depth dimension, Buddhists insist, time is overcome.

Another theme of contention is that for Whitehead, the entry of novelty into concrescence is said to be the presence of God in that concrescence. Even if Whitehead's notion of God, as nonsubstantial and process in terms of concrescence, is very similar to the Buddhist notion of codependent origination, Buddhists do not agree with Whitehead's notion of concrescence for the following reason. In Buddhism time is realized in and through the realization of the impermanency of everything in the universe, especially through the realization of our living-dying: we are fully living and fully dying at each and every moment. If we grasp our lives not objectively from without but subjectively from within, we are not moving from life to death but are in the midst of this process of living-dying. Therefore, we must also realize the process of our living-dying as being without beginning and without end. Because of the absence of any notion of a God as creator and ruler of the universe, for Buddhists there is no beginning of the universe in terms of creation, and no end in terms of a last judgment. Accordingly, we must realize the beginninglessness and endlessness of samsara, that is, the transmigration of living-dying.

This realization is essential to overcoming time because it implies at least two things. First, each and every moment can be a beginning and an end in itself: time begins and ends at each moment. Accordingly, time is not understood to be an unidirectional movement but is seen as a sheer series of moments that can move reciprocally. Here a sort of reversibility of time is realized. Second, if we clearly realize the beginninglessness and endlessness of living-dying *at this particular moment,* the whole process of living-dying is concentrated within this moment. In other words, each moment embraces the whole process of beginningless and endless time within itself. Thus, one can in fact transcend time at this very moment. Therefore, to me, the notion of concrescence still retains traces of dualism and is not completely organic. For Whitehead's system to be completely organic and dynamic, time must be realized as completely reversible and reciprocal, and concrescence must be fully realized between God and the world.

CHAPTER 8:
William R. LaFleur, "Interpretation as Interlocution"

William R. LaFleur presents powerfully and beautifully his understanding of the problem of textual hermeneutics. First, he presents a dilemma he experienced with me: he was fascinated and yet frustrated by my approach to teaching Buddhist texts. LaFleur states that while not denying the value of what we often call our "modern" and "critical" approaches to texts, I refuse to let the intentionality of a writer/interlocutor such as Dōgen get lost in the bramble of historical and critical textual questions. And he is correct in saying that for me the matter of Dōgen's "intentionality" was itself not so much a textual question as it was an existential one.

In this regard, I clearly remember LaFleur and I having long conversations at the blackboard, even after all the students had left, during the two years I was a visiting professor at Princeton. This encounter with LaFleur was one of the most important and significant pedagogical experiences for me throughout my many years of intercultural dialogue.

CHAPTER 9:
David W. Chappell, "A Tribute to 'Mr. Dialogue'"

David W. Chappell mentions four areas where my ideas persistently raise questions for him. He writes: "One of these areas concerns the use of paradoxical logic, another is the claim for ultimacy for his categories (signaled by the adjective *absolute* or *total*), a third is his claim that his views of *Śūnyatā* are the core of Buddhism, and a fourth is his subordination of ethics to *Śūnyatā*." Let me respond to these four questions as follows.

First, concerning the use of paradoxical logic: I am afraid that Chappell takes my statement "the negation of negation is absolute affirmation" merely as a statement of *objective* logic in which double negation indicates an affirmation. But when I speak of the dialectical character of nirvana in terms of "the negation of negation is absolute affirmation," negation here is not merely negation in the logical sense but in an existential sense. In other words, it indicates *self-negation* or *abnegation*. Accordingly, the negation of negation is nothing but the self-negation of self-negation, or the internal abnegation of abnegation. This existential realization of the abnegation of abnegation is the essence of nirvana in the Mahāyāna sense and in Zen Awakening.

David Chappell suggests that the term *Dharma* is a better or more embracing one than *Śūnyatā*. My statement "the ultimate reality for Buddhism is Sunyata" does not necessarily imply that the ultimate reality for Buddhism is *exclusively Śūnyatā*. It is well known in the Buddhist world, as Chappell suggests, that terms such as Dharma, *tathatā,* and so forth also indicate ultimate reality for Buddhism, although they each represent somewhat different aspects of this ultimate reality. The term *Śūnyatā* and the term Dharma are not mutually exclusive. So I agree with Chappell that "Dharma can be used as a term for ultimate reality for Buddhists that would be even more embracing than *Śūnyatā.*" But the reason why I chose the term *Śūnyatā* rather than Dharma to indicate the ultimate reality of Buddhism is that I would like to make the difference between Buddhism and Christianity clear; that is, Buddhism is neither monotheistic nor dualistic.

The most important point of Chappell's discussion on the distinction between *Śūnyatā* and Dharma lies in the area of ethics. Although the term *Śūnyatā* better indicates the nondualistic nature of the Buddhist ultimate than does the term Dharma, the former can lead to a nihilistic and even an anti-ethical understanding of Buddhism. However, as already mentioned, the crucial point of *Śūnyatā* in its true sense lies in the internal double negation. In order to realize true *Śūnyatā,* not only the negation of dualism but also the negation of nondualism is necessary. The double negation is nothing other than an affirmation in which dynamic nondualism makes both dualism and nondualism alive and workable. In the case of the duality of good and evil, in true and dynamic nondualism, this duality is *re*grasped in a new light and is *re*-established in its moral functioning. This dualism regrasped beyond good and evil can strengthen human moral responsibility.

CHAPTER 10:
Ashok K. Gangadean, "Masao Abe and Nishida's Logic of Place"

Ashok Gangadean includes not only his critical evaluation of my work but also his own understanding of Nishida's philosophy, especially Nishida's logic of *basho* (place) and Absolute Nothingness. I think that Gangadean sharply grasps the core of Nishida's thinking when he says that

> He [Nishida] attempted to clarify what he took to be the universal logic at the foundation of Eastern and Western thought: a truly global logic. But it is also clear that in attempting to break new ground in excavating the logic of Śūnyatā, he faced great challenges in thinking and speaking in the ways of nonduality that is the signature of the dialectics of Absolute Nothingness.

Gangadean also accurately states that "the right-minding of Absolute Nothingness requires the most radical transformation of thinking into the methods of nonduality. . . . In making this radical turn . . . Nishida presses the logical subject and logical predicate beyond the dualistic limits, all the way to their transcendental grounding in the universal place of Śūnyatā." And "by pressing the poles of dualistic predication to their absolute limits and alleged origin, Nishida attempts to reach the absolute nondualistic or unitive grounds of predication where the absolute subject and absolute predicate meet and apparently co-arise." It is here that, as Gangadean says, "Nishida speaks of the principle of 'absolute contradictory identity' as the universal principle of all historical existence revealed in the ground of Absolute Nothingness." The real task that now lies before us is to develop Nishida's logic of *basho* or Absolute Nothingness and apply it to the concrete historical reality in which the East and the West coexist.

CHAPTER 11:
Durwood Foster, "Masao Abe as a Zen Teacher in the West"

Upon reading his essay, I was deeply moved by how Durwood Foster and other colleagues have made considerable efforts to create teaching opportunities for me at their respective institutions. I realize that there are special difficulties in teaching Buddhism at Christian seminaries such as the GTU and PSR. At the same time it is a great encouragement for me to learn that not a few students at those institutions evaluated my lectures to be "excellent, stimulating, exciting, effective and extremely helpful." My wife, Ikuko, and I have many fond memories of our three years at PSR.

CHAPTER 12:
Donald W. Mitchell, "Dialogue and Unity"

Donald Mitchell vividly describes his impressions of meeting with me at various conferences in Hawaii, Vancouver, and Purdue. He sympathetically understands my spiritual transformation from Pure Land faith to Zen through my encounter with Shin'ichi Hisamatsu. And he also discloses why and how he came to realize the necessity to respond to the full range of comparisons of Emptiness and kenosis made from within the Kyoto School. In Mitchell's *Spirituality and Emptiness: The Dynamics of Spiritual Life in Buddhism and Christianity,* he correctly demonstrates that this comparison is not merely a matter for theological debate but is more truly a point of spiritual encounter between Christianity and Buddhism to be explored both at the individual and communal levels of experience. It was in this connection Mitchell invited me to Purdue University as a visiting professor for two years.

During those years, Mitchell and I had numerous opportunities to discuss our fundamental experiences of ultimate reality; and the most crucial issue Mitchell raised for me was the following:

> [To Abe] the dynamic of the inner trinitarian kenosis is the same as the dynamic of the creative kenosis. Or the kenotic nature of God in the Trinity is the same as the kenotic action of God in creation. . . . [But] the kenosis between the divine persons is just different in kind from the kenosis between the Creator and creation. And since God is uniquely incarnate in Christ, of course, the kenosis of God in Christ is also different in kind from the kenosis of God in the rest of creation.

To this criticism of Mitchell's I would like to emphasize that God's kenosis must be total, not partial. The kenosis of Christ was accomplished on the basis of God's *will,* but in the case of God, kenosis is implied in the original *nature* of God that is love. God is God, not because God had the Son of God take a human form and be sacrificed while God remained God, but because God is a suffering God, a self-sacrificial God through *total* kenosis. Only through total kenosis and God's self-sacrificial identification with everything in the world is God truly God. Here we fully realize the reality and actuality of God, which is entirely beyond conception and objectification. In short, through complete self-abnegation, God is totally identical with everything, including sinful humans.

To this, Mitchell's response would be as follows (again quoting from his essay): "But for me, as a Christian, while God is certainly found in all things and all things in God, the Trinity also exists apart from creation, a light without darkness in which we find an eternal paradise." If the Trinity is found to exist apart from creation, we must say that the Trinity is somewhat objectified and conceptualized, and thus apart from ultimate reality. This may simply reflect, however, my lack of understanding of Christian spirituality, since Mitchell is careful to add, "The Godhead of this Trinity is not beyond the persons of the Trinity. The Godhead just is the dynamic and kenotic Love of the persons that is expressed in the kenosis of creation. . . . [This creative kenosis] is defined within the Trinity itself as Love which in turn defines creation as an expression of Love." Here we see the heart of Christian spirituality.

In the latter half of his essay, Mitchell reports that he introduced me to the Focolare movement, a unique spiritual community founded by Chiara Lubich that seems to me to be a Christian counterpart to the F.A.S. Society. In Rome I was deeply impressed by the unity, spirituality, and living activities of Love of the people of the Focolare as well as by the sincere and very open attitude of Vatican theologians. As Mitchell says, the Pontifical Council for Interreligious Dialogue entertained me and Ikuko in the Vatican and arranged for us to meet the pope. When Father John Shirieda, a member of the Pontifical Council, introduced me to the pope by saying that "Professor Abe is a pioneering and most active figure in Buddhist-Christian dialogue today," the pope warmly took my hands into his own and uttered a single Japanese word, "*Arigatō.*" He went on to express his deep gratitude for my dialogical work as "a fellow pilgrim." When the pope turned to Ikuko, she told him that his presence was a great encouragement for her life. To this the pope said, in an overwhelming attitude of love, "Let us carry the Cross together." We were deeply moved by the Christian spirituality manifested by the pope. Thus, my visit to Rome in 1993 was a landmark for my career in Buddhist-Christian dialogue.

CHAPTER 13:
John Hick: "The Meaning of Emptiness"

With regard to the uses of the term Śūnyatā, John Hick states in his essay:

> There seems to me to be a distinction between, on the one hand,
> the thought of Śūnyatā as entirely unconceptualizable, "formless,"
> and empty of all humanly conceivable qualities and, on the other
> hand, the thought of Śūnyatā as having the characteristics of wis-
> dom and compassion, as being the activity of making everything
> alive and as being identical with the experienceable state of nir-
> vana and the process of pratītya-samutpāda. For these latter
> appear to me to be ways of conceptualizing, or characterizing . . .
> Śūnyatā.

Hick further suggests that although the great spiritual traditions produce
different forms of religious experience, they produce essentially the same
human transformation. Asking himself how within different religious cultures the same ultimate transforming reality is affecting us, Hick answers
that it is based upon a distinction between the ultimate reality in itself
and that reality as humanly experienced in various ways.

In Buddhism Śūnyatā is entirely unconceptualizable and formless
and is constantly emptying everything—this is the ontological aspect of
Śūnyatā. At the same time it is *emptying itself* and making everything alive
through its wisdom and compassion—this is the soteriological aspect of
Śūnyatā. These two aspects of Śūnyatā are not separate; they are one but
not identical. In other words, Śūnyatā in the authentic sense is not a static state but a dynamic activity constantly emptying everything, including
itself. It is formless as it negates every form, and yet without remaining in
formlessness, it takes on various forms freely to negate its own formlessness. This is the reason that Formless Emptiness or Boundless Openness
is regarded as the ultimate ground that dynamically reveals itself both in
terms of a personal God and in terms of historical religious figures.

This being the case, John Hick states that "[Abe] has seemed to me
to want to identify one particular manifestation of the ultimately Real—
that which is known through his own tradition—exclusively with the Real

in itself." Hick here raises a most significant question as to how I understand the relationship between *Śūnyatā* and the ultimate as experienced by the different great world religions.

To answer Hick's question, I would first like to state that in any religion the realization of the oneness of ultimate reality is of crucial concern because religion must offer an integral and total—rather than fragmental or partial—salvation from human suffering. Yet the particular realization of oneness in a religion can entail exclusiveness, intolerance, and religious imperialism that cause conflict and schism within a given religion and among the various religions. This is a serious dilemma from which no higher religion can escape. How can we believe in the oneness of ultimate reality in our own religion without falling into exclusive intolerance and religious imperialism toward other faiths? What kind of oneness of ultimate reality can solve that dilemma and open up a dimension in which positive tolerance and peaceful coexistence are possible among religions?

In this connection I would like to distinguish two kinds of oneness or unity: first, monotheistic oneness or unity, and second, nondualistic oneness or unity. It is my contention that not the former but the latter kind of unity or oneness can provide a common basis for the contemporary pluralistic situation of the world religions. This is so because monotheistic oneness is realized by distinguishing itself and setting itself apart from any form of dualism and pluralism and therefore stands in opposition to them. Precisely because of this oppositional relation, monotheistic oneness is not a truly ultimate oneness. In order to realize true oneness, we must go not only beyond dualism and pluralism but also beyond monotheism. It is only then that we can realize nondualistic oneness, because at that point we are completely free from any form of duality, including the duality between monotheism and dualism or pluralism. In the nondualistic oneness thus achieved, nonsubstantial Emptiness is clearly realized.

The view of monotheistic unity does not *fully* admit the distinctiveness or uniqueness of each religion, because of its lack of the realization of nonsubtantial Emptiness. By contrast, nondualistic unity thoroughly allows for the uniqueness of each religion without limitation—through the realization of nonsubstantial Emptiness. This is because nondualistic unity is completely free from any conceptualization or objectification and is itself without substance. In this nondualistic unity, all world religions are dynamically united with their uniquenesses and without being reduced to a single principle. However, this unity does not entail an uncritical acceptance of the given pluralistic condition of religions. Instead, nondualistic unity makes a critical acceptance and creative reconstruction of world religions possible because each religion is regrasped in this nondualistic unity. For further discussion of this point, see Masao Abe, "Two Types of Unity and Religious Pluralism," *The Eastern Buddhist* 26, no. 2 (autumn 1993): 76–85 (with response by Donald W. Mitchell, pp. 86–90).

CHAPTER 14:
Thomas J. J. Altizer, "Kenosis and Śūnyatā in the Contemporary Buddhist-Christian Dialogue"

Thomas J. J. Altizer is surprisingly candid while showing deep insight into the contemporary Buddhist-Christian dialogue. He interprets my dialogical work as (1) giving Buddhist witness to the world of Christian theology, (2) employing the deepest Christian language and symbolism as a language of Buddhism itself, (3) opening a way to a language and a vision that will be Buddhist and Christian at once, and (4) doing so in the context of a deeply modern or postmodern thinking, a thinking embodying not only the end of Christendom but also the death of God.

   Altizer also points out that one of the most challenging dimensions of my presence and language is found in my view of the Incarnation as a totally kenotic actualization of God. He appreciates my idea of the kenosis of God and suggests that Christians today can speak of God in the context of Śūnyatā, or Absolute Nothingness. But I wonder how Christ is to be believed in, in this context of Śūnyatā? In this regard, Altizer speaks of "our uniquely modern realization of the death of God." Here we must be very careful to understand how Christ is believed in, in the context of Śūnyatā and in the context of the modern realization of the death of God.

CHAPTER 15:
Heinrich Ott, "The Experience of Neighborhood"

Quoting Heidegger's concept of neighborhood, which especially suggests the neighborhood of poetry and thinking, Heinrich Ott understands "this image of neighborhood as a powerful language-symbol for the essential relation of religions to one another." He means by this experience of neighborhood an experience in which each is open to the other, reaching out to the other, and entrusting self to the other. He further states, "I believe I have had this experience again and again with different worlds of partners and in differing degrees of intensity, yet hardly ever with the same intensity as with the Buddhist Kyoto School to which Keiji Nishitani and Masao Abe belong." Reading these words, I am clearly reminded of the refreshing openness of Heinrich Ott, the successor to Karl Barth, with whom I had an enriching theological discussion in 1978.

There are a number of theological and religious issues to discuss in Ott's essay. However, I would like to restrict my comments to the topic of a Chinese Zen master's discourse and the Christian notion of forgiveness. This Zen discourse by Ch'ing-yuan Wei-hsin of the T'ang dynasty is a favorite of mine that I often cite to elucidate Zen Awakening. It goes as follows: "Thirty years ago, before I began the study of Zen, I said, 'Mountains are mountains, waters are waters.' After I got an insight into the truth of Zen through the instruction of a good master, I said, 'Mountains are not mountains, waters are not waters.' But now, having attained the abode of final rest [that is, Zen Awakening], I say, 'Mountains are *really* mountains, waters are *really* waters.'"

Heinrich Ott says that he also often cites this discourse when discussing the Christian problem of faith in the forgiveness of sin: "God does not annihilate sin. . . . And yet he does annihilate it in the event of forgiveness. He 'forgets' it, as if it had never been. Without both of these aspects, we could not understand the event of forgiveness in its entire depth." Here we see a kind of "neighborhood" between Zen Awakening and Christian forgiveness whereby we can better understand the depth of each other's experience.

CHAPTER 16:
Langdon Gilkey, "A Tribute to a 'Prophetic Rōshi'"

It was a great joy for me to read Langdon Gilkey's essay "A Tribute to a 'Prophetic Rōshi.'" As an eminent Christian theologian, he vividly describes his encounter with me in the United States and Japan. He participated vigorously in the F.A.S. Society meeting in Kyoto and seriously touched the core of F.A.S. I still remember the enjoyable time we spent in Nara when we, together with Mrs. Gilkey, toured that ancient capital of Japan. I hope to continue our Buddhist-Christian dialogue in Japan and the United States.

CHAPTERS 17 & 18:
Eugene B. Borowitz, "Masao Abe's Challenge to Modern Jewish Theology," and Richard L. Rubenstein, "Emptiness, Holy Nothingness, and the Holocaust"

Since the essays by Eugene B. Borowitz and Richard L. Rubenstein somewhat overlap in terms of the issues discussed therein, let me respond to them together.

Borowitz takes my articles, especially "Non-Being and *Mu:* The Metaphysical Nature of Negativity in the East and the West," as a challenge to the basis of the Western philosophical tradition. In particular, Borowitz confesses, "Abe's challenge forced me to think through at least two major aspects of my religious heritage and to ask just how I now felt about them. The first of these was the Jewish understanding of God as, so to speak, Nothing. Offhand, that seems utterly incompatible with the central Jewish affirmation that God is One." Yet Borowitz recognizes that Jewish mysticism, especially the kabbalah, understands God as both the ten *sefirot,* the energy centers of the divine self-manifestation, and the *En Sof,* the No Bounds. Jewish mysticism also asserts that these two understandings of God are, in fact, inextricably one. Here I find a most congenial point of contact between Judaism and Buddhism. I greatly appreciate Borowitz's work and in my dialogues with him—which he discusses in his essay—I have profoundly deepened my own understanding of the relation between Judaism and Buddhism.

Turning now to Rubenstein, he tells us, "My theological position had developed as a result of a progressive liberation from rabbinic theology. . . . Having turned away from theism, I came to comprehend that Nothingness is the Ground and Source of all that exists, a view not unlike the Buddhist teaching about Śūnyatā." Rubenstein sees a close resemblance between his Holy Nothingness and Buddhist Śūnyatā. However, Rubenstein also raises a very crucial problem for Buddhist-Jewish dialogue when he says, "I have some reservations concerning the tendency of Buddhist thinkers to diminish the significance of the sociohistorical dimension of human existence."

Reading this, I got the impression that Rubenstein deals with the sociohistorical dimension and the religious dimension of human existence on the same plane, just with a *quantitative* difference. But I think that these two dimensions of human existence belong to *qualitatively* different planes. The sociohistorical dimension refers to human-human relations and thus refers to the horizontal plane of human existence; whereas the religious dimension indicates a divine-human relationship and thus refers to the vertical plane. The former is conditioned by time and space, whereas the latter is the place of the trans-spatial and transtemporal. These two dimensions are essentially and qualitatively different from each other, yet they are inseparably connected with each other in the living reality of human existence. We are dialectical existences always working at the intersection of the horizontal sociohistorical dimension and the vertical religious dimension. Without the religious dimension as the ground, the sociohistorical dimension is groundless and rootless; whereas without the sociohistorical dimension as a condition or occasion, the religious dimension does not manifest itself. Rubenstein says that I ascribe a lesser significance to the sociohistorical dimension than to *Śūnyatā*. If this is the case, it is because the sociohistorical dimension is neither the "Ground" nor "Source" of human existence.

Rubenstein also expresses surprise about my interest in the Holocaust: "The Holocaust is not a religious problem for Buddhism as it is for Judaism and Christianity. For Jews and Christians alike, the decisive events of Jewish history are part of *Heilsgeschichte*. As such, they have a religio-mythic significance." Since Buddhism has no notion of *Heilsgeschichte*, it is quite understandable that Rubenstein was surprised by my Buddhist interest in the Holocaust. But my interest stems from my concern with the human being as such, particularly from my interest in the collective karma of human being. The Holocaust is a diabolical event that I simply cannot deal with objectively. So instead, I look into the depth of my own being, where I painfully realize the universal or collective karma that is innate in human existence and in which the Holocaust is also ultimately rooted.

Referring to my avowal of responsibility for the Holocaust in terms of this collective karma, Rubenstein states, "I find Abe's explanation of the 'responsibility' for the Holocaust in terms of karma and *avidya* ahistorical. . . . That idea trivializes the distinction between the actual perpetrators and the rest of the world, not to mention the victims." From these remarks it seems that Rubenstein distinguishes individual and collective karma as two separate categories. He believes that individual karma pertains to specific historical events, and collective karma pertains to universal trans-historical reality. In fact, individual and collective karma are inseparably united in the depths of *avidya*—the innate fundamental ignorance of our human condition. Therefore, both types of karma are involved in specific historical events such as the Holocaust.

To address the Holocaust properly, we must also look at its deepest roots . . . in the collective karma innate in human existence. This means that responsibility is shared by all people, not just the perpetrators. But does this realization of collective karma and shared responsibility at the *ultimate* level of human existence reduce the uniqueness of the Holocaust and obscure the particular evil of the Nazis? I think not. Should we reject such a realization at the ultimate level and stay only at the sociohistorical level? I hope not, because if we do, how can we solve the root problem of the Holocaust? Is not religious realization the only legitimate *basis*—as opposed to *condition*—on which we can solve the problem of the Holocaust and work cooperatively to build a better world in the future?

CHAPTER 19:
Joseph A. Bracken, S.J., and Wolfhart Pannenberg, "The Abe-Pannenberg Encounter"

Joseph A. Bracken beautifully summarizes my dialogue with Wolfhart Pannenberg, which appears in the book *Divine Emptiness and Historical*

Fullness: A Buddhist-Jewish-Christian Conversation with Masao Abe. In this response I shall go right to an examination of Pannenberg's criticism of my understanding of the kenosis of God himself.

I am certainly well aware that there is no literal evidence for the kenosis of God in the New Testament and that traditional Christian theology states that the Son of God became a human without God ceasing to be God. Nevertheless, I have argued for the kenosis of God himself for the following two reasons. First, in our society religion is being challenged by antireligious ideologies and is urgently required to elucidate its deepest spirituality by reinterpreting traditional formulations of doctrine and practice. Second, even if reinterpretation is necessary, it should not be arbitrary but should be rooted in the authentic spirit of the religion in question. "God is Love" (John 1:4, 8, 16) is a basic tenet of all Christianity. If God is really love, God does not remain God while having the Son of God empty himself. A God who fully empties himself to become completely identical with humanity is the truly all-loving God. Therefore, self-emptying, or kenosis, is not an *attribute* of God but the fundamental *nature* of God. While the kenosis of the Son of God is based on the *will* of God, in the case of God the Father, kenosis is implied in his original *nature*.

The Buddhist highly appreciates that, as Pannenberg says, "the common essence of the three persons does not have any separate reality prior to them but exists only in their interrelationship." In connection to this notion of *perichoresis*, the Buddhist may ask the Christian, If the common essence of the three persons does not have *any separate reality* prior to them, then are we not here speaking about Absolute Nothingness? Absolute Nothingness indicates the deepest ground or the creative source in which all things, positive and negative, are rooted and from which all things, positive and negative, are generated. The realization of Absolute Nothingness makes the interrelationship clearly possible. Without the clear realization of Absolute Nothingness (*Śūnyatā*) there is no realization of true interrelationship, and without the realization of true interrelationship, there is no clear realization of Absolute Nothingness.

On the other hand, Buddhists must appreciate the Christian notion of *perichoresis* and the divine dynamics of love realized therein. By so doing, I think that, as Pannenberg suggests, we Buddhists can better explore the manifestations of *Śūnyatā* in *interpersonal relationships*.

CHAPTER 20:
Ruben L. F. Habito, "Hans Küng Questions Masao Abe:
On Emptiness and a Global Ethic"

Through carefully and accurately "reading the mind of Hans Küng," Ruben Habito elucidates the crucial points of Küng's question to me: Can Buddhist Emptiness ground a commitment to a global ethic? Habito raises two reasons for answering this question in the negative. First, the standpoint of Emptiness as presented by me is one that subsumes all history in an Eternal Now. This removes the need for social engagement because social transformation necessarily seeks for a "better future." Second, the standpoint of Emptiness as presented by me is one that overcomes all distinctions between good and evil. This makes an objective ethic impossible and blunts one's moral "sense of abhorrence for violence, injustice, exploitation, and oppression—realities that we humans continually come up against."

The following is my Buddhist response to the above criticisms. First, in the Buddhist view of time and history, time is understood to be entirely without beginning and without end. Inasmuch as time is beginningless and endless, it is not considered to be linear, as in Christianity, or circular, as in non-Buddhist Vedāntic philosophy. Being neither linear nor circular, time is understood to move from moment to moment, with each moment embracing the whole process of time. This view of time is inseparably linked with the Buddhist view of life and death. Buddhism does not regard life and death as two different entities but one indivisible reality—that is, "living-dying." For if we grasp our life not objectively from the outside, but subjectively from within, we are fully living and fully dying in each moment. According to Buddhism, we are not moving from life to death but are in the process of living-dying. If we clearly realize the beginninglessness and endlessness of the process of living-dying *at this moment*, the whole process of living-dying is concentrated *in this moment.*

Buddhism can develop its view of history if we take seriously the compassionate aspect of *Śūnyatā*. In the wisdom aspect, one realizes that the beginningless and endless process of time is totally concentrated in each moment. This is why in Buddhism each "now" moment is realized as the Eternal Now in the sense of the absolute present. However, in the compassion aspect, also realized in *Śūnyatā*, one beholds many beings still considering themselves unenlightened and deluded. Such persons are innumerable at present and will appear endlessly in the future. The task for an awakened one is to help these persons "awaken" to their suchness and interpenetration with all other things. Here the progress of history toward the future comes to have a positive significance in Buddhism, and we can see that Buddhist Emptiness can ground a commitment to a global ethics.

Second, in their view of ethics, Buddhists clearly realize that good *should* conquer evil. However, based on the experience of their inner struggle, Buddhists cannot say that good is strong enough always to overcome evil. Good and evil as completely antagonistic principles resist each other with equal force. However imperative it may be from the ethical point of view, in Buddhist experience it is impossible to overcome evil with good and to attain thereby the highest good. Since good and evil are always mutually negating principles with equal power, the pure ethical effort to overcome evil with good never succeeds. It only results in a serious existential dilemma. Realizing this existential dilemma as innate to human existence and characterizing it in terms of the doctrine of original sin, Christians believe that it is through faith in God that humanity is freed from sin by God's redemptive activity.

On the other hand, in Buddhism what is essential for salvation is to be emancipated from the very existential antinomy of good and evil and to awaken to Emptiness, which is prior to this opposition. In the existential awakening to Emptiness, one can be master of, rather than enslaved by, good and evil. In this way, the realization of true Emptiness is the basis for true human freedom and the true ethical life.

This Buddhist realization of Emptiness does not indicate a static *state* of Emptiness but rather a dynamic *activity* of emptying everything, including Emptiness itself. Self-emptying activity is a Grand Affirmation realized through the negation of negation. In the realization of the negation of Emptiness, the distinction between good and evil is made nonsubstantial and empty. But in the Grand Affirmation of Emptiness, the distinction of good and evil is *reestablished and reaffirmed*. Here, too, we can see that the standpoint of Emptiness is able to ground a commitment to a global ethics.

CHAPTER 21:
Harold H. Oliver, "Fritz Buri's Assessment of Masao Abe's Religious Thought"

As one of the outstanding Christian theologians of our time, Fritz Buri is deeply interested in Buddhism and the philosophy of the Kyoto School. In 1982 he published *Der Buddha-Christus als der Herr des wahren Selbst* (*The Buddha-Christ as the Lord of the True Self*), which is a classic work on the Kyoto School and Christianity. I am fortunate to have been personally acquainted with him in Germany, Japan, and the United States since 1957.

Harold Oliver, who has been acquainted equally with Buri and me, elucidates vividly and insightfully the Buri-Abe encounter in terms of both appreciation and sincere criticism. For example, Buri states that I compare East-West responses to the "insufficiency of the world" in the following way. The West "responded . . . by the erection of a Being that sublates what is lacking in beings" in a way that makes use of conceptual thinking "whether by appealing to natural reason or to a supernatural revelation." The East, on the other hand, responded "by an extinction of this thinking that is directed toward [objective] Being."

In response, let me discuss the meaning of Zen's non-thinking. Zen does not establish itself on the basis of either thinking or not-thinking, but rather *non*-thinking, which is beyond both thinking and not-thinking. When not-thinking is taken as the basis of Zen, anti-intellectualism becomes rampant. When thinking is taken as the basis, Zen loses its authentic ground and degenerates into mere conceptualism and abstract verbiage. Genuine Zen, however, takes non-thinking as its ultimate ground, and thus can express itself freely through both thinking and not-thinking as the situation requires. However, precisely because of its standpoint of non-thinking, Zen has in fact not fully realized the positive and creative aspects of thinking and their significance, which have been especially developed in the West. Logical and scientific modes of thought based on objective thinking, and moral principles and ethical theory based on subjective thinking, have been very conspicuous in the West.

Because Zen has thus far not fully realized the positive and creative aspects of human thought, its position of non-thinking always harbors the danger of degenerating into mere not-thinking. That Zen today lacks the method to cope with the problem of modern science, as well as with individual, social, and international ethical problems, may be based partly on this fact. In order for Buddhism to become a formative historical force in the modern world, it must place objective and subjective thinking, which have been so refined and firmly established in the Western world, within its own world of non-thinking. However, to carry out this task, Zen must internally embrace the standpoint of Western "Being" and "ought" in order to concretize and actualize its non-thinking in the present moment of historical time.

CHAPTER 22:
Leslie D. Alldritt, "Masao Abe and Paul Tillich: A Dialogue Toward Love"

Leslie Alldritt offers the following two propositions to explain my great interest in Paul Tillich. The first is that Tillich's analysis of the problematic nature of personal existence resonates with my Buddhist view of the ontic plight of the person, that is, the problem of duality as realized in self-estrangement and anxiety. The second is that Tillich's and my analyses have found commonality in resolutions to this problem that can be characterized as love. I accept both propositions as adequate and would like to make some remarks about the second, that is, the nature of love.

Accordingly to Alldritt, Tillich's answer to the problem of personal existence is God who is defined as "Being itself." Tillich explains that God is love so that God's Being and power is the being and power of love. Therefore, the existential movement toward resolution is a movement of love toward God that is initiated by God's love itself. Alldritt concludes that "for Tillich the Christian resolution is one that results in a personal participation with God; yet it is not a *complete* identification with God— there remains always an 'otherness' in the love relationship."

But the Buddhist resolution of the human predicament is not a personal participation with God but nirvana, which is realized by transcending the realm of transmigration and impermanence, that is, the realm of samsara. However, throughout its long history, Mahāyāna Buddhism has always emphasized "Do not abide in nirvana," as well as "Do not abide in samsara." If one abides in so-called nirvana by transcending samsara, it must be said that one is not yet free from attachment—an attachment to nirvana—and is thus confined by the discrimination between nirvana and samsara. It must also be said that one is still selfishly concerned with one's own salvation, while forgetting the suffering of others in samsara. On the basis of the idea of the bodhisattva, Mahāyāna Buddhism thus teaches true nirvana to be the returning to samsara. Therefore, nirvana in the Mahāyāna sense, while transcending samsara, is nothing but the realization of samsara as samsara, no more no less, through the complete returning to samsara itself. In the returning we see that true nirvana is, according to Mahāyāna Buddhism, the real source of both *prajñā* (wisdom) and *karuṇā* (compassion). It is the source of *prajñā* because by returning to the world one is entirely free without any sense of attachment. It is the source of *karuṇā* because one is also unselfishly concerned with the salvation of all others in samsara through one's own returning to samsara. In true nirvana, *prajñā* and *karuṇā* are dynamically one. It is called *Mahāprajñā* (Great Wisdom) and *Mahākaruṇā* (Great Compassion), in which justice is realized through love and love is supported by justice.

CHAPTER 23:
James L. Fredericks, "Masao Abe and Karl Rahner: On Traces of Dualism and Monism"

At the suggestion of James Fredericks, I read many of the writings of Karl Rahner and came to appreciate Rahner's deep concern for the problem of dualism and his deep understanding of God as "unobjectifiable mystery." I was also impressed with his theological position concerning kenosis, namely, that the self-emptying of the Son has its origins in God the Father.

But Rahner's notion of kenosis, as applied to the Incarnation, is fundamentally different from my own understanding of kenosis because Rahner maintains "traces of dualism." For Rahner, God as the absolute and infinite One can, by dispossessing himself, "become the other." But in so doing, God "always preserves" his infinite unrelatedness. (See Karl Rahner, *The Foundation of Christian Faith: An Introduction to the Idea of Christianity* [New York: Seabury Press, 1978], 220–22.) Here we see that for Rahner, God's infinite Being has priority over God's self-emptying, so traces of dualism are maintained. For me, God's self-emptying must be understood as total. This is especially the case if God is really unconditional love. For this love to be truly complete and unconditional, it must be realized in the total self-emptying of any "unrelatedness" into the complete fullness of loving relatedness.

As for traces of monism in my own view, I have always tried to present a "nondualism" that avoids any monism by affirming the self-emptying of Emptiness itself. This complete self-emptying is expressed as the Grand Affirmation that reaffirms all dualism in its boundless openness. And since this nondualism of Emptiness is fundamental, my intrafaith dialogue with Jōdo Shin-shū always places its dualistic factors in this broader nondual horizon. (For an analysis of my intrafaith dialogue with Jōdo Shin-shū, see Chapter 32.) On the other hand, Fredericks has given me even more to think about in this regard.

CHAPTER 24:
Thomas P. Kasulis, "Masao Abe as D. T. Suzuki's Philosophical Successor"

Reading Thomas P. Kasulis's essay, I had the impression that he deeply understands my work, ideas, and intentions through his keen insight and elucidates well the significance on my work in the West. His evaluation of my work is very encouraging to me. For example, he states:

> *On one hand, [Abe] carried on the tradition of Suzuki and brought to it a new, distinctively philosophical, element on the other. Furthermore, by drawing inspiration from the writings of Dōgen, he has brought a less sectarian perspective to the West's understanding of Zen Buddhism. . . . By bridging the gap between the intellectual worlds of Japan and the West . . . he is a philosopher in his own right, and through the stance he takes, communicative lines between Japan and the West have been established.*

Toward the end of his essay, Kasulis sets up a contrast between two groups of the Japanese thinkers in question: Suzuki/Hisamatsu/Abe and Nishida/Nishitani/Watsuji/Tanabe. According to Kasulis, "the first group advocates [the experience of Emptiness] as beneficial to the resolution of philosophical problems." However, for the second group, "the experience needs to be explained and located in relation to more mundane, more secular, more everyday types of experiences." I find Kasulis's classification of these Japanese thinkers to be very significant and extremely suggestive for our future studies.

CHAPTER 25:
John E. Smith, "Kitarō Nishida, William James, and Masao Abe: Some Comments on Philosophy East and West"

John Smith carefully examines the philosophies of Kitarō Nishida and William James with regard to the notion of pure experience and discusses my role in their encounter. In the first half of his essay, Smith clearly expresses his agreement with Nishida and myself concerning the following:

> I believe that Nishida and Abe are right in attacking the idea . . . that there is "first" an individual who as a subject experiences and comes to know objects in some incorrigible way that is ultimately confined to that individual alone so that the problem becomes that of "transcending" this individual to reach an intersubjective truth.

In the second half of his essay, however, Smith declares, "It is reasonable to conclude that Nishida and Abe are mistaken in the claim that James *assumes* pure experience to be individual at the outset." This is a question we must consider carefully.

According to Smith, for William James "pure experience" is prior to any distinction, including the distinction between subject and object: pure experience for James includes relations, conjunctions, transitions, tendencies, etc., because he did not start with the individual, but with the "stream of thought." For James, therefore, any distinction between subject and object is always consequent and not primordial. If for James pure experience has such a special feature, strictly speaking, Smith is correct in saying it cannot be said to be individual at the outset. When Nishida and I assumed James's pure experience to be individual at the outset, however, we took pure experience to be fundamental to the individual without the slightest attention to its features.

Therefore, to return to the transindividual features of James's fundamental idea of pure experience—where the distinction between subject and object are merely ancillary to primordial experience, and the individual difference is not basic—Nishida called a primordial experience of this order *"direct experience."* When I read where Nishida says that experience exists not because there is an individual, but an individual exists because there is an experience, I, too, arrived at the idea that experience is more fundamental than the individual.

Experience in which not only things but also the self or the individual is experienced is direct, whereas experience that is experienced by a presupposed self is indirect. A direct experience goes beyond the individual—it is fundamentally transindividual. This is why Nishida says that the notion of pure experience enabled him to avoid solipsism. In the end, true directness is realized only from within the actual living reality of experience prior to the separation of subject and object. To grasp pure experience in its strict sense, we must return to the root source of experience that is individual and yet transindividual and universal. On this horizon of pure experience a new metaphysics is possible.

CHAPTER 26:
Thomas Dean, "Masao Abe's Zen Philosophy of Dialogue: A Western Response"

Thomas Dean generates a number of incisive and important questions concerning my approach to Asian-Western dialogue in philosophy based on his penetrating understanding of cross-cultural encounter in the realm of philosophical thinking. Because my response must be short, I limit myself to one of his questions. Dean asks whether my comparative method is judgmental of other philosophical positions from a Zen standard: "[In Abe's effort] there would seem to be a logical inconsistency between maintaining that one is not engaged in judging which system is superior while noting that one's judgments are being made from the standpoint of one's own tradition, particularly with reference to the criterion of how closely that other tradition approximates one's own presumably normative answers."

In my comparative approach, I seek to clarify the differences between various philosophical ways of thinking without compromise.

However, this emphasis on clarifying differences does not intend to exclude or reject the other systems. It is rather an invitation to dialogue beyond the essential differences. Critical questioning of the other traditions will not destroy but rather deepen those traditions. Likewise, I also welcome open criticism from other traditions.

The basic standpoint of my comparative work is but Śūnyatā, or Emptiness, which indicates the complete interdependent co-arising and co-ceasing of everything in the universe. Being itself empty and nonsubstantial, Śūnyatā lets every other position stand and work just as it is. Naturally, Zen Buddhism does not exclude other faiths as false but recognizes the relative truths they contain. This recognition, however, is a starting point, not the end, for Buddhist life. Properly speaking, Zen Buddhism starts to work critically and creatively *through* this basic recognition of the relative truths contained in other positions, hoping for productive dialogue and cooperation with other faiths.

CHAPTER 27:
Joel R. Smith, "Masao Abe on Negativity in the East and West"

Joel R. Smith sharply analyzes my essay "Non-Being and *Mu*—The Metaphysical Nature of Negativity in the East and the West" and criticizes my understanding of the issue discussed therein. In that essay, I tried to clarify what I think to be the most fundamental difference between the Eastern (particularly Buddhist) and Western ways of thinking and to propose a basic standpoint common to them both.

To show my basic position, Smith quotes my statement to the effect that while in the West positive principles (such as being, life, and the good) have ontological priority over negative principles (such as non-being, death, and evil), in the East the negative principles are coequal to the positive principles and *"even may be said to be primary and central."* He then states:

> The crucial point here is that in the passage just cited, Abe concedes, perhaps unintentionally, a point he had denied earlier. The whole thrust of his argument has been to assert that the positive

> and negative principles are coequal so that Buddhism is not onto-
> logically biased toward either positivity or negativity. But in the
> preceding passage, Abe acknowledges that in Buddhism negative
> principles are not only coequal to positive principles but "even
> may be said to be primary and central." He explicitly says that the
> ultimate is "realized in the East in terms of negativity and in the
> West in terms of positivity." Abe seems to contradict himself, claim-
> ing both that Buddhism does not give priority to negativity and
> that it does give priority to negativity. What are we to make of
> this?

Smith presents me with a serious challenge that touches the central point of the issue. When I emphasized that in Buddhism the positive and negative principles are coequal, that Buddhism is not ontologically positive or negative, I was clarifying the *ontological structure* of the Buddhist position. On the other hand, when I said that the ultimate is "realized in the East in terms of negativity and in the West in terms of positivity," I was concerned more with the *practical* and *existential* aspects of the issue. That is to say, in Buddhism the deep realization of negativity is practically crucial to the revelation of ultimate reality. Herein lies the "primacy" of negation.

For example, the ultimate reality in Buddhism is *Śūnyatā*, which is beyond any distinction, including subject and object, positivity and nega-tivity. To existentially realize *Śūnyatā*, it is crucial to realize not only the negation of positivity but also the negation of negativity. This latter dou-ble negation, that is, the negation of negation, is not a logical negation but an existential negation through which one can return to the root-source of both positivity and negativity. On the other hand, in Christianity ultimate reality is God. God is creator and redeemer, the ruler of the world and history, and therefore a "positive principle." However, in Chris-tian mysticism God is undefinable and unnameable. Therefore, as in Buddhism, only the *via negativa* provides a way to reach this ineffable God.

Smith offers two other important criticisms of my discussion. First, he points out, "Abe has not given an adequate account of the ontological nature of relative *mu* to show how it can be more than a privation of *u*. Until he provides this ontological account of relative *mu*, his entire position is weak." My response to this criticism is that *mu* is the complete counter-concept to *u*; therefore, *mu* is more than just a privation of *u*—it is a stronger form of negativity than "non-being" as understood in the West. Further, *u* and *mu* are completely antagonistic principles and therefore inseparable from each other; they constitute an antinomy, a self-contradiction. The Buddhist notion of *Śūnyatā* presents a standpoint that is realized through the overcoming of that antinomy, of the self-contradictory oneness of *u* and *mu*.

The second point of Smith's criticism is that my presentation of Absolute *Mu* bears "traces of negativity" in that it is relative *mu* and not relative *u* that is absolutized in *Śūnyatā*. To this I would like to respond by arguing that in his understanding Smith somewhat *objectifies* Absolute *Mu*. Here, Absolute *Mu* is understood as a static state of Emptiness. But Absolute *Mu* in its authentic sense is not a static *state* but dynamic *activity* of endless self-negation in which any negativity is constantly turned into positivity. Only through the realization of this absolute double negation is Emptiness realized as Fullness.

CHAPTER 28:
Joan Stambaugh, "Masao Abe and Martin Heidegger"

Referring to my essay "The Problem of Time in Heidegger and Dōgen," in *A Study of Dōgen: His Philosophy and Religion,* Joan Stambaugh discusses three issues: (1) the degree of transanthropomorphism, involving a discussion of thinking; (2) the ontological difference; and (3) the priority of time over being. Since these three issues are closely linked, let me respond to them not separately, but together.

For Heidegger, "Being is determined as presence by time." This is a key point to his thinking concerning the problem of being/time. Even in his notion of *Ereignis,* in which being and time are said to belong together, time has priority over being. For example, only being—and not time—disappears in *Ereignis*. This Heideggerian priority of time over being maintains an implicit anthropocentrism because whereas being can be thought of without beings, time cannot be thought of apart from the human self. Therefore, we see that Heidegger's understanding of the identity of being and time is not universally applied to all beings. In

Dōgen's thought, on the contrary, all beings are time, and all moments of time are being. This can be seen in his notion that "impermanence is, as such, Buddha-nature" *(mujō-busshō)*. For Dōgen, the notion of Buddha-nature does not indicate a special supernatural reality, but the original nature of everything, the Thusness *(tathatā)* of all beings.

Also for Heidegger, real thinking is a "recollection of another origin" *(Andenken an den anderen Anfang)*. This thinking is generated because in Heidegger's attempt to discover this origin, he finds it "unthinkable" *(das Unandenkliche)*. Thus, Heidegger's thinking is a new way of thinking beyond "metaphysical" thinking. It is a thinking of this other origin *(den anderen Anfang)* as the ground of metaphysics. For Dōgen, on the other hand, true thinking is a "non-thinking" that is beyond the duality of thinking and not-thinking and yet includes them both. Consequently, despite their resemblance, Heidegger's thinking is different from Dōgen's notion of non-thinking because the former does not reach the unthinkable as the true origin of thinking. For Heidegger, the unthinkable is always encountered from the side of thinking. But for Dōgen, true non-thinking is a self-realization of the unthinkable origin of thinking itself. Further, for Dōgen this unthinkable origin of thinking is the True Self that is realized by breaking through life-and-death.

CHAPTER 29:
Robert E. Carter, "Diagramming the Ultimate: Conversations with Masao Abe"

Robert Carter's essay is an impressive record of a Western intellectual's struggle with the Buddhist notion of Emptiness. The first barrier he faced was the Buddhist notion of ultimate reality, which is neither Being nor God, but *Śūnyatā*, which is entirely unobjectifiable, unconceptualizable, and unattainable by reason or will. Buddhism, especially Zen, is certainly practice and immediate experience rather than intellectual thinking. Zen *kōans*, Zen meditation, and the ordinary life of the Zen Buddhist all strive to break the iron grip of conceptualizing and intellectualizing. However, Zen is not mere anti-intellectualism. It is beyond the duality of thinking and not-thinking. It is non-thinking that, being free from the opposition between thinking and not-thinking, makes them alive and able to work freely according to each given situation. It is true that intellectual understanding cannot be a substitute for Zen's Awakening. But practice without a proper and legitimate form of intellectual understanding is often misleading, and intellectual understanding without practice is certainly powerless.

Buddhism, especially Zen, is full of paradoxical expressions. For instance: "True Emptiness is Wondrous Being." In order to attain true Emptiness, Emptiness must empty itself; Emptiness must become non-Emptiness. In true Emptiness, being becomes empty and emptiness become being; and yet being is being and emptiness is emptiness. Even this reciprocal emptying is also emptied. True Emptiness is paradoxically and self-contradictorily identical. Glancing at the above summary, I feel that Carter is as close as the language and thinking of paradoxicality can take him to an expression of the finger pointing toward the moon of ultimate reality.

CHAPTER 30:
William Theodore de Bary, "Buddhism and Human Rights"

Referring to my talk on "Buddhism and Human Rights" at Columbia University in 1955, in which I proposed that Buddhism could make important contributions to building a more unified and peaceful world where human rights are respected, de Bary raises the question "Is Abe's claim compatible with Buddhist tradition and history?" De Bary then mentions D. T. Suzuki's emphasis on *prajñā*, wisdom, as freedom from illusion and the importance of *upāya*, liberative technique, which the *Vimalakīrti Sūtra* insists upon as the necessary complement to higher wisdom. De Bary understands that through *upāya*, Mahāyāna Buddhism "accepts all states and stages of consciousness as relatively true and none as irremediably false or totally unredeemable." This attitude of acceptance offers a basis for Buddhist religious tolerance. However, de Bary shows the difficulties involved in rendering this implicit belief in the freedom of conscience into an explicit doctrine of human rights.

I generally agree with de Bary's discussion of human rights in the history of Buddhism and appreciate his insightful analysis and elucidation of the issue in question. To me, however, the most fundamental standpoint for a Buddhist view of human rights is still not clear enough.

In my understanding, insofar as the theme "Buddhism and Human Rights" is to be discussed, the *fundamental standpoint* of the Buddhist view of human rights must first be clarified. This is especially important because an exact equivalent of the Western phrase "human rights" cannot be found anywhere in Buddhist literature. The Western notion of human rights pertains only to humans, excluding other creatures. Therefore, the West has an anthropocentric view of human rights.

In Buddhism the human person is understood on a broader trans-homocentric and cosmological basis. Buddhism views human beings as part of all beings, sentient and nonsentient, because both human and nonhuman beings are equally subject to impermanency. The problem of human rights in Buddhism is to be grasped in the context of this transpersonal, cosmological dimension common to humankind and nature, namely, the Dharma or the Suchness (*tathatā*) of everything in the universe. Yet it is also true that only human beings, who alone in the universe have self-consciousness, can define and defend these rights of all beings.

CHAPTER 31:
Arvind Sharma, "A Chrysanthemum with a Lotus Stalk: Reminiscences from a Hindu Perspective"

Reading Arvind Sharma's essay, I strongly sense a special warmth that Hinduism holds in communicating with Buddhism. It is dialogue at its best, full of sensitivity and delicate thoughtfulness! Deeply rooted in Hindu spirituality, Sharma is an excellent dialogue partner not only for Buddhism but for other world religions.

There are a number of issues in his essay to be discussed. But let me restrict my comments to the question of the "indistinguishability" of Hinduism and Buddhism. Sharma confesses that when I asked him, "What do Hindus think of Buddhists?" that "it took me [Sharma] some time even to comprehend the question, for modern Hindus barely differentiate between the two." It is quite easy to point out the affinity between Hinduism and Buddhism. In the phenomenal and historical dimension, these two religions have developed through a long intermingling with each other. However, a question must be raised as to whether this affinity comprises real identity or not.

Emphasis on the similarities between two religions is certainly important, but it does not necessarily create something new. On the other hand, an attempt to disclose the differences, if properly and relevantly done, not only promotes and stimulates mutual understanding but also inspires both religions to seek further developments. In the case of Hinduism and Buddhism, isn't there a fundamental difference beyond their affinity on the phenomenal and historical dimension? That is, while Hinduism is based on the notion of *ātman*, Buddhism clearly denies it and is based on *anātman*. How can Hinduism and Buddhism overcome this fundamental difference and attain deeper developments within themselves? And will these developments create an even deeper unity between them?

Therefore, for the sake of the future of both religions, it is important to differentiate between the present views of each tradition. In fact, Mahāyāna Buddhism severely criticizes equating without discrimination as a false sameness. True interfaith unity dynamically includes sameness and difference. This dynamic unity is possible because it is *nonsubstantial* through a negation of negation. To use the above example, the Buddhist notion of *anātman* is not a mere negation of *ātman*, but being completely nonsubstantial, true *ātman* and true *anātman* are at one and the same time. With the realization of an even deeper unity between Buddhism and Hinduism in mind, I hope, Arvind Sharma, that our dialogue will develop further in the future.

CHAPTER 32:
Steven Heine, "Between Zen and the West, Zen and Zen, and Zen and Pure Land: On Masao Abe's Sense of Inter- and Intrafaith Dialogue"

With deep and thoroughgoing understanding of my work, Steven Heine clarifies my dialogue in the West in a quite unique manner that I appreciate deeply. Referring widely to Christianity and Buddhism, Heine makes a clear distinction between two dimensions of dialogue, that is, interfaith dialogue and intrafaith dialogue. These two dimensions complement, reinforce, and enhance each other.

In this regard, Heine indicates that my involvement with intrafaith dialogue divides into two main levels, both intertwined with interfaith concerns. To him, the first level deals with the dialogue between Zen and the Pure Land Buddhism; the second level is between the two main branches of Japanese Zen, namely, Rinzai and Sōtō. Heine's discussion of my work on both of these intrafaith levels is insightful and correct, so I have no particular disagreement with, nor criticism of, his presentation. Rather, I appreciate his analysis and hope to continue to promote these important dialogues within Buddhism.

CHAPTER 33:
Christopher Ives, "Masao Abe and His Dialogical Mission"

Christopher Ives points out that one of my most important contributions to interfaith and cross-cultural dialogue is the clarification of the nature of Zen Buddhism. However, Ives then questions whether my portrayal of Zen Buddhism is a rather abstract philosophical "composite," created for and by the dialogical context in which I work. Ives warns that my "Zen" is in fact different from the actual Zen of the average Zen Buddhist in Japan today. I will take heed of these remarks with appreciation and as a warning to myself. I believe, however, that my "Zen" is not a philosophical construct created through dialogue with Western thinkers. It is rather an existential outcome of my own long-term research of the history of Buddhism and my actual concrete practice of Zen Buddhism in Japan.

At the very end of his essay Ives expresses his strong desire that I produce "a systematic statement of [my] religious philosophy." It is my own long-cherished desire to produce a systematic presentation of my religious philosophy developed through East-West dialogue. As it would be a systematic work on the basis of *Śūnyatā,* it could be called, as Ives suggests, "Sunyatology."

CHAPTER 34:
Stephen C. Rowe, "A Zen Presence in America:
Dialogue as Religious Practice"

I am most favorably impressed by the words of Stephen Rowe's student who "proclaimed that reading Abe's *Zen and Western Thought* and then seeing Abe at Notre Dame had changed his life." Given the contemporary situation wherein religion is being challenged by secular materialism and antireligious ideologies, I do in fact value, as Rowe points out, interfaith dialogue as a way toward meeting this challenge and changing people's lives.

In this regard, interfaith dialogue must go beyond the goal of better mutual understanding to achieve the mutual transformation of people's lives. Because the criticisms by antireligious ideologies are today so deep and so fatal, to achieve mutual transformation, the prevailing basic assumptions of all religions must be drastically changed and new paradigms created. Thus, Rowe suggests mutual radicalization. In Buddhist terms this means the radicalization of Emptiness and compassion. In such a radicalization, Emptiness negates not only everything else but also Emptiness itself. When Emptiness itself is emptied, Wondrous Being manifests itself. Radicalization of *Śūnyatā* also entails the radicalization of compassion. At this point, John Cobb's criticism that in Buddhism compassion has not generally been applied to ethics and history must be kept clearly in mind.

Rowe correctly perceives that this kind of radicalization is itself a form of religious practice. He states that since this radicalization takes place through dialogue, "dialogue itself is a form of religious practice." He then raises a crucial issue: "And yet I know of nowhere in his [Abe's] writings where he addresses directly and on its own terms this form of practice to which he has contributed to so greatly."

Certainly dialogue is a form of religious practice for me, but it is carried out in the context of my religious practice in the F.A.S. movement. The F.A.S. movement originated as a student group in 1943 under the guidance of Shin'ichi Hisamatsu (1889–1980), the foremost Zen personality of contemporary Japan. This group sought the ultimate Way for human existence through the motto "unity of practice and learning."

What is F.A.S.? *F* stands for "Awakening to the *F*ormless Self," referring to the depth of human existence, i.e., the True Self as the ground of human existence. *A* stands for "Standing within the standpoint of *A*ll Humankind," referring to the breadth of human existence, i.e., human beings in their entirety. And *S* stands for "Creating history *S*uprahistorically," referring to the chronological length of human existence, i.e., Awakened human history. Accordingly, the three aspects of F.A.S. indicate a threefold structure of human existence: the depth, breadth, and length of human existence, or speaking more concretely, self, world, and history. In the notion of F.A.S., these three dimensions of human existence are grasped dynamically and, though different from one another, are inseparably united.

Hisamatsu once stated that if, as has been the case with traditional Zen, the so-called wondrous activity starts and ends only with the so-called practice of compassion involved in helping others to reach Awakening, then such activity remains unrelated to the formation of the world or the creation of history. Thus isolated from the world and history, Zen in the end turns into a forest Buddhism, temple Buddhism, at best a monastery Buddhism. Ultimately, this becomes "Zen within a ghostly cave."

In the F.A.S. movement, the questions of what the self is, what the world is, and what history is are all related. The problem of what the self is cannot be resolved—in its true sense—if it is investigated independently of the problems of the nature of the world and the meaning of history. On the other hand, world peace, for example, cannot be established—in the true sense—nor can history be truly created unless one clarifies what the True Self is. These three problems are inseparably related and united at the root of our very existence.

CHAPTER 35:
Stephen Morris, "The Roar of a Lion: Reflections on a Life Dedicated to What Is Ultimately Real"

Stephen Morris elucidates the form and content of my interfaith dialogical work in the West. Particularly referring to one of my key notions, "the Absolute Present," he states that the Absolute Present both defines my "existential stance" and provides "the pivot and the focus" for my philosophical position. He suggests that from within the Zen perspective, my scholarship "is itself an expression of the Absolute Present." It is indeed from this stance in the Absolute Present, or Emptiness, that my work in interfaith dialogue seeks, as Morris says, to crystallize and clarify the real spiritual project of religion.

Regarding the depth of spirituality in religion, Morris compares me with Meister Eckhart and Emerson, but I am afraid I am not worthy of such comparison. However, Morris argues that we are similar in that we are united in our "stance," that is, we rely on our spiritual experience.

While this may be so, we must carefully scrutinize the affinities and differences between these experiences. As for himself, Morris argues as follows: "Committed myself to neither the Buddhist or Christian perspective, I am, frankly, less interested in religions per se than in the spirituality they hope to foster."

Morris makes here a distinction between religion and spirituality and takes spirituality rather than religion (which is often identified as an institution) as his own stance. Here we are facing the following question: How can we individually and socially foster spirituality? Can we truly foster spirituality without religion? What is the role of religion? What form of practice is appropriate for people today—individually and socially?

To answer these questions, Morris introduces "education." He argues that if a fundamental spirituality can be developed outside of religion, then we no longer have to wait for religion to be radicalized and transformed. We do not have to wait for religion to "catch up." Spirituality in education can "develop people intellectually and socially in the soundest way." I myself well realize the importance of education in contemporary society. But however important education may be, to me it is not sufficient to cope with the current human predicament. In the modern world, because of the remarkable advancement of science and technology and the complexity of social and political systems, spirituality has been largely neglected. Why and how has this neglect of spirituality taken place in religions? Why and how have religious institutions failed today to foster spirituality? These are important questions. Without a serious consideration of these questions, education will not be enough to heal the painful condition of modern humanity.

In the end, we cannot help but face a most serious problem: How can religion be revitalized to meet the contemporary spiritual crisis of humankind? In this connection I completely agree with Morris when he says,

> One must seriously wonder if, in the long run, widespread spiritual change will trickle from the top down, or sprout from the bottom up. And what is advanced here is all in keeping with Abe's own vision of supplying a spiritual ground for the modern world; his very participation in the philosophical religious process is an

attempt to push the highest good within reach of the greatest number of people. Everyone deserves to be provided the wherewithal to retrieve the pearl.

NOTES

CHAPTER ONE

1. Masao Abe, "Toward the Creative Encounter Between Zen and Christianity," in *A Zen-Christian Pilgrimage: The Fruits of the Annual Colloquia in Japan, 1967–1976* (privately printed, 1981), 43.
2. Ibid.
3. Masao Abe, "Hisamatsu's Philosophy of Awakening," *The Eastern Buddhist* 14, no. 1 (spring 1981): 27.

CHAPTER TWO

1. A week-long period designated for intensive Zen meditation.
2. Kira Kozuke no suke (1641–1703) was an official of the Tokugawa shōgunate, assassinated by forty-seven samurai of the Ako clan in the celebrated episode of the *Forty-Seven Ronin*. On the occasion of a reception for imperial messengers at Edo castle in 1701, Kira, commonly disliked for his arrogance, received a slight wound in the forehead at the hands of Asano Takumi no kami (1667–1701), *daimyo* of Ako, who believed that Kira had intentionally withheld from him the fine points of court etiquette needed to avoid error in matters of protocol. In consequence for drawing his sword, Asano was immediately deprived of his domain and ordered to commit suicide. Kira escaped even reprimand, though he was later forced to leave office. Asano's retainers vowed vengeance, which they achieved in 1703, executing Kira in his own home.
3. Ryutarō Kitahara, "Makujikiko [Straight Ahead!]," *Zen Bunka* 97 (June 1980): 35–36.

CHAPTER FOUR

1. Masao Abe and John Cobb interviewed by Bruce Long, "Buddhist-Christian Dialogue: Past, Present and Future," *Buddhist-Christian Studies* 1 (1981): 20.

CHAPTER FIVE

1. Masao Abe, *Zen and Western Thought* (Honolulu: University of Hawai'i Press, 1985).
2. Ibid., ix.
3. Ibid.
4. See his translation of excerpts from Kitarō Nishida, "The Problem of Japanese Culture," in Ryusaku Tsunoda, W. Theodore de Bary, and Donald Keene, eds., *Sources of the Japanese Tradition*, vol. 2 (New York: Columbia University Press, 1958), 350–365.
5. See Shokin Furuta, "Shaku Sōen: The Footsteps of a Modern Japanese Zen Master," *Philosophical Studies of Japan* 8 (1967): 70.
6. Ibid., 69.

7. Ibid., 77; See also Sōen Shaku, "The Law of Cause and Effect as Taught by Buddha," translated by D. T. Suzuki in *The Eastern Buddhist* 26, no. 2 (autumn 1993): 134–37; and the Rev. John Henry Barrows, ed., *The World's Parliament of Religions*, vol. 2 (Chicago: Parliament Publishing Co., 1893), 829–31.

8. Sōen Shaku, *Sermons of a Buddhist Abbot* (Chicago: Open Court Publishing Co., 1906).

9. Ibid., 33.

10. Ibid., 47.

11. Ibid., 144.

12. Ibid.

13. See the discussion below of Nishida's logic of place.

14. Daisetz Teitaro Suzuki, *Açvaghosha's Discourse on the Awakening of Faith in the Mahayana* (Chicago: The Open Court Publishing Co., 1900). Hereafter referred to as *Açvaghosha's Discourse*.

15. Daisetz Teitaro Suzuki, *Outlines of Mahayana Buddhism* (London: Luzac and Co., 1907).

16. *Açvaghosha's Discourse*, 43.

17. Ibid., 152.

18. Ibid., 58–59.

19. Ibid., 58.

20. Daisetz T. Suzuki, *Outlines of Mahayana Buddhism* (New York: Schocken Books, 1963), 295. All further quotations from this work are from this edition.

21. Daisetz T. Suzuki, *Sengai the Zen Master* (Greenwich, Conn.: New York Graphic Society, 1971), 186.

22. Daisetz Teitaro Suzuki, *The Zen Doctrine of No-Mind* (London: Rider and Co., 1949), 59.

23. Daisetz T. Suzuki, *Zen and Japanese Buddhism* (Tokyo: Japan Travel Bureau, 1958), 60.

24. Daisetz T. Suzuki, *Zen and Japanese Culture* (Princeton: Princeton University Press, 1959), 298.

25. Daisetz T. Suzuki, *Essays in Zen Buddhism* (Third Series) (Kyoto: The Eastern Buddhist Society, 1934), 296.

26. Ibid., 228.

27. Ibid., 250.

28. Daisetz Teitaro Suzuki, *Mysticism: Christian and Buddhist* (New York: Harper & Brothers, 1957), 69.

29. *Açvaghosha's Discourse*, 107–108.

30. Ibid., 60.

31. Suzuki, *Essays in Zen Buddhism* (Third Series), 250.

32. Masao Abe, "Double Negation as an Essential for Attaining the Ultimate Reality: Comparing Tillich and Buddhism" (unpublished paper), 8. Hereafter cited as "Double Negation."

33. Masao Abe, "Substance, Process, and Emptiness," *Japanese Religions* 11 (September 1980): 32.

34. May not such a nondualistic self-negating-negation, self-negating-negating, or, therefore, self-negating-self-negating be detected as well in Hinduism's *neti-neti* ("not-this-[very-]not-this," or "not-[even-]this-not-this"), and in the Chinese Taoist Chuang-tzu's *wu-wu* ("self-naughting-self-naughting")?

35. Suzuki, *Outlines of Mahayana Buddhism*, 115.

36. Suzuki, *Zen and Japanese Culture*, 300.

37. Daisetz Teitaro Suzuki, *Essays in Zen Buddhism* (Second Series) (Kyoto: The Eastern Buddhist Society, 1933), 298.

38. *Açvaghosha's Discourse*, 61.

39. Suzuki, *Outlines of Mahayana Buddhism*, 322–324.

40. Bernard Phillips, ed., *The Essentials of Zen Buddhism, An Anthology of the Writings of Daisetz T. Suzuki* (London: Rider & Co., 1963), 25.

41. Suzuki, *Outlines of Mahayana Buddhism,* 100–101.

42. Ibid., 102.

43. Ibid., 105.

44. Ibid., 96.

45. Ibid., 22.

46. Ibid., 106.

47. Kitarō Nishida, *An Inquiry into the Good,* trans. Masao Abe and Christopher Ives (New Haven: Yale University Press, 1990), xii.

48. Ibid., xiv.

49. Ibid., 164.

50. Ibid., xvii.

51. Ibid., xxv.

52. Ibid., 46.

53. Ibid., 82.

54. Ibid., 168.

55. Ibid., xxv.

56. Ibid., x. Shin'ichi Hisamatsu, one of Nishida's leading direct disciples, has spoken of this in terms of "the paradox of sound negating sound." See Jerome S. Bruner, "The Art of Ambiguity: A Conversation with Zen Master Hisamatsu," *Psychologia* 2 (1959): 104.

57. Nishida, *An Inquiry into the Good,* xxii.

58. Ibid., xxiii.

59. Keiji Nishitani, *Nishida Kitarō,* trans. Seisaku Yamamoto and James W. Heisig (Berkeley: University of California Press, 1991), 49–50.

60. Daisetz Teitaro Suzuki, *The Field of Zen* (New York: Harper & Row, 1970), 93. In Hisamatsu's view as well, the "Self-Awakening" of the Self "where mind and body have fallen away" has been "conveyed by such expressions as Emptiness, Nothingness, Suchness, the Dharmakaya, not-a-single thing" (Shin'ichi Hisamatsu, "The Vow of Humankind, Part 3," translated by Christopher Ives in *FAS Society Journal* [autumn 1987]: 2).

61. Abe, *Zen and Western Thought,* 45.

62. Ibid., 158.

63. Ibid., 126.

64. Ibid., 126–127.

65. Suzuki, *The Field of Zen,* 100.

66. Kitarō Nishida, *Last Writings: Nothingness and the Religious Worldview,* trans. David A. Dilworth (Honolulu: University of Hawai'i Press, 1987), 89.

67. Ibid., 68.

68. Ibid., 69.

69. Ibid.

70. Ibid.

71. Ibid.

72. Ibid., 71.

73. Ibid., 110.

74. Ibid., 117.

75. Quoted from Hans Waldenfels, *Absolute Nothingness*, trans. J. W. Heisig (New York: Paulist Press, 1980), 41.

76. Nishida, *Last Writings*, 125.

77. See ibid., "Introduction" by David A. Dilworth, 20.

78. See Nishitani, *Nishida Kitarō*, 162.

79. See Nishida, *Last Writings*, "Introduction," 5.

80. See ibid., "Postscript" by David A. Dilworth, 127.

81. Ibid., 70.

82. Nishida, *An Inquiry into the Good*, 82.

83. Nishida, *Last Writings*, 70.

84. Ibid., 118.

85. Ibid.

86. Ibid., 68.

87. Ibid., 70.

88. That is, Nishida's notions of absolute nothingness, absolute self-negation, absolute self-contradiction, the logic of the place of nothingness, etc., could also, in language already suggested, be understood—and so expressed—in terms of a nondualistic self-emptying-self-emptying or a self-negating-self-negation. For only through negating itself and simultaneously negating its own self-negation is there self-negation-affirmation that veritably constitutes an "absolute contradictory self-identity"—or, in this sense, a "self-identity of absolute contradictories."

89. See a conversation between Dr. Suzuki and the writer in "Oriental Thought and the West" (*Tōyōshisō to Seiyō*), *Asahi Journal* 7, no. 11 (March 14, 1965): 122.

90. Suzuki, *The Field of Zen*, 39.

91. Ibid., 68.

92. Ibid., 15.

93. Daisetz T. Suzuki, *Living by Zen* (Tokyo: Sanseido, 1949), 2.

94. Ibid.

95. Daisetz Teitaro Suzuki, *An Introduction to Zen Buddhism* (Kyoto: The Eastern Buddhist Society, 1934), 48.

96. Daisetz T. Suzuki, "Knowledge and Innocence," in Thomas Merton, *Zen and the Birds of Appetite* (New York: New Directions, 1968), 107.

97. Ibid., 133–134.

98. Ibid., 111.

99. Daisetz Teitaro Suzuki, *Zen Buddhism and Its Influence on Japanese Culture* (Kyoto: The Eastern Buddhist Society, 1938), 28.

100. Suzuki, "Knowledge and Innocence," 109.

101. Daisetz Teitaro Suzuki, *Studies in Zen* (London: Rider and Co., 1955), 204.

102. Suzuki, *Sengai*, 91.

103. Suzuki, *The Field of Zen*, 15.

104. Nishida, *An Inquiry into the Good*, 145, and Nishitani, *Nishida Kitarō*, 91. Shin'ichi Hisamatsu has likewise commented: "We awaken to our Self, and this awakened Self then functions. . . . This amounts to dying absolutely and being reborn, to being reborn through death." ("The Vow of Humankind, Part 3," 4). See also the discussion below and note 147.

105. Nishida, *An Inquiry into the Good*, 77.

106. Keiji Nishitani, *Religion and Nothingness*, trans. by Jan van Bragt (Berkeley: University of California Press, 1982), 58–59.

107. Ibid., 67.

108. Ibid., 105–106.

109. Quoted from David A. Dilworth, "Nishida's Final Essay: The Logic of Place and a Religious World-View," *Philosophy East and West* 20, no. 4 (October 1970): 364.

110. Nishitani, *Nishida Kitarō*, 50.

111. Ibid.

112. Abe, *Zen and Western Thought*, 226.

113. Ibid., 247.

114. Ibid.

115. Ibid., 211.

116. Ibid., xxi–xxii.

117. Ibid., 165. In the words of Abe's Zen teacher, Shin'ichi Hisamatsu: "In Zen, negation is not mere negation. 'Not something' does not mean the negation of something" ("The Art of Ambiguity," 104).

118. Abe, *Zen and Western Thought*, 129.

119. Ibid., 94.

120. Ibid., 131.

121. Ibid., 127.

122. John B. Cobb, Jr., and Christopher Ives, eds., *The Emptying God: A Buddhist-Jewish-Christian Conversation* (Maryknoll, N.Y.: Orbis Books, 1990), and Christopher Ives, ed., *Divine Emptiness and Historical Fullness: A Buddhist-Jewish-Christian Conversation with Masao Abe* (Valley Forge, Pa.: Trinity Press International, 1995).

123. Cobb and Ives, *The Emptying God*, 10.

124. Ibid., 13.

125. Ibid., 14.

126. Ibid., 16.

127. Ibid., 18.

128. Ibid., 17.

129. Ibid., 26.

130. Ibid., 27.

131. See Abe, "Substance, Process, and Emptiness," 22.

132. Ibid., 31.

133. Cobb and Ives, *The Emptying God*, 28. In Hisamatsu's explanation, "The point . . . where form becomes emptiness, where one dies as form and lives in emptiness, is the place where we say, 'Form just as it is, is Emptiness.' . . . What is involved in 'Form just as it is, is Emptiness' [is that] form is transformed into emptiness, changes into emptiness" (Shin'ichi Hisamatsu, "Vow of Humankind, Part 2," *FAS Society Journal* [winter 1986–87]: 27). So, "this is emptiness, and, moreover, existence. In other words, this is . . . expressed in the Heart Sutra [as] 'emptiness in form'" (Hisamatsu, "Vow of Humankind, Part 3," 3). Accordingly, "this is no mere emptiness or nothingness; it is functioning emptiness and functioning nothingness, and this is what the true nature of emptiness must be" (ibid., 4).

134. Abe, "Double Negation," 5.

135. Cobb and Ives, *The Emptying God*, 31.

136. Abe, *Zen and Western Thought*, 257.

137. Ibid., 251.

138. Ibid., 107.

139. Ibid., 150. As Hisamatsu has pointed out, "the Pure Land Buddhist expression, 'the body that is self-effected and void, the self that is boundless' (*jine kyomu-no-shin, mugoku-no-tai*) expresses the body that is spontaneity, nothingness, complete emptiness. Self-effected spontaneity (*jinen*) indicates our original way of being" ("Vow of Humankind, Part 2," 28).

140. Suzuki, *Living by Zen*, 86–87. In another expression, the "Self we awaken to is not something separate from all other things. . . . We can call that Self the absolute Self . . . beyond the distinction of self and other" (D. T. Suzuki, "Kiyozawa's Living Presence," trans. Taira Satō and W. S. Yokoyama, *The Eastern Buddhist* 26, no. 2 [autumn 1993]: 7).

141. Suzuki, *The Zen Doctrine of No-Mind*, 40.

142. Suzuki, *Essays in Zen Buddhism* (Third Series), 237.

143. Suzuki, *Mysticism: Christian and Buddhist*, 153. Clarified further by Hisamatsu: "In the 'I' of Zen there is no opposition externally and no discrimination internally, thus it is called 'nothing' " (Shin'ichi Hisamatsu, "Zen as the Negation of Holiness," trans. Sally Merrill, *The Eastern Buddhist* 10, no. 1 [May 1977]: 12). Put another way, " 'becoming nothing' is the change from the limited I to the unlimited I" (Hisamatsu, "The Vow of Humankind," *FAS Society Journal* [spring 1986], 4). That is, "this nothingness is the True I" (Hisamatsu, "Vow of Humankind, Part 2," 25); "the 'I' that is reborn after death" (Hisamatsu, "Vow of Humankind," 5). So it is a "Nothingness that is Self, or Self that is Nothingness" (Shin'ichi Hisamatsu, "Talks on the Vimalakīrti Sūtra, Part 1," trans. Nobumichi Takahashi, *FAS Society Journal* [summer 1992]: 2). As a consequence, "this Nothingness is no mere logical negation but the way of being of the Self that comes breaking out through the bottom of [what is an] ultimate antinomy" (Shin'ichi Hisamatsu, "Ultimate Crisis and Resurrection, Part I," trans. Gishin Tokiwa, *The Eastern Buddhist* 8, no. 1 [May 1975]: 29).

144. Suzuki, *Zen and Japanese Culture*, 176.

145. Masao Abe, "God, Emptiness, and the True Self," *The Eastern Buddhist* 2, no. 2 (November 1969): 28.

146. Abe, *Zen and Western Thought*, 252.

147. See, for example, Shin'ichi Hisamatsu, "Teaching-Faith-Practice-Awakening," translated by Jeff Shore in collaboration with Fusako Nagasawa and Gishin Tokiwa, *FAS Society Journal* (summer 1985). In this talk, given in April 1960, Hisamatsu emphasized the Zen exhortation: " 'Die the One Great Death! Then there is Rebirth'—that is Awakening to the Formless Self" (p. 38). For this Awakening in which "the original self Awakens itself" only "comes through the complete death of the ordinary self," "where the ordinary self dies completely," (p. 37), or, again, through " 'dying the One Great Death' " (p. 36). See also Shin'ichi Hisamatsu, "Ultimate Crisis and Resurrection, Part II," trans. Gishin Tokiwa, *The Eastern Buddhist* 8, no. 2 (October 1975): 61, and Shin'ichi Hisamatsu, "Ordinary Mind," trans. Gishin Tokiwa and Howard Curtis, *The Eastern Buddhist* 12, no. 1 (May 1979): 27.

148. Masao Abe, "Man and Nature in Christianity and Buddhism," in Frederik Franck, ed., *The Buddha Eye* (New York: Crossroads Publishing Co., 1982), 152.

149. Abe, *Zen and Western Thought*, 166.

150. Ibid., 145.

151. Abe, "Man and Nature in Christianity and Buddhism," 153.

152. Ibid., 156.

153. See also Abe, *Zen and Western Thought*, 220, 222–223.

154. Considered as referring to the function of Nature, *pratītya-samutpāda* could therefore be interpreted as:

> this be-ing, that is,
> this arising, that arises;
> this not-be-ing, that is not,

> *this ceasing, that ceases;*
> *their be-ing, a being-less be-ing,*
> *their not-be-ing, a being-full not-be-ing.*

Or, stated otherwise:

> *in the simultaneity*
> *of their be-ing and not-be-ing,*
> *this be-ing, every-thing is,*
> *this not-be-ing, no-thing is.*

155. In alternate terminology, this has been expressed by Suzuki as "the self-presentation of the great doubt" ("Zen in America and the Necessity of the Great Doubt: A Discussion Between D. T. Suzuki and Shin'ichi Hisamatsu," trans. Jeff Shore, *FAS Society Journal* [spring 1986]: 22), and by Hisamatsu as "the ultimate antinomy realizing itself" ("Ultimate Crisis and Resurrection, Part II," 49).

156. As articulated by Hisamatsu, "It does assume one particular form, but it is not a particular . . . . Rather . . . it [is] the root source of all particularity . . . a freely functioning root-source" ("True Sitting: A Discussion with Shin'ichi Hisamatsu," translated by Jeff Shore in collaboration with Fusako Nagasawa and Gishin Tokiwa, *FAS Society Journal* [autumn 1984]: 27).

CHAPTER EIGHT

1. Donald Keene, trans., *Essays in Idleness: The Tsurezuregusa of Kenkō* (New York: Columbia University Press, 1967), 12.

2. This is, of course, what gives special distinction to Abe's *A Study of Dōgen: His Philosophy and Religion,* ed. Steven Heine (Albany: State University of New York Press, 1992).

3. Masao Abe, *Zen and Western Thought,* ed. William R. LaFleur (London: Macmillan, 1985).

4. Probably the best-known demonstration of this theory is Stanley Fish, *Is There a Text in This Class? The Authority of Interpretive Communities* (Cambridge: Harvard University Press, 1980).

5. As used, for instance, in Kitarō Nishida, *An Inquiry into the Good,* trans. Masao Abe and Christopher Ives (New Haven: Yale University Press, 1990), 145.

6. Naoki Sakai, *Voices of the Past: The Status of Language in Eighteenth-Century Japanese Discourse* (Ithaca: Cornell University Press, 1991), 299.

7. I discuss this as problematized within medieval Japanese aesthetic theory in my *Karma of Words: Buddhism and the Literature Arts in Medieval Japan* (Berkeley: University of California Press, 1983), 100. My writing about this owed much to essays by Jin'ichi Konishi and conversations with Masamichi Kitayama.

CHAPTER NINE

1. Masao Abe, "The End of World Religion," *The Eastern Buddhist* 13, no. 1 (spring 1980): 31–45.

2. Masao Abe, *Zen and Western Thought,* ed. William R. LaFleur (Honolulu: University of Hawai'i Press, 1985), 178.

3. Masao Abe, "God's Total Kenosis and Truly Redemptive Love," in Christopher Ives, ed., *Divine Emptiness and Historical Fullness: A Buddhist-Jewish-Christian Conversation with Masao Abe* (Valley Forge, Pa.: Trinity Press International, 1995), 253.

4. See Neil Donner, "Chih-i's Meditation on Evil," in David W. Chappell, ed., *Buddhist and Taoist Practice in Medieval Chinese Society* (Honolulu: University of Hawai'i Press, 1987), 49–64.

5. Abe's claim that the experience is a privileged first-order viewpoint that undercuts all others is perceptively analyzed by Thomas Dean in his article "Masao Abe on Zen and Western Thought," *The Eastern Buddhist* 22, no. 2 (autumn 1989): 48–77.

6. John B. Cobb, Jr., and Christopher Ives, eds., *The Emptying God: A Buddhist-Jewish-Christian Conversation* (Maryknoll, N.Y.: Orbis Press, 1990), 11.

7. Ibid., 17.

8. Ibid., 15–16.

9. See this helpful and revealing description in ibid., 188.

10. Ibid.

11. Ibid., 11.

12. Ibid., 27.

13. Ibid., 29–32.

14. Leonard Swidler, *Toward a Universal Theology of Religion* (Maryknoll, N.Y.: Orbis Books, 1987), 98.

15. Ibid., 110.

16. Lawrence Kohlberg, *The Philosophy of Moral Development: Moral Stages and the Idea of Justice* (San Francisco: Harper & Row, 1981), 344–45.

17. Ibid., 345.

18. See especially Carol Gilligan, *In a Different Voice* (Cambridge: Harvard University Press, 1982).

19. Abe, *The Emptying God,* 123.

20. See Tanabe Hajime, *Philosophy of Metanoetics* (Berkeley: University of California Press, 1986).

21. This issue of Zen ethics is being discussed in Zen circles, however, and was formulated as the topic for group study at the Fourth International Buddhist-Christian Conference held in Boston in the summer of 1992 by the Zen Symposium of Hanazono University. See also Bernard Faure, "The Kyoto School and Reverse Orientalism," in Charles W. Fu and Steven Heine, eds., *Japan in Traditional and Postmodern Perspectives* (Albany: State University of New York Press, 1995).

22. See Shioiri's complete bibliography in his memorial volume edited by Muranaka Yusho, *Shioiri Ryōdō sensei tsuito ronbunshu: Tendai shiso to To Ajia bunka no kenkyu* (Tokyo: Sankibo, 1991), 1–6.

23. In addition to the "formless repentance" advocated by Chih-i in his *Mo-ho chih-kwan,* the Lotus Samadhi repentance ritual has confession of individual sins requiring tearful remorse. See a translation by Daniel Stevenson, "The T'ien t'ai Four Forms of Samadhi and Late North-South Dynasties, Sui, and Early T'ang Buddhist Devotionalism" (Ph.D. diss., Yale University, 1987), 500–511.

24. For a sweeping consideration of the tensions between Zen ideology and Buddhist morality, see Bernard Faure's recent book *The Rhetoric of Immediacy: A Cultural Critique of Chan/Zen Buddhism* (Princeton: Princeton University Press, 1991), 231–57.

25. See the superb article by Luis Gomez that places the issues of this debate in a larger historical perspective: "Purifying Gold: The Metaphor of Effort and Intuition in Buddhist Thought and Practice," in Peter Gregory, ed., *Sudden and Gradual: Approaches to Enlightenment in Chinese Thought* (Honolulu: University of Hawai'i Press, 1987), 67–165.

26. Frank E. Reynolds, "Ethics and Wealth in Theravada Buddhism: A Study in Comparative Religious Ethics," in Russell F. Sizemore and Donald K. Swearer, eds., *Ethics, Wealth, and Salvation: A Study in Buddhist Social Ethics* (Columbia: University of South Carolina Press, 1990), 59–76. I am indebted to Donald Swearer for pointing out this reference.

CHAPTER TEN

1. Kitarō Nishida, *Last Writings: Nothingness and the Religious Worldview,* trans. David Dilworth (Honolulu: University of Hawai'i Press, 1987), 126.

2. Ibid.

3. This and the next two quotations are from Masao Abe's draft of his essay "Sunyata and the Logic of Absolute Nothingness—The Logic Expounded by the Kyoto School," which he presented to the American Philosophical Association, Eastern Division, Washington, D.C., December 27–30, 1992. Abe was kind enough to share a draft of this essay with me. This version was adapted by Abe from his published essay "Nishida's Philosophy of 'Place,'" *International Philosophical Quarterly* 28, no. 4 (December 1988): 355–371.

4. Ibid., 8.

5. Ibid., 9.

6. Ashok K. Gangadean, *Meditative Reason: Toward Universal Grammar* (New York: Peter Lang Press, 1993).

CHAPTER TWELVE

1. The proceedings of this theological encounter group have been published in various issues of *Buddhist-Christian Studies* since 1985.

2. The Purdue meeting of the Abe-Cobb group, by then called the International Buddhist-Christian Theological Encounter Group, was held on October 10–12, 1986. The proceedings of this encounter are published in *Buddhist-Christian Studies* 8 (1988): 45–168, and 9 (1989): 123–229.

3. See Donald W. Mitchell, "Compassionate Endurance: Mary and the Buddha, A Dialogue with Keiji Nishitani," *Bulletin of the Vatican Secretariat for Non-Christians* 21, no. 3 (1986): 296–300; Donald W. Mitchell, "A Dialogue with Kobori Nanrei Sohaku," *Japanese Religions* 20, no. 2 (July 1986): 19–32; Donald W. Mitchell, "Unity and Dialogue: A Christian Response to Shin'ichi Hisamatsu's Notion of F.A.S.," *FAS Society Journal* (spring 1986): 6–9.

4. These persons included Marcello Zago, John Shirieda, and Giuseppe Zanghi.

5. Abe's stay at Purdue and his four dialogues were funded by a generous grant from the Lilly Endowment, Inc. The Rubenstein and Pannenberg dialogues are published in Christopher Ives, ed., *Divine Emptiness and Historical Fullness: A Buddhist-Jewish-Christian Conversation with Masao Abe* (Valley Forge, Pa.: Trinity Press International, 1995). Abe's responses to Suchocki and Egan are published in Masao Abe, *Buddhism and Interfaith Dialogue* (Honolulu: University of Hawai'i Press, 1995).

6. See Donald W. Mitchell, *Spirituality and Emptiness: The Dynamics of Spiritual Life in Buddhism and Christianity* (New York: Paulist Press, 1991), 142–181.

7. See Mitchell, "Compassionate Endurance."

CHAPTER THIRTEEN

1. Masao Abe, in Arvind Sharma, ed., *Our Religions* (New York: HarperCollins, 1993), 114.

2. Masao Abe, *Zen and Western Thought* (Honolulu: University of Hawai'i Press, 1985), 167.

3. Masao Abe, in John Cobb and Christopher Ives, eds., *The Emptying God: A Buddhist-Jewish-Christian Conversation* (Maryknoll, N.Y.: Orbis Books, 1990), 27.

4. Ibid.

5. Abe, *Zen and Western Thought*, 198.

6. Ibid., 133.

7. Abe, *The Emptying God*, 32.

8. Ibid., 33.

9. Abe, *Zen and Western Thought*, 211.

10. Ibid., 223.

11. *Yogavasistha*, I:28.

12. Yoshifumi Ueda in his introduction to the English translation of Shinran's *Notes on "Essentials of Faith Alone"* (Kyoto: Hongwanji International, 1979), 4.

13. Ibid., 5.

14. The Dalai Lama, *A Human Approach to World Peace* (Boston: Wisdom Publications, 1984), 13.

15. Abe, *Zen and Western Thought*, 189.

CHAPTER FIFTEEN

1. *Japanese Religions* 11, no. 2/3 (September 1980).

2. Martin Heidegger, *On the Way to Language* (Pfullinger: Neske, 1959), 186ff. and 209ff.

3. Ibid., 187.

4. Ibid., 210.

5. Ibid., 211.

6. See Keiji Nishitani, *Religion and Nothingness* (Berkeley: University of California Press, 1982).

7. Heidegger, 211.

8. B. Buddhadāsa, *Christianity and Buddhism* (Bangkok, 1967).

9. Saint Augustine, *Confessions*, Book IV.

CHAPTER EIGHTEEN

1. Telephone conversation between Masao Abe and the author, September 11, 1993. Abe was at home in Kyoto; I was in Tallahassee.

2. I describe the impact of that course in the chapter entitled "Tillich and Harvard" in Richard L. Rubenstein, *Power Struggle: An Autobiographical Confession* (New York: Charles Scribner's Sons, 1974).

3. The encounter is described in the chapter entitled "The Dean and The Chosen People" in Richard L. Rubenstein, *After Auschwitz: History, Theology and Contemporary Judaism*, rev. ed. (Baltimore: Johns Hopkins University Press, 1992), 3–13.

4. Richard L. Rubenstein, *The Age of Triage: Fear and Hope in an Overcrowded World* (Boston: Beacon Press, 1983), 131–133.

5. Masao Abe, "A Rejoinder," in John B. Cobb, Jr., and Christopher Ives, eds., *The Emptying God: A Buddhist-Jewish-Christian Conversation* (Maryknoll, N.Y.: Orbis Books, 1990), 186.

6. Abe, "Kenotic God and Dynamic Sunyata," in ibid., 60.

7. Rubenstein, *Power Struggle: An Autobiographical Confession.*

8. Abe, "Kenotic God and Dynamic Sunyata," 27.

9. Ibid., 28.

10. Abe, "A Rejoinder," 174.

11. Ibid., 184.

12. Eugene B. Borowitz, "The God Who Fills the Universe," in Cobb and Ives, *The Emptying God*, 81.

13. Ibid., 82.

14. Ibid.

15. Abe, "Kenotic God and Dynamic Sunyata," 29.

16. John B. Cobb, Jr., preface to Cobb and Ives, *The Emptying God*, xi.

17. According to Abe, the religious dimension "signifies that which is neither the divine nor the human, neither the sacred nor the secular, neither the supernatural nor the natural, and that which is neither absolutely good nor absolutely evil—Sunyata." (Abe, "Kenotic God and Dynamic Sunyata," 49).

18. The distinction between the *En Sof* and the *sefirot* is one of the most complex in all of Jewish mysticism. I merely want to draw attention to the distinction between the *Urgrund* and the manifestations of divinity that are revealed to humanity. For a brief discussion of the distinction between the *En Sof* and manifest divinity, see Gershom Scholem, *Sabbatai Sevi: The Mystical Messiah, 1626–1676* (Princeton: Princeton University Press, 1973), 119–23.

19. Borowitz, "The God Who Fills the Universe," 84.

20. Ibid.

21. Richard L. Rubenstein, *After Auschwitz*, 1st ed. (Indianapolis: Bobbs-Merrill, 1966), 154.

22. Christopher Ives, ed., *Divine Emptiness and Historical Fullness: A Buddhist-Jewish-Christian Conversation with Masao Abe* (Valley Forge, Pa.: Trinity Press International, 1995).

23. Ibid., 93–112.

24. It is certainly not the fashion of nonmystical Orthodox Jews, whose understanding of God and the covenant are far more literal than Borowitz's.

25. Abe, "A Rejoinder," 187.

26. Ibid., 188.

27. Japanese-Jewish relations during World War II are discussed in Marvin Tokayer and Mary Swartz, *The Fugu Plan: The Untold Story of the Japanese and the Jews during World War II* (New York: Paddington Press, 1970); David Kranzler, *Japanese, Nazis and Jews: The Jewish Refugee Community of Shanghai, 1935–1945* (Hoboken, N.J.: KTAV, 1988); and Ben-Ami Shillony, *The Jews and the Japanese: The Successful Outsiders* (Rutland, Vt.: Charles E. Tuttle Co., 1992), 178–89.

28. Abe, "Kenotic God and Dynamic Sunyata," 50.

29. Abe, "A Rejoinder," 186.

30. John B. Cobb, Jr., "On the Deepening of Buddhism," in Cobb and Ives, *The Emptying God*, 93.

31. Richard L. Rubenstein, *The Cunning of History* (New York: Harper and Row, 1975). In addition to my research, my activities in the domain of public affairs have included serving as president of the Washington Institute for Values in Public Policy, a Washington-based policy research institution, since 1981. I also serve as editor of *In Depth: A Journal of Values in Public Policy* and as chairman of the Editorial Advisory Board of the *Washington Times*.

32. Emil L. Fackenheim, "Transcendence in Contemporary Culture: Philosophical Reflections and a Jewish Theology," in Herbert W. Richardson and Donald R. Cutler, *Transcendence* (Boston: Beacon Press, 1969), 150.

33. Abe, "A Rejoinder," 188.

CHAPTER NINETEEN

1. Wolfhart Pannenberg, "A Search for the Authentic Self," *Christian Spirituality* (Philadelphia: Westminster Press, 1983), 93–110.

2. Ibid., 97. Cf. Masao Abe, "Man and Nature in Christianity and Buddhism," *Japanese Religions* 7 (1971): 8.

3. Pannenberg, *Christian Spirituality*, 99.

4. Ibid., 99–100.

5. Ibid., 101. Cf. Abe, "Man and Nature in Christianity and Buddhism," 9.

6. Pannenberg, *Christian Spirituality*, 104.

7. Ibid., 105.

8. Ibid., 106. Cf. also Abe, "Man and Nature in Christianity and Buddhism," 22.

9. Pannenberg, *Christian Spirituality*, 107.

10. Ibid.

11. Ibid., 110.

12. Ibid., 108.

13. Cf. Masao Abe, "Kenotic God and Dynamic Sunyata," in John B. Cobb, Jr., and Christopher Ives, eds., *The Emptying God: A Buddhist-Jewish-Christian Conversation* (Maryknoll, N.Y.: Orbis Books, 1990), 3–65. A shorter, earlier version of the same essay was published in Roger Corless and Paul Knitter, eds., *Buddhist Emptiness and Christian Trinity: Essays and Explorations* (New York: Paulist Press, 1990), 5–25.

14. Cf. Wolfhart Pannenberg, "God's Love and the Kenosis of the Son: A Response to Masao Abe," and Masao Abe's rejoinder, "God's Total Kenosis and Truly Redemptive Love," in Christopher Ives, ed., *Divine Emptiness and Historical Fullness: A Buddhist-Jewish-Christian Conversation with Masao Abe* (Valley Forge, Pa.: Trinity Press International, 1995), 244–259.

15. Pannenberg, "God's Love and the Kenosis of the Son," 246. Cf. Abe, "Kenotic God and Dynamic Sunyata," 28.

16. Abe, "Kenotic God and Dynamic Sunyata," 28.

17. Donald W. Mitchell, *Spirituality and Emptiness: The Dynamics of Spiritual Life in Buddhism and Christianity* (New York: Paulist Press, 1991), 55.

18. Abe, "Kenotic God and Dynamic Sunyata," 27. Cf. Pannenberg, "God's Love and the Kenosis of the Son," 246.

19. Pannenberg, "God's Love and the Kenosis of the Son," 246. Cf. Abe, "Kenotic God and Dynamic Sunyata," 38.

20. Pannenberg, "God's Love and the Kenosis of the Son," 247. Cf. Abe, "Kenotic God and Dynamic Sunyata," 32, 60.

21. Pannenberg, "God's Love and the Kenosis of the Son," 247.

22. Ibid., 248.

23. Ibid. Cf. Abe, "Kenotic God and Dynamic Sunyata," 13.

24. Pannenberg, "God's Love and the Kenosis of the Son," 249.

25. Ibid.

26. Ibid., 250.

27. Ibid.

28. Ibid. Cf. Wolfhart Pannenberg, *Systematic Theology* I, trans. Geoffrey W. Bromiley (Grand Rapids, Mich.: William B. Eerdmans, 1991), 382–384.

29. Pannenberg, "God's Love and the Kenosis of the Son," 250.

30. Ibid.

31. Abe, "God's Total Kenosis and Truly Redemptive Love," 253.

32. Ibid.

33. Ibid., 255.

34. Ibid., 256.

35. Ibid., 257.

36. Ibid., 258.

37. Pannenberg, *Systematic Theology* I, 320.

38. Ibid., 324.

39. Saint Thomas Aquinas, *Summa Theologiae* I, Q. 29, a. 4, resp.

40. Cf. on this point my book *Society and Spirit* (Cranbury, N.J.: Associated University Presses, 1991), 129–39, in which I, too, set forth the nature of God as an underlying force-field but from the perspective of a neo-Whiteheadian process-oriented metaphysics rather than from analysis of the Stoic notion of *pneuma* as does Pannenberg.

41. Cf. *Sacred Texts of the World: A Universal Anthology,* ed. Ninian Smart and Richard D. Hecht (New York: Crossroads, 1982), 246: "Form is emptiness, and the very emptiness is form; emptiness does not differ from form, form does not differ from emptiness."

42. Abe, "God's Total Kenosis and Truly Redemptive Love," 255: "There is an agent who abandoned his Sonship of God and resurrected as the redeemer. He is not an agent in the ordinary sense. He is an agentless agent: that is, a self-emptying and yet self-fulfilling agent."

CHAPTER TWENTY

1. Hans Küng, "Towards a Global Ethic," paper delivered at the 1993 Parliament of the World's Religions, August 28–September 5, 1993, Chicago, Illinois.

2. "God's Self-Renunciation and Buddhist Emptiness: A Christian Response to Masao Abe," in Roger Corless and Paul Knitter, eds., *Buddhist Emptiness and Christian Trinity: Essays and Explorations* (New York: Paulist Press, 1990), 26–43.

3. Hans Küng, *Christianity and the World Religions: Paths of Dialogue with Islam, Hinduism and Buddhism* (New York: Doubleday, 1986), xiv.

4. Hans Küng, *Theology for the Third Millennium: An Ecumenical View* (New York: Doubleday, 1988), 123–206.

5. Ibid., 220.

6. Küng, *Christianity and the World Religions,* xiv.

7. Küng, *Theology for the Third Millennium,* 227–256.

8. Ibid., 238–239.

9. Hans Küng, *Global Responsibility: Toward a New World Ethic* (New York: Crossroads, 1991) [Original: *Projekt Weltethos* (Munich: Piper, 1990)].

10. Küng, *Theology for the Third Millennium,* 251.

11. Ibid., 253–256.

12. Küng, *Christianity and the World Religions.*

13. Küng, "God's Self-Renunciation and Buddhist Emptiness," 26–43.

14. Ibid., 42–43.

15. Ibid., 37.

16. Ibid.

17. Masao Abe, "Nishitani's Challenge to Western Philosophy and Theology," in Taitetsu Unno, ed., *The Religious Philosophy of Nishitani Keiji: Encounter with Emptiness* (Berkeley: Asian Humanities Press, 1989), 13–45; Masao Abe, "Will, Sunyata, and History," in ibid., 279–304. Abe's thinking on the question of human rights and ethics is presented in his "Religious Tolerance and Human Rights: A Buddhist Perspective," published in Leonard Swidler, ed., *Religious Liberty and Human Rights in Nations and Religions* (Philadelphia: Ecumenical Press, 1986), 193–211. He has also delivered a paper on this question at the UNESCO-sponsored colloquium in Germany, published in Hans Küng and Karl Joseph Kuschel, eds., *Weltfrieden durch Religionsfrieden—Antworten aus den Weltreligionen* (Munich: Piper, 1993), 109–40. (I thank Professor Christopher Ives of the University of Puget Sound for information on the above article in English and Professor Hans Küng himself for the information on Abe's article in German.)

18. Abe, "Will, Sunyata, and History," 269.

19. Abe, "Kenotic God and Dynamic Sunyata," in John Cobb, Jr., and Christopher Ives, eds., *The Emptying God: A Buddhist-Jewish-Christian Conversation* (Maryknoll, N.Y.: Orbis Books, 1990), 3–65.

CHAPTER TWENTY-ONE

1. Masao Abe, "Zen Is Not a Philosophy, but . . ." *Theologische Zeitschrift* (Basel) 33 (1977): 251–68.

2. Translated by Harold H. Oliver, *Buddhist-Christian Studies* 12 (1992): 83–102. Henceforth I refer to this essay as *TS*.

3. Fritz Buri, *Der Buddha-Christus als der Herr des wahren Selbst: Die Religionsphilosophie der Kyoto Schule und das Christentum* (Bern: Paul Haupt Verlag, 1982). Translated by Harold H. Oliver as *The Buddha-Christ as the Lord of the True Self: The Religious Philosophy of the Kyoto School and Christianity* (Macon, Ga.: Mercer University Press, 1997). Henceforth, I refer to this work as *BC*.

4. *TS,* 85.

5. Ibid., 96.

6. *BC,* 323ff.

7. Ibid., 324.

8. Ibid.

9. Ibid., 325.

10. Ibid.

11. Ibid.

12. Ibid., 326.

13. Ibid.

14. Ibid., 328.

15. Ibid., 329.

16. Ibid., 330.

17. Ibid.

18. Ibid., 336.

19. Ibid., 339.

20. Ibid., 340.

21. Ibid.

22. Ibid.

23. Ibid.

24. Ibid.

25. Ibid., 344.

26. Ibid.

27. Ibid., 345.

28. Ibid., 347.

29. Ibid.

30. Ibid., 348.

31. *TS,* 96

32. Ibid., 97.

33. Ibid.
34. Ibid., 98.
35. Ibid.
36. *BC,* 357.
37. Ibid.
38. Ibid.
39. Ibid., 358.
40. Ibid.
41. Ibid., 359.
42. Ibid.
43. Ibid., 360.
44. Ibid., 361.
45. Ibid.
46. Ibid.
47. Ibid., 362.
48. Ibid.
49. Ibid., 363.
50. Ibid.
51. Ibid., 364.
52. Ibid., 365.
53. Ibid.
54. Ibid., 367ff.
55. Ibid., 368.
56. Ibid., 369.
57. Ibid., 370.
58. Ibid., 372.
59. Ibid.
60. Ibid., 374.
61. Ibid., 375.
62. Ibid.
63. Ibid., 377.
64. Ibid., 379.

CHAPTER TWENTY-TWO

1. Masao Abe, "Zen and Compassion," *The Eastern Buddhist* 2, no. 1 (August 1967): 64.
2. Masao Abe, "Zen and Buddhism," *The Eastern Buddhist* 26, no. 1 (spring 1993): 26–49.
3. In Abe's most recent book, *Buddhism and Interfaith Dialogue* (Honolulu: University of Hawai'i Press, 1995), he devotes several chapters to exploring Tillich's theology and its importance for Christian-Buddhist dialogue. Throughout these readings, the richness of Tillich's religio-philosophy is again apparent as it enables Abe to penetratingly analyze and articulate the basic differences and similarities between the Christian and Zen Buddhist ontic positions.
4. Masao Abe, "In Memory of Dr. Paul Tillich," *The Eastern Buddhist* 1, no. 2 (September 1966): 128. This article was recently reprinted in Abe, *Buddhism and Interfaith Dialogue,* 120–123.

5. Masao Abe, "In Memory of Dr. Paul Tillich," 131. Much could be said about Tillich and his interest in interreligious dialogue; however, since the paper is focused on Masao Abe's dialogue with Tillich, the matter will have to be taken up on another occasion.

6. Masao Abe, *Zen and Western Thought* (Honolulu: University of Hawai'i Press, 1985), 171–185.

7. Ibid., 171.

8. "Human personal existence" indicates the ontological status of a human being that has actualized self [personal]-consciousness. Hereafter, the term *person* will be utilized to indicate this status.

9. Paul Tillich, *Systematic Theology*, vol. I (Chicago: University of Chicago Press, 1951), 49. (Hereafter *Systematic Theology* will be referred to as *ST*, with volume and page numbers following.) "Life remains ambiguous as long as there is life" (*ST*, II, 4); ". . . life at every moment is ambiguous" (*ST*, III, 32).

10. *ST*, I, 170.

11. *ST*, II, 34 (my italics). For Tillich, awareness of finitude is awareness of being. Correspondingly, the awareness of finitude is accompanied by the awareness of infinitude (non-being). It is only by the awareness of infinitude that we can realize our own finitude—only in non-being do we find the possibilities, and the limitations, of being: "Only because we look at something infinite can we realize we are finite. Only because we are able to see the eternal can we see the limited time that is given us. . . . Our melancholy about our transitoriness is rooted in our power to look beyond it." (Paul Tillich, *The Shaking of the Foundations* [New York: Charles Scribner's Sons, 1950] 67.)

12. Paul Tillich, "What Is Man? A Symposium on the Individual in Modern Society" (unpublished broadcast transcript), *Yale Christian Association*, January 4, 1957, Tillich Archives, 407:108, p. 3.

13. Paul Tillich, *Love, Power, and Justice* (New York: Oxford University Press, 1954), 33, 34. (Hereafter referred to as *LPJ*.)

14. Abe, *Zen and Western Thought*, 6.

15. Ibid., 6.

16. Ibid.

17. *ST*, I, 61, 62.

18. *ST*, I, 211.

19. D. MacKenzie Brown, *Ultimate Concern: Tillich in Dialogue* (New York: Harper & Row, 1965), 7, 8.

20. *ST*, I, 235; *LPJ*, 107.

21. *LPJ*, 109.

22. *ST*, I, 244.

23. *ST*, I, 272.

24. *ST*, I, 279 (my italics).

25. Paul Tillich, *The New Being* (New York: Charles Scribner's Sons, 1995), 26.

26. *LPJ*, 25.

27. Tillich, *The Shaking of the Foundations*, 156.

28. *ST*, I, 286.

29. *ST*, I, 49.

30. Paul Tillich, "The Importance of New Being for Christian Theology," in *Man and Transformation*, ed. Joseph Campbell (Princeton: Princeton University Press, 1964), 174.

31. For a full discussion of the kenotic quality of Jesus as the Christ, see *The Emptying God: A Buddhist-Jewish-Christian Conversation*, ed. John Cobb and Christopher Ives (Maryknoll, N.Y.: Orbis Books, 1990).

32. In terms of ontology, Abe holds that for Buddhism, consistent with *pratītya-samutpāda*, being is not ontologically prior to non-being; instead, being and non-being are codependent. As Abe explains this difference in regard to the Zen resolution,

> *in Buddhism, since the polarity of being and nothing is a symmetrical polarity, with equal weight for being and nonbeing, the overcoming of this symmetrical polarity entails us* straightforwardly *to go beyond the horizon of polarity itself to a new horizon which is neither being nor nothing—that is, to a realization of* Sunyata. (Buddhism and Interfaith Dialogue, *106, 107)*

As Abe goes on to say, this Emptiness (*Śūnyatā*) must be "emptied" as well. The Zen Awakening destroys the simple objectification of self, others, and God that is necessarily restricted to relatedness between two "others" and instead provides a consciousness that is complete identification with the other, while still engaging in relative participation—thus, an identification-participation. As Abe states, the Awakened person is "now [and originally] *both* being and nothing at one and the same time" (ibid., 107).

33. This characterization of Awakening as "nondualistic duality" is from the writings of Richard DeMartino.

34. Shin'ichi Hisamatsu, "Ultimate Crisis and Resurrection, Part 1," trans. Gishin Tokiwa, *The Eastern Buddhist* 8, no. 2 (May 1975): 28.

35. Richard DeMartino, ed. and trans., "D. T. Suzuki, Oriental Thought and the West," unpublished manuscript of original interview that appeared in the *Asahi Journal* 7, no. 11, March 14, 1965.

36. "Love corresponds to the Buddhist ideal of *mahākaruṇā*, and according to Buddhists the Buddha-heart is no other than *mahākaruṇā* itself" (D. T. Suzuki, "Human Values in Zen," in Abraham Maslow, ed., *New Knowledge in Human Values* [New York: Harper & Row, 1959], 97).

37. Abe, "Zen and Compassion," 66.

38. Ibid.

39. DeMartino, "D. T. Suzuki, Oriental Thought and the West," 22, 23. DeMartino goes on to add that "though Buddhism has laid much formal stress on undifferentiated-differentiations, it seems not to have worked this out sufficiently as regards the specific relation between love and justice."

40. Cobb and Ives, *The Emptying God*, 60.

41. Ibid., 61.

42. This criterion is one espoused by Robert McAfee Brown in his recent book *Liberation Theology* (Louisville, Ky.: Westminster/John Knox Press, 1993), 27. As indicated by such books as *Asian Christian Spirituality*, ed. Virginia Fabella et al. (Maryknoll, N.Y.: Orbis Books, 1992), there is profound need by Asians for a spirituality of liberation, and Christian liberation theology is active in supporting the development of spirituality. Zen, and Buddhism as a whole, must similarly answer the spiritual needs of the poor and oppressed in Asia with much greater vivacity and urgency than in the past.

CHAPTER TWENTY-THREE

1. "Kenotic God and Dynamic Sunyata," in John B. Cobb, Jr., and Christopher Ives, eds., *The Emptying God: A Buddhist-Jewish-Christian Conversation* (Maryknoll, N.Y.: Orbis Books, 1990), 3–65.

2. See *Foundations of Christian Faith: An Introduction to the Idea of Christianity* (New York: Seabury Press, 1978), 63.

3. Perhaps in the case of Zen, it is more accurate to speak of narrative and rhetorical strategies. Take, for example, the famous poetry contest in the *Platform Sūtra of the Sixth Patriarch* ("Where then is a grain of dust to cling?") or the much-quoted maxim "When all is reduced to one, to what is the one to be reduced?"

4. "Buddhism Is Not Monistic, but Non-dualistic," *Scottish Journal of Religious Studies* 1, no. 2 (fall 1980): 97–100.

5. "Buddhism and Christianity as a Problem for Today: Part II," in *Japanese Religions* 3, no. 3: 8–31. Also, Masao Abe, *Zen and Western Thought* (Honolulu: University of Hawai'i Press, 1985).

6. Abe, "Buddhism and Christianity as a Problem for Today: Part II," 24.

7. Abe, *Zen and Western Thought,* 161. Later in this text, Abe states that "Zen transcends not only dualism, but also monism and monotheism" (p. 187).

8. Abe, "Kenotic God and Dynamic Sunyata," 27–33.

9. Masao Abe, "Memories of Daisetz Suzuki Sensei," in Masao Abe, ed., *A Zen Life: D. T. Suzuki Remembered* (New York: Weatherhill, 1986), 218.

10. For Abe's reflection on the relationship between Zen and Jōdo Shin-shū, see "The Problem of 'Inverse Correspondence' in the Philosophy of Nishida: Toward a Critical Understanding," trans. James Fredericks, in the *International Philosophical Quarterly* 35, no. 4, issue 140 (December 1995): 419–436. Here Abe insightfully explores the intrinsic connection between Zen and Jōdo Shin-shū. His standpoint remains that of Nishida's Absolute Nothingness. What if Abe were to interpret Absolute Nothingness from the standpoint of "other power?"

11. To be sure, Abe has published articles having to do with Jōdo Shin-shū thought. In 1963 and again in 1964, articles appeared in Japanese on Dōgen and Shinran. These articles have recently been translated by Steven Heine and are included as the final chapters of Masao Abe, *A Study of Dōgen* (Stony Brook: State University of New York Press, 1992). Of course, in these early articles no attempt is made to connect Shinran's notion of "other power" with a dynamic approach to *Śūnyatā.*

12. Jan van Bragt, "Buddhism-Jōdo Shin-shū-Christianity: Does Jōdo Shin-shū Form a Bridge between Buddhism and Christianity?" *Japanese Religions* 18, no. 1 (January 1993): 47–75.

CHAPTER TWENTY-FIVE

1. Kitarō Nishida, *An Inquiry Into the Good,* trans. Masao Abe and Christopher Ives (New Haven: Yale University Press, 1990).

2. Ibid., xxv.

3. Ibid., xii.

4. Ibid.

5. Ibid., xxx.

6. Ibid., xv (Abe's introduction); xxx (Nishida's preface).

7. William James, *Essays in Radical Empiricism* (New York: Longmans, Green and Co., 1943), 9. The above quotation is in italics in the original.

8. Ibid., 23.

9. Ibid., 40.

10. Nishida, *An Inquiry into the Good,* xv.

11. Ibid., xviii.

12. Ibid., xix.

13. Ibid., 135.

14. Ibid., 161.

15. Ibid., 150.

CHAPTER TWENTY-SIX

1. Masao Abe, *Zen and Western Thought* (Honolulu: University of Hawai'i Press, 1985).
2. Ibid., 152.
3. Ibid., xxi.
4. Ibid., xxii, 152, 170.
5. Ibid., 152.
6. Ibid., 186.
7. Ibid., 202.
8. Ibid.
9. Ibid.
10. Ibid., 186.
11. Ibid., 172.
12. Ibid., 169.
13. Ibid.
14. Ibid., 109.
15. Ibid., 74.
16. Ibid., 74, 189; cf. p. 31.
17. Ibid., 188–189; cf. p. 202.
18. Ibid., 120.
19. Ibid.
20. Ibid., xxiii.
21. Ibid., xxii.
22. Ibid., 210.
23. Ibid.
24. Ibid.
25. Ibid., 209.
26. Ibid., 85.
27. Ibid., 261–265.
28. Ibid., 266, 268.
29. Ibid., 192–193.
30. Ibid., 193.
31. Ibid.
32. Ibid.
33. Martin Heidegger, "A Dialogue on Language between a Japanese and an Inquirer," in *On the Way to Language,* trans. Peter Hertz (San Francisco: Harper & Row, 1982).
34. Ibid., 4–5.
35. Ibid., 5.
36. Ibid., 2–3.
37. Ibid., 8.
38. Ibid., 12–13.
39. Abe, *Zen and Western Thought,* 131.

CHAPTER TWENTY-SEVEN

1. Masao Abe, "Non-Being and *Mu*—The Metaphysical Nature of Negativity in the East and the West" in Masao Abe, *Zen and Western Thought* (Honolulu: University of Hawai'i Press, 1985), 121–134.

2. Ibid., 122–123.

3. Ibid., 121.

4. Ibid.

5. Masao Abe, "Zen and Western Thought" in Abe, *Zen and Western Thought*, 109.

6. Abe, "Non-Being and *Mu*—The Metaphysical Nature of Negativity in the East and the West," 133–134.

7. Ibid., 130.

8. Ibid., 127.

9. Ibid., 130–131.

10. Abe, "Zen and Western Thought," 94.

11. Abe, "Non-Being and *Mu*—The Metaphysical Nature of Negativity in the East and the West," 126.

12. Ibid.

13. Ibid., 127.

14. Ibid.

15. Ibid., 128.

16. Ibid., 130.

17. Ibid., 128.

18. Ibid., 126–127.

19. Ibid., 130.

20. Abe, "Zen and Western Thought," 102.

21. Abe, "Non-Being and *Mu*—The Metaphysical Nature of Negativity in the East and the West," 131–132.

22. Ibid., 133.

23. Ibid., 124.

24. Ibid., 125.

25. Ibid., 133.

26. Ibid.

27. Ibid., 121.

28. For the text of and a commentary on the *Heart Sūtra* or *Hṛdaya Prajñāpāramitā,* see Geshe Rabten, *Echoes of Voidness,* trans. Stephen Batchelor (London: Wisdom Publications, 1983), 15–45.

29. For Nāgārjuna's statement of this point, see the quotation from *Madhyamakasātra* in Hans Wolfgang Schumann's *Buddhism: An Outline of Its Teachings and Schools* (Wheaton, Ill.: Theosophical Publishing House, 1974), 146.

30. Abe, "Non-Being and *Mu*—The Metaphysical Nature of Negativity in the East and the West," p 223.

31. Alan Watts, *The Way of Zen* (New York: Vintage Books, 1957), 126.

32. Ibid.; the *Diamond Sūtra* or *Vajracchedikā Prajñāpāramitā* emphasizes this movement of negation of substance deepened by a second, self-emptying negation that gives rise to, or is, the positive realization of dependent co-arising.

33. Rabten, *Echoes of Voidness,* 35.

34. Ibid., 26–27.

35. Ibid., 33–34.

36. Ibid., 33.

37. Abe, "Non-Being and *Mu*—The Metaphysical Nature of Negativity in the East and the West," 132.

38. Ibid., 124 (figs. 5.1 and 5.2).

39. Ibid., 128 (fig. 5.3).

40. Ibid., 129 (fig. 5.4).

41. Ibid., 123, 128.

42. Ibid., 133.

CHAPTER TWENTY-EIGHT

1. Masao Abe, *A Study of Dōgen* (Albany: State University of New York Press, 1992), 141.

2. Martin Heidegger, *Aus der Erfahrung des Denkens* (Pfullingen: Neske, 1954), 21.

3. Ibid., 15.

4. Heidegger, *Gelassenheit* (Pfullingen: Neske, 1954), 27.

5. Ibid., 34.

6. Ibid., 52–53.

7. Stambaugh, *Thoughts on Heidegger* (Washington, D.C.: University Press of America, 1991), 123–136.

8. Quoted in Abe, *A Study of Dōgen*, 123.

9. Ibid., 57.

10. Heidegger, *Vier Seminare* (Frankfurt: Klustermann, 1977), 104.

11. Heidegger, *On Time and Being*, trans. Joan Stambaugh (New York: Harper & Row, 1972), 43.

CHAPTER TWENTY-NINE

1. Masao Abe, "Zen Is Not a Philosophy, but . . . ," in Masao Abe, *Zen and Western Thought* (Honolulu: University of Hawai'i Press, 1985), 26.

2. "Kenotic God and Dynamic Sunyata," in John B. Cobb, Jr., and Christopher Ives, eds., *The Emptying God: A Buddhist-Jewish-Christian Conversation* (Maryknoll, N.Y.: Orbis Books, 1990), 27.

3. Ibid.

4. Ibid., from the *Prajñāpāramitā Sūtra*. Taisho 8:250b.

5. Ibid., 26.

6. Ibid., 27.

7. See Abe, *Zen and Western Thought*.

8. Ibid., 24.

9. Thomas R. Martland, Jr., *The Metaphysics of William James and John Dewey* (New York: Philosophical Library, 1963), 92.

10. William James, *The Principles of Psychology*, vol. I (New York: Dover Publications, Inc., 1950 [first published in 1890]), 467.

11. Masao Abe, *Zen and Western Thought*.

12. Ibid.

13. Ibid.
14. Ibid., 129.
15. Ibid.
16. Ibid., 4.
17. Ibid., 128.
18. Ibid., 129.
19. Shizuteru Ueda, "'Nothingness' in Meister Eckhart and Zen Buddhism," in Frederick Franck, ed., *The Buddha Eye: An Anthology of the Kyoto School* (New York: Crossroads Publishing, 1982), 160.
20. Cobb and Ives, *The Emptying God*, 29.
21. Abe, *Zen and Western Thought*, 256.
22. Ibid., 257.
23. Shin'ichi Hisamatsu, *Zen and the Fine Arts* (Tokyo: Kodansha International, 1971), 52.
24. Ibid.
25. Kitarō Nishida, *Intelligibility and the Philosophy of Nothingness*, trans. Robert Schinzinger (Honolulu: East-West Center Press, 1958), 137.
26. Abe, *Zen and Western Thought*, 167.
27. Ibid., 49.
28. Ibid., 67.

CHAPTER THIRTY

1. Robert A. F. Thurman, *The Holy Teaching of Vimalakīrti, a Mahāyāna Scripture* (University Park, Pa.: University Pennsylvania Press, 1976), 46.
2. Ibid., 47.
3. Ibid., 46.
4. Ibid.
5. Ibid., 47.
6. W. T. de Bary et al., *Sources of Chinese Tradition* (New York: Columbia University Press, 1960), 320–322.
7. On the relatively weak position of the Buddhist *saṅgha* in China, see Erik Zürcher, "Buddhism in China: The Limits of Innovation," unpublished paper contributed to the Conference on the Historical Experience of Change and Patterns of Reconstruction in Selected Axial Age Civilizations, Jerusalem, December 28, 1983–January 2, 1984.
8. Kakuyei Tada, "Buddhism in China Today," *Pacific World* 1, no. 3 (spring 1984): 28–30.
9. Ibid., 28.
10. Ibid., 29.
11. Ibid., 30.
12. Ryusaku Tsunoda et al., *Sources of Japanese Tradition* (New York: Columbia University Press, 1958), 50–51. Translation adapted from W. G. Aston.
13. Ibid., 53.
14. Ibid., 50.

CHAPTER THIRTY-ONE

1. See D. T. Suzuki, *Living by Zen* (London: Rider & Co., 1972), 172, for another version.

2. Kitarō Nishida, *An Inquiry into the Good* (New Haven: Yale University Press, 1990).

3. *Hinduism Today* 15, no. 3 (March 1993): 27 reports that the Dalai Lama recently complained: "When I say Buddhism is a part of Hinduism, certain people criticize me. But if I were to say that Hinduism and Buddhism are totally different, it would not be in conformity with truth. I have always described Hinduism and Buddhism as twin brothers. The only difference is in the concept of *ātman* [the individual soul]. Buddhism does not believe in *ātman*." Perhaps the question of Brahman also needs to be addressed.

4. I offer some of my own thoughts to begin with. Some have plausibly suggested that Hinduism and Buddhism are two distinct but complementary ways of looking at the world and its underlying reality. These ontological approaches in turn mold their soteriological approaches, but the goal of *mokṣa* or *mukti* remains the same for both. Both, in a sense, are *upāyas*. The parallel from the world of science that suggests itself is that of the wave and particle theories of light as two ways of understanding the behavior of light, whose property of revealing things is not affected by these theories. The action of switching on the light is to be distinguished from that of understanding the behavior of light. Both Hinduism and Buddhism, on this analogy, are capable of switching on the light but explain the phenomenon of light rather differently.

   Some have argued that the differences between the two are minimal, that Brahman and *Śūnyatā* for all intents and purposes can be identified as already mentioned. Other have argued that this is not so, that "Samkara differentiates his doctrine from the sunya-vada of the Madhyamika. . . . If according to the Madhyamika it is impossible for thought to rest in the relative, it is equally impossible for it, according to Samkara, to rest in absolute nothing. . . . Or as an old writer has observed, while the Advaitin negates only distinction *(bheda),* the Madhyamika negates it as well as the distincts *(bhidyamāna)*" (M. Hiriyanna, *Outlines of Indian Philosophy* [London: George Allen & Unwin, 1932], 372–373).

   One also sometimes wonders whether Hinduism and Buddhism chose not merely to describe the same phenomenon differently but rather chose to identify different phenomena on the same occurrence. Let us suppose that one is describing the images on a TV screen. As the images disappear completely once the TV is switched off, the images are totally empty; they possess no self-existence and may be described as empty. However, if the view is entertained that no image can appear without the screen, then it will be implicated in all the images. The first description would then correspond to Buddhist *nairātmya,* and the second to the Hindu *jīvātman,* the descriptions reflecting a kind of choice.

   One final comment may not be out of place. A fundamental contribution that Masao Abe made to my understanding of *Śūnyatā* was by highlighting its dynamic nature, as the realization that one finally abides neither in samsara nor nirvana. By contrast, the Brahman of Hinduism is understood as immutable, as uncontradicted in all three dimensions of time and therefore as "static" (for want of a better term). In Śamkara's Advaita change is ultimately illusory; in Mādhyamika Buddhism permanence is ultimately illusory; however, as both admit the ultimate reality to be beyond description, are both the descriptions illusory and common in their illusoriness?

5. Tu Wei-ming, "Confucianism," in Arvind Sharma, ed., *Our Religions* (San Francisco: Harper-Collins, 1993), 199.

CHAPTER THIRTY-TWO

1. Masao Abe, *A Study of Dōgen: His Philosophy and Religion,* ed. Steven Heine (Albany: State University of New York Press, 1992), 167.

2. See Tamura Yoshirō, *Kamakura Shin-Bukkyō no Kenkyū* (Kyoto: Heirakuji Shoten, 1965), and Tamura, "Critique of Original Awakening Thought in Shōshin and Dōgen," *Japanese Journal of Religious Studies,* 11, no. 2–3 (June – September 1984): 243–266.

3. Dōgen, *Shōbōgenzō Bendōwa,* trans. N. A. Waddell and Masao Abe, *The Eastern Buddhist* 4, no. 1 (May 1971): 144 (the term *realization* has been changed to *attainment*).

4. Dōgen, *Shōbōgenzō* "Gyōbutsuigi," *Dōgen Zenji Zenshū,* vol. I, ed. Ōkubo Dōshū (Tokyo: Chikuma Shobō, 1970), 345.

5. Yoshinori Takeuchi, *The Heart of Buddhism: In Search of the Timeless Spirit of Primitive Buddhism* (New York: Crossroads, 1983), 135.

6. Abe, *A Study of Dōgen,* 14.

7. Ibid., 120.

8. Cited in ibid., 219.

9. Ibid., 213.

10. Ibid., 216.

CHAPTER THIRTY-FOUR

1. Masao Abe, "The Interfaith Encounter of Zen and Christian Contemplation: A Dialogue between Masao Abe and Keith J. Egan," in Masao Abe, *Buddhism and Interfaith Dialogue,* ed. Stephen Heine (Honolulu: University of Hawai'i Press, 1995), 171.

2. Ibid., 172.

3. Ibid.

4. Ibid.

5. Ibid., 171.

6. Masao Abe, "Education in Zen," *The Eastern Buddhist* 9, no. 2 (October 1976): 66.

7. Ibid.

8. Ibid.

9. Masao Abe, "Kenotic God and Dynamic Sunyata," in John B. Cobb, Jr., and Christopher Ives, eds., *The Emptying God: A Buddhist-Jewish-Christian Conversation* (Maryknoll, N.Y.: Orbis Books, 1990).

10. References in this paragraph and the next four are from Abe's paper, which was read and distributed informally at the Third North-American Buddhist-Christian Theological Encounter. This event was held at Purdue University on October 10–12, 1986. The organizer was Professor Donald W. Mitchell.

11. Masao Abe, *Zen and Western Thought* (Honolulu: University of Hawai'i Press, 1985), 274–75.

12. See especially John B. Cobb, Jr., *Beyond Dialogue: Toward a Mutual Transformation of Christianity and Buddhism* (Philadelphia: Fortress Press, 1982).

13. Cobb and Ives, *The Emptying God,* 11.

14. Abe, *Zen and Western Thought,* 236.

15. Ibid., 148. See also Cobb and Ives, *The Emptying God,* 11.

16. Abe, *Zen and Western Thought,* 126.

17. Ibid., 79.

18. John B. Cobb, Jr., "On the Deepening of Buddhism," in Cobb and Ives, *The Emptying God,* 91–101.

19. Masao Abe, "A Rejoinder," in Cobb and Ives, *The Emptying God,* 178.

20. In my *Rediscovering the West: An Inquiry into Nothingness and Relatedness* (Albany: State University of New York Press, 1994), I address dialogue as religious practice. See also David Tracy, *Dialogue with the Other: The Inter-Religious Dialogue* (Grand Rapids, Mich.: William B. Eerdmans, 1990); Leonard Swidler, John B. Cobb, Jr., Paul F. Knitter, and Monica K. Hellwig, *Death or Dialogue: From the Age of Monologue to the Age of Dialogue* (Philadelphia: Trinity Press International, 1990); and Donald W. Mitchell, *Spirituality and Emptiness: The Dynamics of Spiritual Life in Buddhism and Christianity* (New York: Paulist Press, 1991).

CHAPTER THIRTY-FIVE

1. Quoted from *A Zen Forest: Sayings of the Masters,* trans. Sōiku Shigematsu (New York: Weatherhill, 1981), 87.

2. *The Complete Writings of Ralph Waldo Emerson* (New York: Wm. H. Wise & Co., 1929), 144.

3. *A Zen Forest,* 37.

4. D. T. Suzuki, *Essays in Zen Buddhism* (First Series) (New York: Grove Press, Inc. 1961), 265 (my italics).

5. Masao Abe, *Zen and Western Thought* (Honolulu: University of Hawai'i Press, 1985), 161.

6. Ibid., 12.

7. For a detailed discussion of how Abe and Emerson stand side-by-side in contrast to traditional Christianity, see my "Beyond Christianity: Transcendentalism and Zen," *The Eastern Buddhist* 24, no. 2 (autumn 1991): 33–68.

8. Matthew 10:39.

9. Luke 17:20–21.

10. John B. Cobb, Jr., and Christopher Ives, eds., *The Emptying God: A Buddhist-Jewish-Christian Conversation* (Maryknoll, N.Y.: Orbis Books, 1990), 11.

11. Ibid., 17.

12. Stephen Morris, "Buddhism and Christianity: The Common Ground. A Study of the Radical Theologies of Meister Eckhart and Abe Masao," *The Eastern Buddhist* 25, no. 2 (autumn 1992): 89–118.

13. *A Zen Forest,* 68.

14. See Abe's preface to Donald W. Mitchell's *Spirituality and Emptiness: The Dynamics of Spiritual Life in Buddhism and Christianity* (New York: Paulist Press, 1991), x.

15. Masao Abe, "Beyond Buddhism and Christianity—'Dazzling Darkness'" in Masao Abe, *Buddhism and Interfaith Dialogue* (Honolulu: University of Hawai'i Press, 1995), 138–139.

16. Abe, *Zen and Western Thought,* 274.

17. Ibid., 224.

18. Ibid.

LIST OF
CONTRIBUTORS

LESLIE D. ALLDRITT is associate professor of philosophy and religion at Northland College in Ashland, Wisconsin. His dissertation concerned the relationship between Paul Tillich and Zen Buddhist religio-philosophy. His current research interest is Japanese religiosity.

THOMAS J. J. ALTIZER, a retired theologian who, after completing his doctorate in the history of religions at the University of Chicago, has devoted a substantial part of his work to the Buddhist-Christian theological dialogue. This began with his first book, *Oriental Mysticism and Biblical Eschatology,* and is recently represented in *The Contemporary Jesus.* As a radical Christian theologian, a crucial dimension of this work has been an attempt to seek a genuinely Buddhist ground for Christian theology.

STEVE ANTINOFF lives and works in Tokyo.

EUGENE B. BOROWITZ serves as the Sigmund L. Falk Distinguished Professor of Education and Jewish Religious Thought at Hebrew Union College, Jewish Institute of Religion, New York. His most recent book was *Renewing the Covenant, a Theology for the Postmodern Jew.* In the spring of 1999, he and Francie Schwartz will publish *The Jewish Moral Values.*

JOSEPH A. BRACKEN, S. J., is professor of theology at Xavier University, Cincinnati, Ohio. He previously taught at Marquette University, and at Saint Mary of the Lake Seminary, Mundelein, Illinois. Author of several books on the relation between process theology and trinitarian theology, Bracken is interested in the philosophical foundations of the notion of ultimate reality in the various world religions. His most recent book in this regard is *The Divine Matrix.*

ROBERT E. CARTER is professor of philosophy at Trent University in Canada. He studied at Tufts, Harvard and Toronto Universities, with degrees in both philosophy and theology. He has authored and jointly authored eight books, including *The Nothingness Beyond God,* which is a study of the Japanese philosopher Kitarō Nishida, and a comparative work entitled *Becoming Bamboo.* Carter is a joint-translator of Tetsurō Watsuji's *Rinrigaku* (Japanese Ethics). He has researched extensively in Japan and is currently working on a study of Japanese ethics.

DAVID W. CHAPPELL teaches Chinese Buddhism at the University of Hawai'i where he is professor and graduate chair in the department of religion. He did his doctoral work at Yale University on the Chinese Pure Land pioneer, Tao-ch'o. His publications include *T'ien-T'ai Buddhism: An Outline of the Fourfold Teachings,* and as editor, *Buddhist and Taoist Practice in Medieval Chinese Society.* He was the founding editor of the journal, *Buddhist-Christian Studies.*

JOHN B. COBB, JR. is professor emeritus of the Claremont School of Theology. As a Christian theologian, renown for his contribution to process theology, he has been active in interfaith dialogue, especially with Buddhists. He published *Beyond Dialogue: Toward a Mutual Transformation of Christianity and Buddhism.* He worked with Masao Abe to initiate theological dialogue between leading Buddhists and Christian theologians especially in North America, and he co-edited with Christopher Ives *The Emptying God: A Buddhist-Jewish-Christian Conversation,* focusing on Abe's work.

THOMAS DEAN is associate professor of religion at Temple University. In 1989–90 and again from 1991–1994, he taught at Temple University Japan in Tokyo. His publications include "Masao Abe on Zen and Western Thought" in *The Eastern Buddhist* (Part One, Autumn 1989; Part Two, Spring 1990), "Enlightenment or Liberation? Two Models of Christ in Contemporary Japanese Theology" in *Fukuin to Sekai* (October, November, December 1994) with the English version in *The Japan Christian Review* (December 1995), and an edited volume, *Religious Pluralism and Truth: Essays on Cross-Cultural Philosophy of Religion.* Dean's area of research is cross-cultural philosophy of religion, and he is currently engaged in a study of Heidegger and the Kyoto School.

WILLIAM THEODORE DE BARY is John Mitchell Mason Professor and Provost Emeritus, Columbia University. He was president of the Association of Asian Studies 1969–70, and is the author of *Waiting for the Dawn: A Plan for the Prince, The Trouble With Confucianism,* and *The Buddhist Tradition.*

RICHARD J. DeMARTINO is associate professor emeritus (religion) at Temple University, and has known Masao Abe since 1952. Besides publishing extensively in the West on Zen Buddhism, DeMartino collaborated with Abe on the English translation of Shin'ichi Hisamatsu's "The Characteristics of Oriental Nothingness," published in Japan by the Ministry of Education in *Philosophical Studies of Japan* (II, 1960).

DURWOOD FOSTER is professor emeritus of Christian theology at Pacific School of Religion, where he was also dean. An ordained United Methodist, he earlier taught at Union Theological Seminary in New York and at Duke University. Among various writings he has authored *The God Who Loves* on the theology of Paul Tillich. The wider ecumenism of interfaith dialogue, especially with Buddhism, has been a main commitment for some years.

JAMES L. FREDERICKS is associate professor in the department of theological studies at Loyola Marymount University, Los Angeles, where he teaches comparative theology. He is a specialist in the area of Christianity and Japanese Buddhism, and is a member of the Los Angeles Buddhist-Catholic dialogue group. Fredericks has known Masao Abe since 1984 when he studied with Abe as a graduate student at the University of Chicago. His topic for his doctoral research was the Kyoto School. Since that time, he has translated a series of Abe's more technical articles on the philosophy of Kitarō Nishida for the *International Philosophical Quarterly,* and has edited several of Abe's papers. They have appeared frequently on panels together. Currently Fredericks is editing a book by Abe on the Kyoto School.

ASHOK GANGADEAN is professor and chair of philosophy at Haverford College where he has taught for the past twenty-nine years. He was the first director of the Margaret Gest Center for Cross-Cultural Study of Religion at Haverford, and has participated in numerous professional conferences on interreligious dialogue and East-West comparative philosophy. He is founder-director of the Global Dialogue Institute which seeks to embody the dialogical powers of global reason in all aspects of cultural life. His book, *Meditative Reason: Toward Universal Grammar,* attempts to open the way to global reason; and a companion volume, *Between Worlds: The Emergence of Global Reason,* explores the dialogical common ground between diverse worlds. His forthcoming book, *The Awakening of the Global Mind,* further develops these themes for the general reader.

LANGDON GILKEY was for many years the Shailer Mathews Professor of Theology at the Divinity School of the University of Chicago. Through a grant from the Japan Society in the spring of 1976, he was a visiting professor at Kyoto University. There he and his wife, Sonya Gilkey-Weber, became friends with Masao Abe and participated under his watchful but kind direction in *zazen*. This trip inspired among others an interest both in interchange with Buddhist thinkers such as Abe, and in the philosophy of the Kyoto School. Gilkey's publications include: *Naming the Whirlwind* and *Society and the Sacred*.

RUBEN L. F. HABITO completed doctoral studies in Buddhism at Tokyo University. After teaching at Sophia University in Tokyo (1978–1989), he took a position at Perkins School of Theology, Southern Methodist University, where he is now professor of world religions and spirituality. He is the author of *Total Liberation: Zen Spirituality and the Social Dimension, Healing Breath: Zen Spirituality for a Wounded Earth, Original Enlightenment: Tendai Hongaku Doctrine and Japanese Buddhism,* as well as many other volumes in Japanese.

STEVEN HEINE is professor of religious studies at Florida International University. His recent publications include *The Zen Poetry of Dōgen, Japan in Traditional and Postmodern Perspectives,* and *Dōgen and the Kōan Tradition.* His current research is on the relation between philosophy and folklore in Zen Buddhist *kōan* literature.

JOHN HICK was a colleague of Masao Abe's at the Claremont Graduate School, of which he is now an emeritus professor, and a member with Abe of the International Buddhist-Christian Theological Encounter. The author of a number of books on the philosophy of religion, Hick is currently a fellow of the Institute for Advanced Research in the Humanities at the University of Birmingham, U.K. He gave the Gifford Lectures in 1986–87, and received the Grawemeyer Award in Religion for the book resulting from them, entitled *An Interpretation of Religion* in 1991.

CHRISTOPHER IVES is associate professor of religion at the University of Puget Sound. Author of *Zen Awakening and Society,* Ives edited *Divine Emptiness and Historical Fullness: A Buddhist-Jewish-Christian Conversation with Masao Abe,* and, with John B. Cobb, Jr., co-edited *The Emptying God: A Buddhist Jewish-Christian Conversation.* His scholarship focuses on Japanese Buddhism and ethics, especially the relationship between Buddhism and the state in Japanese history.

THOMAS P. KASULIS is professor of comparative studies in the humanities at Ohio State University, where he teaches courses in religious studies, philosophy, and East-Asian studies. He has written or edited five books, including *Zen Action/Zen Person* and *Self as Body in Asian Theory and Practice*, and published over three dozen articles in scholarly journals, books, and encyclopedias, including the article "Japanese Philosophy" for the forthcoming *Routledge International Encyclopedia of Philosophy*.

WILLIAM R. LaFLEUR is professor of Japanese studies and the Joseph B. Glossberg Term Professor of Humanities at the University of Pennsylvania. He received degrees from the University of Michigan and the University of Chicago. He has taught at Princeton, U.C.L.A., and Sophia University. He was the recipient of the Watsuji Tetsurō Prize for scholarship in 1989. His books include *The Karma of Words: Buddhism and the Literature Arts in Medieval Japan*, and *Liquid Life: Abortion and Buddhism in Japan*. He edited Masao Abe's *Zen and Western Thought*, and *Dōgen Studies*.

DONALD W. MITCHELL is professor of comparative philosophy of religion at Purdue University where is also chair of the religious studies program. He has been active in the Society for Buddhist-Christian Studies, and associate editor of its journal, *Buddhist-Christian Studies*. Mitchell is author of *Spirituality and Emptiness: The Dynamics of Spiritual Life in Buddhism and Christianity*, and co-editor of *The Gethsemani Encounter: A Dialogue on the Spiritual Life by Buddhist and Christian Monastics*.

STEPHEN MORRIS graduated from Harvard's Program on Religion and Education and taught in various public schools in the United States and Japan. He also studied comparative philosophy and received his doctorate from the California Institute of Integral Studies. Today he lives and writes in North Billerica, Massachusetts.

HAROLD H. OLIVER is professor emeritus of philosophical and comparative theology and New Testament at Boston University School of Theology. He is author of *Relatedness: Essays in Metaphysics and Theology*, and translator of Fritz Buri's *The Buddha-Christ as the Lord of the True Self: The Religious Philosophy of the Kyoto School and Christianity*.

HEINRICH OTT has been successor to Karl Barth as Ordinary Professor of Systematic Theology at Basel University since 1956. He was appointed chair of systemic theology at Basel University in 1962. Ott has been a visiting professor at universities in Europe, the United States, and East Asia. From 1979 to 1990, Ott was also a member of the Swiss Parliament. Among his many publications are books on Rudolf Bultmann, Dietrich Bonhoeffer, and Martin Heidegger. His work in ecumenism includes *Glaube und Bekennen: Ein Beitrag zum kumenischen Dialog.*

WOLFHART PANNENBERG, with a doctor's degree in theology from Heidelberg, became an ordained minister of the Evangelical-Lutheran Church in 1955, the same year he became dozent in the field of systematic theology at Heidelberg. In 1961, Pennenberg accepted the chair in systematic theology at the University of Mainz. Since 1963, he was visiting professor several times at American universities, such as the University of Chicago, Harvard University, and the Claremont Graduate School of Theology. In 1967, he accepted the chair in systematic theology at the University of Munich, where he also served as director of the Institute of Ecumenical and Fundamental Theology until he became a professor emeritus in 1994. Most of Pannenberg's publications are available in English, the most important of them being his *Systematic Theology* in three volumes.

FELIX E. PRIETO is now retired and living in Spain where he has translated many of the works of Masao Abe into Spanish.

STEPHEN C. ROWE is professor and chair of the department of philosophy at Grand Valley State University, and coordinator of the liberal studies program. His previous books include *Leaving and Returning, Rediscovering the West: An Inquiry Into Nothingness and Relatedness,* and *The Vision of William James.*

RICHARD L. RUBENSTEIN is president and CEO of the University of Bridgeport. He is professor emeritus of religion at Florida State University where he worked in the fields of theology and the history of religion. Rubenstein is the author of eight books and editor of five books. His most recent book is *After Auschwitz: History, Theology and Contemporary Judaism.* During his career, Rubenstein has made fifteen visits to Japan, and has maintained a strong interest in Buddhism.

ARVIND SHARMA received his early education in India, where he served in Gujarat as an I.A.S. officer. He resumed higher studies in the United States, and obtained his doctorate in Sanskrit and Indian Studies, specializing in Hinduism, at Harvard University. Sharma began his career in Australia at the University of Queensland in Brisbane and also taught at the University of Sydney before moving to McGill University in Montreal, Canada. He is currently Birks Professor of Comparative Religion in the faculty of religious studies at McGill. Sharma is the author of several books as well as the editor of a trilogy on women and religion, and *Our Religions*.

JEFF M. SHORE is associate professor of English and Zen Buddhism at the Rinzai Zen-affiliated Hanazono University in Kyoto, Japan. Originally from Philadelphia, he has undertaken Zen study and practice for over twenty-five years, the last seventeen in Zen monasteries in Japan. Shore has translated, written, and lectured extensively on Zen Buddhism and the F.A.S. Society, and has edited the *FAS Society Journal* for the last fifteen years.

HUSTON SMITH is Thomas J. Watson Professor of Religion and Distinguished Adjunct Professor of Philosophy, Emeritus, Syracuse University. For fifteen years he was professor of philosophy at M.I.T., and for a decade before that he taught at Washington University in Saint Louis. Most recently he has served as visiting professor of religious studies, University of California, Berkeley. His eight books include *The World's Religions, The Illustrated World's Religions, Forgotten Truth, Beyond the Post-Modern Mind*, and *One Nation Under God: The Triumph of the Native American Church*.

JOEL R. SMITH is associate professor of philosophy at Skidmore College in Saratoga Springs, New York. He received degrees in religion and in philosophy from Vanderbilt University. His work in comparative philosophy of religion includes articles comparing Nietzche and Nishitani, and comparing Kierkegaard and Shinran. He is co-founder and board member of the New York State Independent College Consortium for Study in India.

JOHN E. SMITH is Clark Professor Emeritus of Philosophy at Yale University. He is a past president of the American Philosophical Association, Eastern Division, and general editor emeritus of *The Works of Jonathan Edwards*. His books include *Experience and God, Purpose and Thought: The Meaning of Pragmatism*, and *Quasi-Religions: Humanism, Marxism, Nationalism*.

JOAN STAMBAUGH is professor of philosophy at Hunter College of the City University of New York. She is author of *Impermanence is Buddha Nature* and other works on comparative philosophy. She is also translator of numerous works by Martin Heidegger, including *On Time and Being*.

VALDO H. VIGLIELMO received his advanced degrees from the department of Far Eastern languages of Harvard University. He has specialized in the field of Japanese literature and thought, with emphasis on the literature and thought of the modern period, and especially the philosophy of the Kyoto School. He has also translated numerous works by such authors as Sōseki Natsume, Yasunari Kawabata, Kitarō Nishida, and Hajime Tanabe. He has taught at Harvard University and Princeton University as well as at Meiji Gakuin University, Tokyo University, Tokyo Women's Christian College, and International Christian University in Japan. He is currently professor of Japanese literature at the University of Hawai'i at Manoa.

HANS WALDENFELS is professor of fundamental theology, theology of non-Christian religions, and philosophy of religion in the faculty of Roman Catholic theology, University of Bonn. He is a member of the Society of Jesus, and has twice been dean of the faculty at the University of Bonn. His many publications include *Absolute Nothingness: Foundations for a Buddhist-Christian Dialogue*.

A MASAO ABE
BIBLIOGRAPHY:
PUBLICATIONS IN ENGLISH

BOOKS

Zen and Western Thought, William R. LaFleur, ed. Honolulu: University of Hawai'i Press, 1985.

A Zen Life: D. T Suzuki Remembered, Masao Abe, ed. Tokyo and New York: Weatherhill, 1986.

A Study of Dōgen: His Philosophy and Religion, Steven Heine, ed. Albany: State University of New York Press, 1992.

Buddhism and Interfaith Dialogue: Part I of a Two-Volume Sequel to Zen and Western Thought, Steven Heine, ed. Honolulu: University of Hawai'i Press, 1995.

Zen and Comparative Studies: Part II of a Two-Volume Sequel to Zen and Western Thought, Steven Heine, ed. Honolulu: University of Hawai'i Press, 1997.

CHAPTERS IN BOOKS

"The Idea of Purity in Mahayana Buddhism," in *Guilt or Pollution Rites Of Purification*. Proceedings of the llth International Congress of the International Association for the History of Religions 2, 1968, 148-151.

"A Buddhism of Self-Awakening, not a Buddhism of Faith," in J. Tilakasiri, ed., *Anjali: A Felicitation Volume Presented to Oliver Hector de Alwis Wijesekera on his Sixtieth Birthday*. Peradeniya, Ceylon: University of Ceylon, 1970, 33-39.

"The Buddhist View on Inter-Religious Dialogue," in *Report of the Consultation on Inter-Religious Dialogue with Special Reference to World Peace*. Kyoto: N.C.C. Center for the Study of Japanese Religions, 1970, 32-35.

"Buddhist Nirvana: Its Significance in Contemporary Thought and Life," in S.J. Samartha, ed., *Living Faiths and Ultimate Goals*. Lausanne, Switzerland: World Council of Churches, 1974, 12-22.

"Education in Zen: Centering Around the Role of the Master," in S. Lee and K. Rhi, eds., *Buddhism and the Modern World*. Seoul, Korea: Dongguk University, 1976, 176-181.

"Buddhist Nirvana: Its Significance in Contemporary Thought and Life," in H. Das,

C. Das, and S. Pal, eds., *Buddhism and Jainism*. Cuttack, India: Institute of Oriental and Orissan Studies, 1976, 61-67.

"Non-being and *Mu*: The Metaphysical Nature of Negativity in the East and the West," H. Das, C. Das, and S. Pal, eds., *Buddhism and Jainism*. Cuttack, India: Institute of Oriental and Orissan Studies, 1976, 52-60.

"Man and Nature in Christianity and Buddhism," in George F. McLean, ed., *Man and Nature*. Calcutta: Oxford University Press, 1978, 165-172. And in George F. McLean and Hugo Meynell, eds., *Person and Nature*. Boston: Boston University Press, 1978, 161-167.

"Religion and Science in the Global Age: Their Essential Character and Mutual Relationship," in *International Conference of Scientists and Religious Leaders*. Tokyo: *Proceedings of the International Conference of Scientists and Religious Leaders on Shaping the Future of Mankind*, 1978, 24-29.

"Toward the Creative Dialogue between Zen and Christianity," in *A Zen-Christian Pilgrimage: The Fruits of Ten Annual Colloquia in Japan, 1967-1976*. Tokyo: Zen-Christian Colloquium, 1981, 36-44.

"Zen and Nietzsche," in Nathan Katz, ed., *Buddhist and Western Philosophy*. New Delhi: Sterling Publishers, 1981, 1-17.

"God, Emptiness, and the True Self," in Frederick Franck, ed., *The Buddha Eye: An Anthology of the Kyoto School*. New York: Crossroads, 1982, 61-74.

"Man and Nature in Christianity and Buddhism," in Frederick Franck, ed., *The Buddha Eye: An Anthology of the Kyoto School*. New York: Crossroads, 1982, 148-156.

"Emptiness is Suchness," in *The Buddha Eye: An Anthology of the Kyoto School*. New York: Crossroads, 1982, 203-208.

"Zen in Japan," in H. Brinker, R. P. Kramers, and C. Ouwehand, eds., *Zen in China, Japan, and East Asian Arts*. New York: Peter Lang, 1984, 47-72.

"The Oneness of Practice and Attainment: Implications for the Relation between Means and Ends," in William R. LaFleur, ed., *Dōgen Studies*. Honolulu: University of Hawai'i Press, 1985, 99-111.

"A Dynamic Unity in Religious Pluralism: A Proposal from the Buddhist Point of View," in John Hick and Hasan Askari, eds., *The Experience of Religious Diversity*. Gower, Vermont: Ashgate Publishing Co., 1985, 163-190.

"The Problem of Evil in Christianity and Buddhism," in Paul O. Ingram and Frederick J. Streng, eds., *Buddhist-Christian Dialogue, Mutual Renewal and Transformation*. Honolulu: University of Hawai'i Press, 1986, 139-154.

"Religious Tolerance and Human Rights: A Buddhist Perspective," in Leonard Swidler, ed., *Religious Liberty and Human Rights in Nations and in Religions*. Philadelphia: Ecumenical Press, 1986, 193-211.

"A Buddhist Response to Dr. Mohamed Talbi's Paper, 'Religious Liberty: A Muslim Persective,'" in Leonard Swidler, ed., *Religious Liberty and Human Rights in Nations and in Religions*. Philadelphia: Ecumenical Press, 1986, 189-193.

"The Problem of Time in Heidegger and Dōgen," in Alistair Kee and Eugene Thomas Long, eds., *Being and Truth: Essays in Honour of John Macquarrie*. London: SCM Press, 1986, 200-244.

"The Problem of Evil in Christianity and Buddhism," in G. McLean and H. Meynell, eds., *Person and Society*. Washington, D.C.: University Press of America, 1988, 125-142.

"Nishitani's Challenge to Western Philosophy and Theology," in Taitetsu Unno, ed., *The Religious Philosophy of Nishitani Keiji: Encounter with Emptiness*. Berkeley: Asian Humanities Press, 1989, 13-45.

"Will, *Śūnyatā*, and History: Nishitani's View of History and its Examination," in Taitetsu Unno, ed., *The Religious Philosophy of Nishitani Keiji: Encounter with Emptiness*. Berkeley: Asian Humanities Press, 1989, 279-304.

"Kenosis and Emptiness," in Roger Corless and Paul Knitter, eds., *Buddhist Emptiness and Christian Trinity: Essays and Explorations*. Mahwah, N.J.: Paulist Press, 1990, 5-25.

"Self-Awakening and Faith: Zen and Christianity," in Paul Griffiths, ed., *Christianity through Non-Christian Eyes*. Maryknoll, N.Y.: Orbis Books, 1990, 171-180.

"Kenotic God and Dynamic Sunyata," in John B. Cobb, Jr. and Christopher Ives, eds., *The Emptying God: A Buddhist-Jewish-Christian Conversation*. Maryknoll, NY: Orbis Books, 1990, 3-65.

"A Rejoinder," in John B. Cobb, Jr. and Christopher Ives, eds., *The Emptying God: A Buddhist-Jewish-Christian Conversation*. Maryknoll, N.Y.: Orbis Books, 1990, 157-200.

"Preface," in Donald W. Mitchell, *Spirituality and Emptiness: The Dynamics of Spiritual Life in Buddhism and Christianity*. Mahwah, N.J.: Paulist Press, 1991, ix-xvi.

"The Self in Jung and Zen," in Robert L. Moore, ed., *Self and Liberation: The Jung-Buddhism Dialogue*. Mahwah, N.J.: Paulist Press, 1992, 128-140.

"Negation in Mayahana Buddhism and in Tillich." in R. Scharleman, ed., *Negation and Theology*. Charlottesville: University of Virginia Press, 1992, 86-99.

"A Rejoinder," in R. Scharleman, ed., *Negation and Theology*. Charlottesville: University of Virginia Press, 1992, 142-148.

"God and Absolute Nothingness," in A. Sharma, ed., *God, Truth and Reality*. New York: St. Martin's Press, 1993, 69-134.

"Buddhism," in A. Sharma, ed., *Our Religions*. San Francisco: HarperSanFrancisco, 1993, 69-137.

"The Buddhist View of Human Rights," in Abdullahi A. An-Na'im, ed., *Human Rights and Religious Values*. Grand Rapids: William B. Erdmanns, 1995, 144-153.

"Critical Reflections on the Traditional Japanese View of Truth," in Charles W. Fu and Steven Heine, eds., *Japan in Traditional and Post-modern Perspectives*. Albany: State University of New York Press, 1995, 297-312.

"Kenotic God and Dynamic Sunyata," in Christopher Ives, ed. *Divine Emptiness and Historical Fullness: A Buddhist-Jewish-Christian Conversation with Masao Abe*. Valley Forge, P.A.: Trinity Press, 1995, 25-90.

"A Rejoinder," in Christopher Ives, ed., *Divine Emptiness and Historical Fullness: A Buddhist-Jewish-Christian Conversation with Masao Abe*. Valley Forge P.A.: Trinity Press, 1995, 175-204.

"Beyond Buddhism and Christianity: 'Dazzling Darkness,'" in Christopher Ives, ed., *Divine Emptiness and Historical Fullness: A Buddhist-Jewish-Christian Conversation with Masao Abe*. Valley Forge, P.A.: Trinity Press, 1995, 224-243.

"God's Total Kenosis and Truly Redemptive Love," in Christopher Ives, ed., *Divine Emptiness and Historical Fullness: A Buddhist-Jewish-Christian Conversation with Masao Abe*. Valley Forge P.A.: Trinity Press, 1995, 251-259.

ARTICLES

"A Living-Dying Life," *Pacific Philosophy Forum* 3, no. 4 (May 1965): 96-102.

"Buddhism and Christianity as a Problem of Today," Part I, *Japanese Religions* 3, no. 2 (summer 1963): 11-22; Part II, 3, no. 3 (autumn 1963): 8-31.

"Review Article: Paul Tillich's Christianity and the Encounter of the World Religions," *The Eastern Buddhist*, n.s. I, no. 1 (September 1965): 109-122. Reprinted in *Indian Philosophy and Culture* 19, no. 2 (June 1974): 107-124.

"In Memory of Paul Tillich," *The Eastern Buddhist*, n.s. I, no. 2 (September 1966): 128-131.

"Professor Abe's Reply to the Debate," *Japanese Religions* 4, no. 2 (March 1966): 26-57.

"Zen and Buddhism," *Japan Studies*, no. 11 (1966): 1-11.

"The Idea of Purity in Mahayana Buddhism," *Numen 13*, no. 3 (October 1966): 183-189. Reprinted in *The Middle Way* 42, no. 4 (February 1968): 158-162.

"Zen and Compassion," *The Eastern Buddhist*, n.s. II, no. 1 (August 1967): 54-68.

"Christianity and Buddhism: Centering around Science and Nihilism," *Japanese Religions* 5, no. 3 (July 1968): 36-62.

"'Life and Death' and 'Good and Evil' in Zen," *Criterion* 9, no. 1 (autumn 1969): 7-11. Reprinted in *The Young Buddhist* (1973): 41-45.

"God, Emptiness, and the True Self," *The Eastern Buddhist*, n.s. II, no. 2 (November 1969): 15-30.

"Zen and Western Thought," *International Philosophical Quarterly* 10, no. 4 (December 1970): 501-541.

"Man and Nature in Christianity and Buddhism," *Japanese Religions* 7, no. 1 (July 1971): 1-10. Reprinted in *The Young Buddhist* (1972): 37-40.

"Dōgen on Buddha Nature," *The Eastern Buddhist*, n.s. VI, no. 1 (May 1971): 28-71.

"Zen and Nietzsche," *The Eastern Buddhist*, n.s. VI, no. 2 (October 1973): 14-32.

"Buddhist *Nirvana*: Its Significance in Contemporary Thought and Life," *The Ecumenical Review* 25, no. 2 (April 1973): 158-168. Reprinted in *Dialogue*, no. 20-21 (June 1970): 8-10.

"Religion Challenged by Modern Thought," *Japanese Religions* 8, no. 2 (November 1974): 2-14.

"Zen as Self-Awakening," *Japanese Religions* 8, no. 3 (April 1975): 25-45. Reprinted in *The Young Buddhist* (1980): 99-105.

"Non-Being and *Mu*: The Metaphysical Nature of Negativity in the East and in the West," *Religious Studies* 11, no. 2 (June 1975): 181-192.

"Mahayana Buddhism and Whitehead: A View by a Lay Student of Whitehead's Philosophy," *Philosophy East and West* 25, no. 4 (October 1975): 415-428.

"The Crucial Points: An Introduction to the Symposium on Christianity and Buddhism," *Japanese Religions* 8, no. 4 (October 1975): 2-9.

"Zen and Buddhism," *Journal of Chinese Philosophy* 3, no. 3 (June 1976): 64-70.

"Education in Zen," *The Eastern Buddhist*, n.s. IX, no. 2 (October 1976): 235-252.

"Zen is not a Philosophy, but....," *Theologische Zeitschiift* 33, no. 5 (September/October 1977): 251-268.

"Emptiness is Suchness," *The Eastern Buddhist*, n.s. X, no. 2 (October 1973): 132-136. Reprinted in *The Young Buddhist* (1979): 35-37.

"The End of World Religion," *The Eastern Buddhist*, n.s. XIII, no. 1 (spring 1980): 31-45. Reprinted in *World Faiths Insight* I (spring 1980): 1-34.

"Substance, Process, and Emptiness," *Japanese Religions* 11, nos. 2 and 3 (September 1980): 1-34.

"Buddhism is not Monistic, but Non-dualistic," *Scottish Journal of Religious Studies* 1, no. 2 (fall 1980): 97-100. Reprinted in *The Young Buddhist* (1981): 87-88.

"Sovereignty Rests with Mankind," *World Faiths Insight* I (autumn 1980): 31-36.

"Hisamatsu's Philosophy of Awakening," *The Eastern Buddhist*, n.s. XIV, no. 1 (spring 1981): 26-42.

"Hisamatsu Shin'ichi, 1889-1980." *The Eastern Buddhist*, n.s. XIV, no. 1 (spring, 1981): 142-149.

"Buddhist-Christian Dialogue: Past, Present, and Future," Masao Abe and John Cobb interviewed with Bruce Long, *Buddhist-Christian Studies* 1 (1981):13-29.

"Comments on 'Christian and Buddhist Personal Transformation,'" *Buddhist-Christian Studies* 2 (1982): 45-49.

"God, Emptiness, and Ethics," *Buddhist-Christian Studies* 3 (1983): 53-60.

"A History of the FAS Zen Society," *FAS Society Journal* (autumn 1984): 1-12.

"The Self in Jung and Zen," *The Eastern Buddhist*, n.s. XVIII, no. 1 (spring 1985): 57-70.

"John Cobb's *Beyond Dialogue*," *The Eastern Buddhist*, n.s. XVIII, no. 1 (spring 1985): 131-137.

"Responses to Langdon Gilkey," *Buddhist-Christian Studies* 4 (1985): 67-100.

"The Japanese View of Truth," *Japanese Religions* 14, no. 3 (December 1986): 1-6.

"The Problem of Death in East and West: Immortality, Eternal life, and Unbornness," *The Eastern Buddhist*, n.s. IXX, no. 2 (autumn 1986): 30-61.

"Shin'ichi Hisamatsu's Notion of FAS," *FAS Society Journal* (winter 1986-87): 21-23.

"Shintō and Buddhism: The Two Major Religions in Japan," *The Scottish Journal of Religious Studies* 8, no. 1 (spring 1987): 53-63.

"Philosophy, Religion, and Aesthetics in Nishida and Whitehead," *The Eastern Buddhist*, n.s. XX, no. 2 (autumn 1987): 53-62.

"Transformation in Buddhism," *Buddhist-Christian Studies* 7 (1987): 5-24.

"Sunyata as the Formless Form: Plato and Mahayana Buddhism," *Avaloka* (winter 1987): 41-66.

"Nishida's Philosophy of 'Place,'" *International Philosophical Quarterly XXVIII*, no. 4 (December 1988): 355-371.

"Kitarō Nishida Bibliography," with Lydia Brull, *International Philosophical Quarterly XXVIII*, no.4 (December 1988): 373-381.

"Transformation in Buddhism in Comparison with Platonic and Christian Notions," *Concilium* (April 1988): 41-60.

"Response to John Cobb," *Buddhist Christian Studies* 8, (1988): 65-74.

"Spirituality and Liberation: A Buddhist Christian Conversation: A Buddhist Perspective," *Horizons: The Journal of the College Theology Society* 15 (fall 1988): 350-354, 358-364.

"The Concept of Self as Reflected in Zen Buddhist Literature," *Wind Bell XXII*, no. 1 (spring 1988): 3-9.

"Spirituality and Liberation: A Buddhist-Christian Conversation with Paul F. Knitter," *Horizons 15*, no. 2 (1988): 347-364.

"Dōgen's View on Time and Space," *The Eastern Buddhist XXI*, no. 2 (autumn 1988): 1-35.

"The Problem of Self-Centeredness as the Root-Source of Human Suffering," *Japanese Religions 15*, no. 4 (July 1989): 15-25.

"There is no Common Denominator for World Religions: The Positive Meaning of this Negative Statement," *The Journal of Ecumenical Studies 26*, no. 1 (winter 1989): 72-81.

"The Impact of Dialogue with Christianity on my Self-understanding as a Buddhist," *Buddhist Christian Studies 9*, (1989): 62-70.

"God and Absolute Nothingness," *Studies in Interreligious Dialogue 1*, no. 1 (1991): 58-69.

"Nishitani Keiji 1900-1990," *The Eastern Buddhist XXIV*, no. 2 (autumn 1991): 149-152.

"'Inverse Correspondence' in the Philosophy of Nishida: The Emergence of the Notion," *International Philosophical Quarterly XXXII*, no. 3 (September 1992): 325-344.

"What is Religion," *The Eastern Buddhist XXV*, no.1 (spring 1992): 51-69.

"Zen Buddhism and Hasidism—Similarities and Contrasts," *Religious Traditions 15-17* (1992-1994): 6-13.

"Response to Eugene B. Borowitz," *Buddhist Christian Studies 13* (1993): 227-231.

"Zen and Buddhism," *The Eastern Buddhist XXVI*, no. 1 (spring 1993): 26-49.

"Two Types of Unity and Religious Pluralism," *The Eastern Buddhist XXVI*, no. 2 (autumn 1993): 76-85.

"A Report on the 1993 Parliament of World Religions," *The Eastern Buddhist XXVI*, no. 2 (autumn 1993): 73-75.

"Suffering in the Light of our Time, Our Time in the Light of Suffering," *The Eastern Buddhist XXVII*, no. 2 (Autumn 1994): 1-13.

"The Logic of Absolute Nothingness, as Expounded by Nishida Kitarō," *The Eastern Buddhist XXVIII*, no. 2 (autumn 1995): 167-174.

"The Problem of 'Inverse Correspondence' in the Philosophy of Nishida: Toward a Critical Understanding," *International Philosophical Quarterly XXXV*, no. 4 (December 1995): 419-436.

TRANSLATIONS

Nishida Kitarō, "The Problem of Japanese Culture," trans. with Richard DeMartino, in *Sources of the Japanese Tradition*. NewYork: Columbia University Press, 1958, 350-365.

Hisamatsu Shin'ichi, "The Characteristics of Oriental Nothingness," trans. with Richard DeMartino, in *Philosophical Studies of Japan* 2 (1960): 65-97.

Dōgen, *Bendōwa*, in *The Eastern Buddhist*, n.s. IV, no. 1 (May 1971): 124-157.

Dōgen, *Shōbōgenzō Ikkamyōuju*, in *The Eastern Buddhist*, n.s. IV, no. 2 (October 1971): 108-118.

Dōgen, *Shōbōgenzō Zenki* and *Shoji*, in *The Eastern Buddhist*, n.s. V, no. 1 (May 1972): 70-80.

Dōgen, *Shōbōgenzō Genjōkōan*, in *The Eastern Buddhist*, n.s. V, no. 2 (October 1972): 129-140.

Dōgen, *Shōbōgenzō Zazengi* and *Furkanzazengi*, in *The Eastern Buddhist*, n.s. VI, no. 2 (October 1973): 115-128.

Dōgen, *Shōbōgenzō Sammai-ō-Zammai*, in *The Eastern Buddhist*, n.s. VII, no. 1 (May 1974): 116-123.

Dōgen, *Shōbōgenzō Buddha-nature*, Part I, in *The Eastern Buddhist*, n.s. VIII, no. 2 (October 1975): 94-112; Part II, IX, no. 1 (May 1976): 87-105; Part III, IX, no. 2 (October 1976): 71-87.

Kitarō Nishida, *An Inquiry into the Good*, trans. with Christopher A. Ives. New Haven: Yale University Press, 1990.

INDEX

454 *index*